Twentieth
Century Theology
in the Making

Also available

**VOL II THE THEOLOGICAL DIALOGUE
ISSUES AND RESOURCES
VOL III ECUMENICITY AND RENEWAL**

Twentieth Century Theology in the Making

1 Themes of Biblical Theology

EDITED BY JAROSLAV PELIKAN

TRANSLATED BY R. A. WILSON

Harper & Row, Publishers
New York, Evanston, San Francisco, London

This translation is a selection from the second edition of Die Religion in Geschichte und Gegenwart *published by J. C. B. Mohr (Paul Siebeck) in Tübingen 1927-32*

TWENTIETH CENTURY THEOLOGY IN THE MAKING:
Volume I

English translation
Copyright © 1969 by William Collins Sons & Co., Ltd., London, and Harper & Row, Publishers, Inc., New York. All rights reserved. Printed in the United States of America. No part of this book may be used or reproduced in any manner without written permission except in the case of brief quotations embodied in critical articles and reviews. For information address Harper & Row, Publishers, Inc., 49 East 33rd Street, New York, N.Y. 10016. Published simultaneously in Canada by Fitzhenry & Whiteside Limited, Toronto.

First HARPER PAPERBACK edition published 1971.

LIBRARY OF CONGRESS CATALOG CARD NUMBER: 72-178974

STANDARD BOOK NUMBER: 06-139220-0

Contents

General Introduction   *page* 13
Introduction to Volume I   15

1 Biblical Theology and the
  History of Biblical Religion   23
  by Martin Dibelius
   I THE OLD TESTAMENT   23
   II THE NEW TESTAMENT   27

2 Prophets   32
   I PROPHECY IN THE HISTORY OF RELIGION   32
   by Alfred Bertholet
    1 The Definition and Nature of Prophecy   32
    2 The Spread of Prophecy   35

   IIA THE EARLIEST ISRAELITE PROPHECY BEFORE   38
     AMOS
   by Hans Schmidt
    1 The Sacred Ecstasy of the Bands of Prophets   38
    2a The Prophets as Givers of Oracles   43
    2b The Prophets as Miracle-Workers   44
    3 The Political Prophets   45
    4 The Origin of Classical Prophecy   46

   IIB THE ISRAELITE PROPHECY FROM THE TIME OF   48
     AMOS
   by Hermann Gunkel
    1 The Secret Experiences of the Prophets   48
    2 On the History of Prophecy   55
    3 The Literary Methods of the Prophets   61

Contents

IIC THE RELIGION OF THE PROPHETS   *page* 76
  by Ernst Sellin
  1 General Features   76
  2 The Religious Ideas of the Individual Prophets   78

3 The Gospels (Form)   86
  by Rudolf Bultmann
  1 The Task of the Form Criticism of the Gospel   86
  2 The Literary Category of the Gospels   86
  *3 The Material of the Gospel Tradition, its
    Literary Form and its History*   90

4 Jesus Christ   93
  by Karl Ludwig Schmidt
  I JESUS AND THE TRADITION CONCERNING HIM   93
  1 The Methodological Dispute   93
  2 The Gospels as Sources for the History of Jesus   97
  3 The Setting out of the Material   114

  II THE HISTORY OF JESUS IN OUTLINE   117
  1 Absolute Chronology   117
  2 Relative Chronology   119
  *3 The Principal Dates and the Beginning of
    Jesus's Ministry*   121

  III THE PREACHING OF JESUS (HIS WORDS): THE
    IMMINENCE OF THE KINGDOM OF GOD AND
    MAN'S REPENTANCE   122
  1 The Link with Judaism   122
  2 The Content of Jesus's Preaching   128

  IV THE ACTS OF JESUS: THE SIGNS OF THE
    KINGDOM OF GOD   152
  1 Jesus's Miracles   152
  2 The Purification of the Temple   160

Contents

V JESUS HIMSELF (HIS PERSON): THE MESSIAH
OF THE KINGDOM OF GOD   *page* 161
 1 The 'Church'   163
 2 The Suffering and Death of Jesus   164
 3 Jesus's Messianic Secret   165

VI CONCLUSION   168

5 Paul   169
 by Rudolf Bultmann
 I SOURCES   169
 II LIFE   170
 1 Background and Training   170
 2 Conversion   171
 3 Career as Apostle   175
 III THEOLOGY   182
 1 Presuppositions   182
 2 Content   190

6 Eschatology   215
 I ESCHATOLOGY IN THE HISTORY OF RELIGION   215
 by Alfred Bertholet
 1 Origin and Dispersal   215
 2 Signs of the End   220
 *3 The End of the World as a Result of
 Natural Catastrophes*   222
 *4 The End of the World Brought about by
 Living Agents*   225
 5 The Renewal of the World   226

 II ESCHATOLOGY IN THE OLD TESTAMENT AND
 JUDAISM   230
 by Otto Procksch
 1 The Beginning and the End of History   230
 2 The Elements of Israelite Eschatology   231
 3 Hosea and Amos   234
 4 Isaiah   236
 5 The Seventh Century   238

Contents

6 *Deutero-Isaiah* *page* 240
7 *Canonical Apocalyptic* 242
8 *Extra-canonical Apocalyptic* 245
9 *The Calculation of the Date of the End* 247

III THE ESCHATOLOGY OF PRIMITIVE CHRISTIANITY 249
by Kurt Deissner
  1 *Significance* 249
  2 *Old and New Material* 251
  3 *Basic Features* 256
  4 *Realistic Eschatology and the Future Hope of the
    Individual* 259

IV CHRISTIAN ESCHATOLOGY AND THE HISTORY OF
  DOCTRINE 260
by Paul Althaus
  1 *The Eschatology of the Early Church* 260
  2 *Augustine and the Middle Ages* 264
  3 *The Reformation and Protestant Orthodoxy* 266
  4 *From Pietism to the Present Day* 269

V ESCHATOLOGY IN THE PHILOSOPHY OF RELIGION
  AND DOGMATIC THEOLOGY 276
by Paul Althaus
  1 *The Concept of Eschatology* 276
  2 *The Origin of Eschatology* 277
  3 *Christian Eschatology (Methods and Principles)* 280
  4 *The Criticism of the Eschatology of the
    Final Phase of Time* 283
  5 *The Truth contained in Chiliasm* 289
  6 *Eschatology and Ethics* 292

7 Baptism 294
  I BAPTISM IN PRIMITIVE CHRISTIANITY 294
  by Ethelbert Stauffer
    1 *Pre-Christian Baptismal Practices* 294
    2 *The Beginnings of Christian Baptism* 298
    3 *Paul* 305

8

Contents

4 Post-Pauline Churches   *page* 307

II THE HISTORY OF THE DOCTRINE OF BAPTISM   311
by Friedrich Wiegand
1 The Earliest Period   311
2 Augustine   313
3 The Doctrine of the Catholic Church   314
4 Protestantism   316

III THE DOGMATIC THEOLOGY OF BAPTISM   318
by Arnold Meyer

IV THE LITURGICAL HISTORY OF BAPTISM   321
by Hans Hohlwein
1 The Formation of the Rite of Baptism   321
2 The Further, Formal Development of Baptism   323
3a Baptism in the East   324
3b Distinctive Features found in the West   326
4 Roman Catholic Baptism   327
5 Different Types of Protestant Baptism   330
6 Baptismal Customs   333

V PRESENT DAY LITURGICAL PRACTICE   335
by Paul Graff
1 The Presence of the Congregation   335
2 Baptism in Emergency   336
3 The Baptism of Adults and Re-Baptism   336
4 Present-day Needs   337

VI BAPTISM IN CANON LAW   338
by Martin Schian

8 The Eucharist   341
I THE EUCHARIST IN THE NEW TESTAMENT AND
    THE PRIMITIVE CHURCH   341
by Karl Ludwig Schmidt
1 Jesus and the Eucharist   341

Contents

*2 The Eucharist in the Church of Jerusalem
(and Palestine)*   *page* 350
*3 The Eucharist in St. Paul and in the
Hellenistic Churches*   352
*4 The Eucharist in the Post-apostolic Churches
and in the Fourth Gospel*   357

II THE HISTORY OF THE DOCTRINE OF THE
     EUCHARIST   358
by Friedrich Wiegand
1 The Earliest Period   358
2 The Greek Development   362
3 The Western Church   367
4 Eucharistic Disputes in Protestantism   373

III THE SIGNIFICANCE OF THE EUCHARIST
     AT THE PRESENT DAY   379
by Arnold Meyer

IV THE LITURGICAL HISTORY OF THE EUCHARIST   385
by Hans Lietzmann
1a The Breaking of Bread in the Primitive Church   385
1b The 'Eucharist' of the Didache   386
2 The Pauline 'Lord's Supper'   388
3 The Formation of the Sunday Morning Celebration   389

V PRESENT-DAY LITURGIES   391
by Paul Graff
*1 The Historical Origin of the Present Protestant
Eucharistic Liturgies*   391
2 The Reform of the Eucharist   396

VI THE EUCHARIST AND CANON LAW   401
by Martin Schian

Bibliography   403
Index   405

Acknowledgements

The editor, translator and publishers wish to acknowledge their indebtedness for permission to use copyright material contained in this volume as follows: the article *Paul* translated by Schubert M. Ogden and reprinted from *Existence and Faith:* Shorter Writings of Rudolf Bultmann, with the permission of Hodder & Stoughton Ltd., London, and of World Publishing Co., Cleveland and New York.

Scripture quotations from the Revised Standard Version of the Bible, copyrighted 1946 and 1952 by the Division of Christian Education of the National Council of the Churches of Christ in the United States of America, are used by permission.

General Introduction

An encyclopedia can be a piece of high-level hack work, warming over and serving up the conventional wisdom, factual or not, contained in previous works of reference— or it can be an active partner in creative scholarship, giving thinkers at the growing edge of research an opportunity to state the results of that research for the nontechnical reader and to correlate their results with the work of men in related fields.

A splendid example of the second type of encyclopedia is *Die Religion in Geschichte und Gegenwart*, a multivolume reference work on religion and theology. Its first edition was published by J. C. B. Mohr (Paul Siebeck) in Tübingen from 1909 to 1913; the second edition from 1927 to 1932; the third edition from 1956 to 1962. Thus its first edition was published in the German Empire, the second in the Weimar Republic, the third in the German Federal Republic; there was no new edition during either of the World Wars or during the Third Reich.

More even than the vicissitudes of the German people and state over the past half-century, it is the scarcely less turbulent changes in German Protestant theology that are reflected in the successive editions of the *R. G. G.* When the first volume of the first edition appeared in 1909, Paul Tillich and Karl Barth had just completed their schooling, and Rudolf Bultmann was still a graduate student. When the last volume of the third edition appeared in 1962, all three were emeriti, and they and their colleagues had meanwhile changed the shape of theology so drastically that every major article had been radically revised as the result of their work.

The second edition of the *R. G. G.*, therefore, occupies a special place in the making of twentieth-century theology. For here many of the men who re-drew the theological map have set down their thought on the key issues of theology. Most of them wrote full-length books on those issues. While some of the books have been translated into English, others have not. As a result, the articles in this edition provide a unique wealth of materials, from which the selections in these three volumes have been made.

These selections are based on the conjunction of several criteria: the issues that have, since *R. G. G.*[2], become or continued to be dominant in theological discussion; the men who wrote for *R. G. G.*[2] who have shaped the development of twentieth-century theology; the resources that have been drawn upon for that development. In many cases, the article by *the* man on *the* issue in *R. G. G.*[2] is the best available summary of his position; practically all of them appear here in English for the first time. Thus here, and perhaps nowhere else, the present-day reader may study Paul Tillich on *Myth* and on *Revelation*, Rudolf Bultmann on *Gospels* and on *Paul*, Friedrich Heiler on *Catholicism*, Paul Althaus on *Eschatology*, Nathan Søderblom on *Union Movements*, Adolf Harnack on *Origen*, and many other seminal thinkers of the twentieth century on the questions which have made them important, but which have also shaped us and our time.

Each volume is supplied with a brief introduction both to the men and to the movements it sets forth, and with a bibliography of works in English pertinent to both. But these have been deliberately held to a minimum, in order to permit the material to speak for itself.

J. P.

Introduction to Volume I

The Christian theology of the twentieth century has been characterized by an unprecedented development of biblical theology. The notion of 'biblical theology' is itself a product of the Enlightenment; and in a real sense, of course, theology has always dealt primarily with the themes of biblical literature. The golden ages of the history of theology have been times of a new and deeper study of Scripture. Irenaeus and Athanasius, Augustine and Thomas Aquinas, Luther and Calvin, Wesley and Kierkegaard—despite the radical differences among them, all these thinkers would deserve to be called 'biblical theologians' and wanted to be known as such. Indeed, some have argued that the very emergence of the idea of 'biblical theology' as distinguished from other kinds of theology is itself a testimony to the theological poverty of our time, for previous centuries were engaged in the study of biblical theology whenever they 'did theology' at all.

Separating our time from previous centuries, however, is a revolutionary change in the method of studying the Bible and therefore of 'doing theology.' The theological scholarship of the eighteenth and especially of the nineteenth century undertook to examine the literary remains of the Christian past in greater historical detail than had ever been done before. Among those literary remains, the Bible occupies a special place, and the historical-critical method of modern theology analysed the Old and New Testaments with the care and precision made possible by new tools and new materials. More has been learned about the historical environment of Israel and early Christianity during the past century or so than in all the history of scholarship before. The analogies and contrasts between the Old Testament and the religious literature of the ancient Near East can now be made the subject of historical investigation, rather than merely of competing apologetic claims. Similarly, the echoes of the Greek mystery religions and of Gnosticism in the language and thought of the New Testament may now be evaluated in a disciplined manner. The distinctive literary forms of the Bible have been isolated and classified, with the result that we can read the text in its context with a new sensitivity to the nuances of meaning produced by these forms.

One natural reaction to all this historical research could be, and in fact was, to give up the theological task as quite impossible as well as presumptuous. The rich variety of biblical myth and narrative, poetry and apocalyptic, could not be forced into the static categories of the dogmatic theologian without doing violence to what the historian had discovered about the Bible in its setting. As Karl Barth has put it, 'in the history of Protestant theology the nineteenth century brought with it the none too dignified sight of a general flight, of those heads that were wisest, into the study of history. From the safe, distant regions of the history of religion, the Church, dogma, and the mind, the practice of theology is a gentle exercise, if one has the necessary equipment.' But Barth adds the warning: 'What decides whether theology is possible as a science is not whether theologians read sources, observe historical facts as such, and uncover the nature of historical relationships, but whether they can think dogmatically.' It was understandable that for a time the study of the Bible in what was thought to be a purely historical way should simultaneously fascinate the scholar and intimidate the systematician, but eventually the question whether theologians can think dogmatically, or at least doctrinally, had to reassert itself.

When it did, however, the theologian could not proceed in the same old way. It simply would not do any longer to treat the Bible as a seamless robe or to pick a verse here and a verse there as proof texts for traditional dogmas. The historical method of studying the Bible had permanently amended the ground rules of theology. If one was to 'do theology', one must go beyond historical criticism; one could not go behind it. The realization of this may not have dawned on some churches or some Christians even today, but that does not alter the stubborn reality of the predicament of post-critical theology. The emergence of modern biblical theology is one of the ways theology has found for coping with that predicament. Biblical theology claims to be a way of thinking doctrinally on the basis of Scripture without doing violence to the assured results of historical scholarship. The historians were not always convinced of this claim or impressed with its concrete expressions. They saw biblical theology as an attempt to reintroduce dogmatics through the side entrance after it had been ejected through the front. Justified though this criticism may have been in certain instances, it will be clear from the article on *Biblical Theology and the History of Biblical Religion* that the new 'biblical theology' did not look upon 'the history of biblical religion' as an embarrassment to be overcome, but as a critical methodology to be exploited.

In the new situation, certain traditional themes of dogmatics were discarded. In the article on *Jesus Christ*, for example, the doctrine of the two natures in Christ, the divine and the human, and the analysis of the reciprocal relations between them, is no longer a tool for the interpretation of the random data we have about the life of Jesus. (It is discussed at considerable length in the article on *Christology* in Volume II of this set.) For after those data had been pored over by the historical critics 'from Reimarus to Wrede', to quote the title of Albert Schweitzer's classic on the subject, the religious mystery and the theological problem represented by the doctrine of the two natures were, to be sure, still unresolved. But the dominant category for the theologian's reflection on that mystery had become 'history' rather than 'nature,' the dynamic rather than the static, time rather than eternity. And problematical though such distinctions still are, they do indicate both the extent and the direction of the reorientation.

A similar reorientation is visible in the article on *Prophets*. Much of the history of biblical interpretation in Christianity had been devoted to the 'messianic prophecies,' which, beginning with the so-called 'protevangel' in Genesis 3.15, were thought to run as the crimson thread throughout the Old Testament. Events in the life of Jesus or in the subsequent history of the Church were found to be fulfilments of such prophecies; conversely, one found prophetic anticipations for such events also when the New Testament itself did not quote the prophetic passage in question (consider the use of Isaiah 9.6 in the liturgy for Christmas). Even in the hands of the most skilful of Christian allegorists, however, this definition of the role of the 'prophet' left large portions of the prophetic literature untouched. The historical criticism of the eighteenth and nineteenth centuries, therefore, deepened an insight to which interpreters of that literature had come earlier: that the prophets were 'forthspeakers' and not merely (or even primarily) 'fore-tellers.' Their writings deserved to be studied on their own terms and in relation to the historical situation of Israel. If a Christian exegete found the application of certain prophecies to Jesus Christ unavoidable (as most did, for example, with Isaiah 53), that was now regarded as an extension of the primary, that is, the historical, sense of the passage.

While certain themes of dogmatics have been discarded, others have become much more prominent than they had been before. They had always been a part of traditional summaries of Christian teaching, but for a variety of reasons they had risen and fallen in importance during the course of theological history. Now they have acquired a new importance, thanks to the historical-critical study of the Bible. Probably the best instance of such a theme is to be found in the article on *Eschatology*, the doctrine of 'last things'. Because it dealt with 'last things', this doctrine had usually appeared at the end of a book on theology or of a series of classroom lectures; and as 'that little chapter at the very end', it was sometimes disposed of quite summarily. When it was given a fuller exposition, moreover, the theologian tended to concentrate on a description of the afterlife that matched Dante in precision of detail if not in power of language. But the contention of Johannes Weiss, Albert Schweitzer, and others that Jesus had expected the end of this age to come very soon and had taught his disciples to look for the messianic kingdom, thrust the 'little chapter at the very end' into the very centre. Even those who did not accept that contention in so radical a form were compelled to reconceive the problem of eschatology to meet it. They were compelled to do so also by a growing realization that the man of the twentieth century did not look at nature, history, and time as his ancestors had, and that therefore an eschatology still cast in the older framework did not make much sense to him.

Still other themes continued to be as important as they always had been, but they had to be played in a new key. As part of the sacramental system of the Church, the sacred rites described in the New Testament have always been a subject for churchly theologians to discuss.

But the articles on *Baptism* and on *Eucharist* show that these rites must now be viewed in the light of discoveries about the New Testament in its setting. The career of John the Baptist and statements of the Church Fathers had long made it clear that Christian baptism was not altogether unique. But the new interest in the relation between primitive Christianity and both its Jewish and its gentile environment stimulated the historical investigation of other baptisms and their possible significance for the Christian rite of initiation. Historical investigation of the eucharist did not pay attention only to non-Christian parallels, whether in the Jewish Passover or in the sacred meals of certain mystery religions, but also to the cultic and dogmatic evolution of the memorial meal said to be instituted by Jesus 'on the night in which he was betrayed' into the Divine Liturgy of the Eastern churches and the solemn Mass of the Western. The theological implications to be drawn from this investigation were, and still are, a matter of vigorous controversy; the propriety of the investigation itself is not.

Historical investigation has left its mark on the themes of biblical theology in another way, too: the organization of theological material under historical rather than doctrinal categories. The article on *Prophets*, already referred to, or the article on *Gospels*, may seem to be predominantly literary rather than theological and thus to be concerned with form at the expense of content. But the literary analysis both presupposes and produces theological judgements about the content of the biblical books. The proper way to organize and present that content is determined by the historical and literary study of the Old and New Testament. The literary form of the books, then, is not a barrier to their theological use, but a tool for their theological analysis. The gospels do not tell us about the teachings of Jesus in isolation from the early

Christian community, and only an awareness of how the community remembered the words and deeds of its Lord will enable us to get at the 'theology' of the gospels. For the same reason, the article on *Paul* carries out a theological task by means of a literary and historical examination of the Pauline epistles. Such traditional and controversial questions as the meaning of the doctrine of justification by faith in the epistle to the Romans, so long a matter of debate between Roman Catholic and Protestant theologians, take on a different appearance when priority is given to the historical assignment.

Thus the biblical theology that came out of historical criticism looked markedly different from its ancestors, yet not so different that all family resemblance was lost. The authors of the chapters in this volume all claimed to be engaged in the delicate assignment of thinking historically as they wrote theologically. By no means may they all be said to have belonged to a single theological party or even to have followed the same method of relating historical investigation to theological exposition. The bibliography appended to this volume includes those works by them which have appeared in English and, in some instances, works in English that deal with them. Some of their names have become famous during the past generation; others are familiar only to a few:

Althaus, Paul, b. 1888 (*Eschatology*), professor of systematic theology at Rostock and Erlangen.

Bertholet, Alfred, 1868-1951 (*Prophets, Eschatology*), professor of Old Testament at Basel, Tübingen, Göttingen, and Berlin.

Bultmann, Rudolf, b. 1884 (*Gospels, Paul*), professor of New Testament at Breslau, Giessen, and Marburg.

Deissner, Kurt, b. 1888 (*Eschatology*), professor of New Testament at Greifswald.

Dibelius, Martin, 1883-1947 (*Biblical Theology*), professor at Berlin and Heidelberg.

Graff, Paul, 1878-1955 (*Baptism, Eucharist*), pastor in Klein-Freden and Hanover-Limmer.

Gunkel, Hermann, 1862-1932 (*Biblical Theology, Prophets*), professor of Old Testament at Berlin, Giessen, and Halle.

Hohlwein, Hans, b. 1902 (*Baptism*), pastor in Eilenburg.

Lietzmann, Hans, 1875-1942 (*Eucharist*), professor at Jena and Berlin.

Meyer, Arnold, 1861-1934 (*Baptism, Eucharist*), professor of New Testament and practical theology at Zürich.

Procksch, Otto, 1874-1947 (*Eschatology*), professor of Old Testament at Greifswald and Erlangen.

Schian, Martin, 1869-1944 (*Baptism, Eucharist*), professor of practical theology at Breslau and Giessen, and general superintendent of the Lutheran churches of Breslau.

Schmidt, Hans, 1877-1953 (*Prophets*), professor of Old Testament at Tübingen, Giessen, and Halle.

Schmidt, Karl Ludwig, 1891-1956 (*Jesus Christ, Eucharist*), professor of New Testament at Giessen, Jena, Bonn, and Basel.

Sellin, Ernst, 1867-1946 (*Prophets*), professor of Old Testament at Vienna, Rostock, Kiel, and Berlin.

Stauffer, Ethelbert, b. 1902 (*Baptism*), professor of New Testament at Erlangen.

Wiegand, Friedrich, 1860-1934 (*Baptism, Eucharist*), professor at Erlangen, Marburg, and Greifswald.

J. P.

I

Biblical Theology and the History of Biblical Religion

I THE OLD TESTAMENT

1. The science of 'biblical theology' has its origin in the early period of rationalism, when people began to realize that the dogma of the Church was not simply equivalent to the content of the Bible, and tried to distinguish between *dogmatic* theology and *biblical* theology. In the expression 'biblical theology', therefore, the emphasis is on the distinctive term 'biblical'. The intended purpose of this science was to draw together in a systematic whole, that is, in logical order, the doctrines which occur, according to the occasion and the purpose of the author, scattered throughout all the biblical writings. The view of that period, then, was that the material for study consisted of biblical *doctrine*, and the framework in which it was set out was taken from that of contemporary *dogmatic* theology.

2. There is no doubt that the setting up of biblical theology as a special discipline, distinct from dogmatic theology, was a great step forward, which can never be reversed. But, now that biblical theology has been of importance for almost two centuries, in the past generation more and more scholars have demanded the renewal of this discipline. It has constantly become more clear that a mistaken view is implied both by the word 'theology' and by the word 'biblical'.

First, the word '*theology*'. Since the work of Schleiermacher an increasingly clear distinction has been made between 'religion' itself and its scientific and cognitive treatment, that is 'theology'; and in the present case it is quite clear that living religion, springing from the heart, is one of the main concerns of the Old Testament, wh ile intellectual reflection about religion plays a comparatively small part. Neither the characteristics of the Israelite people, nor the period in which they lived were favourable to reflective thought. Thus, in order to do justice to the material in the Old Testament, it is necessary to lay all the emphasis on the *religion* to which it bears witness.

3. At the same time the limits implied by the word *'biblical'* are beginning to be of less and less significance. The religion that grew up and flourished amongst the people of Israel forms an extraordinarily complex pattern, which must be studied in all its manifestations and tendencies, in its achievements and in its depths. Every piece of evidence which will further this study is equally acceptable, whether it comes from the Bible itself or from outside it. Thus the results of archaeological excavations are automatically taken into account. The importance of this principle is made particularly clear when we consider the post-biblical writings of the *Apocrypha* and *Pseudepigrapha*. They were formerly excluded from biblical theology, but are now widely used in the work of exegesis, for in the history of religion as it actually took place, there was no abrupt break such as would justify the exclusion of these later writings.

4. Above all, however, scholars have begun to *order the material* of biblical theology differently. Biblical theology formerly set out its subject matter in the order of dogmatic *loci* (the subject-headings of dogmatic theology) and therefore dealt first with God, his nature, his attributes and his works, and went on to the angels, then to the creation and sustaining in being of the world, and

then to man, his original condition, sin, etc. This ordering of the material can properly be objected to on the
grounds that the principal object of the study, the living
religion, is dealt with inadequately. In particular, conventional biblical theology does not give adequate
treatment to *persons* who are of great religious significance, and who are themselves a powerful and abundant
source of religious devotion. This is particularly true of
the *prophets*. The reason for this is not that scholars are
incapable of it but because the way in which their material is ordered prevents it. Similarly, the great *periods* of
the history of religion fall entirely or almost entirely into
the background, in spite of the fact that the last generation realized quite clearly that marked divisions had
occurred in the course of Israel's religion.

5. If one looks closer at the ultimate reasons for this
inadequacy of biblical theology, it becomes evident that
it is still under the influence of the Church's traditional
doctrine of inspiration. The result is that all the material
in the Bible is treated as though it were on the same level,
and the unity of thought which it is assumed exists in the
Bible leads to a unified and systematic ordering of the
material. If this method is rejected at the present time,
the ultimate reason is that the spirit of *historical* investigation has been introduced into this study. The phenomenon observable in the present generation, the re-
placement of biblical theology by the *history of Israel's
religion*, is explained by the fact that the doctrine of
inspiration is now beginning to be superseded by the
spirit of historical investigation. We see the same change
taking place in other fields. An older work on Christian
dogma such as that of Luthardt's *Dogmatik* is set out
according to the *loci*, with the result that all psychological
connections are disrupted. For a considerable time, however, it has taken the form of a 'history of dogma' with a
strict historical approach, especially in the work of Adolf

Harnack. Accordingly, therefore, the 'Introduction to the Old Testament', dealing with individual books in turn, is tending to be replaced by a 'History of Israelite Literature'; and even in the field of archaeology, which previously consisted of the accumulation of individual facts, the historical outlook is beginning to creep in. The same change as has taken place in the sphere of Old Testament religion has come about simultaneously in the case of the New Testament. In consequence, one might expect that in the immediately foreseeable future biblical theology may take the general form of a 'History of Israelite Religion'. This term is first met in the work of K. Marti (1897, 1907) as a consequence of the work and influence of Wellhausen; the same approach is made by R. Smend (1893, 1899) under the title of *The History of Old Testament Religion*; E. König (1912, 1924) takes the same line; the last 'biblical theologies' of the Old Testament, or similar works, are those of A. Dillmann, 1895; B. Stade (who includes, however, a section on the history of Israelite religion) I, 1905, and E. Kautzsch, 1911.

6. But however serious an attempt is made to understand the religion of Israel as an historic process, our study cannot be restricted to Israel alone, but must place that religion in the context in which it belongs, and which alone can provide a proper historical understanding of it. This means that it must also include the *religions of other nations*, and above all of course the religions of the great civilizations of that period, especially Babylon, Egypt and Persia. In this way, a complete picture will be obtained of the general level of religion we are dealing with, the mutual dependence and similarities that exist, and equally of the differences between the religion of the Bible and that of other nations. Since the religion of Israel retains a great deal of material from the very earliest times, a comparison has also to be made with *primi-*

tive religions. The custom has recently grown up of referring to this method of adducing extraneous material for comparison as 'The History of Religion'; the term is misused in this sense, and is much more appropriate to the whole conception we have discussed. The sense in which it is possible to speak of revelation when the religions of the Bible are regarded from this historical point of view, must be decided by dogmatic theologians (*cf.* Vol. II *Revelation*).

II THE NEW TESTAMENT

1. The 'biblical theology' of the New Testament has the same background as the Old Testament theology described in the first section of this article. Both studies began with mere collections of scriptural proof texts for dogmatics, the so-called *dicta probantia*, arranged according to dogmatic *loci* and set out with explanations; *cf.* S. Schmidt, *Collegium Biblicum*, 1671. The title 'biblical theology' seems first to have been given to such a work by Haymann in 1708. The close attachment of pietism to the Bible then brought into being a theology which, by contrast to the prevailing dogmatic theology of the time, sought only to set out the doctrinal content of the Bible (Büsching, 1756). The transformation of biblical theology from a subordinate discipline of dogmatic theology into an *historical* science was completed in its main outlines by the 'rationalist' J. P. Gabler in his inaugural lecture when he became Professor at Altdorf in 1789. In practice its separation from dogmatic theology came about only gradually. But more and more, the goal that was aimed at was that of presenting 'The Original Countenance of Christianity' (as in the title of a work by Cludius published in 1808). It was true that the declining influence of dogmatics was often replaced by a kind of objectivity

which equated the spirit of the classical age with the outlook of the contemporary scholar. Besides, primitive and later material, major themes and side issues were still discussed on the same level. The separation of the two parts of the Bible within the field of biblical theology had gradually come about since the beginning of the nineteenth century, first by devoting different volumes of the same work to the Old and New Testaments, and then by complete specialization ('Old Testament and New Testament Theology').

2. The infusion of a profounder historical sense into biblical theology in the course of the nineteenth century owes most to the work of F. C. Baur. For he was the first to attempt to understand the writings of the New Testament not as 'books' but as the product of the numerous historical movements of primitive Christianity. His use of Hegelian categories, and his conception of the writings of the New Testament as polemical writings defending particular tendencies, was soon improved upon. His representation of primitive Christianity as a conflict between Jewish Christianity and gentile Christianity was a construction which has largely been superseded; but the way Baur posed the question has been of decisive influence for the later history of biblical theology. At the same time as biblical theology became an historical discipline in this way, the associated theological question in the narrower sense of the word was tackled by J. C. K. Hofmann in Erlangen; his very individual understanding of the concept of revelation is still influential at the present day. But the whole development of biblical theology up to the turn of the century took place under the influence of Baur, and was marked by distinctions between the different personalities and tendencies of primitive Christianity. There was an attempt to individualize the historical phenomena in terms of

what were called the doctrines of a particular writer, and by this process to discover the personal characteristics of the New Testament writers, and even to distinguish the different periods of Paul's life from one another.

The *objections* which were aroused by this method, which had become widely known in the manuals of B. Weiss and H. J. Holtzmann, were first expressed in the methodological study of W. Wrede published in 1897. Following the same lines as the contemporary development of the study of the Old Testament (*cf.* I, 2 above), he objected above all to the doctrinaire fashion in which it was presumed that the New Testament writings were mainly doctrinal in content, as well as to the isolation of each work, which forced scholars to approach each one with the same questions. In place of a 'succession of doctrines' he contended that scholars had to turn their attention to the living development of the primitive Christian *religion*, and that in addition they ought not to restrict their studies to the limits of the scriptural canon, but should pay attention to every piece of writing that bears witness to primitive Christianity. It was only possible to show any development in terms of the origin of the ideas under discussion. 'It is Judaism, and not directly the Old Testament, which is the basis of Christianity from the point of view of the history of religion'; the origin of the religion of primitive Christianity was to be understood in relationship to Judaism and to the spiritual situation of *hellenism*. These two latter demands, the inclusion within the field of biblical theology of the extra-canonical writings and of the problems of the history of religion, are characteristic of the new approach, which could be described as 'the history of primitive Christian religion', or as 'the history of early Christian religion and theology'. Up to the present time, the greatest use of this approach has been made by Wernle (*Die*

Anfänge unserer Religion, 1901), Weinel in his manual (3rd ed. 1921) and Bousset in his work *Kyrios Christos* (2nd ed. 1921).

3. But even with this, and apart from the numerous and complex problems raised by the study of the history of religion (Iran, Hellenism, Judaism; apocalyptic, gnosis), certain *methodological questions* remain undecided, and their discussion belongs to the future of biblical theology. *a.* There is first of all the question of the importance of *persons* in primitive Christianity. Not every leading personality is a living figure for us from his own literary testimony (Peter); not every important writer is an historical leader (Luke, Ignatius); and one, who was a prophet and writer of the first rank, Paul, had comparatively little effect upon the generation which followed him. But Paul is also a witness; for in parts of his letters, the general moral exhortations (parenesis), he often simply reproduces traditional material. Thus even his letters are also a source for the belief of innumerable unknown Christians; and their historical influence is important, for the beginnings of gentile Christianity, of gnosticism and of early Catholicism are their work. *b.* While the appropriate distinctions have to be made in treating different texts, the *synthesis of what is common to them all* must not be neglected: the essence of primitive Christianity, the 'religion of the New Testament' (books with this title were produced by B. Weiss and Feine; but *cf.* also the *Theology of the New Testament* by Schlatter) is a reality. And if historical study is not to be content with being merely antiquarian, even a purely historical approach must ask which features of this general picture explain the *universal significance of Christianity;* almost imperceptibly, this question then becomes related to the *evaluation* of these ideas, the question as to whether these features and their meaning are truly 'enduring'. From this point of view, it is easy to understand that the extra-

canonical literature takes second place to the New Testament. The final problem, that of faith, is an even thornier one. For the relationship of a Christian to the gospel 'does not permit a continuous attitude of vacillation and reservation' (Schlatter). The demand that theology must be able to raise *revelation* above the level of the historical picture study was pressed by Karl Barth and his followers; amongst the manuals in general use, those of Feine and of Hofmann have made an attempt in this direction. The danger of such an attempt lies in the uncritical confusion of historical and 'theological' points of view. The recognition that the scholar himself is caught up in the course of history, shows that this danger can never be completely excluded. In spite of this, we must advocate the separation of the two points of view, because they belong to different levels, and the more the scholar retains the freedom and the opportunity to emphasize the *supra-historical content of the New Testament*, the more he will be able to maintain untarnished the integrity and the purity of his historical study of the New Testament.

Martin Dibelius

2
Prophets

I PROPHECY IN THE HISTORY OF RELIGION

1. The Definition and Nature of Prophecy

Prophecy is a difficult concept, because the *word* is applied to different things, and because from the impression made by prophecy as it is found in the Old Testament, it is very easy to adopt a one-sided idea which is by no means appropriate to all cases. Thus, for example, the Egyptian 'prophets' cannot be compared with the Hebrew prophets, because there prophet is nothing but a word for priests; thus for example, the 'first', 'second', and 'third' prophets form the first three of five classes in the priesthood of Amon-Re. And although perhaps the original idea may have been that of a priest who gave oracles, the prophets of Isis and Serapis in Rome were not even that, but simply priests. Even from the linguistic point of view the word 'prophet', which is taken from the Greek, is ambiguous. Does it mean someone who 'speaks forth' or someone who 'speaks in advance'? In the first case the simplest paraphrase would be that which can be drawn from a combination of two passages in the Old Testament (Exod. 7. 1 and 4.16): the mouth of God, that is, his *instrument of revelation*. In the second case, the particular task of the prophet would be to foretell the future. Clearly, conventional usage provides examples of both. We hear of prophets of salvation and doom, and of weather prophets, etc., and understand by them persons who are able to foretell good fortune or bad fortune, or at least the

32

weather; whereas Mohammed is called a prophet, without any implication that he foretold the future. But one thing is common to both conceptions: what the prophet proclaims is more than what is known to ordinary persons; the prophet has a special gift. This is expressed by primitive people by saying that the prophet is someone who is able as a matter of course to exert or pour out his *orenda* (his inner spiritual power) and so to learn the secrets of the future. In other words, the eyes and ears of the prophet are open to things which the everyday person neither sees nor hears: the element from which he lives is vision and hearing, and in so far as these are exercised in an ecstatic condition, the prophet is an *ecstatic*. The underlying psychological structure is usually constant: 'There is always a powerful sub-conscious experience, ecstatic in nature, in which a superhuman power seizes the prophet who has been called, and forces him into its service whether he will or not' (Hauer).

Depending upon the degree of his psychic endowment, the prophet's ecstasy can attain one of several stages. They can perhaps to some extent be distinguished according to the degree in which his own activity is involved in his experience: there are cases where the person of the prophet seems to be completely absorbed by the spirit that controls it; the spirit possesses him completely, so that his personality is filled with God ('enthusiasm'); it destroys and replaces his personal individuality in order to speak through him completely unhindered; and there are other cases where this individual personality can nevertheless remain so strongly interposed that it seems in some way to govern from within the spirit that speaks through the prophet. Between these two extremes, there lies the whole wide variety of individual cases. But the constant feature is always that the prophet, in so far as he genuinely deserves this name, is *inspired*. 'Without the spirit there is no prophet' (Hauer). Thus the prophet speaks from the inspiration of spirit by which he is distinguished from ordinary men: a characteristic of the prophet is the *differentiation of the individual*, even though, by the use of suggestion—the power of which is extraordinary, especially in primitive civilization—the impulse to form a collective grouping with other prophets is occasionally evident. But another aspect of this differentiation brought about by the inspiration of the spirit is that one characteristic of prophetic preaching is its proclamation of something *new*, hitherto unknown or unrecognized. Usually, in fact, its content is the *future*. The future is hidden from ordinary mortals, but is revealed to the specially gifted beings among them, the prophets. The prophet has the power of divination, at least that of 'inspired divination', and what is true of mantics (those who carry out divination), that their talents need to be cultivated by a form of training, and that where the gift begins to fail increasing use is made of artificial means, is also extensively true of the prophets. In itself, the prophetic gift is independent of sex—there are numerous *prophetesses*—and of age, although there seems to be a preference for youth, at least in the case of the calling of a first-born son. The fact that a prophet needs *vocation*, that is, that on principle he cannot take upon himself what must be given to him, means that he is usually imbued with a powerful *consciousness of mission*. This is the point which makes most clearly evident how false it is to suppose that prophecy is mere illusion and deception. This makes no sense at all of the powerful urge, the sacred and sometimes terrible *necessity*, to which prophets in so many cases feel themselves subject. There is far more tragedy than pleasure in prophecy. 'What good word ever came to mortal men from prophets? Through evil portents the many oracles of their art teach us the fear of prophecy'; these words from the *Agamemnon* of

Aeschylus, spoken with regard to the message of Cassandra, not only reflect the impression made by prophetic preaching upon innumerable hearers, but also that made upon those who utter them, as can be seen from the words with which Cassandra immediately continues: 'Woe upon me and my merciless lot; for mine too is bound up with it'. That the prophet can utter an oracle concerning his own person is a sign of the true significance of prophecy in the history of religion. This lies in the progressive element of which the prophet becomes a spokesman, so that the prophetic genius has always been a creative force in religion.

2. The Spread of Prophecy

Prophecy is *world-wide*. The only question is, how much can be included within this concept; for example, whether it should be extended to shamanism and other similar phenomena in primitive societies. But it is difficult to exclude these ecstatics, who were conscious of receiving a revelation concerning the future in the form of visions and voices, and Hauer's statement must be accepted: 'If we are to understand *primitive* religion aright, and wish to appreciate the outlook of primitive religion, then we have to take its prophecy as seriously, for its own stage in development, as we do the prophets of higher religions.' It is a fact that it was taken seriously in its own environment, in a way which gave its occurrence the character of a direct divine revelation. This evaluation of prophecy can be traced throughout the most widely differing *popular religions*, which can only be mentioned briefly here: the Chinese Taoist prophets and Japanese religion, Indian religion (*cf.* the statements concerning prophecies in the Puranas), Roman religion (*cf.* the prophecy of Anchises in the *Aeneid* VI), Germanic religion (*cf.* the *Völuspá*), and Slavic and Celtic religion. Amongst the Greeks, according to the detailed study of

Fescher, three groups of prophets can be distinguished: 1. Legendary figures of pre-history such as Orpheus, Musaeus, Bacis, Epimenides, and the Sibyllae, who were a special group. 2. Seers who appear in poetry, such as Teiresias, Calchas, and Cassandra. 3. Temple prophets, who answer specific questions, but who have no personal standing apart from their oracles. These do not prophesy the future (that is rather the task of the μάντεις); their particular task is to proclaim on feast days the ἱερὸς λόγος which every great sanctuary possessed. Thus Pindar regards himself as a τιροφάτας, when he re-shapes a passage out of a heroic saga. Thus a writer describing Greek religion can say that no prophet appeared in Greece, if he means a prophet in the sense of someone 'who came into conflict with older conceptions of belief and preached instead a new revelation'; but the same writer can describe Xenophanes as a prophetic figure, because he taught of a God who was similar to mortals neither in his form nor in his thoughts, and attacked the worship of idols and mythology, especially in the form in which they were related by Homer or Hesiod.

The fundamental difference between Greek prophecy and that of Israel has been described as its impersonal and unhistorical nature. This cannot be said of a prophet with the consciousness of mission of the *Iranian* prophet *Zarathustra*, who was 'the first to think of the good, the first to speak of the good, and the first to carry out the good . . . the first to bring revelation'. He is said to have received the revelation which bestowed upon him all wisdom, in conversations with Ormazd himself in heaven, where he had been taken up by angels. This revelation gave him such assurance that he was willing to confirm the truth of his promises at the decisive moment by submitting to an ordeal in his own person. Later Parsee writings tell of other prophets who save the faithful in the miseries of the final age, and the value placed on prophecy is so high that the angels who belong to the first prophets are regarded by the orthodox as the strongest. It is a matter of opinion whether the founder of *Manichaeism* can be called a prophet; the use of his own intellect is much more strongly developed, and he is one of the few of his kind who have read and written a great deal. On the other hand Mohammed is regarded in a special sense as 'the prophet'. By Islam he is regarded above all as him whom God has sent (rasûl), and in the same way God has revealed his will by means of human messengers to individual ethnic or local groups (ummak's), who admittedly usually greet them with deaf ears or with actual resistance. Islamic doctrine reckons the total number of prophets (nabî's) at 124,000, of whom 313 have been given a message, and so much reliance is placed on these messages that the later dogmatic development could not but regard those who brought them as sinless. By contrast to all earlier prophets, Mohammed was regarded as the final and ultimate manifestation, the 'seal of the prophets' (*Koran* 33.40). The right of intercession was regarded as a special privilege of the prophet (*shafa'a*; cf. Jer. 15.1). The picture of *Buddha* has also been enriched with prophetic features. He prophesied that those who carried out devout actions would become Buddhas in a future era; as he did this, he smiled and rays proceeded from him, such that when they returned to him, depending upon the subject of the particular prophecy, they disappeared into one or another of the parts of his body. He is even said to have prophesied the decline of his religion. In Japan in modern times, the appearance of prophetesses, uneducated women, such as Shimamura Mitsuko (ob. 1868) and especially Deguchi Nao (1836-1918), resulted in the setting up of sects.

Alfred Bertholet

IIA THE EARLIEST ISRAELITE PROPHECY BEFORE AMOS

It is a characteristic of the *earliest prophets before Amos* that none of them wrote anything. From the time of Amos on the prophets formed one of the classes which produced literary works. In other respects, the differences within the periods we have distinguished are greater than, for example, the difference between Elijah and Amos.

1. The Sacred Ecstasy of the Bands of Prophets

The first time we hear of 'prophets' (Hebrew, *nāb'ī* plural *n*e*bī'īm*) is 1 Sam. 10. Here Samuel prophesies to Saul, who has just been anointed king by him: 'After that you shall come to Gibeathelohim, where there is a garrison of the Philistines; and there, as you come to the city, you will meet a band of prophets coming down from the high place with harp, tambourine, flute and lyre before them, prophesying. Then the spirit of the Lord will come mightily upon you, and you shall prophesy with them and be turned into another man' (vv. 5 f.). V. 10 tells of the exact fulfilment of this prophecy: 'The spirit of God came mightily upon him, and he prophesied among them.' The first thing that this story tells us is that the *n*e*bī'īm* used to live together in bands. In 2 Kings 2.7 we hear of more than fifty, and in 1 Kings 22.6 of four hundred *n*e*bī'īm* in one place. They did not just meet together on certain occasions: the *guilds of prophets* lived close together. If their company grew too great, part of it might migrate into another place, in order to found a new settlement there (2 Kings 6.1 ff.). It was possible to enter the guild in youth (2 Kings 5.22; 9.4). In their external appearance, those who belonged to a band of prophets could be distinguished by a special dress, a shaggy garment of hair cloth and a leather girdle (2 Kings 1.8 and Zach. 13.4), and apparently also by a special way of cutting their hair, a tonsure (*cf.* 2 Kings 2.23, where Elisha is called 'bald head'). Their community was not monastic: the $n^eb\bar{\imath}$'$\bar{\imath}m$ had wives and children and their own possessions. We hear of the debts of a $n\bar{a}b$'$\bar{\imath}$, which the creditor was collecting from his widow after his death (2 Kings 4.1 ff.). At the head of the community was a person who was its 'master', and was addressed by the others and also by outsiders as 'lord' and 'father' (2 Kings 2.3; 4.1; 6.21; 8.9; 13.14). What was the *occupation* of these people who lived together? In the first instance, it was religious in nature. The settlements of the $n^eb\bar{\imath}$'$\bar{\imath}m$ of which we are told were all found at places which are famous as sanctuaries: in Gibeathelohim (1 Sam. 10.10), in Ramah (1 Sam. 19.18), in Bethel (1 Kings 13.11; 2 Kings 2.3), in Gilgal, and in Jericho (2 Kings 2.5). Saul met the $n^eb\bar{\imath}$'$\bar{\imath}m$ when they came down from the 'high place', and the place of worship. What they did in common, and what distinguished them as $n^eb\bar{\imath}$'$\bar{\imath}m$ from others, was regarded as due to the 'spirit of Yahweh' or the 'spirit of God' (1 Sam. 10.6,10).

This common activity, this behaviour as a prophet, seems to be something *alien* by contrast with the usual behaviour of men. Through it, one became 'another man' (1 Sam. 10.6). It was possible to come to this state, even against one's will; for the behaviour, or rather particular condition of those people was very infectious (1 Sam. 10.5 f.; 19.20 ff.). Nothing is more characteristic of this than the fact that it came upon the $n\bar{a}b$'$\bar{\imath}$ *by force*, sometimes against his will, but always as the effect of a power outside him. The spirit of Yahweh 'came upon man', like a beast of prey (1 Sam. 10.10). This did not exclude people from sometimes making *preparation* for it. When the $n\bar{a}b$'$\bar{\imath}$ Elisha wished to 'prophesy' he had a minstrel play before him (2 Kings 3.15); in 1 Sam. 10, we also hear of music, played before the *nᵉbî'îm*. We may suppose that rhythmical movements—a passionate dance—were used as a preparation for the prophetic state, as is explicitly stated of the prophets of Baal (1 Kings 18.26). On the other hand, the *holding of the body tense and still* could also serve to induce the condition of prophecy. Before a prophetic esctasy, Elijah sat for a long time and crouched down with his head between his knees (1 Kings 18.42 ff.). The person who was the head of the 'band' (1 Sam. 19.20) would have led the exercises that induced the coming of the spirit.

What did a nāb'î do when the 'spirit came upon him'? This question can best be answered by the story of the flight of David to Samuel (1 Sam. 19.18-24). David fled before King Saul to Samuel, who appears here as the master of a band of prophets. When this was reported to Saul he sent out messengers to seize David. These came face to face with the *nᵉbî'îm*, who were prophesying at the time. Samuel, however, stood before them. Then the spirit of God also came upon Saul's messengers, so that they too fell into the *hitnabbê'*, the prophetic state. Finally, after sending messengers a third time in vain, the king himself set out. But while he was still making his way, 'the spirit of God came upon him also, and as he went he prophesied'. But when he arrived, 'he too stripped off his clothes, and he too prophesied before Samuel, and lay naked all that day and all that night'. From this story we learn—as is also clear from 1 Sam. 10 and elsewhere—that one could prophesy and move at the same time, but that this state reached its highest point when the prophet lay on the ground. It was possible for someone to lie there for a day and a night—without any control over himself—in ecstasy. Consequently, it is natural that the condition of the *nāb'î* should have appeared to the ancient Israelites as related to madness, and that *prophetic inspiration and madness* were sometimes identified. The mental illness of Saul was called *hitnabbē'*, prophecy. Anyone who spoke in contempt of a prophet, in fact, called him 'mad' (2 Kings 9.11; Jer. 29.26 and Hosea 9.7). A prophet, like someone mad, could not be made responsible for his actions: when he had promised to remain in a place, 'the spirit of Yahweh would carry him who knows where' (1 Kings 18.12). Who could reproach the prophet for this, when the force under which he acted was so strong that when a prophet could not be found, it was supposed that his bones were scattered in some abyss into which his sacred madness had cast him (2 Kings 2.16 and *cf.* 1 Kings 18.46)? Even the Israelite *neḇī'īm* seem like the prophets of Baal (1 Kings 18.28) to have inflicted wounds upon themselves at the beginning of their ecstasy (*cf.* Zach. 13.6 and 1 Kings 20.41).

This religious frenzy and the value placed upon it is *not something specifically Israelite* (*cf.* 1,2 above). The Old Testament recognizes this phenomenon amongst Israel's neighbours, and calls those amongst them who underwent this 'frenzy' by the same name as its own prophets, *neḇī'īm*. But as early as the ancient Egyptian of the journey of Wen-Amon from the eleventh century B.C., we hear of a sacrifice at night at *Byblos*, during which the 'god seized one of the great servants of the king, so that he went into a frenzy'. There were bacchantes and maenades in *Greece*, and epidemics of dancing and the phenomenon of the flagellants in the *Middle Ages*, which also provide parallels. But the clearest surviving parallel to ancient prophecy is found in the cultic practices of the oriental *monasteries of dervishes*, which take place under the guidance of a leader, are induced by music and rhythmical movements, and go to the extent of the self-infliction of wounds and to ecstasy—in which the dervish is 'out of his senses'. Again, amongst so-called *primitive peoples*, all the details of prophecy described above can still be observed: the stimulating music, dancing that becomes more and more passionate, the brooding (with the head between the knees and the hand before the face, as we hear of a 'prophetess' in Guinea), and then the epileptic trance, in which the prophet lies on the ground, his face and limbs twitch, his veins swell up, his eyes stand out from his face and his voice changes. All this takes place, even at the present day, amongst primitive people of various races and in distant parts of the world, and is understood by them in a religious sense.

It is a feature common to all religions at a certain stage of their development, that *psychic abnormality*, madness, epilepsy, hysteria and melancholy are regarded as *caused by the deity*. It is perfectly obvious—so the people of the ancient world would have said—that someone in such a frenzy is not acting and speaking on his own initiative. Something has 'taken him over' (in Greek 'ἐπιληψία), is moving his limbs without his consent, 'speaking from him with a strange voice' and 'is looking with other eyes than his own' (*cf.* Philostratus, in his *Life of Apollonius of Tyana* III, 38). Even in the ancient world, such 'possession' as it was called, was felt to be something terrifying. People spoke of an *evil spirit*, or of an 'impure spirit', which had overpowered the person, and longed greatly for him to 'go out of him', so that the person could return 'to his own nature'; *cf.* the driving out of demons in the New Testament and Josephus, *Ant.* VIII. 2.5. But in other religions, and also in the Old Testament itself, the mysterious and awesome states into which the prophets fell were regarded as *effected by the highest deity himself*. In this context, it is noteworthy that the Old Testament nevertheless—by contrast to the religion of Cybele or Dionysius—displays from the very start the feeling that God himself is too great to enter into a person in this way. The expression is not that it is Yahweh who had taken possession or come upon a person, but the 'spirit of Yahweh' (1 Sam. 10.6,10; 11.6; Judges 14.6; Ezek. 11.5), or 'the hand of Yahweh' (2 Kings 3.15; Ezek. 1.3; 3.22; Isa. 8.11). In one passage there is even mention of 'an evil spirit from Yahweh' (1 Sam. 16.14). Here we are approaching the view of late Judaism and the New Testament on the subject of the demonic. But this is an exception; in general, ecstasy, even in its most terrible form, is regarded as the work of Yahweh, and consequently as a blessing to be desired. It is not surprising that the words and actions of ecstatics were carefully noted.

2A. *The Prophets as Givers of Oracles*

When the deity is speaking through the mouth of the *nāb'î* inspired by him, he must want to say something definite. Consequently, the *disconnected sounds* which came from the mouth of the person lying in an ecstasy were listened to in fearful suspense. However confused or incomprehensible they were, they might signify something of the future. Thus the prophets, whose ecstasy at first seems to have been an end in itself, became givers of oracles. It is not to be expected that such confused outcries, proceeding from an ecstasy, would have been preserved in any great number in literature. The strange names Hosea and Isaiah gave to their children (Hosea 1.4,6,9; Isa. 7.3; 8.3) and the strange combinations of words which Isaiah (30.7) and Jeremiah (20.3) uttered as curses against their enemies, may be regarded as isolated examples of such words, uttered in ecstasy; *cf.* also the speaking with tongues in the New Testament.

A decisive reason why the prophets came to be valued as givers of oracles was the fact that at that time, as today, a peculiar faculty of receiving presentiments or of clairvoyance, or of experiencing *hallucinations in the form of visions and voices*, often seems to have been found amongst those persons who had a tendency to fall into ecstatic states. We can clearly see in the stories of prophets in the books of Samuel and Kings that it was conviction confirmed by experience that during an ecstasy prophets could see through closed doors and walls and into the far distance; *cf.* 2 Kings 6.12. The knowledge possessed by the prophets is always the seeing and hearing of individual concrete things. In the earliest times, visions seem to have been much more frequent than auditory phenomena (*cf.* Vol. II, *Revelation* II, 2.3). Far more frequent than the apprehension of something distant in space was the revelation to the prophet of the *future*. Prophets seem to have imparted their secret experiences in metrical speech from the very earliest times. Ultimately, even in this period the prophets were conscious of *seeing God* in their ecstasy: 'I saw the Lord sitting on his throne, and all the host of heaven standing beside him,' said the prophet Micaiah ben Imlah (1 Kings 22.19). In 2 Kings 6.17 it is assumed that the prophet *constantly* sees the invisible supernatural beings who, hidden from ordinary men, hold sway throughout the world.

2B. *The Prophets as Miracle-Workers*

It is natural that when men could see and hear such wonderful things, there should be stories about their *wonderful acts*. Someone who has the spirit of Yahweh within him is capable of more than other men. The stories of the ancient *nᵉbi'im* rest on the assumption that *their words* do not merely proclaim the future, but *bring the future about*. When King Ahab said that he did not ask the *nābi'* Micaiah ben Imlah about the future, because all he ever foretold was evil, the assumption is that the word of this man brought about evil, otherwise there would be no point in not calling for his oracles. In 1 Kings 18.17 Ahab refers to Elijah as the 'troubler of Israel'. This is only meaningful if the drought from which the country was suffering at that time had not only been foreseen by the prophet, but brought about by his words; *cf.* 2 Kings 6.31. Elijah is represented as having power to call down fire from heaven (2 Kings 1.10). The word of Elisha is obeyed by the bears in the forest (2 Kings 2.24). Even the later writing prophets had this view of their work. On one occasion, Jeremiah tells how he uttered the following word against an opponent: 'This very year you shall die', and he adds: 'In that same year, in the seventh month, the prophet Hananiah died' (Jer. 28.16 ff.). On some occasions, the prophet was able to accompany his miracle-working word with an *action* which also worked the miracle (*cf.* 2 Kings 13.14-19). The last echoes of such actions are probably to be found in the 'symbolic' actions of the later prophets (*cf.* II B, 1 g. below). We often find the belief that the *bodies* of the prophet or the objects which he always carries with him can work miracles merely through contact. For example, Elijah wore a cloak, which amongst other things had the power to divide the waters of the Jordan when he struck the water with it (2 Kings 2.8), while Elisha had a staff, contact with which caused an iron axe to float (2 Kings 6.6). The story is told of both these prophets that they stretched themselves out over a dead body and by contact with their own body brought it back to life (1 Kings 17.19; 2 Kings 4.34). It is easy to understand that men of whom such things were believed were treated with *veneration*, mingled with terror. It is small wonder that we can see how some of them came to have a powerful influence upon the destiny of their people.

3. The Political Prophets

As far as we can see, the majority of the $n^eb\bar{\imath}'\bar{\imath}m$ used their power for nothing more than to *earn their living*, which apart from this may have been a poor one (*cf.* Amos 7.12). There were various ways of inquiring into the future, and one of them was to go to the $n\bar{a}b\bar{\imath}'\bar{\imath}$, if one perhaps wanted to know where something was that had been lost, or if one sought a healing or information about the future. It was customary to bring a present on certain occasions (Num. 22.5,7; 1 Kings 14.3 ff.; 2 Kings 4.42; 5.22; Ezek. 13.19). There were even prophets who gave a favourable or unfavourable oracle depending upon the value of this present (Micah 3.5).

There is a clear distinction between the great mass of the *nebi'im* and certain individual personalities, who, aware of their mysterious experiences and supported by the veneration that they were accorded as a result, disdained to concern themselves with minor everyday affairs. These men went in for *politics*. The subject of their secret visions was the destiny of their people. They were to be found at the court of the king, and at the head of the army as it went out into battle. The king himself had to submit to their will, and if he refused, they were powerful enough to incite revolutions. Such a political prophet was Elisha, who, according to 2 Kings 9.1 ff. brought down the dynasty of Omri and then accompanied King Jehu on his campaigns. The title 'the chariots of Israel and its horsemen' (2 Kings 13.14), borne by Elisha in history, and by Elijah, though in his case only in saga, shows most clearly the importance such a 'political prophet' could have for the history of his people. In the Old Testament, in addition to Elisha and perhaps Nathan, we have only one other example of a prophet who went out into battle with the king: *Jonah ben Amittai*, who accompanied Jeroboam II on his victorious campaigns (2 Kings 14.25) and made such a powerful impression upon the memory of his people, that centuries later he became the hero of a poem (the Book of Jonah).

4. *The Origin of Classical Prophecy*
The question as to where the real *origin* of prophecy should be sought is a difficult one. Is it to be found in the

46

religious world of the ancient Canaanite civilization, or is it a distinctively Israelite phenomenon? The whole nature of the religion of the oldest $n^ebi'im$, the practices aimed at depriving them of consciousness, and also their dances, belong in the realm of Near Eastern nature religion, into which Israel entered when it conquered the country. On the other hand, one can list a whole series of features which point to the rise of the prophecy of the $n^ebi'im$ in the ancient Israelite religion of the tribes who migrated from the desert: their clothing (a cloak of skin, a leather girdle, and especially their tonsure) is most easily explained as the ancient Bedouin form of dress maintained as a protest against the civilization of a settled nation. The prophets were particularly vigilant in preserving ancient Israelite practices: the prophet Samuel hewed in pieces with his own hand the king of the Amalekites, Agag, who had been spared by Saul, because he regarded the ancient and barbaric custom of the 'ban', the utter destruction of everything living amongst the conquered people, as an inexorable religious duty (1 Sam. 15.32 ff.). The prophet Ahijah incited the revolution which led to the separation of Israel and Judah, in anger against the foreign and new-fangled culture at the court of Solomon. Finally, the prophet Elijah, the greatest prophet of this whole age, fought against the nature religion of the Baal of Tyre on behalf of the Yahweh of the desert, whom according to the sage, he went to seek himself at Sinai.

We also find that these earliest prophets have a powerful awareness of the close relationship between *religion and morality*. It was a prophet who condemned the sin of King David in the story of Bathsheba. A prophet faced King Ahab when he had obtained for himself Naboth's vineyard. That Yahweh was a god of righteousness, and that even kings might not pervert this righteousness with impunity, and that this God would even abandon his

47

own people to the enemy for the sake of his righteousness, is a lofty conception, which is voiced by the prophets even as early as the period we are discussing. Of course in all these points—in the rejection of nature religion, in the veneration of Yahweh alone, and in the conviction that God protects righteousness, this earlier prophecy was expressing a traditional point of view. Behind them there towers the mighty figure of Moses, who—in the view of the later Deut. 18.15—was himself a 'prophet', and who in a way which we can no longer grasp in detail, already seems to have possessed the goal of the development we have been describing, if only in a rudimentary form.

Hans Schmidt

IIB. THE ISRAELITE PROPHECY FROM THE TIME OF AMOS

1. The Secret Experiences of the Prophets

a. PROPHETIC REVELATION. *The fundamental conviction* of all the prophets who produced literary works was that their ideas came from Yahweh himself. They quite regularly begin their teaching with the phrase: 'Thus has Yahweh spoken to me', that is, 'Yahweh inspired these ideas'. And anyone who heard the voice of the prophet had to face the question whether or not he believed that this was true. Everything else stood or fell with the answer. Thus the prophet demanded a belief in his person, in his *divine inspiration*. And this inspiration was so conceived that it excluded all human co-operation. Anyone who spoke 'of their own minds', 'prophesied lies' (Jer. 23.16; Ezek. 13.2). Jeremiah confesses that of himself he would have wanted something quite different than what Yahweh was now inspiring him to say (Jer. 17.16). And even the fact that the prophet uttered such ideas was not his own free decision; necessity was laid upon him (1 Cor. 9.16).

> *'The lion has roared; who will not fear?*
> *The Lord God has spoken; who can but prophesy?'*
> *(Amos 3.8).*

As when a lion roars no one asks whether or not one should be frightened, but anyone feels involuntarily afraid, so everyone becomes a prophet who hears Yahweh's voice. He is filled by a sea that must overflow, a fire that cannot be controlled; he can do nothing else, he must cry out. Thus Jeremiah tells us himself that, as Moses had done before, he had refused to become a prophet; but of what use was human resistance when God laid his mighty hand on the man whom he had destined from his mother's womb (Jer. 1.5)? On another occasion he tells how, depressed by the sorrowful calling, which brought only persecution and distress of the soul, he had constantly attempted to be rid of it all:

> *'There is in my heart as it were a burning fire*
> *shut up in my bones,*
> *and I am weary with holding it in,*
> *and I cannot' (Jer. 20.9).*

When the prophet was asked when and how Yahweh's word came to him, he was able to tell of certain dark hours when he was lifted out of himself in an ecstasy, when something mighty pressed down upon him (Isa. 8.11), where the spirit fell upon him; then he saw and heard a *mystery*. Most prophets either did not speak of these matters or only hinted at them, out of reverence and awe. The people had to be satisfied by hearing the content of the revelation, while the form of the revelation concerned only the prophet and his God. But a few prophets, especially the later ones, have left us more detailed descriptions.

b. VISIONS. In such circumstances the prophet had visions. Such visions are quite regularly associated with *verbal re-*

velations. The prophet saw Yahweh seated upon his high and lofty throne, and then he heard the spirits who surround him, and who spoke to him themselves (Isa. 6.1 ff.). He saw the mounted messengers of Yahweh and received the knowledge that they brought him (Zach. 1.7-11). Now it is significant that the principal emphasis in this association of vision and words that are heard is almost entirely upon the words, especially in the early period: to the prophet, the important thing was not Yahweh's appearance, but what he said; not the description of the appearance of the messengers, but their message. The precedence of verbal revelations over visionary appearances means that there are far more words than visions, and that the most frequent oracles are those which lack any detail about how they were received. Here again it can be seen that the prophets placed the whole value on the ideas which they had received, and not upon the marvellous way in which they came to them; ideas are much more easily represented to the ear than to the eye. Isa. 21.1-10 tells us a great deal about the mental life of the prophets; it is a passage which in its miraculous and poetic form gives us a deep insight into prophecy. There the assumption is that the prophet could send out another self, the watchman, who saw secret things and heard hidden words. Thus the prophet had the ability to prepare himself for the revelation (Hab. 2.1). Sometimes this second self forgot what it had seen; but here it is commanded before it goes out to watch to make the revelation known to the other self; thus one might compare the procedure to 'post-hypnotic suggestion'. At a later period the form of the vision came to be something very close to an artificial setting for the ideas, without a real experience lying behind it.

c. THE VERBAL REVELATIONS, which, as we have seen, were sometimes associated with visions, usually occur *independently.* Yahweh opened the prophet's ears so that he might perceive the mysterious voices. He heard the spirits speaking amongst one another (Isa. 40.3 ff.). He heard the words which were spoken 'in the council of God'. He was even now able to hear future voices: the trumpets that should one day ring out, already sounded in his ears (Jer. 4.21). He already heard the snorting of the enemy horses (Jer. 8.16) and the terrified cry of the fallen city (Jer. 4.21). He could also perceive things which were far off; he heard the moaning of the exiled people in Canaan (Jer. 31.18 f.).

Often the prophet heard immensely *loud sounds* and saw exceedingly *bright lights*: a roar like the roaring of mighty waters, the thundering roar of whole nations (Isa. 17.12), the shaking and rattling of Yahweh's chariot (Ezek. 3.12), and the glory of God a thousand times brighter than all earthly light (Ezek. 1.4 ff.).

d. OTHER PROPHETIC EXPERIENCES. There were also other prophetic experiences, such as do not belong to the fields of hearing and seeing. Thus in a vision a strange taste was imparted to Ezekiel: he was given to eat a book in the form of a roll, which tasted to him as sweet as honey (Ezek. 3.3). Or we hear of miraculous journeys or travelling. When Ezekiel had received the first revelation and the mighty vision had left him, we read: 'The spirit lifted me up and took me away, and I went in bitterness in the heat of my spirit, the hand of the Lord being strong upon me; and I came to the exiles of Telabib' (Ezek. 3.14 f.). A flood of anger had swept over the prophet. Now he must go to the stubborn people that they might hear. Then he was seized, the spirit took hold of him, and he raged about, up hill and down dale, careless of where he was going, crying out, striking about himself, and deeply agitated.

e. ENERVATION AFTER ECSTASY. Such strange experiences had a terrible effect upon the body and soul. For one cannot hear divine things in peace of soul, especially if the content of revelation is distress and ruin, and catastrophe; *cf.* Isa. 21.3 f. Jeremiah gives a moving description of how the fearful vision pursued him, and how the human instrument, too weak to bear the enormous weight of the divine message, had to succumb to it (Jer. 4.19-21). And when the ecstasy then left him, he felt as though he had been beaten with clubs. The apocalyptic writers were particularly fond of describing this condition of *stupefaction*.

f. NERVOUS DERANGEMENTS. Thus we need not be surprised to hear on occasion of phenomena in the prophets which we would at once term *mental illness* or at least *nervous derangements*. Thus Ezekiel tells how for a long time he felt as though he were bound, and how when a divine power had put cords about him, he could not turn from one side to the other (Ezek. 4.8). The same prophet was unable to speak for a time, until suddenly his mouth opened (Ezek. 3.26; 24.27). Finally one must also remember the striking sexual images which play so important a part in Ezekiel, and which may display something of his personal, and perhaps unconscious life.

g. SIGNS. Again, some of their signs are as strange as many of these experiences. Isaiah once went naked for three years (Isa. 20.3). Jeremiah one day appeared in the forecourt of the temple with a yoke upon his shoulders (Jer. 28.10). Ezekiel once took his household chattels upon his shoulder and forced himself with them through a hole in the wall (Ezek. 12.1 ff.). He represented the siege of Jerusalem by besieging a brick with a pan (Ezek. 4.1 ff.). These were things which were done by children, fools and prophets in Israel! It was formerly believed that the prophets did not really do these things, but only described them as means of expression for their ideas. But how could they have lit upon such astonishing stories, if it had not been the custom of prophets to do such remarkable things in fact? It may well be asked whether the prophets carried out such 'signs' under a force that constrained their soul, and in obedience to the spirit, or whether they only did so in order to attract attention. For we may certainly imagine that crowds of children ran after the prophet where he showed himself naked, and that all respectable people shook their heads over him. But the question we have posed cannot be answered with a simple yes or no. Ezekiel gives the impression of being an ecstatic personality, from whom such strange actions were to be expected. But persons of clear intellect such as Isaiah and Jeremiah were different; they probably quite consciously imitated the weird actions of the earlier half-mad ecstatics (*cf.* IIA, 1 above) for particular purposes. But we must not forget that between the two extreme cases numerous intermediate phenomena are possible.

h. LESS DRASTIC MANIFESTATIONS. But the experiences of the prophets were not always so remarkable. In the case of the literary prophets there were a great many more which were much less unusual. Only at the beginning of the activity of a literary prophet was it expected of him that he should have experienced a vision; this is what we nowadays call the *vocation vision* (Isa. 6; Jer. 1; Ezek. 1). There, as it were, the electric charge that filled the prophet was discharged with a single powerful flash. Throughout the rest of his life, the forms taken by his revelation then became less powerful. This is something clearly associated with a change that took place in the content of prophecy. The earlier prophets prophesied individual events in the immediate future; the later literary prophets certainly did not cease to speak in the first instance of the future, but they were able to do more than this: they were also capable of giving the reasons why Yahweh was sending the event they prophesied; they knew his thoughts and they felt his moods. It is true that the strangeness, however much it was mitigated by

53

them, was still constantly present: even though the extraordinary forms of revelation which were a reality in the earlier prophets were tending to become merely stylistic forms, they never completely disappeared even amongst the later prophets. They were not thoughtful and dispassionate thinkers or even disinterested instruments of God, to whom he could proclaim what he wished; they were always full of an inner fire, overflowing with fierce anger or burning enthusiasm, and they experienced what they preached as 'the word of Yahweh'. They were drawn by a marvellous certainty: they were sure that they knew the secret plans of Yahweh. They had a feeling of power (Micah 3.8), a certainty that they were able to utter commands in the name of God to kings upon their thrones, and defy their whole nation. Thus they cared nothing for persecution, imprisonment and death. The physical necessity that constrained the earlier prophets was here on the point of becoming a moral necessity. A person such as this was not merely aware of a few isolated moments in which God spoke to him; his whole life was full of revelations, and ultimately he thought only what God thought. Thus a prophet of this kind remained in the service of God throughout the whole of his life. He regarded as God's thoughts all the thoughts which he was bound to think if he was to make sense of God at all, everything that had come upon him in the great moments of exaltation and inspiration. Thus the prophets also heard the voice of God in the events of their own lives: Jeremiah once recognized God's word in a strange offer for a sale which a relation made to him (Jer. 32.6 ff.). Thus the psychically abnormal falls into the background, to be replaced by a moral and religious demand made on the whole personality. Jeremiah even reached the point of recognizing the law of God's ordering of the whole world (Jer. 18), despised dreams and sought to discern the truth of all other prophets by inquiring whether they served the true purpose of God, to convert Israel (Jer. 23.23 ff.).

i. CONCLUSION. Thus we see in the history of prophecy a *rapid transition from the prophet to the religious thinker.* This must not lead us to overlook the demonic elements in the Old Testament prophets, but we must not overestimate them or be too surprised at them. Factors that dissuade us from giving too great a weight to the elements of psychic abnormality are that the same phenomena occurred throughout the whole world, that they occur even in lower regions, and in these above all, that similar phenomena such as those of clairvoyance or fortune-telling have nothing to do with a higher conception of religion as such, and finally that many of them have a suspicious similarity to mental disease. But one cannot accept a crude supernaturalist view, because of the wide variety and different levels of thought displayed in the sayings of the prophets, as well as the observation of the great differences in style between different prophets, which reveals how important a part was played by the prophet himself in his sayings. The prophets sometimes foresaw the future in the most marvellous way, but they were also often wrong. Thus although there may be much that is wonderful in prophecy, something that we do not wish to deny, what is of constant value to us is not its form, but content: we recognize the revelation of God in these profoundly inspired and devout persons, and in the eternal thoughts which they uttered.

2. On the History of Prophecy

a. PROPHETS OF GOOD FORTUNE AND OF DOOM. Jeremiah distinguished two kinds of prophet: those who prophesied good fortune and those who prophesied doom (Jer. 28.8 f.). This distinction, drawn from the Old Testament itself, is entirely justified. At almost every period we find the two types side by side. At the very earliest period of prophecy, before the appearance of the literary prophets, we find both together: the mighty Elijah, the enemy of King Ahab, who is an example of the prophecy of doom, and Elisha, who brought favour to Jehu and his house.

Even after the appearance of the great literary prophets and prophets of doom, the prophecy of good fortune still continued. Certainly, it would be easy to conclude from the Bible itself that during this period there was only a series of *prophets of misfortune*: Amos, Hosea, Isaiah, Jeremiah and Ezekiel. This impression is explained by the fact that history justified these prophets of doom— Israel and Judah were in fact conquered by the world empires, as they had prophesied—and by the fact that as a result of this, when Judaism drew up the canon, practically the only prophets chosen from before the Exile were those who had proclaimed misfortune. But if we look closer, we see everywhere traces of the existence, during the very same period, of an important body of *prophets of good fortune*, who had been a powerful force. We learn from Amos that his contemporaries spoke a great deal of 'the day of Yahweh' and longed for it to come (Amos 5.18): thus the prevailing prophecy at that time was of good fortune. And from the end of Judah's history we hear that Jeremiah and Ezekiel fought against an influential and certainly powerfully inspired prophecy. But from the Persian period on, the prophecy of good fortune obtained undisputed dominance; beginning with the great 'Deutero-Isaiah', all the prophets of Judaism were prophets of good fortune, right up to their later successors, the apocalyptic writers (*cf. Eschatology* II p. 230, below). But even from the pre-exilic period we have the prophets of good fortune, and prophecies of good fortune, in the canon: men such as Nahum and Habakkuk prophesied the fall of the world empires, as do many passages prophesying good fortune which are now found as interpolations in the books of the prophets of doom. For it is by no means to be taken for granted, as is usually done, that such additions all belong to the post-exilic period; rather, we must accept the possibility that they are the work of the prophets of good fortune, who are contemporary or who lived not long after. But there is a further consideration. Like an individual, a nation can only live when it possesses a hope. The prophets who proclaimed hope, therefore, must always have been the rule in a nation that was so forceful and so convinced of itself, while the prophets of doom are only conceivable as a terrible exception. In fact, we must go on to recognize that even the prophecy of doom was only enabled to survive permanently by the fact that the longer it continued, the more it borrowed from the prophecy of good fortune. Thus this tendency, which for the earlier period is played down by the canon, we must imagine as being much greater, if we are trying to achieve an understanding of the true history of prophecy. Naturally, this tendency was simply branded by its opponents, the prophets of doom, in the passionate language of ancient Israel as 'lying prophecy' (Jer. 23.21 ff.; 29.8 f.; Ezek. 13). Nevertheless, we have to acknowledge that in their manifestations they could not be distinguished from their opponents, and even more, that they gave expression to ideas that are at the very heart of religion, such as that of Yahweh's dominion over the whole world, and of the conversion of the heathen; and no one spoke so wonderfully as they did of Yahweh's love for Israel.

Much more important, of course, than these prophets were their opponents, the *prophets of doom*. The mass of the people heard the prophets of good fortune with enthusiastic rejoicing; the prophets of doom were despised and slandered, imprisoned and slain. But at the same time, it was they who proclaimed lofty ethical ideas, and who were the true instruments of revelation. It is they who at the period of the Assyrians and Babylonians

57

preached the fearful message of the fall of the state and the nation. They were locked in a struggle which lasted for a century with the prophets of good fortune. And yet both schools of thought had things in common: both shared in an extensive popular eschatology which ultimately went back to foreign conceptions (*cf.* 2*b*. below). And even the most terrifying prophets of doom almost all saw salvation as the conclusion of what God was doing, and so found their way back to the prophecy of good-fortune, from which they had so widely separated themselves. Thus we can tell from the hope of salvation expressed by the prophets of doom, what was proclaimed at that time by the prophets of good fortune. For a long time both parties seem to have tolerated each other. This was during the period of the Deuteronomic reform, which seemed to have realized the ideal of the prophets of doom, and when it was possible to believe that Judah had become a devout nation which from henceforth could expect good fortune. But then came the parting of the ways once again, between the two schools of thought. As the Babylonians drew near, the prophets of good fortune proclaimed the salvation of Jerusalem, while Jeremiah prophesied its fall. At this point what was more or less true even of the preceding period became clear: the prophets of doom laid more emphasis on the demands of religion, especially upon its *ethical demands*—Jeremiah threatened ruin, because the unrighteousness of the people was necessarily bringing judgement upon them— while the prophets of good fortune tended more to proclaim the consolation of religion: Yahweh would not abandon his people or let his sanctuary fall into the hands of the heathen. Jeremiah was justified by what happened; Judah fell. Now the ideas uttered by the prophets of doom became a force in the community that was being built up in exile. But by the very victory which they had so evidently won, the prophecy of doom ceased to exist.

It was now no longer sufficient to speak of God's anger; consolation had to be given and salvation to be proclaimed, if the nation and its religion were to survive at all. Thus the Exile signified the victory of the prophecy of doom, and also the moment of its disappearance. The prophecy of good fortune had brought Judah to ruin, but now it raised its head with renewed force. The prophecy of doom had seen a terrible fulfilment. The dream of the glorification of Zion never came to reality. But the greatest conception of the prophets of salvation, that the religion of Yahweh would become a world religion, was fulfilled when the time came.

b. THE EARLY HISTORY OF THE LITERARY PROPHETS. It follows from what we have said above that the *previous history* lying behind the prophecy of someone like Amos was a prophecy of good fortune which struck a responsive chord amongst his people. But we can go even further than this. The whole of the material which we find in the prophetic books can be divided without distorting it into three groups; (a) *political* prophecies and advice given by the prophets; (b) their *ethical* and *religious* ideas; (c) various oracles *non-political* in content, dealing with the destiny of the country, the earth and the universe. Such themes, dealing especially with the end of the world and the coming into being of a new world, form a strange contrast to the other expectations of the canonical prophets, which in general were concerned with *politics*. This leads to the conclusion that they must have belonged to a general pattern of prophecy taken over by these prophets. Since it is quite evident that there are mythical elements in these cosmic oracles (*cf.* Vol. II, *Myth and Mythology* III A, 5), it seems likely that this eschatology was not created in Israel but was borrowed from other nations. Thus the whole development probably took place as follows: (a) somewhere in the East—it is not possible at the moment to say where—there existed an eschatology with a powerful mythological tendency, which spoke of the passing away of the old world and the coming into being of a new world: (b) this teaching concerning the end of the world was brought to Israel and adopted by an enthusiastic prophecy of good fortune which prophesied ruin upon the nations round about, through such events as the coming of an enemy from the north (Gog and Magog), and salvation to Israel in the midst of all this horror; (c) at this point, the prophets of doom who shared the same basic pattern of ideas as their predecessors, took the step of including Israel in the universal disaster.

c. THE DIFFERENCE BETWEEN THE LITERARY PROPHETS AND OTHER PROPHETS. In their religious ideas the literary prophets are closely related to such figures as Ahijah and Elijah. But they differ from these early prophets in the following respects. Whereas previously the prophetic movement, as far as we can tell, had only made any decisive advance on isolated occasions, there now came into being an almost uninterrupted series of dominant men. Again, while the earlier prophets attacked one point or another with passionate force—Ahijah turned on the forced labour of Solomon, Elijah on the temple of Jezebel and the murder of Naboth—the later prophets laid down general principles, in the same spirit as their predecessors but with far greater clarity. Thus, for example, they did not fight against one god or another who may happen to have been contesting Yahweh's position in Israel at that time, but against polytheism as a whole. In the same way, they did not announce isolated events in the future, as Elijah had prophesied the famine; instead, they saw a whole vision of the future, a great 'plan of Yahweh', a 'mighty work' of God—this is particularly evident in Isaiah. It is characteristic of these men that they committed their prophecy to writing: it is possible to attack a single wrong or prophesy an isolated event by the spoken word, but a whole series of ideas can only be communicated in writing. In politics, the difference between the older and the new approach is that the former was concerned with the internal affairs of Israel, while in the latter the dominant theme is international politics; it was the approach of the might of Assyria which brought about this change in Israel's intellectual life. In the strictly ethical and religious field the characteristic of the later movement is its prophecy of the fall of Israel on account of its sins, the battle against sacrifices and ceremonies, the intervention of the prophets on behalf of the oppressed in the social distress of their time, and their 'ethical monotheism' (*cf.* II C below).

3. The Literary Methods of the Prophets

a. THE PROPHETS AS ORATORS. Originally, the prophets were not writers, but became such towards the end of their history. They were originally orators, as can be seen from the expression 'Hear!' with which their speeches begin. We must try and imagine their sayings being uttered orally, and not as they stand on paper, if we are to understand them. Their public was the people, either in the market place or in the forecourt of the temple (Jer. 7.2). We must not imagine that their manner of delivery, especially in the case of the older prophets, was as deliberate and solemn as that of modern preachers, and in fact the comparison between the prophets and preachers (and even more between them and teachers) has greatly hindered our understanding. We learn of Ezekiel (6.11) that as he spoke he stamped on the ground and clapped his hands, and Jeremiah (23.9) compares himself to a drunken man; and there are passages in the prophets which are derived directly from prophetic ecstasy (Isa. 21.1-10). The 'signs' of the prophets, which we discussed above (1g), and which are often totally extraordinary, imply indirectly that we should conceive

of the whole behaviour and activity, including the manner of speech, of such men as being strange, agitated and
emotional. Thus unbelievers who were contemptuous of
prophetic utterances were able to dismiss them as
meaningless gibberish (Isa. 28.10 f.). On the other hand,
the normal opening words of prophetic oracles, 'Thus
Yahweh *has spoken* to me', show that the prophets usually
used to speak not during their ecstasy, but after. And
from the content of their speeches, we can perceive a
gradual transition from a passionate to a completely
calm mode of speech; we find the latter, for example, in
the concluding passages of Ezekiel.

b. THE PROPHETS AS WRITERS. In the course of a long history the prophets ceased to be orators and became
writers. The earliest prophets, such as we see in the story
of Saul's meeting with Samuel (1 Sam. 10.5) did not
yet write, and had nothing to write (*cf.* II A, 1 above).
But men such as Elijah and Elisha were not writers
either: they came forward in their own person, and did
not think of any effect they might have had over a wider
area; and probably not many of the people to whom they
addressed themselves were able to read. Of course, we
can see from the later literary prophets that even in this
early period the prophetic style had taken on a clearly
developed form, but this does not mean that a great deal
was written at that time; even as the spoken word, their
style could still take on fixed forms. But even from this
early period we have some written passages; these are
the Blessing of Jacob (Gen. 49), the Blessing of Moses
(Deut. 33) and the Blessing of Balaam (Num. 23 f.), the
style of which unites the imitation of the artistic forms
of the prophets with the form of a blessing by a distant
ancestor or man of God.

Even *persons such as Amos and Isaiah* were not writers at
first. We have an express statement that Jeremiah had
already been active for twenty-three years, when he con-

ceived the idea of gathering his oracles together, even though he may have made isolated written notes previously, and he took on the task of gathering them together only because he was prevented from speaking personally to the people (Jer. 36). Amos must have turned to writing when he was expelled from the Northern Kingdom. Isaiah set up an inscription in public (8.1) or wrote down a short oracle before witnesses (8.16; 30.8), in order to be able to display even to the most confirmed unbelievers in the future, that he had prophesied a particular event; thus it was because of those who would not believe him that the prophet became a writer. In general, the literary activity of the prophets was encouraged by the fact that times had changed since their predecessors had prophesied; by this time, writing was much more used in other spheres than during the early period (Isa. 10.1).

We can still trace the process by which this literary activity began with small passages and ended up by producing large books. It began with the writing down of *short sayings*, such as Isaiah displayed or wrote down and sealed, or with brief poems and oracles (an example is the oracle against the steward Shebna, Isa. 22.15-19). A writing such as this would go through the country as a *pamphlet*, and would be read, repeated, and copied, and if it came to pass, would certainly have a powerful effect. Of course the procedure employed by the prophets with these pamphlets, which are so precious to us, was very casual; they thought only of its immediate effect, and not of later generations. And even when the prophet himself, or a devoted disciple, in order to increase this effect, drew up *collections*, they had no interest in arranging passages in chronological order or according to their content. Moreover, the prophets were not concerned to write passages down exactly as they had been uttered at first; they left words out or added them as they fancied. An example of such a later amplification by the prophet himself is found in the oracle concerning Shebna mentioned above: the original oracle, 22.15-19, a short pamphlet, prophesied that the steward would be driven into exile. Not long after, Isaiah added a supplement (which in other respects is certainly genuine), in which in the name of Yahweh he designated Shebna's successor (vv. 20-53). This oracle was fulfilled; but the new minister practised such nepotism that the prophet added yet another oracle, in which he announced the deposition of the new steward as well (vv. 24 f.). Sooner or later, and in part only after several centuries, the *present books* of the prophets were formed from such original collections, and in this process a great deal which did not come from the prophet himself was included. Thus, for example, the Book of Isaiah could be called a review of Hebrew prophecy rather than the 'Book of Isaiah'. The first prophet to alter this situation is Ezekiel. This man was a priest and a lawyer used to scrupulous order, and was convinced that his promises concerning Israel would only be fulfilled decades later, and therefore wrote the first prophetic book, arranging his work on the pattern of a contemporary collection of documents.

c. THE LITERARY UNITS IN WHICH THEY WRITE. Since it is characteristic of every literary category, that the units within the category are of a specific form and extent, and since if these units are not identified, it is impossible to understand the style in question, the study of the style of the prophets must begin with the units in which their utterances were made. This study is all the more valuable, in that in general they are not indicated in the tradition of the text we possess, and many scholars, who have not yet realized the necessity of this task, and following modern ideas of style, still think in terms of units which are much too large, and display great uncertainty in the distinguishing and identification of the passages.

The *short enigmatic words and combinations of words* such as

Jezreel, Lo-ammi, Lo-ruhamáh (Hosea), Emmanuel, Shear jashub (Isaiah), Maher-shalal-hash-baz—'the spoils speed, the prey hastes' (Isa. 8.1), Rahabhammosh-bath ('Rahab who sits still', the bound dragon of chaos; Isa. 30.7) are examples of the very earliest prophetic style. In such mysterious words the literary prophets, imitating the cries of the ancient ecstatics (*cf.* II A, 2*a.* above), summed up their ideas. A further step was taken when the prophets expressed themselves with greater clarity in *short oracles*, extending to two, three or a few more lines. Examples of these are Isa. 1.2 f.; 3.12-15; 14.24-27; 17.12-14; Amos 1.2; 3.1f.; 5.1-3; 9.7. Such oracles are not, as is usually suggested, fragments or summaries of original prophetic 'speeches', but are themselves these speeches. Then the prophets learnt to compose *longer speeches*, of approximately the length of a chapter. But even such speeches are rarely arranged with one clear purpose in mind, as would be demanded by our own ideas of style, based on the example of the Greeks, but mostly consist of a greater or lesser number of oracles strung together. A clear movement of thought is quite frequently absent; the speech takes up the notion of the moment, and comes to an end when the prophet considers the subject has been exhausted. A typical example is Isa 13. The internal ordering of a passage is replaced by a formal and external ordering: one method which is applied several times is that of the *refrain*. Examples of poems with a refrain are Amos. 1.3-2.16 and 4.6-12, and also 7.1-9; 8. 1-3; and also Isa. 2.6-21; 9.7-10.4; 5.24-30. The seven woes (Isa. 5.8-23) were probably first brought together by a compiler. It was the later prophets who first learned to bring extensive material into a coherent order and to write true books; but even in these, the order is not so much by subject as by chronology. This is the case with Ezekiel and Zachariah (1-8). On the other hand, Deutero-Isaiah writes entirely in the old manner:

his work can be compared to a diary, in which he noted down words which came to him each day without any further attempt to arrange them. This heaping up of isolated units is a procedure that can be observed elsewhere in Israelite literature.

d. POETRY AND PROSE. Another line of development in the prophetic writings is that which leads from poetry to prose. Of its nature, enthusiastic inspiration speaks in poetic form, and rational reflection in the form of prose. Consequently, in form the prophetic 'speech was originally a poem. People like the prophets, who received their ideas in times of exalted inspiration and uttered them under the impulse of an over-flowing emotion, could only speak in poetic rhythms. Here, again, our feeling for style, derived from the Greeks, differs from the Hebrew, where oratory and poetry were not mutually exclusive. As far as the metrical form is concerned, two categories can be distinguished in the poems of the prophets: a stricter style, in set rhythms, and a more free style which, depending upon the fluctuation of the prophet's mood, used a mixture of different verse forms. Examples of the first category are Isa. 1.10 ff.; 3.12-15; Jer. 2.1-3; Micah 4.1-3, and of the second such passages as Isa. 1.2 f. and 29.1-8. From the aesthetic point of view, these poetic compositions of the prophets reach extraordinarily high standards, and represent the most sublime element in the Old Testament, which is full of the sublime. We have seen above (1*h.*) how the prophets turned from ecstatics into preachers and religious thinkers. In accordance with this change, the form of their utterances gradually became more calm: the rhythm became more and more free, until it ultimately turned into prose, or else they adopted such categories (*cf.* 3*m.* below) as that of the '*tōrāh*', or that of historical narrative, which of their nature made use of prose. This did not prevent the later prophets from constantly making use of ancient poetic forms, so that in such prophets as Jeremiah and Ezekiel poetry and prose are found side by side.

e. THE VARIOUS LITERARY CATEGORIES THEY USE. If we now attempt to describe the material of the prophetic books and to arrange it according to its literary categories, we are immediately faced by an almost insuperable difficulty. For we are faced with such an *infinite variety*, that it seems to resist any attempt at organization. We find stories of the deeds and events of the prophet's life, told by contemporary or later disciples, and beside them passages which they produced themselves; amongst these are passages which they wrote for themselves and for God, and with them others which were meant for the people, and which form the real substance of their writings. But these prophetic oracles fall into two classes, depending upon the way in which the revelation was received: *visions* and *verbal revelations*, what the prophets saw and what they heard, characterized by their opening words: 'Thus Yahweh showed me' and 'Thus Yahweh spoke to me'. As we have shown above (1*b.*) the verbal revelations were the most frequent.

f. THE STYLE OF THE VISIONS. The content and form of visions are not dealt with in this article.

Dreams are related to visions; Jeremiah (23.25 ff.) was not prepared to consider them as a form of revelation, but they must formerly have been very frequent and very highly regarded.

g. VERBAL REVELATIONS. Much more important than visions are verbal revelations, which for the most part are the revelations of the words of *Yahweh*. Here the prophet regards himself as the 'messenger' of Yahweh—a favourite and characteristic image from an early period—and just as a messenger reports the words of his master exactly as he has heard them from him, so the prophet also has the right to speak in the first person in the name of Yahweh himself. 'Thus has Yahweh spoken', his oracle begins, and at certain points at the end of the sections he adds 'says the Lord' (*n$e^,$um jhwh*). This can alternate at will with another form, in which he speaks about Yahweh's thoughts in his own name, and so speaks of Yahweh in the third person. Thus there is a gradual transition from words heard in ecstasy (Isa. 20.6) to sermons, poems and meditations such as occur, for example, in the book Deutero-Isaiah, which the prophet himself can scarcely have regarded any longer as inspired by God.

Up to this point, the division of the prophetic material into categories has offered no particular problem. We now pass to a series of prophetic sayings which seem to present an almost incalculable variety: we find promises and threats, description of sin, exhortations, priestly injunctions, historical descriptions, disputes, songs of every kind, both religious songs and imitations of secular songs, songs of lamentation and rejoicing, short lyrical passages and whole liturgies, parables, allegories etc. The task of scientific study in interpreting the text is to arrange these individual passages according to their literary categories, and to interpret them according to the context to which they belong; in so far as this study is that of the 'history of literature', however, its task, if it is to be worthy of this name, is to study the history which produced such a variety. The fundamental principle to be recognized in this history is that most of the categories we have named are not originally prophetic, but that *prophecy adopted a very wide range of alien categories.* Originally, the prophets were certainly not composers of songs, story-tellers, or proclaimers of the *tōrāh*, but only became such subsequently (*cf.* 3*m.* below). And the reason why they became such is evident: the prophets were driven to it by their burning desire to gain power over the minds of their people. The fact that they mastered such an extraordinary number of literary categories is a sign of the zeal with which they struggled with the hearts of their people. This makes even more acute the question as to which was the *original and genuinely prophetic category*, on which everything else was based. The answer is clear when we recall the nature of the preaching and the revelation of the earlier prophets (*cf.* 1*a.-g.* above).

The earliest prophets were *foretellers of the future*. This is the popular view at the present day, though scholars have recently disagreed with this, and it is wholly correct to say that there never arose a prophet in Israel whose first saying was not the foretelling of an event of the immediate future. Consequently, we may accept that the earliest prophetic style is to be found in passages in which the future is described. It is characteristic that particularly clear examples of this style are found in the *oracles concerning foreign nations* (Isa. 13-21; Jer. 46-51; Ezek. 25-32 etc.). The new forms of which the prophets made use are naturally to be found in the main in the passages directed towards Israel; however, the passages aimed at foreign nations represent a category which by the time they wrote was completely dead, but which reveals to us the concerns of an earlier period. If this assertion is correct, then the genuinely prophetic descriptions of the future must also provide the clearest examples of the genuinely prophetic form of revelation. We can see that this is entirely the case if we go on to describe the *style of the oracles*.

h. THE OLDEST STYLE: THE MYSTERIOUS. Revelations were received in mysterious times of ecstasy; they appeared obscure and shadowy before the soul of the prophet. This is faithfully reflected in the style of the visions of the future, and explains the strange *demonic and enigmatic* tones of these passages. As far as possible, *names* are avoided; even those which were perfectly well known are not named. Thus in the oracles against Edom in Obadiah, against Egypt (Isa. 19) and the Philistines

(Isa. 14.29 ff.), the enemy from whom the threat comes is not named. Amos and Isaiah, the latter in his earliest period, avoid the name of Assyria. Similarly, exact *figures* are not permitted. Only very approximate figures are given: in three years, forty years, or seventy years' time; when a child who is now conceived is born; when the child can call his father and mother by name (Isa. 7.14; 8.4) etc. *Indirect expressions* are used where one would expect a specific term; thus Hosea (3.1) speaks of 'an adulteress', when he means someone quite specific, his own unfaithful wife. *Images* conceal more than they reveal, or else they are only comprehensible to the initiated: the prophet says 'harvest' when he means judgement, or 'yoke' when he means servitude. Thus ultimately there developed a whole prophetic language of images, and a preference on the part of the prophets for an allegorical form of speech. This obscurity is usually to be found at the beginning of the oracle, which then becomes clearer towards the end; thus, for example, Isaiah 13 begins in a very mysterious way, and the names 'the Medes' and 'Babylon' are not mentioned until vv. 17 and 19. This mysterious tone is particularly appropriate when the *intervention of the divine* in history has to be described (Isa. 10.33 f.), and especially when the prophets make use of ancient mythological material; they tremble to the very depths of their being at what is to come, and so find it only possible to give distant hints. Thus the prophet speaks with the deepest mystery of the child who is to be born to us (Isa. 9.5 ff.), of him who is to come, 'whose origin is from of old' (Micah 5.1 ff.), and of 'the servant of Yahweh', who, going to his death unknown, bears our sins (Isa. 53).

There is no doubt that the prophets often consciously concealed even what was clear to them; Isaiah thought that Assyria would sack Damascus and Samaria, but he said in quite indefinite terms, 'the spoil speeds, the prey

hastes' (Isa. 8.1). The present-day scholar, if he knows
the time and circumstances of an oracle, is able to supply
the appropriate name to what is not named in it; but
when the tradition on the matter is inadequate, our explanations often grope in total uncertainty. In any event,
we ought to read such passages in the prophets with a
different attitude than has obtained up to now: we ought
to recognize that mysteries are being presented to us, and
take care not to destroy with our own over-hasty explanations the impression that the prophet is trying to
achieve.

i. THE FRAGMENTARY NATURE OF THEIR STYLE. Another
sign of the genuine prophetic style is *the way it leads
from one subject to another.* Prophetic apprehension does not
form a coherent and self-contained whole, but consists of
a sudden illumination like lightning. The style of the
oracles reflects this. That is why they display so marked a
movement from one subject to another. Isolated individual elements, uprooted from their context, are abruptly
placed together. One stone is heaped upon another,
mere fragments, which, however, sometimes succeed in
producing an artistic unity, in the spirit that pervades
the whole. The discontinuity is particularly marked
when the prophet turns from the prophecy of doom to
proclaim salvation, giving the impression that Yahweh is
creating something new. An example of this is the final
phrase of Isa. 6.13. These observations mean that an
alleged 'incoherence' should not lead to the conclusion
that a passage is not genuine. The reading of such magnificent passages as Jer. 64.3 ff., Joel 4.9 ff. and Nahum 3.1 ff.
is sufficient to show that this very heaping up of apparently incoherent elements is a genuinely prophetic trait.

j. THEIR CONCRETE FORMS OF EXPRESSION. The occurrence
of the vision as a form of revelation also explains why the
prophetic oracles are so extraordinarily concrete; they
abound in utterly concrete and visual images. The pas-

sage does not say that deserted Babylon will be the possession of 'animals from the marsh', but of 'bitterns' (R.S.V.: 'hedgehogs', Isa. 14.23). If their subject is not in itself visible, it is replaced by a visual image, described as closely as possible: Israel will become as small 'as when one gleans on the ears of grain in the Valley of Rephaim . . . as when an olive tree is beaten—two or three berries in the top of the highest bough, four or five branches of a fruit tree' (Isa. 17.4 ff.); this is concrete language indeed. As we have seen (*cf.* 3*i*. above) it is not the prophets' way to describe a whole circumstance at length; but the prophets have the ability of boldly picking a small scene out of the whole and describing it in concrete terms in such a way that everything else is made clear in it, and it is a reflection of the audacious spirit and determination with which they carry everything to its conclusions, that this scene is usually the last (e.g. 1 Kings 22.17).

k. THEIR PASSIONATE EXPRESSION. No characteristic, however, is so evident as the profound and passionate intensity of the prophets. No word is too terrible or too cruel for the prophets of doom, and nothing too extravagant for the prophets of good fortune. Time and again the climax of a prophecy is formed by marvellous mythological images which horrify the human heart, or inspire and delight it. Or else their passion is relieved in a spate of puns, of reminiscences of other material, allusions, ironical and sarcastic turns of phrase, sometimes in mighty periods as majestic as the waves of the ocean (as in Isaiah), and sometimes in a disquiet that flares up intermittently and a constant shift of attention (as in passages in Jeremiah and even in Hosea). They address everyone with whom they are dealing in the second person: a relic of the ancient prophetic practice of coming face to face with those to whom Yahweh had sent them. They are extraordinarily addicted to the *imperative* form of speech; sometimes whole passages consist of a string of such imperatives (e.g. Jer. 46.3 f.); this too is genuinely prophetic, and the prophet feels justified in giving commands to the whole world in the name of Yahweh (Jer. 1.10). Or else they may break into a series of questions, astonished outcries of the visionary amazed by what he sees and hears (e.g. Jer. 46.5; Isa. 63.1 f., etc.). All the characteristics which we have described, and to which it would be an easy matter to add many other similar features, show the considerable degree to which the prophets' revelations of the future display the original and genuine prophetic style.

l. THE MORE DEVELOPED PROPHETIC STYLE. The earliest prophetic style never completely disappeared, but was used continually up to the date of the latest period of prophecy. But great writers added to it new *literary categories.* Most of these had already existed before their time, and were now filled by them with a new prophetic spirit.

In this process, two different lines of development can be distinguished: the prophets became both poets and preachers. We turn first to the *prophets as poets.* Long before the time of the prophets, there must have existed in Israel a richly developed lyrical literature, both secular and religious in content. Naturally, the prophets drew deeply on both sources, and ornamented their practices with many songs. Thus from secular literature, we find on occasions in their works a *sentry's song* (Isa. 21.11 f.), *drinking songs* (Isa. 22.13; 21.5; 56.12), and even a *song mocking a harlot* (Isa. 23.16); they made particular use of the *funeral elegy,* which even before their time had been given a political significance (Isa. 14.4 ff.; Amos 5.1 f.; Ezek. 19; 27; 28.11 ff.; 32). Besides these, there are a great number of imitations of forms used in worship; hymns, found particularly in the prophets of good fortune, and especially in Deutero-Isaiah (Isa. 42.10 ff.;

44.23; 40.22 ff.; 42.5; 43.16 f.), *laments of the people,* either those which they now use as intercessions for the misfortunes of their people (e.g. Jer. 14.2 ff., 19 ff.), or those which they present as uttered by the people, as prophecies of the future (Hosea 6.1 ff.; 14.4; Jer. 3.22 ff.), *hymns for a thanksgiving sacrifice* (Jer. 33.11), *pilgrimage songs* (Isa. 2.1 ff.; Micah 4.1 ff.), *tōrāh's for entry into the sanctuary* (Isa. 33.14 ff.), and finally even *individual laments,* made use of by Jeremiah (Jer. 15.15 ff.; 17.14 ff.; 20.7 ff.). They also imitated the forms of *liturgical worship* (Isa. 33.1 ff.; Micah 7.7 ff.) and by so doing often achieved their most telling effects. The poetry of the prophets is of an equally high standard both from the religious and aesthetic point of view, and forms one of the most precious treasures of the Old Testament.

However rich these borrowings are, they by no means exhaust the fullness of the prophetic movement. For there is a second line of development; the prophets became *preachers, teachers and thinkers.* They were not satisfied merely with foretelling the future, although this always remained their principal purpose; but they also began to give the *ethical reason* why what they prophesied had to come to pass (e.g. Zeph. 2.10; Jer. 2.17; 13.22; 16.11 ff.; Nahum 3.4; Micah 1.5). Thus they added to their threats *reproaches,* in which they described Israel's wrongdoings (e.g. Isa. 1.2 f.; Jer. 2.10-13), and used for preference the style of an accusation before a court (e.g. Isa. 3.13-15; Micah 6.1 ff.). For the great prophets of doom, this revealing of sin formed one of the main parts of their preaching (Micah 3.8); there are whole prophetic books which consist essentially of these two categories, the threat and the reproach; an example is the book of Amos. Furthermore, it was an ancient prophetic practice to answer questions and give advice (Jer. 42.1 ff.; Zach. 7.1 ff.; Micah 6.6 ff.); making use of this right, the prophets uttered *exhortations,* and so found an opportunity of developing their great religious and ethical ideas in a positive sense; such exhortations are characteristic of the style of Jeremiah (Jer. 7.1-15; 11.1-8; 18.11; *cf.* also Amos 5.4 f.; Isa. 1.10-17). On other occasions, they came into conflict with their opponents in angry *disputes*; sometimes the situation which gave rise to these disputes is described (Amos 7.10 ff.; Isa. 7; Jer. 28), and sometimes the words of their opponents were also recorded (Amos 5.14; Jer. 7.10; 28.9 ff. etc.; especially Haggai and Malachi); mostly the latter are left out, but whole passages in the prophets read like the answers of the prophets to objections on the part of their audience, as it were a transcription of the prophet's part (e.g. Jer. 2.14 ff.). Many of the strangest turns of phrase in the prophets can only be understood when it is realized that they are drawn from such dialogues. Finally, prophecy became a form of *philosophy of religion*: the prophets proclaimed the law of God's rule (Jer. 18; Ezek. 18). To this end, they adopted the style of the priestly *tōrāh*: in the doctrinal statements of Ezekiel the style of the legal ordinances is particularly evident (Ezek. 18). Again, in order to express their ideas, they made use of *historical accounts* (Amos 4.6-12; Jer. 3.6 ff.), though of course they were not concerned with recounting facts, but in presenting a certain view of them. Ezekiel in particular contains extensive historical surveys of the whole past since the Exodus, by preference in the form of *allegory* (Ezek. 16; 20; 23).

This is the way in which the marvellous profusion of the later prophetic styles came into being; we have only been able to mention a few of the principal literary categories which occur there. Some of the categories which came to being in this way, especially the prophetic lyric and the prophetic *tōrāh*, continued to be used by the successors of the prophets, and exercised a great influence.

Hermann Gunkel

IIC. THE RELIGION OF THE PROPHETS*

1. General Features

The *religion of the prophets* is best understood if it is contrasted with that of their people, both with that of the mass of the people, a synthesis of Yahwehism and Baalism, and with the official Yahwehist cult which predominated at the sanctuaries. Now the prophets had no intention of founding a new religion; they too based their religion on the great and miraculous acts of Yahweh in the past, the salvation of their people from Egypt, the choosing in the desert, the sending of Moses, the proclamation through him of the will of God, and the giving of the promised land to Israel; *cf.* Amos 2.9-11; 3.1 ff.; 5.25; Hosea 2.17; 6.5 f.; 8.12; 12.10 f., 14; 13.4 f.; Micah 6.4,8; Isa. 1.2; Jer. 2.2 f.; 7.22 ff.; 31.32 etc. But they reproached both the people and the priests with having perverted the will of Yahweh from the earliest times, and with having replaced him by Baal (Hosea 4.6,10; 7.13; 8.14; 9.10; 11.2; Jer. 23.27) or by human ordinances (Isa. 10.1 ff.; 29.13; Jer. 8.8 f.). Consequently the *characteristic feature of* the religion of the prophets is not so much the name of Yahweh and the many elements in their picture of Yahweh which they shared with the religion of the people, but a different and distinctive faith in Yahweh. More precisely, this was a faith in a God who was in the first place ethically holy, who excluded the worship of any other God besides himself, and who sought from his worshippers only the service of ethical religion, and not a sacrificial cult or any other external ceremony. The kingdom of such a God could

---

* See also *Eschatology* II, 3-6, pp. 234-241 below; and Vol. II—
Revelation II, *Sin and Guilt* IIA, *Grace* II.

naturally not be limited to a single nation. It was for all
nations, for humanity, and both for nations as a whole
and for individuals as well; it was an ethical monotheism,
both universalist and individualist. The prophets regarded as certain a fearful judgement upon a nation
which had fallen away from the true will of Yahweh; but
it could be followed by salvation, by a new nation created
by God, a new community, and a new covenant on an
earth transformed into paradise.

The seed of this religion was sown by Moses in the
simple conditions of the desert, and came to fruition
above all in that section of the people who even after the
entry into Canaan remained faithful to the outward
features of the life of the fathers, amongst shepherds and
herdsmen far from the cities that were so powerfully influenced by Canaanite culture. This simple religion,
based entirely upon obedience to the God of Sinai, by
contrast to the world of religious, political and social
innovations into which Israel had been drawn, was
repeatedly manifested in isolated prophetic figures such
as Samuel, Nathan, Ahijah, Elijah and Elisha. But it was
not until the eighth to the sixth centuries, as the end of
Israel's ancient national life drew near, that it reached
the climax of its *classical period* in an almost continual
series of powerful personalities. Its inspiration ran out in
the community founded in the fifth century by Ezra and
Nehemiah, but, through the writing produced by that
community, it continued to exercise a powerful effect
on various occasions in the centuries that followed.

There is no uniformity amongst the representatives of
this religion, but rather a wide and living variety. The
orientation of one is more strongly ethical or social, and
of another, more religious; one seems to foresee almost
exclusively a judgement on the abandonment of the
religion of Sinai, while another lays strong emphasis
on the salvation that will follow; the historical vision

of one is more limited to Israel, whereas that of another extends to the whole gentile world; one takes an entirely negative view of the popular and priestly religion, while another adopts various elements from it. It is also possible to trace a certain development of individual religious ideas in the course of this classical period, until the period of decadence begins. Ultimately, the foundation on which they all stand is the same; they had a real experience of one and the same holy God, and had heard and accepted his voice.

2. *The Religious Ideas of the Individual Prophets*

It is not possible to describe the religion of the prophets systematically, but only to draw out the main points of its realization in *the mighty individual figures who proclaimed it, in historical sequence*:

a. AMOS. For Amos, Yahweh was in the first instance the stern and inexorable judge, who demanded justice and righteousness (5.24; 6.12), who rejected the whole cult at Bethel etc., and in fact hated it (4.4 ff.; 5.4 ff., 21 ff.), and who desired only what is good (5.14). The struggle of Amos was constantly aimed mainly at the rich, the exploiters, and the unjust judges; he was the advocate of the poor. He prophesied that after Yahweh, who ruled the destiny of the nation, had first passed judgement, in his 'day', over Israel (5.18) and destroyed the kingdom with sanctuaries, and had exiled the people, he would himself recreate and rebuild the ancient kingdom of David in a Palestine transformed into paradise. (9.11-15).

b. HOSEA. Hosea regarded Yahweh as in the first place the loving spouse and father of Israel, who was filled with passionate jealousy, and who nevertheless constantly prevailed (3.1; 11.1,8 f.). His struggle was aimed principally against the whole cult adopted in Canaan, which with its images and sacrifices, sacred prostitution and ecstasy, was an idolatrous cult of Baal, and at the same time

Prophets

against the earthly kingdom and secular politics. Consequently, his principal enemies were the priests (4.4 ff.), the kings and their officers (7.3; 8.4; 10.3; 13.10 ff.). Yahweh demanded no sacrifice, but a devotion actively expressed in the love of one's neighbour and inner abandonment to himself (6.6). Yahweh would make Palestine a desert, but would himself lead a remnant of Israel into the desert, where a new and untroubled communion of love between himself and the nation would come into being in the conditions of paradise (2.16 ff.; 12.10; 14.2 ff.).

c. ISAIAH. Isaiah's experience of Yahweh was above all that of the supernatural and holy God who cast down everything that was exalted to the earth (6.3; 2.6 ff.) and to whom man owed a blind faith (7.9; 28.16; 30.15). Consequently, like Amos, he sharply opposed the cult and stood for ethical worship, justice and righteousness (1.10 ff.; 28.7,17; 28.13). His vision extended to the gentile world, he saw there too the hand and the counsel of Yahweh, (10.5 ff.; 17.12 ff.; 2.1 ff.). He too looked forward to the return of the kingdom of David, and even shared with popular religion a belief in Zion as the dwelling place of Yahweh (8.18; 31.4 f.,9), but in positive terms emphasized that justice and righteousness would be the sole foundation of the new kingdom, and that its boundaries would extend to the end of the earth (9.6; 11.1 ff.).

d. MICAH. Isaiah's contemporary Micah to some extent represents a contrast to him. For Micah the great cities were the real dwelling place of sin, in particular Jerusalem with its temples, over which he prophesied an irresistible ruin (1.5,13; 3.10 ff.). His main enemies were rapacious rulers of the cities, but priests and prophets had made common cause with them (3.1 ff.,5 ff.). The will of Yahweh consisted in doing good, practising love and walking humbly with God, not in sacrifice (6.18). Be-

cause the people had rejected him, Zion would fall
(3.12; 6.9 ff.), while redemption would take place outside
in open country (4.10), while from the country town of
Bethlehem the second David would come and set up
his kingdom of peace from there to the ends of the earth
(5.1-3).

e. ZEPHANIAH, like Amos and Micah, was in the first instance the advocate of the proletariat against the cour-
tiers and the prosperous, the whole ruling class of Jerusalem (1.9-13; 3.1-5). He regarded the day of Yahweh,
which would bring an end to all who were lofty and rich
and would even extend to the gentile world, as imminent
(1.8,14-18; 2.4-15). But Yahweh would then create on
Zion a new community from the poor and humble, a
devout nation with pure lips, which would honour him
alone, and would rule over it as its king (2.3; 3.9-19).

f. NAHUM and HABAKKUK, the first the author of the festal
liturgy for the celebration of the fall of Nineveh, and the
latter of a prophetic liturgy for a day of prayer at the
time of the threat from Babylon, are closest to the popular prophets; they do not mention the sin of Judah. Their
whole anger is directed towards the Assyrian and Babylonian conquerers of the world, for whom they prophesy
a cruel end at Yahweh's hands. But it must be noted that
they too contain much more than national hatred of
foreign oppressors. Rather, they both speak in the name
of a moral order of the world, which is valid for the whole
world; they attack the hybris and insatiability of the two
world powers, and proclaim Yahweh as the God who
restores justice to all oppressed nations.

g. JEREMIAH. In Jeremiah the prophetic religion reaches
its climax. For him, as for Hosea, by whom he was profoundly influenced, the whole religion of his people had
turned to the religion of Baal in Canaan. This had destroyed the first love of the people for their God (2.1-11).
Yahweh did not desire any sacrifice, but ethical obedi-

ence (6.20; 7.21 ff.). Consequently, the prophet saw everywhere degeneration and sin, especially amongst the priests and the ecstatics; judgement was bound to come, and the temple to fall. But Yahweh, who had constantly loved Israel, would bring salvation after the catastrophe, not only with the blessings of paradise, but also in the form of a new covenant with the people, in which the law would be written in their hearts, and every individual would acknowledge Yahweh and receive the forgiveness of sins, so that all human mediation would be superflous (31.31 ff.). It cannot be denied that the seed first sown by Moses here reached the highest point of its development. In a lifetime full of ignominy and persecution, Jeremiah learned that there was only one defence for the devout believer, the dialogue of the individual in prayer with his God, who tries his heart and reins. But he did not regard religion merely as the dialogue of the individual with God; like all the prophets, he saw salvation in a new society of those who knew the way to Yahweh, and experienced his forgiveness. And he too could see the future as a kingdom under the just rule of the scion of David, who characteristically would bear the name 'Yahweh is our righteousness' (23.5 f.).

h. EZEKIEL. With Ezekiel, in exile in Babylon, the decline begins. It is true that at first sight his belief in God was still that of Isaiah, a belief in a holy and absolute lord. But both in the conception of God and in the motives given for his actions—the decisive object was that of his honour—and in the way in which man was to serve him —cultic and ritual requirements were of equal importance to ethical demands, and even superseded them in Ch. 40-48—we can see that something foreign was beginning to find its way into the world of prophetic ideas from the priestly religion. There is no question that in one sense this represented a step forward, and that Ezekiel brought the individual face to face with God much more than had previously been the case, and made him responsible to God. But on the other hand, the schematic standard of 'righteous' and 'godless' which he gave, set up a doctrine of reward and retribution which lacked any religious profundity, and could not be maintained in practice, where it led inevitably to doubt and confusion (14.12 ff.; 33.1-20). Ezekiel believed in a restoration of his people, and in a new kingdom under Yahweh and his representative, the shepherd David (37.1-28); but here again, any profundity of thought or wide range of vision was lacking. Nevertheless, it is true that in the great heathen city he too inexorably proclaimed the ethically holy will of God, and above all the idea of the necessity of the total inward rebirth of the nation, which ultimately only God could bring about through a miracle (11.19).

i. DEUTERO-ISAIAH. More than in any other prophet, we find in the religion of Deutero-Isaiah the immediate juxtaposition of the highest flights of prophetic thought and the phenomenon of decline. This is the prophet who on the one hand took the work of all his predecessors to its ultimate conclusion. He gave Israel the task in world history of being the servant of Yahweh in the gentile world. He joyfully proclaimed that Yahweh is simply the only God, that the universe, which he alone has created, belongs to him, and that consequently all nations of the earth must bow down in adoration before him, their king. Besides this, he gave a wonderful description of everlasting grace and the mercy of Yahweh (49.15; 55.8 ff.). But it cannot be denied that the basis he gives to these ideas is sometimes rationalistic, and sometimes quite superficial, and that some of his hymns of rejoicing anticipate the arrogance towards the gentiles which became more and more intolerable during the post-exilic period (45.14; 49.22). It must also be emphasized that his description of the salvation to be given in the era that was now beginning contains little of the ethical profundity of Isaiah or Jeremiah, but is frequently ornamented by apocalyptic descriptions of material prosperity (54.12 f.).

And yet his work contains something which, together with Jeremiah's prophecy of the new covenant, must be regarded as the crowning achievement of the whole of prophetic religion. This is found in the songs of the servant of Yahweh (42.1 ff. etc.), in which he proclaims not only the extension of the justice and salvation of Yahweh to all nations through the mysterious figure of the servant of God—as a prophet like Moses—but also the redemption of his people by the voluntary and innocent suffering and death of this man. In these passages he not only gave to humanity a new ideal of life, that of the patient martyr, but in a way far more profound than the prophets who preceded him, with their expectation of the king of righteousness and peace, showed mankind the way of life and salvation intended by God, the way through the death and the burial of *one* righteous person, who would be the founder of a new and righteous humanity (53.11 f.)

j. With HAGGAI and ZECHARIAH there begins the period of the successors and imitators of the prophets. They continue to look forward to salvation through a particular person chosen by Yahweh, and attempt to identify him with Zerubbabel (Haggai 2.23; Zech. 6.12), and also to a universalist religion in the future, but both these elements are inseparably linked with the new temple of Jerusalem (Zech. 2.15; 6.13; 8.20 ff.), and in both, their hope of salvation is beginning to be directed towards material prosperity (Haggai 2.7). And however forcibly Zechariah may emphasize that the true will of Yahweh requires morality and not ceremonies, he says himself that in this respect he can only repeat what the great prophets have said before him. He has nothing new or original to add (1.4; 7.7 ff.). For him, God is remote; angels mediate between God and man.

k. TRITO-ISAIAH AND MALACHI. The same is true of these two prophets. They both sharply condemn the sins of their contemporaries, especially their ethical transgressions. Sometimes a brilliant idea flashes forth from them; above all, they cling firmly to the hope that their religion is not destined merely for the small community of Jerusalem, but for the whole earth (Isa. 60.1 ff.; 66.19; Mal. 1.11); but this religion, in which rites and sacrificial worship are beginning to play an increasingly powerful role, had lost the power to respond to this destiny, and its expectation of salvation was becoming more and more material (60.16 ff.).

l. JOEL. We see the degeneration of prophetic religion in the Book of *Joel.* In the face of an immense plague of locusts, the true prophetic note seems to ring out once again: 'Rend your hearts and not your garments. Return to the Lord' (2.13); but according to 2.12, this is a matter not of a return to righteousness and love, but of fasting, weeping and mourning. The punishment of which the plague is a sign is certainly meant to teach the people righteousness; but this righteousness only consists of the proper practice of the cult (2.23). And the second half of the work shows definitely that the period of prophecy was over, and that it had been replaced by apocalyptic expectations of miraculous signs and a bloody judgement over other nations. This is the conscious rejection of universalism.

This is an outline of the religion of the prophets. For all the differences in outlook between different prophets, they are ultimately all aiming at one and the same *goal,* the kingdom of a holy God upon earth. What is the *origin* of this religion? Since the time of Moses, there had always actually existed a spiritual current in Israel directed towards this end, although its representatives were frequently not yet conscious of the ultimate consequences of it, but limited their ideas to a narrower scope. And as in every spiritual movement, each naturally influenced his successors. A degree of historical development is unmistakable: the link between Moses, Hosea and Jeremiah is particularly clear; parallel lines of development run from Isaiah through Zephaniah and Habakkuk to Deutero-Isaiah, and again from Amos through Micah to Jeremiah, not to speak of the dependence of Zechariah upon the 'former prophets'. But this is not the end of the matter. Ultimately, in the case of everyone who proclaimed this religion, his source must be looked for where he himself found it; that is, all these men drew not merely on human tradition, but at the same time, and above all, on what was given them directly by someone greater, who constantly reassured them anew of his will and his plan (Amos 3.8; 7.15; Hosea 1.2; Isa. 6.8; 8.11; Micah 3.8; Jer. 1.5; 15.16; 20.9 etc.).

If this is the case, then we need not be astonished that although the driving force of this religion disappeared in the community founded by Ezra, it suddenly burst forth again in its original power, when the time was fulfilled, and broke down all the barriers of a world that had grown old.

Ernst Sellin

3
The Gospels (Form)

1. The Task of the Form Criticism of the Gospel
It is the purpose of *literary criticism* to study the mutual
relationship of the different gospels, to look for their
possible sources, and to decide the date of their composition. To some extent the results of this approach
are accepted and applied by form critical study and to
some extent complemented. The first task of form criticism is to describe the literary character of the gospels as
a whole, and to determine their place in the general
course of the history of literature. Its second task is to
describe the history of the traditional material which
has been incorporated into the gospels, from its pre-
literary origins up to the point at which it took a fixed
literary form in the different gospels. It is recognized that
the traditional material originally consisted of single
items whose origin and history may be explained by the
study of their literary form. The guiding insight of form
critical study is that a particular literary form has a
particular context in which it is used (its *Sitz im Leben*);
that is, its origin and history are associated with particular situations or procedures in the history of a nation, a
group, or a community (e.g. a war, a harvest, worship,
etc.).

2. The Literary Category of the Gospels
Εὐαγγέλιον, originally occurring only in the singular, was
not at first used to describe a literary category, but
referred to the content of the Christian proclamation; it
was only later that the word *evangelion* came to mean the

86

gospel book, and so became *the name of a literary category*. There had been no such thing as a gospel in the previous history of literature, nor was there at any later period; the writing of gospels flourished into the second century, but the Church brought this process to an abrupt conclusion by canonizing four gospels, and excluding the rest, of which we now only possess fragments. Later compositions such as the Old High German *Heiland,* or Klopstock's *Messias,* can no more be regarded as gospels than can later descriptions of the life of Jesus, leading up to modern novels on the subject. The question whether there are other *analogies to the gospels* in the history of literature leads us to a clearer view of their distinctive nature. They cannot be included in the category of biographies, which did not exist in Judaism, but were highly developed by the Greeks. For the gospels show no interest in historical or biographical matters; they contain no account of Jesus's human personality, his origin, education or development, or his appearance and his character. In no sense do they belong to the category of major literature, characterized by a skilful technique of composition, the display of the personality of the author, and aesthetic or scientific concerns. They have only one feature in common with the literature of memoirs and lives of philosophers, in that these are collections in a loose form of the tradition of the conversations, and episodes from the life, of important persons; but again, they differ from them in lacking any historical and scientific character, and do not reveal the individuality of their authors. On the other hand, collections of episodes and conversations in a popular form, like Aesop's fables, or the stories of a miracle-worker such as Apollonius of Tyana, a category of *minor literature* which was taken up again later in certain Christian lives of monks and saints, do in fact provide an analogy to the gospels. They are probably even more closely related to the oriental *popular books,* of which we can only try to imagine the form, on the basis of the only one which has been preserved, the *Story of Ahikar.* This is similar to the gospels in that the accounts of individual episodes are joined together by interpolated sayings and parables. Finally, analogies to the gospels can be found in popular collections of the works and deeds of highly admired persons from different periods and cultures, such as the tradition concerning Francis of Assisi, the book of Doctor Faust, the Chassidic legends of the great Maggid, and also certain parts of the Buddhist canon.

However all these analogies are valid only to a certain degree. The gospels resemble them in so far as their authors are in no sense literary personalities, in so far as they gather together a tradition consisting of individual deeds and sayings of their hero without any scientific purpose, and in so far as they lay no value on chronology, consistency of content, or psychological motivation and characterization. The gospels differ, however, not only in that they have no interest in story-telling for its own sake (apart from later imitations), which is a frequent element in the analogous literature, and provides a luxurious growth of incident in the later apocryphal Acts of the Apostles, but above all in that in the gospels the material is ordered from one dominant point of view. This distinction does not lie simply in the fact that they are intended to provide religious edification, and to be used as readings in worship, so that they do not really tell a story, but preach; for they have this in common with numerous lives of monks and legends of the saints. But the principal distinction is that they do not tell of their hero because he was an historical personality whose life and sayings were edifying, but because for them he is *the Son of God, the Lord.* They grow up from the *cult of Christ,* and their unity is provided by the Christ myth (*cf.* Vol. II, *Christology* I). They are the cult *legends* of

Christian worship; but they are distinguished from other cult legends in that their deity is not a mythical figure; but the Christ myth is associated and forms a unity with the historical tradition of Jesus Christ. Thus they are a unique phenomenon in the history of literature, and at the same time are symbolic of the distinctive nature of the Christian religion as a whole. The first gospel was written, as far as we can see, amongst hellenistic Christians, and is that of *Mark,* which has been called the book of the secret epiphany, because in it Jesus reveals himself as the Christ, and at the same time conceals himself. *Matthew* and *Luke* heightened this mythical character by numerous new miracle stories, and the miraculous infancy and resurrection narratives, but also added other historical material from the tradition, especially the sayings of Jesus. *Matthew* laid a new emphasis on the miracles by relating them to prophecy, while *Luke* tried to write as a historian, to relate the life of Jesus to contemporary history (1.5; 2.1-3; 3.1-2), and to continue it in the Acts of the Apostles; he is also the only evangelist to make any mention of himself in the first person (1.1-4). In *John* we find the use of 'we'; however, it is not the author who is speaking, but the community (1.14,16; 21.24); for John is a further development of the type of gospel created by Mark: the unity of myth and history is obtained by restricting the amount of traditional material; the discourses of Jesus which form its principal content are revelation discourses which use the sayings found in the synoptic gospels only occasionally. As far as we can tell from the extant fragments, the apocryphal gospels show a further development of the original type of gospel; in their details, they show evidence of an interest in story-telling for its own sake, and even of an attempt to build up an extended story like a novel; there are numerous legendary themes; Jesus is credited with all kinds of revelations, often gnostic in content.

3. The Material of the Gospel Tradition, its Literary Form and its History

If it is recognized that the *traditional material* consisted of small individual passages, which were worked into their present context by the evangelists, and by redactors before them, then the first task is to separate the individual passages from this context, in order to *distinguish between tradition and redaction* and get back to the earliest tradition; naturally, it is part of this task to obtain some idea of the purpose and technique of the redactor. Then we go on to examine *the form of the individual passages of the tradition*, not just because this is the only way in which the text can properly be understood in detail (e.g. the parables), but above all in order to understand *the history of the tradition*. Thus by bearing in mind the relationship between the form and its *Sitz im Leben* it is possible to recognize the origin of individual passages, to distinguish hellenistic material from Palestinian, and to see where there is a pure example of a form and where it has been modified by the tradition, and to judge what is primary material and what is a secondary addition. Such an inquiry must go hand in hand with the study of the laws of popular story-telling tradition (folk-tales and anecdotes).

In general, it is clear at once, from the literary form and the language of individual passages in the tradition, that their origin is the *oral* spoken word, and that the language of the earliest stratum of the tradition was Aramaic. Thus the gospel tradition did not arise within a literary movement, but had its origin in the preaching of Jesus in the life of the community of his followers, in their preaching, teaching, missionary work and apologetics. This is what one would expect not only from the oriental origin of Christianity, but above all from the ministry of Jesus as a prophet and teacher, and from the fact that the earliest community formed part of Judaism and carried out its activity in the forms of Judaism, which were those of the synagogue and the teaching of the scribes. The spoken word was dominant, fixed forms had come into being, great use was made of the memory in preserving and reproducing what was heard, and the basis of everything was the scripture. This stratum of the tradition can be distinguished from other material which sometimes reproduces the older forms, and sometimes makes use of hellenistic themes, especially in miracle stories and legends. The material can be grouped in a number of particular *categories*. One must distinguish between the words of Jesus and stories about him. This can be divided, by form and content, into three groups. 1. *Sayings (logia)*, which belong to the category of 'proverbial wisdom' (*cf.* Proverbs and Ecclesiasticus). In formal terms, the parables also belong to this category. It is a category which was widespread in Israel and throughout the Near East, and in Judaism was also used by the scribes (*cf.* the *Sayings of the Fathers* and the *Mishnah*). It is 'wisdom', the content of which is prudence in daily life, morality and piety, and which in the East possesses something of the status accorded to philosophy by the Greeks. 2. *Prophetic and apocalyptic sayings*, which proclaim the coming kingdom of God, and contain a call to repentance. They renew the eschatological message of the older prophecy (*cf. Eschatology* II p. 230 below), but also contain elements of Jewish apocalyptic. Many apocalyptic sayings with which Jesus is credited have their origin in the community. 3. *Legal sayings and community regulations*, some of which have their origin in the disputes of Jesus and the Christian community with Jewish piety based on the law, while others spring from the life of the community and express its interests, the interpretation of the scripture, discipline, and missionary work. Many of the sayings of Jesus are transmitted in a brief framework which gives the situation in which the saying was uttered. They can be called *apophthegmata*; they are found almost everywhere in the literature of the world, but were especially popular with the rabbis. They can be divided into didactic dialogues, disputes and biographical apophthegmata. In many cases the framework is secondary, and many have been expanded by the interpolation or addition of other sayings of Jesus. Stories of Jesus properly speaking consist in the first place of *miracle stories*, many of which are told at length and with the use of many of the story-teller's devices, and show the stylistic characteristics of hellenistic miracle stories. Then there are the *legends* (e.g. the stories of Jesus's baptism, temptations, transfiguration and of the last supper); they consist in part of frequently recurring legendary themes, and in part have their origin in the worship of the community. Naturally, not all the material in the gospel falls into these groups; they also contain historical tradition belonging to no fixed category, but (as in the account of the passion) heavily overlaid with legendary themes. This is true of the traditional material used in the synoptic gospels. *John* draws on this, and he probably made some use of the synoptic gospels, from which he takes a number of sayings and stories. Apart from this, he seems to have made use of a collection of miracle stories that had undergone a considerable stylistic development. Finally, one of his sources must have been a collection of revelation discourses, stylistically completely different from the synoptic material, but manifesting such oriental forms of composition as were used in gnostic literature (e.g. in the *Odes of Solomon*). However, the study of this matter has not yet reached firm conclusions. The material of the *apocryphal gospels* is too fragmentary to provide any fresh information; in general they developed further the older categories, especially those of legend and apocalyptic.

Rudolf Bultmann

4
Jesus Christ

I. JESUS AND THE TRADITION CONCERNING HIM

By 'and' we do not wish to imply that we shall deal first
with one and then with another. This approach is both
possible and necessary in many other branches of scientific historical study. The procedure is first to establish
the extent of the sources and test their value, and then to
describe the personality and activity described in the
sources. But the word 'and' implies here a very special
relationship and mutual influence: we are inquiring into
the significance of the formation of the tradition concerning Jesus for our understanding of the personality, or
to be more precise, the figure of Jesus, and at the same
time we are examining his ministry in its significance for
the form of the tradition concerning him.

1. The Methodological Dispute

Considerations of this sort are clearly necessary, as can
be seen from the uncertainty and confusion of the *different methods of approach*, which have been used in an attempt
to master the problem presented by Jesus. We can see
how, ever since Jesus has been the subject of scientific
historical study, a vacillation between many variations of
the *individualist* and the *collective* approach. An admirer
of Carlyle regretted that, in spite of his piety, the Scottish
historian had not included Jesus in his book *Heroes,
Hero-worship and the Heroic in History*, since from Carlyle's
point of view 'the history of the world is basically the

history of the great men who carried out creative work in it'. Renan, in his famous *Life of Christ*, filled in his own way the historical gaps which so many people found distressing. In contrast to this individualistic approach, collective views regarded the figure of Jesus in its place in the history of human thought, in its mythical aspects, or in its place in historical and economic development. For Hegel, what mattered was not the person of Jesus, but the idea which he enshrined: 'let history and exegetics make what they wish of Jesus, the only question is the idea he stands for'. For those who dispute the historicity of Jesus (*cf.* Vol. III *Christianity* I), amongst whom the best known modern scholar is Arthur Drews, the story of Jesus we find in the gospel is an adaptation of a syncretistic myth, while for those who support the economic view of history, and in particular, for Marxist Socialists, the whole New Testament and especially what is contained in the gospels, is no more than an example of a universal truth, and represents the product of a change in the balance of economic forces, regardless of the influence of any personality. The individualistic and collectivist approaches have been advanced at various times and in different forms against the 'corporate' treatment of the problem of Jesus which is the customary theological method. It is alleged that theologians, and historians and philologists who have followed them, have proved unable to distinguish the historical facts concerning Jesus; typical representatives of this point of view are the adherents and followers of Renan down to Emile Ludwig, a Renan *predivivus* in a more modest form. Others suggest that theologians have failed to give full weight to the sublime and supra-historical in Jesus; this is the assumption in Georg Brandes' *Jesus-Sage*, a literary work forming a complete contrast to that of Ludwig. This is a fruitless argument, but it is symptomatic: we must remember that even amongst theologians the study of Jesus has made use of these two approaches in the past, and has continued to do so. The more recent theological 'liberalism', with its emphasis on personality even in the history of religion and in primitive Christianity, is concerned in the first place with understanding the *personality* of Jesus in its inner and outward development. It must of course be admitted that as a much more searching approach has been adopted, this kind of language has gradually become fossilized, and is much less important in an increasingly radical study of the gospels. By contrast, the older theological liberalism which followed Hegel was concerned not with the individual approach, but with the *idea*. The radical approach based on the study of *comparative religion* is associated with this, and is also found amongst theologians. Thus a duality is produced in theological study which is so acute that theologians who adopt very different positions have put forward, with weighty arguments but not always with complete methodological clarity, a synthesis *between history and what is beyond history*, between history as it happened and the interpretation of history, between Jesus and Christianity. The question is whether such a synthesis, attractive in itself, accurately represents the confession of primitive Christian faith found in the gospels. Apart from this attempt to obtain a unified solution to the problem by dialectic methods, another approach tends more to a compromise, and attempts to evade the choice between an individual personality and a collective force by pointing to the special relationship between *personality and community*, in which the first is a function of the second. On the other hand, modern man, strongly influenced by Nietzsche, is faced once again with the direct choice, an Either-Or. Can modern man, with his concentration on the growth of personality—something true of every person regardless of what metaphysical views he may

95

also hold—find in the New Testament and the gospels anything which is meaningful to him? Nietzsche says not, and rightly so. But the question is whether the lack of interest in personality in the gospels can be explained by any particular psychological theory, such as Nietzsche's theory of *Ressentiment*, the disgust with life and the body that leads to the celebration of the 'pure spirit', or by any of the other approaches mentioned above, which ignore the factor of personality.

2. The Gospels as Sources for the History of Jesus
(Their portrayal of him; the development and framework of the history of Jesus; the evangelists as authors; the theme of the gospels; the unity and diversity of the traditions; are there older sources?; the primitive Christian kerygma and the summaries in the gospels; the growth of the tradition; the birth narratives of Jesus; Jesus's journey to the temple at the age of twelve; the sifting out of the main content of the tradition.)

This is a summary of the questions we have in mind when we turn to the sources. We shall look for an answer in the gospels themselves, and shall examine them in the framework of the New Testament, and of primitive Christian writing as a whole. It is immediately obvious on reading the *gospels* that these writings are in *no sense biographies*, and that their authors are not biographers (*cf. Gospels, Form* p. 86 above). This observation has a particular importance and application beyond the conclusions usually drawn from the fact. A personality is generally presented in a writing in what is known as a literary *portrait*. There is no such portrait in the gospels. A thorough and honest comparison between the gospels and ancient biographies and memoirs reveals a decisive difference. The question of whether or not the gospels should be described as biographies, becomes a purely verbal dispute, depending upon how a biography is defined. But a full scale biography at least is a work of historical art portraying a person's life at length. It describes both the outward and inner *development* of the personality described. To attain this end, questions such as the ordering of the material (whether it is arranged by subject or chronologically), or the practical lessons to be drawn from the events of the subject's life, his psychology, and other characteristics are of decisive importance. All these questions are virtually absent from the gospels. In most stories in the gospels the people who come into contact with Jesus are not individualized at all. Basically we are told nothing about all these people, the many sick who are healed, the relations, friends, disciples and opponents of Jesus. Now and again we are told their names; more often they are not mentioned. But that this is by no means an automatic procedure can be seen from the fact that individual traits appear in later redactions of the gospels, that a portrait comes into being, and we meet new names, such as are known to us from Christian legends. And these Christian legends, stories of famous and saintly men and women with their actions and deeds, are secondary; they take us away from the primary sources of the earlier, non-literary period, into the realm of the Greek minor literature concerned with the portrayal of individual personalities in such stories. Nor do the gospels present a portrait of Jesus himself; we are told next to nothing of his outward and inner development. The hellenist Luke attempted to change this by arranging his traditional material in periods, with some psychological comment. In the account of Jesus's infancy, which he alone presents in the form of a continuous narrative, he twice notes, as he has done once already in the story of the infancy of John the Baptist, that the child grew, became strong in spirit and increased in wisdom (Luke 1.80; 2.40, 52) Luke is the only evangelist to introduce any further account of the youth of Jesus, in the story of his visit to the temple at the age of twelve (Luke 2.41-52). The apocryphal gospels described his youth in much greater detail. Thus, for example, miracles performed by the child Jesus are described in exact detail. The later gospels gave a very clear representation of the earthly appearance and character of Jesus.

The same is true of *details of time and place* in the gospels. Looking at the matter as a whole, one can only speak of an outline *of the life of Jesus*, which is a secondary editorial addition. The gospels contain not the life-story of Jesus, but stories about Jesus. Whenever the evangelists, especially Luke, have attempted to arrange and evaluate the fragmentary information that has come down to them about time and place, to give something like a continuous narrative, this attempt must be regarded as having failed. In fact in the case of Mark and Matthew it is exceedingly doubtful whether they ever seriously considered such an attempt—though historians would like to believe that it might have succeeded in the case of a hypothetical proto-Mark. But this state of affairs does not mean that all the individual details of the outline that is given are necessarily secondary and therefore of no historical value. Many of them are so distinctive, and yet receive so little emphasis, that there is every likelihood of their being part of the original tradition. This is so, for example, in the mention of the place in an important pericope such as that of Peter's confession at Caesarea Philippi (Mark 8.27-30 and parallels). If all such details were secondary additions, first made when the individual stories were gathered together as one, then the outline of the life story of Jesus would appear much more as a unity, that is, individual items of information concerning the time, place and situation of particular events would possess a unified character not only in short passages but throughout. The important point is that in every case the passages that provide the outline are not strongly emphasized. This confirms that while in one sense they are unreliable, in the other sense they are nevertheless trustworthy. It is easy to understand that both Matthew and Mark felt it necessary to order the individual stories which record the words and acts of Jesus not chronologically, but according to their content. And even when a description of Jesus's itinerary is given —such descriptions are much less full in Matthew than in Mark, while they occur again in Luke—we must again ask whether they do not in fact represent an arrangement according to subject. Such a case is found in the three stories of Mark 4.35-5.43, the storm on the lake, the Gerasene possessed by an unclean spirit, and Jairus's daughter and the woman with a flow of blood. If this itinerary, which seems at first to be self-consistent, is examined more closely, no sense can be made of it, and its only point is clearly that three stories of events which took place on, or on the shore of, the Sea of Galilee, and which could perfectly well have happened in different years, are placed together. Sometimes stories in the gospel are provided with such a framework, and sometimes not. The evangelists—again excluding Luke—regarded all this as of no significance. This explains the great complexity of the details of time and place that we are given. Although it is not possible to be certain about any individual case, nevertheless, as the tradition developed, many place names were added to stories. The attempt that can be seen in early Christian accounts of pilgrimages, to identify all the holy places in the story of Jesus, is very ancient. From very early times Christianity recognized Tabor as the mountain of the Transfiguration; in the New Testament itself Tabor is not named.

This peculiarity of the gospels, their unreliability as a source for the portrayal of the character and development of Jesus or for a description of the situations in which

Jesus found himself, and of his environment, becomes clear by a comparison with *parallels from popular literature* of different periods and civilizations, including the ancient world, and with innumerable popular works which are not literature in the strict sense. But at the same time we must be quite clear that the analogy is only partial. The gospels, and the stages that preceded them, originated amongst a particular group of authors, a particular community, in a similar way to popular histories and many legends of saints. This form was clearly the only one appropriate to the material which went to make up the gospels. Their distinctive features were decisively affected by the character of the community we are dealing with, that is, the community which regarded itself as the people of God (Church) of the old and new covenants.

At this point it becomes clear that the *evangelists* were on the whole *not literary personalities, but compilers* of traditional material. But as time went on, the interests which appear in Luke in gentle touches of no particular importance, become more prominent. The fidelity to the material which characterizes all popular tradition, and particularly the esoteric tradition of Jesus, increasingly declined. From the purely formal point of view there is an increasing use of the first person, which is naturally associated with the frequent occurrence of ornamental details of psychological interest. Nevertheless, the fourth evangelist, who must be mentioned in this context, was far from adopting the conventional attitudes of secular literature described above. His notably concrete and indeed worldly gospel is in the end completely unworldly; for its decisive characteristic is that of the confession of faith of the visionary, or of a small visionary community, so that this gospel is remote from the concerns of secular literature.

As we have seen, then, the gospels are not biographies,

and the evangelists are not biographers; the object of the evangelists is not to produce a literary portrait, and they are not literary personalities; this state of affairs only began to alter on the fringes of primitive Christianity, and was associated with the hellenization, that is, the secularization of the primitive Christian movement. All these factors must be borne in mind when we are looking for the essential *context* of the gospels. They were not and could not have been intended to portray a towering personality, a hero, and to reveal his mind and heart to the reader. It is the truly radical critic who has to admit that nothing can be gained by the use of psychological categories.

It is understandable that the great critical scholars have never ceased to refer to the *Christ myth*. The first assertion that must be made is that everything that concerns particular situations, topography, chronology and psychology, is both present and yet absent. In so far as it is present at all, there is no emphasis upon it. The *principal and dominant theme* is something different: the Johannine proclamation of the *Logos*, who became flesh and dwelt among us (John 1; *cf.* Vol. II *Christology* I, 5*b*.) is also the hidden theme of the synoptic gospels. They do not contain stories of an individual who was the founder and originator of Christianity, but consist of numerous individual reflections on the theme of the *incarnation of the Logos*. The purpose of the oldest strata of the gospel, which existed before the primitive Christian community was conscious of such a conception, may have been to tell of a teacher and prophet, Jesus of Nazareth, who disputed publicly and did marvellous things. But these older strata did not long survive in use. We can no longer clearly distinguish them. They were absorbed or submerged by the account of the Messiah who had appeared in Jesus or—to use a more hellenistic term—the epiphany of the Son of God. The oldest gospel we possess, that of

Mark, assumes belief in the Messiah, the worship of Christ and the Christ myth, all of which lie quite beyond the realm of personality and psychology. The Messiah, Christ, is regarded as an *ordinary human being* (ψιλὸς ἄνθρωπος) who as such was no different from other men. The incarnation of the *Logos* was manifested in true humanity. 'In the days of his flesh, Jesus offered up prayers and supplications, with loud cries and tears, to him who was able to save him from death . . .'; these words of Hebrews 5.7 describe the suffering servant of God at Gethsemane (Mark 14.32 etc. and parallels), whose battle of prayer was both human and divine. It is the man Jesus of Nazareth of whom Paul speaks in Phil. 2.5-11: 'Christ Jesus, who, though he was in the form of God, did not count equality with God a thing to be grasped, but emptied himself, taking the form of a servant, being born in the likeness of men. And being found in human form, he humbled himself and became obedient unto death, even death on a cross . . .'. An ordinary man with all his limitations was revealed as he in whom God was acting. According to the proclamation of Peter in Acts 2.22 Jesus of Nazareth was 'a man attested to you by God with mighty works and wonders and signs which God did through him . . .'. Those who handed on the gospels saw God, and only God, at work here. There is no suggestion of the acts of a personality concerned with his future and the effect of what he does on posterity. By the standards of primitive Christianity, to seek to present Jesus in this sense as the originator of Christianity and the founder of the Christian Church is a misleading and Pelagian idea. Much is often made of the idea that a dominant personality, who becomes a myth, increases in stature in people's memories. This does not seem to have happened very much in the case of Jesus. The formation of legend concerning him was remarkably modest. The possibility of a luxurious growth of legend was hampered by the fact that from the very first the Church was concerned with something that represented for it both the judgement and the grace of God: *God become man*. The historian who is seeking to distinguish a clear pattern, and tries to illuminate his subject with concepts such as 'personality', 'genius', and 'hero', finds himself faced here with a mysterious obscurity in which anonymous persons, negative personalities, the poor in spirit as Jesus called them in the Beatitudes, become important. This casts a special light on the theme of 'Jesus and his disciples': the twelve apostles, whom according to tradition Jesus gathered round himself, never take on flesh and blood. It was more important to the primitive community that the word of God through his Messiah should be proclaimed in its midst, in the 'Church', by twelve apostles, than that they should try to find out anything more detailed about their individual personalities. It is the apocryphal Acts of the Apostles, which have virtually become hellenistic travel stories, that first recount concrete personal details. Even the 'prince of the apostles', Peter, does not receive a great deal of attention in the framework of primitive Christianity: more important than his vacillating character was his God-given destiny.

Though these conclusions may seem very negative to an historian, their background is a very positive belief: if all primitive Christians, including the evangelists, were convinced that the gospel was the act of God in him whom he had sent, his Messiah, his Son, then it was not possible to make statements about Jesus of Nazareth such as are made about other historical personalities. There is no point in regarding the affirmation of this state of affairs as an excessive scepticism, and in attempting to counter it by digging down to the original bedrock of historical truth in the gospel. Mark, the first evangelist, may have been preceded by a proto-Mark.

There may have been a Hebrew proto-Matthew underlying the written tradition which we possess. It may be
possible to distinguish in the gospel of Luke a basic
synoptic work, related to certain parts of the fourth
gospel. Such literary work is possible and necessary; what
is not justified is the idea that it often conceals, that
it is possible in this way to uncover an original account
which is historically more reliable. From the very first
there must have been *numerous and varied traditions*, all of
which were intended to illustrate the one theme of Jesus
Christ. It is only when this is understood, that we can
see why the evangelists themselves were not conscious of
the problem of the gospels, whether the synoptic problem
or that of the relation between John's gospel and the
synoptic gospels. They were aware of the *unity of theme* and
did not object to *numerous variations in this theme*. What
Goethe once said of the legend of St. Roch, which he
was investigating, is true here. 'There were no contradictions, but innumerable variations, which probably
arose from the fact that each mind assimilated the story
of his life, and its individual events, in a different way, so
that one circumstance would be ignored, and another
brought into prominence, just as the various travels of
the saint and his stay in various places were confused and
interchanged.' Anyone who attempts to portray the life
story of Jesus from the gospels must first obtain a clear
understanding of this unity in diversity, which is the very
nature of the synoptic problem. This is the only way in
which the sifting of essential and secondary matter becomes possible.

That there must be a *sifting of the gospel material*,
preceding any attempt to portray the life history of
Jesus, is obvious from the above observations on the
different strata that can be seen when one gospel is
compared with another, and within individual gospels.
It is also obvious that within the framework of the gospels

we possess, from Mark and Matthew, through Luke to
John and on to the apocryphal gospels, the gospel
material alters. On the other hand, we must always be
ready to accept that a passage in the gospels which took
on a literary form at a later date may well reflect what
is actually a better and more original tradition. This
caution must always be borne in mind when we consider
the difference between the gospel of John and the three
synoptic gospels. The use we make of sources must vary
from one case to another, depending upon whether they
seem to be primary or secondary. It is also true that
within primitive Christianity there were great variations
in the degree of interest paid to the gospel tradition. Even
hellenistic Christianity, which was essentially where the
gospels—written in Greek—were inspired and produced,
was of various types, two of which can be clearly distinguished. There were churches which were close to
the pattern of the hellenistic mystery religions (one thinks
at once of the Pauline churches). There were also
churches which were associated with the type represented
by the hellenistic Jewish synagogues (*cf.* the figure of
Stephen). The transmission and elaboration of the gospel
tradition seems to have been the work of the latter. Thus
if, as we have suggested above, it is possible to distinguish
within a single gospel, even that of Mark, a distinctive
stratum which portrays Jesus as teacher and prophet,
we have then to ask *how* such a stratum must be regarded.
Assuming that a group of people within primitive
Christianity regarded Jesus principally or even solely as a
teacher of wisdom, and that the historian has here come
upon the *oldest stratum we can distinguish*, it does not necessarily follow that a chronologically later stratum emphasizing Jesus as prophet and then as Messiah, must
be regarded as of less value. We must also remember
that a conscious recognition of what Jesus had really
been only developed gradually, stage by stage, and on

the basis of fresh acts of revelation, notably the resurrection (*cf.* Vol. II *Christology* I,2*b*). Again, we must bear in mind that an opinion such as that which held that Jesus had been a teacher and prophet, or even only a teacher, did not simply arise in primitive Christianity in isolation, but in relation to statements and professions of belief which went beyond what was implied by these titles, and led to a higher christology.

What is positively stated in the oldest comprehensive proclamation concerning Jesus of Nazareth, in what is called the *primitive Christian kerygma*—what is unequivocably placed in the foreground? The oldest passage of this nature, Phil. 2.5-11, which we have already quoted, presents Jesus Christ, that is, Jesus the Messiah, as the servant of God who died and ruled again. This agrees with the statement of 1 Cor. 15.3 ff., which Paul himself presents as a traditional formula, in that this also speaks of the *death* and the *resurrection* of Jesus Christ. In accordance with the context of 1 Cor., Paul here is only talking about the resurrection, but in order to explain it he includes with it the statement that Christ 'died . . . and was buried'. The complete formula may also have contained some information about the life history of Jesus. But this is uncertain; it may also have been the case that Paul never made any specific statements about the life history of Jesus, but at the most simply affirmed that this Jesus Christ had led his life in the world as the servant of God. The proclamation of Jesus Christ in the speeches of Acts are constructed in a similar way: 2.22 ff.; 3.13 ff.; 10.36 ff.; 13.23 ff. Once again the main emphasis is on the death and resurrection.

We also learn the following about the life of the servant of God (3.13): that Jesus of Nazareth was a man through whom God had done mighty works, wonders and signs (2.22); that he travelled throughout all Judaea after he had been baptized by John and begun his own ministry in Galilee; and that he preached good news of peace and healed all that were oppressed by the devil (10.36-8; 13.24 f.). If this is how Jesus was preached, the growth and nature of the gospels becomes clear: their message is that Jesus of Nazareth, attested as the Messiah by word and deed, died and rose again.

Thus the special position accorded to the *passion narrative* is derived from this primitive Christian preaching; in the whole structure of the earliest preaching, the emphasis was on the passion. This is in accord with the nature of the narrative of the passion and death of Jesus, in which we possess the only section of the gospels which in spite of numerous additions and alterations, and in spite of the interpolation of a number of passages, must have been fixed in its present structure from the beginning. This is the reason for the high degree of agreement in the three synoptic gospels, which even extends to the fourth evangelist. Details of place and time, even the very day and hour, are given with great accuracy.

As far as the material that precedes the narrative of the passion is concerned, in their *summaries* the evangelists reproduce the emphasis of the preachers of the gospel in Acts on the close association between words and deeds, emphasizing in any given passage either his words (*cf.* Mark 1.14 f.; 1.21 f.; 2.13; 6.6 f; 10.1; Matt. 4.12-17; 7.28 f.; 11.1; 19.11; Luke 4.14-44.; 8.11; 21.37 f.; John 4.41) or his deeds (Mark 3.7-12; 6.53-6; John 2.11) or both (Mark 1.39; 6.12 f.; Matt. 4.23-5; 9.35 f.): 'Jesus went about all Galilee, teaching in their synagogues and preaching the gospel of the kingdom and healing every disease and every infirmity among the people.' And in the passage which contains Jesus's testimony concerning John the Baptist all this is expressly related to the person of Jesus: 'The blind receive their sight and the lame walk, lepers are cleansed and the deaf hear, and the dead are raised up, and the poor have good news preached to them. And blessed is he who takes no offence at me' (Matt. 11.5 f.). It was this interweaving of *word and deed* which, for primitive Christianity and even for Jews who were not Christians, revealed the authority of Jesus (Mark 2.5 ff.) and showed that 'he who was to come' was there (Matt. 11.2 ff.). There is no basis in the facts for giving greater weight to Jesus's preaching at the expense of his acts, or to treat the latter as incidental. In both, and to the same extent, the decisive issue is their relationship to him who as Messiah possesses authority. Any or all of his words could have been spoken by another teacher and prophet; but here someone was endued with a unique authority. Any or all of his acts might have been carried out by some other miracle-worker; but these were the acts of one who came at the onset of the kingdom of God, which in him became a reality, and that is why he forgave sins. None of this implies any explicit statement about any consciousness of his own vocation and mission on the part of Jesus, his so-called *messianic consciousness*. This is a secondary issue which was not regarded as of great importance in the Church's earliest confession of faith. As the life history of Jesus grew with the development of oral and written tradition, and not always in a legitimate direction, but with the addition of legendary elaborations, so did the tradition of the words and acts of Jesus.

Scholarly study of the life of Jesus lays particular stress on the investigation of this *growth of the tradition*, and the distinguishing of individual strata according to their degree of originality. The criterion which is normally used is the comprehensive preaching of Jesus Christ described above, which is to be found in the preaching of the apostles and in the summaries of the evangelists. There is no doubt that much that is in the gospels goes beyond the limits of this criterion. Of course the evangelists clearly held the view that everything they reported was in accord with the content of their summaries. They attempted to adapt the gospel material they received to the purposes of a comprehensive profession of faith in Jesus Christ. But in reality a delight in storytelling, which was not always very restrained, gave rise to anecdotes and legends; the concern to safeguard the inner consistency and outward evidence of the faith that was proclaimed led to apologetic and polemic elaborations; the necessity of employing authoritative words of Jesus in the context of moral instruction (parenesis) did not merely preserve the tradition of his words which were used for this purpose, but increased it. All this can not only be deduced from this state of affairs, but can be seen directly in a synoptic comparison of the frequently contradictory versions of the same narrative. The result is that the sifting of the gospel material is not only possible but essential.

The oldest preaching of Jesus Christ we possess contains no mention of the *narrative of Jesus's birth*. Thus the emphasis of the oldest account of the proclamation of the gospel, Mark 1.1 ff., is the same as that of Acts 13.23 ff., and it begins with the narrative of the baptism of Jesus as a grown man by John; it contains no mention of the birth and childhood of Jesus. Furthermore, the narratives of Matt. 1 f. and Luke 1 f. cannot be reconciled. They have very little in common, and are in many respects contradictory. Both accounts in the text we possess tell of the conception of Jesus through the Holy Spirit by the Virgin Mary. Now the two principal sources which underlie the synoptic gospels, Mark, and the collection of Jesus's sayings, Q, not only make no mention of the miraculous origin of Jesus, but even contain an implicit contradiction of it, if we read between the lines. Mark 3.21—significantly, the passage which was left out by Matthew and Luke—shows at least that Mary and the brothers and sisters of Jesus knew nothing of this. There is also the positive fact that in Mark 1.11 and parallels (*cf.* esp. Luke 3.22 in the version given in ms. D) his status as Messiah and Son of God are explained on the basis of his adoption by God in the act of baptism (*cf.* Vol. II, *Christology* I, 1*a*).

The gospel of John departs from the idea of the Virgin Birth in a different way, referring to Jesus in 1.45 and 6.42 as the son of Joseph and Mary of Nazareth. Furthermore, the point of the genealogies, Matt. 1.1 ff. and Luke 3.23 ff., is that Jesus is a scion of the royal house of David, in that Joseph is shown to be the father of Jesus and at the same time a descendant of David. Later on, when belief in the Virgin Birth had become established, Mary was said to be a descendant of David, in contradiction to the original intentions of the genealogy (*cf.* Justin *Dialogue* 43. 45. 100 and the *Protoevangelium of James* 10). The Lucan tradition itself, a poetic tradition which probably grew up amongst Jewish Christians, betrays the fact that it originally spoke of Jesus as the son of Joseph and Mary promised by the angel of God. In fact in the whole literature of the New Testament only Luke 1.34 ff. and Matthew 1.18-25 tell of the Virgin Birth. By contrast, the oldest Palestinian community regarded Jesus as the son of Joseph and Mary.

The origins of the idea of the Virgin Birth are to be sought not in the prophecy of Isaiah 7.14, which is referred to in Matthew 1.22 f., but in syncretistic conceptions of the birth of sons of the gods (*cf.* Vol. II, *Christology* I, 5*a*; II, 1*c*). The impulse may have been given by the messianic title 'Son of God', because in pagan regions this was no longer understood in its proper sense. The talents and development of a person do not depend in the first place on his education and environment, but are given him from the very first in his mother's womb, and this was considered to be particularly true of Jesus: the miracle of his manifestation as Messiah was already present in the womb of his mother, Mary.

That Jesus was of the house of David—the second point on which the birth narratives of Matthew and Luke are based—was the general view of primitive Christianity, which regarded the Messiah as the son of David. But the two genealogies, Matt. 1.1 ff. and Luke 3.23 ff., are so different that no definite conclusion can be drawn from them at all. The statements of Rom. 1.3 ('descended from David according to the flesh') and Mark 10.47 ('Jesus, son of David, have mercy on me!') are far more important as evidence of the earliest traditions. Forgetting for the moment that we are dealing here with an important article of messianic faith, we may suppose that the family of Jesus believed that they were descended from David. Jesus's own view could be seen from the passage Mark 12.35-7 if only its meaning were clear. Its probable sense is that Jesus was denying that the Messiah must be a son of David—in contradiction to the view of the Rabbis with their national and political messianic hope. This would mean that even if Jesus regarded himself as the Messiah, he was denying that he was himself the son of David. On the other hand, we may well ask whether this whole scholastic dispute between Jesus and his opponents can carry such a weight of meaning.

The third point on which the narrative of Jesus's birth agree is the reference to the Judean town of Bethlehem as the place of his birth. Once again, Matt. 1.18 ff. and Luke 2.1 ff. are completely isolated in the context of primitive Christian tradition, and also contradict each other in the point that they are trying to make. According to Matthew, the parents of Jesus lived in Bethlehem; and they only went to Nazareth in Galilee after their return from Egypt, from fear of Archelaus. But according to Luke, the parents of Jesus lived in Nazareth, and were only temporarily and by chance in Bethlehem at the time the child was born, on account of the census imposed upon Palestine by the Roman authorities. Even when we ignore legends on which no historical check is possible, and which have found their way into the birth narrative (the wise men from the East, the massacre of the infants at Bethlehem, the flight into Egypt), the census described in Luke 2.1 ff. is highly unlikely, if not altogether impossible. This event in the history of the Roman Empire, with which Luke characteristically links his description of Jesus's earliest days, is found in no other tradition, which is only to be expected, since during the lifetime of Herod the Great (died B.C.) and his son and successor Archelaus (died A.D.) a Roman census in Judaea would not have been permitted. The Jews did not have to undergo such a census until 6/7 A.D. under Quirinius (this is attested by Josephus, *Antiquities* xvii, 13,5; xviii, 1,2; xx, 5,2; *Jewish War* vii, 8,1). We cannot ignore the chronological and practical impossibility of Luke's account of the Roman census. But in primitive Christianity the dominant view was in fact that Jesus's home was in the Galilean village of Nazareth (Nazareth, Nazara, Nazarat, Nazarath; Mark 1.9; Matt. 2.23; 4.13; Luke 4.16; *cf.* Luke 1.26; 2.4). He is consequently described as 'from Nazareth' (ὁ ἀπὸ Ναζαρέθ Matt. 21.11) or the 'Nazarene' (ὁ Ναζαρηνός Mark 1.24; 14.67; 16.6) or again as 'the Nazaraean' (Mark 10.47; Matt. 26.71; Luke 18.37, etc.). The evangelists associate these titles with the village of Nazareth, which is not mentioned in the Old Testament, in the Talmud or by Josephus, but nevertheless existed and can be regarded as Jesus's home village. The title 'Nazaraean' is nevertheless a special case. The linguistic link between 'Nazareth' and 'Nazaraean' is very uncertain. It is possible that 'Nazaraean' may have meant something else before it was associated with 'Nazareth'. Furthermore, it is noteworthy that the

Mandaeans call themselves 'Nazaraeans'; on this basis, Jesus the 'Nazaraean' can perhaps be regarded as an adherent of the baptist sect (as a result of his baptism by John) which is associated with the Mandaeans.

Apart from these two points which they have in common, the birth narratives of Matthew and Luke are completely different. The individual passages are associated with numerous different themes drawn from Old Testament stories and prophecies, from Messianic doctrine, and also from Jewish stories. Amongst these are the story of *Jesus's visit at the age of twelve to the temple* (Luke 2.41-52), the only story of Jesus's boyhood in the New Testament, which differs in this from the rich inventiveness of the extra-canonical gospels. The third evangelist, with the interest in chronology and psychology which we have already mentioned, was clearly trying to fulfil an aim which was important to him, in saying something at least about the youth of Jesus, for which there was no other tradition.

All these critical studies of the sources bring us back to the comprehensive proclamation of Jesus Christ in the preaching of the apostles and in the summaries in the gospels. But we have already emphasized the necessity of *sifting the principal contents of the gospel tradition,* which begins with Mark 1.1 and parallels. This task will be undertaken as we go on to describe this material in the sections that follow.

3. The Setting out of the Material

Our *procedure* will be as follows: We shall first give an account of the external features of the life history of Jesus. This is inevitably only possible in broad outline; for such an outline, with few fixed dates, is all that was established and transmitted to us by early Christianity. Then we shall go on to describe the preaching, the actions and the person of Jesus, and of course it is not of any importance in which order we do this. It cannot be said that one aspect is more important than another. But for methodological reasons, we shall deal with the question of the person of Jesus, which is not that of his personality, but that of his status as Messiah, after the others. What is important is that the *Messiah Jesus preached and acted.*

By way of an excursus we must give a brief account of the non-Christian sources for the life story of Jesus. The above discussion of Jesus and the tradition concerning him shows that non-Christian evidence concerning Jesus, so far as it is authentic, is not very abundant. A brief survey of the sources in question confirms this conclusion. Roman historians have very little to say of Jesus, and it is all in very general terms. It is not certain whether or in what way a remark of *Suetonius* in his life of the Emperor Claudius (Ch. 25), where a certain Chrestus is mentioned, refers to Jesus Christ. More important is the testimony of *Tacitus*, who in his great historical work (*Annals* 15.44), describing the persecution of Christians by Nero after the disruption of Rome by fire, says 'the originator of this name, Christ, was executed during the reign of Tiberius by the Procurator Pontius Pilate'. There is little to be said for the argument frequently advanced that this is a later Christian interpolation. But assuming that the passage is authentic, what does it really tell us? Basically only this, that a Roman historian at the beginning of the second century A.D. held the opinion that Christianity derived its origin from one who claimed to be the Messiah and was executed during the reign of the Emperor Tiberius. This only confirms what we learn from earlier Christian sources, quite apart from the gospels, which are the case under discussion. For Tacitus the question was of so little importance that he was content merely to repeat what Christians themselves held about the origin of their faith, and found no contradiction in it. The same is true of an isolated remark, clearly referring to Jesus, in the letter of a certain Syrian, *Mara*, to his son Serapion. Its date is unknown (the second or third generation after Christ), and it remarks that the Jews had executed their 'wise king'. More remarkable than the lack of more detailed testimony concerning Jesus in ancient pagan historians is the absence of any such evidence in the Jewish historian *Josephus*. The passage in *Antiquities* xviii. 3.3, which mentions Jesus, has either suffered much interpolation by a later Christian hand, or is an interpolation in its entirety, like the more detailed mention of Jesus in the Slavonic translations of Josephus's *Jewish War*. The passage in *Antiquities* xx. 9.1, where James, 'the brother of Jesus, the so-called Christ' is named, is more likely to be genuine. It is astonishing to the outside observer that Josephus should have said virtually nothing about Jesus. And even stranger is the fact that Josephus is completely silent about the primitive Christian Church, although as early as the seventh decade of the first century it had come to the notice of the Roman public authorities, considering that his work was written in Rome in the last third of this century. It seems that Josephus, the Jewish apostate and friend of Rome, preferred for political reasons not to mention the dangerous messianic movements of his people.

Finally, there is a good deal about Jesus in the *Talmudic tradition* (the Mishna etc.) but it is all caricature, and worthless as information. The pagan and Jewish testimonies only tend to confirm the historicity of Jesus in so far as they make it quite clear that in spite of the acute struggle with Christianity, the fact of the life and ministry of Jesus was never disputed by the pagan and secular opponents of the Church. But even such a cautious valuation of the ancient testimonies to Jesus means that the doubt which has constantly been re-expressed in modern intellectual history as to whether Jesus ever existed at all, can be fully allayed and does not require a specific and detailed denial. Our own attitude to this question is implicit in our discussion of the relationship between Jesus and the tradition concerning him.

II. THE HISTORY OF JESUS IN OUTLINE

1. Absolute Chronology

The year in which Jesus was born cannot be decided for certain. According to Matthew 2.1 and Luke 1.5 Jesus was born under Herod the Great. But Herod was already dead by the year 750 *ab urbe condita* (after the foundation of Rome), that is, by 4 B.C. This implies that *the year of Jesus's birth* is wrongly equated with the first year of our era. Luke 3.1, relating the events of Jesus's life to secular history in the way characteristic of the third gospel, solemnly states that the year in which John the Baptist began his ministry was the fifteenth year of the Emperor Tiberius (that is, between August 28th and 29th). Furthermore, Luke 3.23 states that when Jesus began his ministry he was 'about thirty years old'. Apart from the approximate nature of this statement, it must be pointed out that it is in no way related to that of 3.1. According to the synoptic tradition (*cf.* Mark 1.14) Jesus began his ministry after the imprisonment of the Baptist (but when did this take place?), while according to the Johannine tradition Jesus and the Baptist were both active at the same time. It is possible that Jesus may have begun his ministry as early as the year 28/29. But since he was about thirty years at that time he must have been born before the year 1 (the attempt which is often made to fix the year of Jesus's birth by relating the mention of the star in Matt. 2.1 ff. to astronomical computations falls down because of the nature of this story, which in no way offers any basis for such calculations). The *year of Jesus's death* is also uncertain. A statement which recurs in the tradition of the early Church (Tertullian, *adversus Judaeos* 8; *adversus Marcionem* 1.15) which refers to the consulate of the Gemini (29) cannot properly be reconciled with Luke 3.1 (28/29). It is certain that Jesus was executed during the period of the office of the 'Procurator' Pontius Pilate (26/36). Since Pilate was no longer in office at the Passover of the year 36, while John the Baptist began his ministry in the year 28/29, the possible years are 29-35 A.D. It is impossible to work out the year in which Jesus's life ended because we are uncertain not only of the date when his ministry began but also of its duration. Another much disputed detail of absolute chronology is the problem of the *day of Jesus's death*: all the gospel narratives agree that Jesus was crucified on a Friday (Mark 15.42; Matt. 27.62; 28.1; Luke 23.54; John 19.14,31; *cf.* also the *gospel of Peter*), but they differ in the day of the month they give. According to the synoptic account Jesus ate the Passover lamb with his disciples (Mark 14.12,17), was taken prisoner and brought before the Sanhedrin on the Passover night, and was condemned by Pontius Pilate and put to death immediately on the following morning, that is on the 15th Nisan. But the gospel of John, agreeing with the *gospel of Peter*, records that Jesus was taken prisoner on the night of the 14th Nisan (John 13.1,29; 18.28; 19.31). Here the date given by the synoptic gospels presents great practical difficulties. The first day of the Passover (from 6 o'clock in the evening of the 14th Nisan up to the same time on the 15th Nisan) was regarded as holy like the Sabbath, and in particular could not be broken by legal proceedings. From this point of view, the Johannine chronology is to be preferred, although one must remember that from the point of view of the fourth gospel the crucifixion of Jesus on this day, the 14th Nisan, had a deeper significance: Christ is the true Passover lamb (John 19.36; *cf.* 1.29). Furthermore, Mark 14.2 records that the Jewish authorities wanted to avoid dealing with Jesus on the feast day itself. This seems to be a reflection of the older tradition that Jesus was crucified before the

Passover (here again, the attempt to fix the date by astronomical calculations of the year in which the 14th or 15th Nisan fell on a feast day must be regarded as of no avail). A more exact solution of the problem of *absolute chronology* is not possible (*cf.* Vol. III, *Christianity* I, 6*a*).

2. Relative Chronology

The tradition concerning Jesus is of no greater help with regard to *relative chronology*. Here we come to the question of the *place* and the *duration of the public ministry of Jesus*. The first three gospels present the following picture: Jesus's ministry began and was mainly carried out in his own home province of Galilee, especially around the sea of Galilee; then he travelled for a time outside Galilee, which was governed by the Tetrarch Herod Antipas; finally, he went to Jerusalem for the feast of the Passover which was the Passover of his death; his stay in and around Jerusalem lasted from the first to the sixth day of the Jewish week, from Palm Sunday to Good Friday of the Christian calendar. By this reckoning, the whole ministry of Jesus lasted less than *one* year. It would be possible to divide the individual passages as they stand between a few months of the year. But the story of the plucking of corn on the Sabbath (Mark 2.23-8 and parallels) brings us into the period of the Palestinian harvest, which it is quite certain took place in the period between the beginning of April and June. This raises the question whether this story should be placed at the beginning or the end of Jesus's ministry. If we accept that the present tradition of the passage implies the beginning, then the date of the harvest means that his ministry lasted almost a full year. On the other hand, if we ignore its present 'chronological' context, which in any case is wholly uncertain, and place it at the end of his ministry, then it occurred in the very last days of

Jesus's life. A different picture of the place and duration of Jesus's ministry is given in the gospel of John. Here Jesus goes to Jerusalem and Judaea three times before the Passover at which he died. His last visit to this region did not last a single week, but about half a year, if we take the feast of Tabernacles (7.1 ff.) as the time at which it began. The further peculiarity of this chronology is that Jesus's journeys to Jerusalem do not appear as an interruption in his stay in Galilee; rather, the real scene of his ministry is Jerusalem and Judaea; only a few events take place in Galilee. In this contradiction between the synoptics and John it is the former which should be followed on the whole, as far as the scene of Jesus's ministry is concerned. It is obvious that the Johannine picture is strongly influenced by the desire to answer the Jewish reproach that Jesus was no more than an up-country prophet from Galilee, by showing that Jesus's public ministry in Jerusalem was of longer duration (*cf.* John 7.1 ff.). Nevertheless, even the synoptic gospels reveal a number of hints of Jesus's earlier connections with Jerusalem, implying that his ministry was of longer duration. When in Matt. 23.37 (=Luke 13.34) Jesus says: 'Jerusalem . . . how often would I have gathered your children together?' it must be admitted that there is an obvious possibility that he had several times been in Jerusalem and round about. Or it may be that his last stay there lasted for a longer period than would be supposed from the synoptic gospels. We must also remember that Jesus evidently had a long acquaintance with families in and near Jerusalem (Mark 11.1 ff.; 14.14; Luke 10.38 f.).

What is the situation with regard to *place names* in the gospels? The most prominent in the synoptics is *Capernaum*. On the whole, this presumably reflects a historical reality, though we must bear in mind that some passages originally associated either with no special place or with another place, were later linked with Capernaum. The small number of other places which are mentioned, without being especially emphasized, thereby produce a much less suspect impression. There are, however, constantly recurring elements which do not fit the synoptic outline as it is usually accepted; an example of this is the woe which Jesus called down upon Bethsaida and Chorazin, which are worse than Tyre and Sidon (Matt. 11.21 = Luke 10.13). Jesus may have come into contact with Chorazin or may even have worked there, without this being mentioned in any passage. The form of the tradition of these isolated passages makes it impossible to introduce any order into the way they are arranged (*cf.* I 2 above p. 97). The attempts made by the third evangelist in this direction are not so successful that one can trace the influence of a trustworthy earlier tradition. This is true both of the shorter and of the more extensive passages into which he rearranged the material, and above all of his travel narrative 9.51 ff., in which he attempts to include Samaria in the area covered by Jesus's ministry.

3. The Principal Dates and the Beginning of Jesus's Ministry
The result of our examination is that the statements made in the gospels as a whole are consistent, but that it is *no longer possible to establish their order in detail*: as a man of about thirty years of age, about whose outward and inward preparation we can say nothing, Jesus began his public ministry, working for a few years, principally in Galilee and sometimes beyond the boundaries of the province (in the region of Tyre and Sidon, and Caesarea Philippi and in Decapolis) and in Jerusalem, to which the conclusion of his work was restricted. Thus there is no indication of any outward development, far less any inner development, in the pattern of the public ministry

of Jesus. In attempting to elucidate the latter, and trace it back into Jesus's youth, it is perhaps possible to draw one or two indirect conclusions (such as that Jesus was raised in a Jewish family and instructed in the synagogue) but nothing of decisive importance is known.

This makes the *beginning of Jesus's ministry* even more significant. The movement of repentance and baptism begun and sustained by John the Baptist, also gave Jesus the opportunity to preach repentance, taking up the cry of the Baptist: 'Repent, for the kingdom of God is at hand' (Mark 1.15; Matt. 4.17). Here we encounter the *preaching of Jesus.*

III. THE PREACHING OF JESUS (HIS WORDS)

The Imminence of the Kingdom of God and Man's Repentance

1. The Link with Judaism
(The Messianic Movements; The Law and the Promises; Rabbinism and Apocalyptic; John the Baptist.)

Jesus was not the first to speak of the *kingdom of God*; nor was John the Baptist. The theme of their preaching was not: I proclaim to you that there is a kingdom of God, and that it is like this; but rather: I proclaim to you that 'the kingdom of God' is at hand. They were talking about something already known to their audience, their Jewish contemporaries. This concrete starting point is of decisive importance in the preaching both of John the Baptist and of Jesus himself.

We can best explain what the Jews had in mind at that time by discussing first the word used to describe it. The Greek word $\beta\alpha\sigma\iota\lambda\epsilon\acute{\iota}\alpha$, which we usually translate 'kingdom', means in itself the being, the nature, the status of a king. Since it refers to a king, perhaps we do best to say that it denotes his rank and power. The second meaning of the word follows naturally from this: the authority of the king extends to the territory he rules, his kingdom. An examination of the canonical Old Testament in its Hebrew text and its Greek translation (the Septuagint), and of the Pseudepigrapha, the Apocrypha and the rabbinic literature shows that the most important meaning is that of 'rank', 'authority'. It mainly refers to an eschatological concept going back to the preaching of the prophets and elaborated by the apocalyptic writers, in which the expressions 'kingdom of God' (βασιλεία τοῦ θεοῦ=in Hebrew, *malkūt yahwēh*, and in Aramaic *malkūtā di'elāhā*) and 'kingdom of heaven' (βασιλεία τῶν οὐρανῶν, *malkūt hašāmayim, malkūtā dišmayya*) are used in the same sense. All the same, the second expression has a particular implication of its own, referring to the rule which comes from heaven and enters the world. In fact the expression, 'kingdom of heaven', reveals two important facts. Once again, it makes it clear that the essential significance is not 'kingdom' but 'kingly rule'. Secondly, it follows that such a kingly rule from heaven cannot by its very nature signify a kingdom brought into being by the natural development of the earthly situation, or by human exertion, but only by the intervention of God from heaven.

The Jewish people, as the chosen people of God, looked forward to this intervention of God. An enthusiastic revival, but also a morbid darkening of hope, is characteristic of the *messianic movements* at the beginning of the present era. By contrast with other nations, the Jewish people saw their true being not in their physical and intellectual achievements, however powerful and talented their nation may have been, but in something else which was greater than themselves, in the calling of God which constituted them as the 'people of God'.

Their possession was the *law*, their hope the *promise*—as it were the two focal points of an ellipse that included the whole national life. The law and the promise are inseparably related to one another in that in both, God, and God alone, speaks in uncompromisingly radical terms. God the Lord is not a tyrant, but the Father, who loves his people as his first-born son, and for this reason has given them his law: a law in which ethical and juridical principles are united, and which leads man, in all his activities, away from the material and even the spiritual world, and guides him to God, demanding obedience to his will. Only from this point of view does the nation have a future, a promise to be realized in the fulfilment not of human ideals, but of the will of God. God, to whom the last word belongs, will bring into being his day, the day of God, through his anointed, his *Messiah*: the world will come to an end, but God in his glory will remain, and with him will be his people, who serve him. This prophetic certainty, this preaching of salvation and disaster, of judgement and grace, was accepted in all its complexity by late Judaism, but was not maintained in its proper significance. A quietism on man's part, and also, by contrast, a fierce activism, not to speak of human individualism, became powerful forces at the expense of the calling of God manifested in the law and the prophets. The Judaism of the scholarly scribes, *Rabbinism*, as it is called, is known to us from written records only from the post-Christian centuries, but was certainly widespread even in Jesus's lifetime. It did not of course abandon this hope on principle, but was preoccupied with striving zealously to establish what was the will of God here and now, and in practice declined increasingly into a calculating human casuistry. Others, in contrast to this, adopted an apocalyptic which set great store by the calculation of the events of the future, and concocted fantastic dreams and visions on the basis of all sorts of conceptions adopted from oriental religions. More or less in association with such oriental mythology, there came into being the hope of the restoration of the former glories of David, in which the dominant note was automatically formed by political ideas and desires, based on the longing for the end of Roman rule, ideas which were paralleled in statements made by the prophets in similar circumstances.

Not all the Jews shared in this attitude, with its numerous detailed variations. Groups in official positions, such as the *Sadducees*, disassociated themselves from them; they had come to terms with Roman rule, and in any case were unsympathetic to apocalyptic ideas, which had found their way relatively late into Judaism. It was quite different with the mass of the people, whose whole life and thought was filled by the hope of the end. The same is true of the *Pharisees*, who did not exercise official leadership in Jerusalem—this was in the hands of the Sadducees as the representatives of the ancient priestly families—but who, as lay people who were not priests, and also as scribes learned in the scriptures, were a pattern and example to the people. It was amongst them that the burning messianic hope was often transformed into an activism which brought political passions to fever pitch. We know of numerous such messianic movements about the beginning of the Christian era. Apart from a number of individuals who claimed to be the Messiah, there was also the party of the *Zealots*, associated with the Pharisees, as well as the *Sicarii*, whose attitude was similar, and who gave a great deal of trouble to the Romans. Other eschatological movements were not political in nature, but nevertheless came under political suspicions as can be seen from the fact that the non-political leaders of such movements, John the Baptist and Jesus, fell prey to political forces.

John the Baptist proclaimed the imminence of the end,

and on the basis of this conviction he preached repentance. As a prophet like the great prophets of Israel, he looked forward to the day of Yahweh (*cf. Eschatology* II, 2 p. 231 below), which was to be a day of repentance and judgement. He thundered against the self-complacency and self-assurance of the people which was particularly widespread amongst the Pharisees with regard both to their legalism and also to their apocalyptic expectation: 'Do not presume to say to yourselves, "We have Abraham as our Father"; for I tell you, God is able from these stones to raise up children to Abraham' (Matt. 3.9= Luke 3.8). Repentance was necessary for the Jews as well as for the Gentiles: and both could share in the kingdom of God. Repentance was also extended to the ordinary actions of everyday life, in which we conduct our affairs with our neighbours; those who possessed goods were told to renounce them (*cf.* the Baptist's 'sociological' sermon, Luke 3.10-14). This prophetic approach, proclaiming the calling of God, to whom obedience is due, and not the distinctive national individuality of the people of God, that is, the 'Church', was adopted in the same way by Jesus of Nazareth, who fulfilled it both in his words and actions: 'Truly, I say to you, not even in Israel have I found such faith. I tell you, many will come from east and west and sit at table with Abraham, Isaac, and Jacob in the kingdom of heaven, while the sons of the kingdom will be thrown into the outer darkness' (Matt. 8.10-12; *cf.* 15.28; Luke 13.28 f.; Matt. 22.1-14=Luke 14.16-24; Isa. 49.12); and he healed the servant of the Roman centurion in whom he had found 'such faith' (Matt. 8.5-13=Luke 7.1-10), and also the daughter of the gentile Syrophoenician woman (Mark 7.24-30; Matt. 15.21-8). When, later in the course of his ministry, Jesus had to describe the status of the Baptist, and saw in him 'more than a prophet' (Matt. 11.9=

Luke 7.26), he was expressing his agreement with the basic preaching of John the Baptist. When emphasis is laid in the same context on statements of Jesus according a low status to the Baptist (Matt. 11.11=Luke 7.23: he who is least in the kingdom of heaven is greater than John, who is the greatest to be born of woman; Matt. 11.12 f.=Luke 16.16: the difficult saying about the taking of the kingdom of heaven by force), it is later anti-Baptist polemic which lies behind one or both of the statements. But the tradition is unanimous that Jesus drew away from the Baptist, in spite of his agreement with his preaching. Two peculiarities of this prophet, his *asceticism* and the *practice of baptism*, were not adopted by Jesus, or at least not emphasized. Jesus and his disciples were not ascetic, and they did not fast like John and his disciples (Mark 2.18 ff., and parallels). Baptism is of no importance in the ministry of Jesus (*cf. Baptism* I p. 294 below; the contrary Johannine tradition grew up as a result of anti-Baptist polemic: not only the Baptist but Jesus also baptized). Jesus fulfils the kingdom of God (*cf.* Mark 2.19 and parallels) over and above asceticism, seen as man's effort to sanctify himself, and over and above baptism as a ritual action on the part of man (here at least we can see the danger in the practice of baptism which lay behind Jesus's misgivings). The special claim of Jesus was made known in the context of John's baptismal movement, and the Baptist himself recognized the provisional nature of Jesus's intention in associating with him, something that is far more clearly seen and portrayed in the fourth gospel than in the synoptic tradition; and John pointed to him who was greater than himself, him who was bringing fulfilment, although the contradictions of the tradition do not make it clear whether and to what extent he regarded Jesus of Nazareth as the Messiah.

2. *The Content of Jesus's Preaching*

a. GRACE AND JUDGEMENT. (The negative and positive nature of the kingdom of God; Jesus and the ancient world.)

Jesus preached the *imminence of the kingdom of God*, which signifies *grace* and *judgement*, salvation and repentance, at one and the same time. The statement made in the evangelist's summary at the beginning of the account of Jesus's ministry (Matt. 4.17), recurs again and again: 'Blessed are the eyes which see what you see' (Luke 10.23), blessed are the poor, the humble and those that mourn (Luke 6.20 f.). This blessing and salvation, this invitation to the kingdom of God, has to be accepted through repentance; that is, men have to turn their back on everything else in the world, and therefore they have not to act like those who were invited to a banquet but found all kinds of excuses (Matt. 22.1-14=Luke 14.16-24). This is why this invitation is so serious, even terrifying. For the sake of this great gain, which is like a treasure hidden in a field or a precious pearl for which a merchant sells all his possessions (Matt. 13.44-6), one must be prepared to tear out an offending eye, or to cut off an offending hand (Matt. 5.29 f.). There is a reminder that many have made themselves eunuchs for the sake of the kingdom of God (Matt. 19.12.). This means that there is a very strict separation of the few from the mass of the many (Matt. 22.14; *cf.* the saying concerning the narrow gate and the wide road, Matt. 7.13 f.=Luke 13.23 f.). A stern Either-Or demands an inexorable decision: 'no one who puts his hand to the plough and looks back is fit for the kingdom of God' (Luke 9.62); and such a decision is not to be made in a moment of ecstasy, but as the result of determined, sober consideration, as a master-builder who draws up a proper estimate of the cost before he begins to build, or as a king who makes his plans before he goes out to battle (Luke 14.28-32). Those who are invited to the kingdom of God have seriously to consider whether they are truly accepting the invitation. And those who accept the invitation but do not realize its compelling demands, that is, those who 'hear' but do not do, are like the man who builds his house on sand (Matt. 7.24-7=Luke 6.47-9). A readiness to suffer the utmost sacrifice is demanded, even to the extent of hating one's own family (Matt. 10.37=Luke 14.26). Jesus himself demonstrated this in his attitude towards his own family (Mark 3.31-5 and parallels).

This radical demand makes clear what are the decisive elements in the *nature of the kingdom of God*. The nature of the situation when God rules is defined in the first place negatively, and also, as a result, in positive terms.

In negative terms, the kingdom of God is something opposed to everything that is here and now, everything present and earthly, so that it is something which is, without qualifications, miraculous. The kingdom of God is not an ideal, a highest good in the ethical sense, towards which one constantly strives, and to which one grows nearer step by step. Its source is in something totally different from us. The question is not whether and to what extent we men have the kingdom of God in our hearts, in our inward disposition, or whether men display the kingdom of God in society. The question is whether, when the kingdom of God comes—and it comes without any action or assistance on our part—men will belong to it or not. To attempt to bring the kingdom of God into being by force is an impertinence on the part of man, a refinement of the attitude of the Zealots, and is self-righteous Phariseeism. The hardest thing of all is the patience which alone guarantees that we are ready for the act of God. Anyone who does not show this patience, against his own desires and in readiness to wait on God, is like the man who sows and does not let the seed which grows—'he does not know how'—sprout and grow on its own (Mark 4.26-9). A miracle is worked before our very eyes, when, without our assistance or understanding, the seed-corn grows into the fruitful ear—that modern science has explained this miracle or is striving to explain it, makes no difference to the point of comparison in this parable; and the same is true of the miracle of the kingdom of God. The parables of the mustard seed (Mark 4.30-2 and parallels) and the leaven (Matt. 13.33=Luke 13.20 f.) contain the same message. Their purpose is also to show how the kingdom of God comes suddenly at a time that cannot be calculated, and with overpowering force, and that in the meantime it is present within the anticipatory signs which are contained in the acts of Jesus. We never hear that men are in a position to build such a kingdom. Only God builds. When the gospels say that we 'enter the kingdom of God' (Matt. 5.20; 7.21; Mark 10.15 and parallels; Mark 10.23 and parallels), we must bear in mind what was said above about the 'kingdom of God' as the 'kingly rule of God'; we are entering the kingly rule of God, we are going where God rules as Lord. We are going into 'life' (Mark 9.43 f.=Matt. 18.8 f.), something which in truth we can neither bring about nor even help in bringing about. We are entering 'the joy of the Lord' (Matt. 25.21,23), which is given to us as a gift.

What, then, is this kingly rule of God in *positive* terms? It is a *cosmic catastrophe*. For in this positive sense it is represented by certain events which form part of the eschatological drama of Jewish apocalypse. Jesus shared in full the hope of his people, so far as this did not consist of the idea of a political Messiah but looked forward to the glory of the 'Son of Man' (Dan. 7.13) who was to come in the clouds of Heaven: the dead would rise again, the judgement would break in upon the world as a blessing for some and a curse for others. Much in this picture (especially in the Synoptic Apocalypse of Mark

13 and parallels) is drawn from the apocalyptic imagery
of ecstatic communities. But Jesus did in fact speak of
eating and drinking in the kingdom of God (*cf.* for
example Luke 22.18). And yet the decisive element in
Jesus's preaching on this subject is something different.
What is important is not that Jesus shared the conceptions of his Jewish contemporaries in this particular
sphere, or far less that he exceeded them. The important
point is that on this subject Jesus remained far behind
his contemporaries, and did so consciously. By contrast
to the true apocalyptic that we encounter in Judaism
and also in early Christianity, Jesus refused to describe
the events of the end and to base a calculation on the
preliminary signs of the end. The mockery of the Sadducees who put to him a problem of apocalyptic belief
and the hope of the resurrection which, by contrast to
the Pharisees, they rejected, failed to find its mark:
'When they rise from the dead, they neither marry nor
are given in marriage, but are like angels in heaven'
(Mark 12.25 and parallels). The emphasis here is quite
clearly laid on the rejection of any speculation, and not
on an exact description of the condition of the angels.
Even more clearly expressed is the rejection of any attempt to determine the date of the approaching end, or
to base a calculation on *signs of the end*, as was normal
practice in Jewish and Christian apocalyptic. 'The kingdom of God is not coming with signs to be observed'—
Luther gives a free translation which makes the point
clear: *nicht mit äusserlichen Gebärden*—'Not with outward
gestures'—'nor will they say "Lo, here is it!" or "There!"
For behold the kingdom of God is in the midst of you'.
(Luke 17.20 f.). The whole point of this frequently quoted
and misunderstood saying lies in the rejection of the
attempt to forecast the end from signs.

The question whether this passage is emphasizing that
the kingdom is present at the moment this saying was

uttered (immanent), is not under discussion, particularly since in the original Aramaic the copula 'is' or 'will be' would not be used. Similarly, the translation 'within you' (A.V., Luther) is incorrect, as can be seen from the fact that the Syriac translation implies a re-translation of the Greek ἐντός (within) into a word in Aramaic—closely related to Syriac—which signifies 'in the midst of'. The same is true of the saying concerning the time of the day of the Son of Man: 'If they say to you, "Lo, he is in the wilderness", do not go out; if they say, "Lo, he is in the inner rooms", do not believe it. For as the lightning comes from the east and shines as far as the west, so will be the coming of the Son of Man' (Matt. 24.26 f.; *cf.* Luke 17.23 f.). That Jesus's contemporaries thought differently about the signs and the nature of the kingdom of God can also be seen from the story of the sons of Zebedee, who wanted to assure for themselves a good place in heaven, and to whom Jesus replied that the according of places of honour was the affair of God alone (Mark 10.40=Matt. 20.23).

In yet another point Jesus is more reserved than his contemporaries. Even where the dominant theme of the future hope was not national and political, and where instead the end was expected to bring salvation to the whole world, that is, where the implications of the saying of John the Baptist that God was able to raise up children to Abraham from the stones were remembered, the *preferential status of the Jewish nation* was nevertheless of importance. It was Israel's right to be restored to its old glory once again: the scattered members of the nation would pour into the new Jerusalem, as would the gentiles. The power of the Romans suddenly brought this hope to an end for ever. On the whole Jesus shared this hope. This explains why he promised to his disciples, the 'twelve', the representatives of the twelve tribes of the people of God, who were a holy people, the office of judges and rulers in the kingdom of God (Matt. 19.28; Luke 22.29 f.). It is in accord with this that Jesus limited his ministry and that of his disciples to Israel: 'Go nowhere amongst the gentiles, and enter no town of the Samaritans, but go rather to the lost sheep of the house of Israel'. (Matt. 10.5 f.; 15.24; *cf.* also the passages concerning the centurion in Capernaum, Matt. 8.5-13= Luke 7.1-10; and the Syrophoenician woman: Mark 7.24-30=Matt. 15.21-8). At the same time, there are limits to the widespread view that these are sayings of Jesus which it would have been impossible for anyone to invent (because of the implied opposition to the Christian gentile mission) for it is possible that Jewish Christian zealots may have put such sayings into circulation. In all these cases, considerable significance attaches to a negative point which had already been made by John the Baptist: the Jew as such has no special claim upon God, if it is possible that he may be put to shame on the day of judgement even by gentiles. The role of Israel is understood in the same way by Paul (Rom. 2: the rejection of Israel; Rom. 9-11: the salvation of Israel). Finally, Jesus's concern for Israel is not aimed against Rome. One has only to compare the widely used Jewish prayers of the *Shemoneh-esreh*, with their patriotic and nationalist outlook, and the Lord's Prayer with its total absence of patriotic and national ideas. There is also the answer made to the trap set for him in the Pharisees' question: 'Render to Caesar the things that are Caesar's, and to God the things that are God's' (Mark 12.13-17 and parallels). God is Alpha and Omega. By contrast with this, friendship to the Romans or hatred of the Romans are equally pointless.

We are brought back time and time again to a negative statement, and the intensity of this statement must be insisted upon, for it is the *status of God* which is at issue. It does not follow from Jesus's rejection of apocalyptic calculations that he preached the immanence of God and his kingdom at the expense of his transcendence. Nor does his indifference to the national and political aspect of the Jewish expectation of the end mean that he held a *universalist* view. The alleged universalism of Jesus's preaching is the same as that of all the great prophets, including John the Baptist. It is recognized that the Jew as such is of no account in the sight of God, but this does not mean that man as such is of any value or has any claim. The very fact that Jesus limited his concrete task to Israel, and in fact to Israel according to the flesh, means that there was no question of an internationalist or universalist ideal based on the nature of man. In the Greek world at that time the universalist attitude went hand in hand with a concern for 'personality' (*cf.* the Stoics), but the preaching of Jesus has nothing to do with this. Jesus's regard for the apocalyptic setting of his preaching, and the emphasis he places on the eschatological drama as the final phase of time, sharply distinguishes his preaching from the *individualism* of the Greeks. Of course it is a misunderstanding of the preaching of the kingdom of God to overlook the disagreement between Jesus and Judaism on this issue. It is even more of a misunderstanding to interpret the disagreement on the basis of Greek thought. Greek thought, which in fact continues to govern our modern thinking, sees in man a character which develops, with the gradual mortification of its bodily and sensible elements and the growth of its spiritual and psychical aspects. Anyone who attempts to place Jesus in this context is sublimating his preaching of the kingdom of God, and thus replacing the human apocalyptic fantasy which Jesus rejected, and the human political dreams he also rejected, by nothing more than a sophisticated ideal of humanity, similar to that contained in the ancient ideal of the *vir bonus*. According to a remark of Epictetus, 'to please oneself' and 'to please

God' are one and the same thing, because the 'law of nature' and the 'law of God' are identical. Neither Jesus nor Paul know anything of such optimism—Paul in fact puts the whole issue much more pointedly and therefore much more clearly than Jesus. However attractive Epictetus' preaching of true freedom may be, it is nevertheless entirely concerned with the condition of the human personality. Man is never liberated from himself, never gets outside himself. The thought of the Greek world culminated in an individualistic ideal of life, the autarky (self-sufficiency) of the philosophical personality, whose cosmic ideal community was not even rooted in a real community. Of course we know that the ancient world also contained *pessimistic* tendencies. The Attic tragic poets (Aeschylus, Euripides and Sophocles) and Plato had already raised serious objections to a philosophy which did not ever look beyond the present world, and founded and developed a psychological and cosmological *dualism*. But even during the period of its decline, the ancient world, which included the hellenistic mysteries with their struggle for purification, clung firmly to its original golden rule, 'Know yourself', and so continued to be based on human *hybris*. The crucial question is, whether the secular arguments of this philosophy ever gave any fundamental recognition to reality, and whether someone like Seneca, with his declamatory philosophy (Nietzsche calls him a 'toreador of virtue') did not carry on his disputation in a rarefied atmosphere beyond all reality. Jesus, who did not share the optimism of the ancient world, was not influenced by a pessimistic cosmological dualism. He did not speak, as the Greeks did, of soul and body, spirit and flesh, but of the whole man who is called to repentance and acts of penance. The saying, 'What does it profit a man to gain the whole world and forfeit his soul?' (Mark 8.36 and parallels) has led some to speak of the doctrine of the 'infinite value of the human soul'. But the word 'soul' here (as the R.S.V. and other modern translations recognize) means no more than 'life' here, so that the meaning of the saying is quite simple: what use are all the goods of this world to a man, when he still has to die? Jesus, whose comment on the conditions of his own life sounds so pessimistic ('Foxes have holes, and birds of the air have nests; but the Son of Man has nowhere to lay his head', Matt. 8.20 =Luke 9.28), accepted an inherited belief in providence, and praised the lilies of the fields and the birds of the air, which are cared for by God (Matt. 6.25-34=Luke 12.22-31). Jesus never speculated on the wickedness of the world in the manner of pessimistic dualism. His observation of reality showed him that there are different kinds of men, good and evil, righteous and unrighteous, just as there are healthy and sick people. But no one can be called good in the sight of God, who alone is good (Mark 10.18 and parallels). In one exhortation he addresses his audience as those who are evil, and are thus different from the heavenly Father (Matt. 7.11=Luke 11.13). This observation of reality is based on the realization that men should regard themselves in a modest and humble way, and not think that others who are severely afflicted are particularly great sinners, worse sinners than themselves (13.1-5), or that someone born blind is atoning for the sins of his parents and himself. (John 9.1 ff.).

One important negative point should be made quite clear: Jesus, the preacher of the kingdom of God, had *no world philosophy and no metaphysic*, and owed allegiance to none of the great human abstractions, neither to nationalism, internationalism, universalism, humanism, individualism, optimism or pessimism, nor to monism or dualism. Because he had not adopted any such position, there is a complete absence of any emphasis in his sayings on any particular mental attitude, the perfectionism of the Pharisee, the asceticism or the libertinism of the gnostics, or the enthusiasm of the fanatic. By contrast with these, his lack of any metaphysics—the same is true of Paul, especially in 1 Cor.—signifies a lack of intellectual commitment even to the most interesting and sublime states and activities that have attracted men; a self-emptying. Jesus's preaching of the kingdom of God is scandal to the Jews and foolishness to the Greeks, just as much as the apostles' proclamation of the cross of Christ.

Jesus's attention is fixed not on the background but on the foreground of reality. But he regards it not with the outlook of an artist or with the naïvety of a child, but as a thinker, as one who makes a conscious decision, as a man. His strictly theocentric point of view was not a speculation, but an insight into the reality of man, who is subject to death, and yet destined for the kingdom of God.

We have already said that these negations assume the status of God as the Lord. But when we have described this in terms of transcendence, of the cosmic catastrophe and of the miracles, we find that such expressions are really inadequate for us, as human beings, to construct from the conceptions associated with them a true picture of the world above. God alone is the future, and he alone has a future. His kingdom is of the future, because it is not interwoven with our human existence. But this future is not completely separate from us; it directly concerns us and defines our present existence. It is not true that we can assist in bringing this future into being by our repentance and good works, or do something for its sake. This would be nothing less than Phariseeism, and one of the sayings of the Pharisees was: 'If Israel kept only *one* Sabbath, it would be redeemed.'

What is asked of men is that they should do the will of God in everyday life. What has Jesus to say about the obedience of man to God in the world?

b. OBEDIENCE TO GOD IN THE WORLD. (The authority of the law; the true interpretation of the law; Jesus's criticism of legalism; the whole demand of God and the Either-Or; reward and punishment; the will of God; the double commandment of love.)

Like his Jewish contemporaries, and especially like the Rabbis, Jesus, who was often himself addressed as 'Rabbi' (Mark 9.5; 10.51 etc.), emphasizes *the authority of scriptures and the law,* in which the *will of God* is set down. He took part in the arguments in the synagogue as a Rabbi, and as a teacher of wisdom put forward many ideas which in form and content are related to Rabbinic sayings or are even identical with them. Of great importance is the obedience to the law which Jesus practised and which was demanded by his audience. A rich man asked him, 'What must I do to inherit eternal life?' Jesus answered, 'You know the commandments', and listed the familiar commandments of the Decalogue (Mark 10.17-19 and parallels). Another man, who was in fact a scribe learned in the law, asked Jesus what was the greatest commandment; Jesus reminded him of two Old Testament passages, Deut. 6.4 f. and Lev. 19.18, where the double commandment of the love of God and the love of one's neighbours is set out (Mark 12.28-31 and parallels). In many important instances Jesus appeals to scripture, as in the question of divorce (Mark 10.1-12 = Matt. 19.1-12), in the story of the plucking of corn on the Sabbath (Matt. 23.26 and parallels), and with regard to his sitting at table with tax collectors (Matt. 9.13; 12.7). Sometimes Jesus cites some scripture passage more in passing, or refers to it indirectly. This is in accord with the practical attitude of Jesus and his disciples. He recognized the temple worship (*cf.* Matt. 5.23 f.), paid temple tax (Matt. 17.24-37). and carried out customary acts of piety such as alms-giving, prayer and fasting (Matt. 6.1-4,5-8,16-18). A note of caution must be sounded in the light of a critical view of the sources: many of these passages are only found in the first gospel. Even if they perhaps represent the product of a later tradition of the community in which this gospel was written it is at least clear that this community had no knowledge of any resistance to the authority of the law on the part of Jesus. The most directly relevant saying in this context also occurs in Matthew: in the introduction to the Sermon on the Mount Jesus describes himself as one who has come not to abolish the law and the prophets, but to fulfil them. The point of course is, what does 'to fulfil' mean here? At least the first evangelist saw no contradiction between this 'fulfilment' and the antitheses that follow, which are aimed against every kind of legalism. In the same way, for Paul, Christ is he who fulfils the law by revoking it. Thus we must ask in what sense the law was authoritative for Jesus, and how he interpreted it.

The Rabbis also argued about the *right interpretation of the law*. There are many strata of rabbinic thought, but, ignoring hellenistic Judaism with its doctrine of the virtues, they are all agreed on one point: man has to carry out what God has commanded him regardless of whether it is a matter of ritual or ethics. While the preaching of the prophets demanded justice and righteousness and mercy, late Judaism emphasized *obedience*, as it were for the sake of obedience itself. This attitude, the intention of which was to give due place to God alone, and to avoid the introduction of human ordinances, led to a remarkable juxtaposition and interweaving of ritual and ethical admonitions, which were given with the formal authority of the law. No distinction was made between ethical and legal considerations. The relationship of man to God is a legal contract; it is to be fulfilled by carrying out the obligatory provisions of the law, and also provisions which go beyond this (e.g. alms, prayer and fasting), which thus require a particularly meritorious character. The zealous endeavour to submit to the authority of the law led to the development of casuistry. On the other hand, many rabbis strove to find a way out of the complexity and fragmentation of comment on the law by raising the question of the most important principle of the law, and answering it with a slogan (e.g. 'Love your neighbour as yourself') or a general rule (e.g. 'What you do not wish to be done to yourself, do not do to anyone else'=The Golden Rule). Rabbinic tradition also contains the saying: 'The Sabbath is given for you and not you for the Sabbath', which is a clear criticism of formalism. A number of statements against the idea of merit are also recorded from the rabbis. But it seems that these were criticisms which were only raised occasionally.

In Jesus's over-riding *criticism of legalism* these occasional comments came to form the central theme. He also appealed to the prophets, who themselves formed part of the scriptures, even, or rather especially, when they came into conflict with another scripture passage. Thus one passage of scripture was set against another. The clearest example of this is the treatment of divorce (Mark 10.1-12=Matt. 19.1-12). Where is God's will to be sought? Moses, of course, had written in his law that a man could put away his wife with a certificate of divorce. But the story of the creation states that man and wife should not be separated. This meant that Moses had given his law only because of the hardness of the Jews' hearts. In simple terms, the procedure Jesus used here implies the necessity of a distinction between essentials and inessentials, which he put very forcibly in his threat to the Pharisees, whom he accused of 'straining out a gnat and swallowing a camel'. He meant that they ignored what was most difficult in the law, justice and mercy and faith (Matt. 23.23 f.=Luke 11.42). Such controversial sayings, arising from numerous conflicts with the scribes and Pharisees, form one of the main themes of Jesus's preaching. While the saying just mentioned is still comparatively reserved in its import: 'One should do this and not omit that', in another passage the scribes are directly challenged with the charge that by a perverse ritual provision they were actually abrogating the fifth commandment (Mark 7.9-13, on saying 'Corban'). It is clear here that in the first instance Jesus is attacking a perverse interpretation of the scripture on the part of the scribes. But in reality his prophetic attack is aimed against the Old Testament itself, in so far as it represents a formal authority. He quotes from Hosea 6.6 the saying 'I desire mercy and not sacrifice' (Matt. 9.13; 12.7). And there is nothing more clear and pointed than this saying: 'There is nothing outside a man which by going into him can defile him; but the things which come out of a man are what defile him' (Mark 7.15= Matt. 15.11). When he leaves the realm of the law, in so far as it is merely the realm of prohibitions, man, who within that realm can never rest assured that he has not done something or other that is forbidden, becomes subject to an all-embracing and constant demand, so that his acts are never neutral: 'Is it lawful on the Sabbath to do good or to do harm, to save life or to kill?' (Mark 3.4=Luke 6.9; *cf.* 14.3). The concern for incidentals, instead of for what is most difficult in the law, and instead of *the command of God in its entirety*, leads man into lukewarmness and hypocrisy. The Pharisees, with their endeavour to carry out all the details of the law and all the ritual provisions, certainly regarded themselves as humble in the sight of God, but set themselves up on a pedestal in the sight of men, and forgot that God looked into their very hearts (Luke 16.15; Matt. 23.25-8=Luke 20.39-44).

There are others who are half-hearted, and cannot overcome their timidity before the decisive *Either-Or*; they are those who are of good will, but whose fatal weakness is that they only accept God's purposes when it suits their own affairs. Thus it was said of the rich young man (Mark 10.17-27 and parallels): 'It is easier for a camel to go through the eye of a needle than for a rich man to enter the kingdom of God.' What matters is that a decision must be made in the heart for God or for the world (Matt. 6.19-21=Luke 12.33 f.). 'No one can serve two masters . . .' (Matt. 6.24=Luke 16.13). The great antitheses of the Sermon on the Mount (Matt. 5) belong here; they draw the contrast between a total and a half-hearted decision, a positive and a negative approach (they demand that one should do good, and not merely avoid evil), and between the spirit of the commandment and the letter: anyone who does not murder, but is angry, is a murderer; someone who does not commit adultery, but harbours a wicked lust in his heart, is an adulterer; someone who obtains a divorce commits adultery, for marriage is not relative but absolute, not partial but a wholeness; someone who merely avoids perjury is ignorant of what truthfulness really means; someone who exacts vengeance for a wrong he has suffered is approving the wrong; someone who only loves his friends does not know about the whole of love, which extends even to one's enemies. Man must bear the full burden of this Either-Or, the decision between good and evil. And in such a *return to first principles*, such an *abandonment of literalism*, such a rejection of the mass of ordinances which is the end-product of the Pharisees' attempt at self-justification, is the substance of the *gospel*, the good news. If the preaching of the kingdom of God means salvation for men, then the conflict with the law we have just described is concerned with this salvation. And if salvation is preached to the poor, the hungry and those who mourn, then this conflict with the law is concerned with them as well. A burden is taken from the poor. The Pharisees and scribes looked with contempt on the 'people' who 'did not know the law', the 'ordinary humble folk', on the tax collectors whose calling brought them into conflict with the ordinances, and on sinners. 'Woe to you, scribes and Pharisees, hypocrites! Because you shut the kingdom of heaven against men; for you neither enter yourselves, nor allow those who would enter to go in' (Matt. 23.13=Luke 11.52). Jesus, as the *friend of tax collectors and sinners* (Mark 2.16 f. and parallels; Matt. 11.18=Luke 7.34) praises the little children, to whom is given what has been hidden from the wise and understanding (Matt. 11.25 f.=Luke 10.21 f.). To those who labour and are heavy-laden the Saviour says: 'My yoke is easy, and my burden is light' (Matt. 11.28-30). In such a period of messianic joy, there is no time for the religious practices that were followed before: 'Can the wedding guests fast while the bridegroom is with them?' (Mark 2.19 and parallels). The similes of the new patch on an old garment and the new wine in old wine-skins (Mark 2.21 f. and parallels) are appropriate to such a time.

All of this forms part of the good news, even the fact that a *reward* is promised to those who do God's will. This does not mean that the promised reward, any more than the *punishment* promised to those who fail, is the motive for the action. In fact it is made quite clear that Jesus demands obedience without any secondary considerations or ulterior motives. A servant has no claim on his master's thanks (Luke 17.7-10); this is made clear by the way the workers in the vineyard are treated (Matt. 20.1-16). But God gives the reward of his own free will to those who have been obedient to him, but not for the sake of any reward.

The question of how men fulfil the *will of God* is not easy to answer, and is not meant to be easy to answer. A general rule is of no help. When someone like the rich young man asks what is the way of life, he can only be referred to the commandments that he already knows. But what happens when men are faced with a particular demand in a particular situation? Will they then act like the merciful Samaritan in the parable (Luke 10.29-37)? The *Either-Or*, the decision which clearly faces man at every turn, cannot be summed up in a universal rule. This can be seen from the fact that Jesus's preaching never mentions any form of asceticism as a universal demand. Poverty is not a guarantee of a state of holiness; what is demanded is sacrifice. Sexual continence may be necessary under certain circumstances; but what is demanded is purity within and outside marriage. Fasting may be a pious and useful practice, but is no more than this: Jesus permitted himself to be described as a glutton and a drunkard (Matt. 11.19=Luke 7.34). As far as economic and political life is concerned, neither a negative reforming or revolutionary programme can be derived directly from God, nor a positive and constructive programme. We have to be constantly aware that the implacable demand of God reaches down into our existing family, social and political situation, though no attack is made on this in itself; and that, for example, someone may be asked to separate himself from his own family (Mark 3.31-5 and parallels). Just as the Samaritan knew that he had to help the wounded man—while the priest and the levite, with their knowledge of the law and their ethical principles had failed in this—so we also must constantly deny ourselves and help and serve our neighbour (Mark 10.42-4 and parallels; Matt. 23.8 f., 11 f.).

Here we come to the *commandment of love*. What we
have just been discussing is essential to the understanding
of this commandment: obedience through self-renunciation. The love of one's neighbour is not the same as the
love of mankind, which was an ethical principle that one
man should regard another as holy. If this idea of human
dignity is a starting point, then the love of *one's neighbour*
is the same as the *love of God*: we love the divine in our
neighbour. In the Old Testament and in the preaching
of Jesus (Mark 12.28-34 and parallels), however, what
we find is a genuine *double commandment* of love: God and
our neighbour. Man's attitude to God is that of obedience; he overcomes himself and is attentive to the needs
of his neighbour. And by loving his neighbour, he carries
out his obedience towards God. In this sense there can
be no love for one's neighbour without the love of God,
and no love of God without the love of one's neighbour.
The question that then arises, how one should love one's
neighbour in this way, is answered simply and decisively
by the phrase 'as yourself'. We know at once how we love
ourselves, and do not need to be taught this. 'So that
whatever you wish that men would do to you, do so to
them; for this is the law and the prophets' (Matt. 7.12=
Luke 6.31). Such a love knows no limits. We must forgive
our brother 'seventy times seven' (Matt. 18.21 f.). Such
a love is not merely affection or merely sympathy for
those we are fond of—this is found also amongst the sinners and the gentiles (Matt. 5.46 f.=Luke 6.36). The
apostle Paul expressed the matter as follows: 'Owe no
one anything, except to love one another; for he who
loves his neighbour has fulfilled the law' (Rom. 13.8).

This is the way in which the judgement of God upon
sinful men is carried out. The kingly rule of God is the
end of man, not his death. For with the end of man this
judgement brings salvation and joy, good news. God
is Lord and he is also our Father.

c. GOD THE LORD AND FATHER. (The Jewish faith in God in
its pure and logical form; faith in prophecy and resignation; belief in miracles; belief in prayer; faith; the forgiveness of sins.)
Jesus's *conception of God* and faith in God are implicit
in what we have already said, in describing Jesus's
preaching concerning God's action and will. But this
does not mean that we now have an independent description of the nature of God. For what God is, he is in
his acts and will. We recognize his acts towards his people;
we obey his will for his people. Only in this way can we
have faith in God and love for God. And this is what
gives us our hope, in so far as the act of God lies in the
future and is coming to us, and in so far as we have not
fulfilled God's will. This shows that it is impossible to
say that Jesus introduced a new conception of God and
a new faith in God, a fact that becomes even clearer
when we consider that it is possible and indeed necessary
to understand Jesus in the *context of Palestinian Judaism,*
for which God was understood neither through the act
of thought involved in theological speculation, nor in the
act of emotion in mysticism. That was done, of course,
by the hellenist Philo, in spite of all his emphasis on the
patriarchal heritage, because the decisive influence upon
him was that of Greek philosophy. It is true that the
impression one obtains from Greek thought is that it
has a purer and finer understanding of the nature of the
spiritual, than is found in the anthropomorphic conceptions of Israelite and Jewish thought. But the inevitable
consequence of these spiritual conceptions is the pan-
theism of the Stoics, which also had a powerful hold on
Philo. And it is apparently primitive anthropomorphic
conceptions which leave the total sovereignty of God untouched, rather than this sublime philosophy. The Israelite Yahweh, the Jewish 'Lord', *is then not the law of the
universe, but a will directed towards the universe.* 'He spoke,

and it came to be; he commanded, and it stood forth'
(Ps. 33.9). The unique will of God makes God the creator
of the world and the Lord of history. He deals with man
as the potter handles his clay pot: 'he will be gracious
to whom he will be gracious, and will show mercy on
whom he will show mercy' (Exod. 33.19; Rom. 9.15).
He who is Lord is also *Father*. This title does not often
occur in the Old Testament, but it is of decisive significance where it does appear. Yahweh is the father of his
people, who form his household, that is, his children and
his slaves. The Father is the creator: 'Is not he your
father, who created you, who made you and established
you?' (Deut. 32.6; *cf.* Jer. 31.9; Isa. 64.3; Deut. 14.1;
Ps. 103.13 f.). As early as the Israelite period, 'Father' is
used as a mode of address in prayer (Isa. 63.15 f.; Ps.
89.27; 68.6; Jer. 3.19; Isa. 64.7; Jer. 3.1). This Father
demands of his people that they should act towards him
as to a father; he demands trust and loyalty (*cf.* Deut.
14.1 f.). This Father is at the same time the Lord; the
Lord is at the same time Father; this can be seen from
the strict parallelism of a saying of the prophet Malachi:
'A son honours his father, and a servant his master. If
then I am a father, where is my honour? And if I am a
master, where is my fear?' (Mal. 1.6; *cf.* 2.10). In later
Judaism the use of the title 'Father' became more
general. Here again, God is Father and Lord (Eccles.
23.1, 4; 51.14; 3 Macc. 5.7; 6.8 ff.; 7.6; Wisdom 2.17).
The title 'Father', of course, also occurs in hellenism,
as for example in the Hermetic literature. But there
God is given this title as a cosmic principle; God the
Father is the physical and metaphysical origin of everything. In a context much closer to Jesus, however, we
find a specifically Jewish prayer: 'Forgive us, our Father,
for we have sinned; pardon us, our King, for we have
done wrong' (the sixth petition of the *Shemoneh-esreh*).
Consequently, both the people and an individual can

be called 'the son of God', 'the child of God' (Eccles. 4.10; *Pss. of Solomon* 17.30; *Jubilees* 1. 24 f.), if they obey God.

In this complex idea of God, the *past*, the *present* and the *future* are related to each other. The 'God of Abraham, Isaac and Jacob' is the God of a history which concerns the people at the present day. And God, who is bringing the events of the world to an end and bringing into being his judgement and his kingdom, is God of a future which in the same way affects his people as the present time. Nevertheless, the actual relationship between the present and the future in the concept of God was a difficult problem for Judaism. A highly developed belief in providence is expressed in the longing of religious hope. Man can look forward to the future through his faith in God as judge. Then God will show his grace and mercy to those who have remained faithful to him. This conception makes it easy for a piety based on good works to creep in, when the attempt is made to assure oneself of the grace of God by the confession of sins and penitential prayer (*cf.* 4 Ezra 8.31-6). The idea of the possibility of good works is never completely excluded. The grace of God is seen more as a benevolent overlooking of sins on which one can rely in fear and hope, in the future, rather than a forgiveness of sins, which is a comfort at the present time.

As we have already said, all this forms part of Jesus's attitude to God. To a considerable degree, Jesus held the ideas we have set out both in form and in content. The only difference between the content of Jesus's belief, and that of Judaism, is that he rejected the false development described in the last paragraph, and therefore *maintained and lived the Jewish concept of God in its purest and most logical form*—that is, he preached the unqualified grace of God towards a wholly sinful mankind (*cf.* Vol. II, *Grace*, III, 1). It is in this that the much vaunted originality of Jesus consists, and not in any new or original ideas about God that he brought forward.

Though he taught that God is both Lord and Father, and described how this was so, this does not mean that Jesus spoke more of God as a loving Father than Judaism as a whole. Judaism also held a *childlike belief in the providence of God*, such as is found in Jesus's sayings concerning worldly cares (Matt. 6.25-34=Luke 12.22-31; Matt. 10.29-31=Luke 12.6 f.; Matt. 5.45). Jesus is particularly close to Judaism in this, because he never relates his sayings to any theory of the working of God in the laws of nature, as did the pantheistic Stoic philosophers, who also described the providential care of God in similar terms. For Jesus, God is a personal will, a holy and gracious will. He is close to men in so far as he has dealings with them. An isolated discourse on the attributes of God is impossible. God is not some kind of higher nature, such that man can take hold of him in worship as a mysterious or even magical instrument, and force him to act. There is *no mystical relation to God*, in which a human being can let his personality be absorbed into the stream of divine being. Instead, Jesus says: 'You shall love the Lord your God with all your heart, and with all your soul, and with all your mind, and with all your strength' (Mark 12.30 and parallels). The belief in providence we have mentioned stands in contrast, as in Jewish proverbial wisdom and that of the East as a whole, to a *resignation* which recognizes the facts of life: 'Foxes have holes . . .' (Matt. 8.20=Luke 9.58); 'Which of you by being anxious can add one cubit to his span of life?' (Matt. 6.27=Luke 12.25); 'Tomorrow will be anxious for itself' (Matt. 6.34 f); 'To him who has will more be given. . . .' (Mark 4.25 and parallels). The question as to how such a resignation is to be understood in conjunction with the optimism which is equally clear is not answered, because it is neither asked nor felt as a problem. When Ecclesiastes utters his *carpe diem* simultaneously with his realization that 'All is vanity', this is not a frivolous Epicureanism, but an insight into the nature of human life, subject as it is to death: when man is fortunate enough to see his wishes fulfilled he is thankful for God's kindness; but he is resigned when God ordains misfortune for him. The ineluctable fact of human suffering, which the Stoics try to argue away but which Jesus does not, is not a basis for doubt in God's rule over the world. The question of the justice of God, the *problem of theodicy* which recurs so often in religious and intellectual history, *is not raised*. Man is struck silent before God: 'Not what I will, but what thou wilt' (Mark 14.36 and parallels).

The same basic insight is found in the *belief in miracles* which Jesus takes for granted. Man may expect miracles. But he has no cause to doubt God when he refuses a miracle. God is omnipotent. But man cannot count on God's omnipotence as on a general fact of nature: 'I believe; help my unbelief!' (Mark 9.24).

The same is true of his *belief in prayer*, which involves an attitude of self-sacrifice and self-renunciation towards God, and at the same time a trustful petition made to God. Jesus inherited from Judaism a rich life of prayer. There are Jewish parallels to every detail of the masterpiece of his prayer, the Lord's Prayer (Matt. 6.9-13; Luke 11.1-4). What distinguishes it is its simplicity and brevity. Jesus taught that in praying we should not heap up empty phrases as the gentiles do (Matt. 6.7), nor make a display of ourselves like the Pharisees; our prayer concerns God alone (Matt. 6.5 f.). More than once it is made clear that prayer is not simply an action to be carried out. In prayer we have recourse to the goodness of God. But no one has the right to do that unless he manifests goodness in his own life; no one has the right to ask forgiveness unless he forgives others (Matt. 6.11

f.=Luke 11.25 f.). And to forgive means to disregard any calculation of the guilt of others; we must forgive not seven times, but seventy times seven (Matt. 18.21 f.=Luke 17.4); we must not act like the wicked servant in the parable (Matt. 18.23-35). A proper petition will move God (*cf.* Matt. 7.7-11=Luke 11.9-13, and the parables of the importunate friend Luke 11.5-8 and the importunate widow, Luke 18.1-8). God can be moved; he is not bound by any (natural) law. In the prayer of petition, the idea of omnipotence is as it were revoked, though only in the sense that the omnipotence of God is free, and is not a universal truth by which we have God tied down. We have to submit ourselves in obedience to the will of God. But this does not mean resignation, but the utterance of what oppresses us, followed by a silence before God himself: 'Not what I will, but what thou wilt'.

This belief in miracles and in prayer are the substance of *faith* for Jesus. Anyone who has this faith only as a grain of mustard seed can move mountains (Matt. 17.20=Luke 17.6); for 'all things are possible to him who believes' (Mark 9.23). Jesus reproaches lack of faith (Mark 9.19 and parallels; Matt. 6.30=Luke 12.28). The summary, Mark, 1.15, refers to the same thing; 'Believe in the gospel'.

Finally, faith is related to the *forgiveness of sins*. Jesus gives no general theory of sin, nor any doctrine of original sin. On the other hand, his understanding of the nature of sin is uncompromisingly radical (*cf.* Vol. II *Sin and Guilt* III): it is not merely a weakness, nor mere error, but so total an alienation of man from God, that only God's forgiveness can be of any help. Judaism abandons the sinner. By contrast, Jesus makes it clear in the parable of the Pharisee and the tax collector (Luke 18.9-14) that it is the sinner who is saved rather than the Pharisee who cannot see that man cannot do more than is asked of him. It remains true that even when we have done the best we can, we are still 'unworthy servants' (Luke 17.10). Because the tax collector and sinner knew something of this, he understood better than the pious and scrupulous Pharisee what it really means to receive the gift of the grace of God. This is why Jesus calls the poor blessed (Matt. 11.5=Luke 7.22; Matt. 5.3=Luke 6.20). A fuller picture is given of this in a number of parables (Matt. 21.28-32: the two sons; Luke 15.4-10: the lost sheep and the lost coin; Luke 15.11-32: the Prodigal Son). Only a sinner knows what grace is. But people like this, who make no claim on their own account, are still only children, which is why Jesus uses children as an example. (Mark 10.13-16 and parallels.) But when and in what way does the forgiveness of sins become manifest? Not in such a way that a general rule can provide a clear standard of judgement. Nor is such a standard given in the death and resurrection of Jesus, the saving acts on which the Church is founded. The question is whether Jesus actually spoke of himself, in this decisive context of the grace of God towards sinful man, as the saving fact (*cf.* V below).

IV. THE ACTS OF JESUS

The Signs of the Kingdom of God

1. Jesus's Miracles
(Miracles and Repentance; God and Nature; The particular Jewish Context by Contrast with the General Context of the Ancient World; The healing of those possessed by Demons).

Jesus did not only speak, he also acted. And just as the climax of his preaching is the forgiveness of sins, the same forgiveness is also closely associated with his acts. The paralytic receives both healing and the forgiveness of sins: 'My son, your sins are forgiven' (Mark 2.1-12 and parallels). Even if the analysis of this story leads to the conclusion that it was the ordering of the material by tradition and redaction which first brought together the miracle of healing and the saying concerning the forgiveness of sins—this analysis is by no means certain—it is nevertheless important that the preaching which summed up the message of primitive Christianity emphasized this particular connection. For *miracles and the word*, related in the primitive Christian kerygma in the way we have described above, are associated with one another. Why does Capernaum bring down such great guilt upon itself? Because it has not been brought to repentance by the signs that Jesus did there (Matt. 11.21-24=Luke 10.13-15). When Jesus, starting from his faith in miracles, reveals the help of God to the people through their faith in miracles, he directly reinforces the call to repentance. When God is revealed, a separation from evil and an adherence to the holy and gracious will of God always takes place. On the other hand, if miracles do not *bring about repentance*, they are of no use, and are not a revelation of God. This mutual relationship is what is essential. Miracles are not a subsequent confirmation and ratification of the preaching of the word. Both repentance and miracles are concerned with faith. Only one who abandons evil and desires good can come to God. Only one who desires the visible help of God experiences the miracle in its fullness. And Jesus is not a miracle-worker manifesting his power, but a helper whose task is laid down by the faith shown towards God in repentance. He refuses to conquer unbelief through revelations of his power. The Pharisees and scribes who clamoured for a miracle were referred to the sign of Jonah, who preached repentance to the people of Nineveh (Matt. 12.38-42=Luke 11-12). Where there is no faith, Jesus cannot do his mighty works (Mark 6.5 f.= Matt. 13.58; *cf.* John 2.18). A faith based purely upon miracles is condemned as inadequate (John 2.23 f.; 4.48). A petition to God which flows from obedience and faith is granted; a demand made to God, which is in fact nothing other than unbelief, is rejected. God's dealings with man are not arbitrary; he is merciful to those who are repentant and judges those who are unrepentant. A faith without repentance, to which God's miracles are accorded, is not faith, but the attitude of a 'perverse and unclean generation'. It is not as though there were another way to God as well as repentance. A sign that was disassociated from repentance would not honour God but dishonour him. To give way to a purposeless hunger for miracles would be to make way once again for Phariseeism, and destroy the force of Jesus's preaching of the kingdom of God. Thus Jesus broke with the rulers of his people and went to his death, actually refusing to work a miracle to save his own life (Matt. 26.53). But it was by this that Jesus fulfilled the scripture; for it is the history of the people of Israel as the people of God which demonstrates that God's great acts of revelation are purposeless without repentance. The fathers ate the miraculous manna in the desert, and yet they died because they were unrepentant (John 6.58).

That Jesus listened to such appeals, and even provided for people's bodily needs, meant that he was calling upon *God's omnipotence*, yet without making a breach between God and nature. In discussing Jesus's concept of God, we saw that he did not regard God as opposed to *nature*, subject as it is to death, and the same close tension is present in the case of miracles. The help of the divine omnipotence is given in appropriate situations. Nothing that threatens human life, either sickness, storms, nature or evil spirits, can place any limit on this help (Matt.

8 and 9). From this point of view, there is no distinction between miracles of healing, and what might be called miracles of God's omnipotence. As soon as the miracle had been worked in a particular concrete situation, Jesus was once again subject to nature like any other human being. It was this that scandalized the Jews: he helped others and could not help himself (Mark 15.31 f. and parallels). Jesus both controlled and obeyed nature. This helps us to understand why Jesus did not go and parade himself as a miracle-worker who could transform the whole course of nature, but left those he had healed at once, and to the astonishment of his disciples, withdrew from the press of the crowd that sought miracles (Mark 1.44 and parallels; Mark 5.19=8.39).

We can now see what is *distinctive in Jesus's miracles,* which makes him different from the ancient world and even from Judaism. If we recall the general context in which the miracles of Jesus appear, we realize that the whole period abounded in miracles. It was not only Jesus who was said to work miracles. Paul and the other apostles were convinced that they had performed miracles (2 Cor. 12.12). The Jews also had miracle-workers (Acts 19.13 ff.). Jesus himself accepted that the Pharisees drove out demons (Matt. 12.27=Luke 11.19). As far as gentile religion is concerned, we can point in particular to the life of the miracle-worker Apollonius of Tyana by Philostratus, and must not forget that even a serious historian such as Tacitus could record that the Emperor Vespasian healed a blind man (*Hist.* IV 81). But the observation that the ancient world had a view of God, man and nature which was foreign to Jesus is not sufficient to explain what was distinctive about his miracles. A more important question is his status as a miracle-worker in the particular context of Judaism. At the time of Jesus, there was a complete cleavage between the function of the teacher and that of the miracle-worker; the Rabbi was not to be identified with the miracle-worker (Chanina ben Dosa and the son of Rabbi Gamaliel; *Mishna*, Tractate *Berakoth* (bab) 34ƒ). In general, the holy men and teachers of the period did not appear as miracle-workers, and were not honoured as such. To suppose that the great holy men of that time must have worked miracles is an unhistorical idea. No miracles are recorded on the part of the famous Rabbis Hillel, Gamaliel, Johanan, Akiba and ben Zakkai. All the tradition tells of is particular cases in which their prayers were heard, and of dreams and prophecies. The Jewish exorcists we hear of used all kinds of formulae and other devices. The characteristics of Jesus's miracles are quite distinct from those of his Jewish background. John the Baptist, to whom no miracles are ascribed in the gospels, belonged to this background. The prophet Jesus is distinguished from him precisely because of his miracles (John 10.41). On the other hand, Jesus's disciples worked miracles just like their master, and these were consistently interpreted as acts of the exalted Christ present in the Church (*cf.* Acts). The preaching of the disciples, like that of Jesus, was simultaneously accompanied by miraculous healings (Mark 6.7; Matt. 10.1,8; Luke 9.1 f.; 10.9). The people saw something that was unprecedented in Israelite history (Matt. 9.33). Some prophets of the Old Covenant had also worked great miracles. But these miracles, and their healings in particular, did not form an essential part of the ministry that they were called to, as was the case with Jesus.

We must now discuss the extent to which the accounts of miracles in the gospels belong to the *general context of the ancient world or the specific context of Judaism*. The evangelists, including John, followed the primitive Christian kerygma in emphasizing the very close relationship between miracles and the word, marvellous acts and the preaching of repentance or the gospel, and they framed their accounts of the miracles in terms evidently drawn from the Jewish context. But in the fourth gospel—frequently to serve the purposes of an allegory—Christ is shown as giving his revelation in stories and miracles which are couched entirely in the style of secular tales and fables—the most typical example is the story of the miracle of Cana, John 2.1 ff.—and similar features have also found their way into the synoptic tradition. The gospel of Mark is emphatic in its portrayal of Jesus as the Saviour (σωτήρ), although this Greek title does not actually occur in the synoptic gospels, and he presents his material according to a single and consistent purpose and plan. But the material as it came to him was markedly varied in form, and must be judged accordingly. The miraculous story of the temple tax, where the coin required was found in the mouth of a fish (Matt. 17.24-7), is strongly reminiscent of the story of the ring of Polycrates. Again, a number of relatively lengthy accounts of miracles are very similar to those of the hellenistic world, in that they describe the technique of the miracle-worker, emphasize how great an act has been carried out, and draw attention to its success. In the story of the healing of one who was deaf and dumb (Mark 7.32-7) something like a magical formula occurs (Ephphatha, 'be opened'); Jesus spits on the eyes of the blind man of Bethsaida and then lays his hands upon them (Mark 8.22-6); the parallel Johannine tradition (John 9.1 ff.) mentions five times in a short space that Jesus made clay and put it on the eyes of the blind man. Or again, the solemn account of the raising of the dead child in the house of Jairus ends with the far from solemn note: 'He told them to give her something to eat' (Mark 5.43; Matt. and Luke lack this sentence). These few examples are sufficient to show clearly that these are conventional stories of a miracle-worker. Many of them are explicitly stories of a divine epiphany. Many, again, are drawn from Old Testament stories. In particular Jewish Christian story-tellers may well have made Jesus the hero of Jewish legends on the pattern of the *Midrash*, in which the patriarchal history was sometimes supplemented with freely invented tales. But in the tradition that grew up in hellenistic areas, the influence of Greek popular tales, myths and fables was an even stronger influence. A thorough and detailed history and stylistic criticism of the material is necessary to sift one stratum from another. But at the same time, it must be clearly understood that such a standard of judgement is not sufficient to distinguish historical and unhistorical material with certainty. Furthermore, however many reminiscences there may be of hellenistic miracle stories, there must be considerable reserve and caution in accepting the presence of secular themes. Just as the evangelists, with their true understanding of Jesus, placed everything in the setting that was the principal and decisive one in his life and ministry, so it is evident that from the first there was a considerable restraint imposed on the element of fantasy and imagination that was at work in the miracle stories.

So when we turn again to the sifting that has nevertheless to be done, there is no question that the stories of the *healings of those possessed by demons* are stylistically the most original, and are the most important with regard to their content. This is in complete accordance with the primitive Christian kerygma: 'He went about doing good and healing all who were oppressed by the devil' (Acts 10.38). The important practical point is that it is quite evident that the healing of those possessed by devils is directly associated with the kingdom of God that is imminent. One of the signs showing that the future salvation is coming into being at the present time is the flight of the demons, whose prince is Satan. Convinced of this, Jesus and his disciples drive out demons in their miracles of healing. 'I saw Satan fall like lightning from heaven.

Behold, I have given you authority to tread upon serpents and scorpions, and over all the power of the enemy; and nothing shall hurt you' (Luke 10.18 f.). 'If it is by the spirit of God (Luke 'by the finger of God') that I cast out demons, then the kingdom of God has come upon you' (Matt. 12.28=Luke 11.20). In the time of Jesus it was believed that much mental illness, the hidden disturbance of the mental life of man, resulted from demonic possession: the sick or possessed person had fallen prey to alien forces that had seized hold of him or entered into him. Jesus accepted this current view, this explanation of a phenomenon which even for modern man is ultimately an enigma, without criticizing it or attempting to seek a different explanation. It was obviously important that Satan was at work here: bodily disturbance was also ethical disturbance. Jesus crushed such monstrous and wicked spiritual forces. He called everyone to the kingdom of God, even those who were in the power of the evil one, of Satan. If the aim of the kingdom of God is the fullness of grace for men, then the force of the mystery is bound to be effective against disorder in the human mind. It is more important to appreciate this essential fact than to go into details of the medical aspects of the matter. There are groups of parallel passages where it is easy to establish similarities to familiar symptoms in the cases they describe, as in some other healings (e.g. Mark 2.1-12 and parallels; 3.1-6 and parallels) where we are reminded of the therapy of compulsive suggestion used for neurosis and hysteria. On the other hand, we ought to use a certain caution in evaluating such parallels. The sensitivity of orientals belonging to a time and place remote from us, and much less complex and more single-minded, may have been far stronger, perhaps making them much better prepared and more receptive subjects. Yet what is at issue in the miracles of Jesus we are discussing is not the question of the single-mindedness or simplicity of those who were healed, but the kingdom of God, which comes from God and not from men, and thus the issue is also Jesus himself as the Messiah. In Jesus's dealings with those possessed by demons, the title of 'Messiah' for Jesus was used: the demoniac of Gadara called Jesus 'Son of the Most High God' (Mark 5.7=Luke 8.28). A normal Jew would pay attention to a teacher who would guide him. The demoniac, whose association with the community had been broken, and who had great doubts of himself, and of all human help, sought the help of God in the Messiah. What did Jesus himself say in this dialogue with the demoniac? He rejected the title he was given, in so far as he did not desire the testimony of the spirits to his lordship over them, but demanded the faith that brings repentance, through which all who are vigilant, and not merely those whose vigilance is recognized and accepted, are brought to God.

2. *The Purification of the Temple*

Are the acts of Jesus exhausted in these miracles, these signs of the kingdom of God? It is evident, and of great importance, that the *acts of Jesus* are *not* to be regarded as the manifestation of a normal, albeit a greatly intensified *activism*. It is understandable that the modern evaluation of Jesus constantly draws attention to the passive aspect of Jesus's work ('Jesus perceived in himself that power had gone forth from him', Mark 5.30) sometimes referring to the demoniac, numinous or even magical aspects, or else to the sharply eschatological concern in Jesus's whole outlook. Though there is much that is both right and important in this, it is fruitless and inappropriate to try and explain everything by the *category of the irrational*. Jesus was not carried along by forces beyond his own control, but spoke and acted consciously to make clear how the kingdom of God affected men, and what the signs of this kingdom signified. His outlook went beyond a purely apocalyptic hope. Jesus went to Jerusalem and *cleansed the temple* (Mark 11.15-19 and parallels). This clearly intelligible action fits into a much larger plan. Jesus travelled to Jerusalem for the feast of the Passover, and was prepared for a battle with the spiritual and secular rulers. What he preached, he put into effect in an action which horrified everyone: this obvious condemnation of the conduct of the temple worship visibly proclaimed the necessity of repentance. He laid down no general doctrinal principles about the nature and value of the temple. He seized on a *single offence* and used it to pose clearly to the Jewish community the question whether they recognized the sin in their worship and would turn from it, or whether they would be hardened, in the face of Jesus's call to repentance. Without debating the matter, Jesus demanded obedience to God, and drove the merchants out of God's temple. This is a central event in the story of Jesus's life, and is the beginning of his passion; that is why the fourth gospel, which sees the whole of Jesus's life in the light of the idea of his passion, places it at the beginning of his ministry.

V. JESUS HIMSELF (HIS PERSON)

The Messiah of the Kingdom of God

The event just mentioned means that Jesus's work took a very personal form, so that the question of the *person of Jesus* becomes unavoidable. It is indeed unavoidable, as we see when we consider the ministry of Jesus as we have described it above. We must limit ourselves here, however, to a brief summary. We have already had less to say about Jesus's acts than about his words, since the association of his acts with the preaching of salvation and repentance in the light of the kingdom of God, which is essential to the understanding of them, was already clear from our previous discussion of his preaching. And after describing Jesus's words and acts we have no right to expect to be able to investigate the person of Jesus and get any clearer picture of one aspect or another of it. Jesus's own view of his task and his calling is clear from what we have said about his preaching and his actions. What Jesus thought about himself, the nature of his *self-consciousness* and his *consciousness of his vocation*, is clearly not an essential question, when we consider that the words and deeds of Jesus in fact point us away from himself and towards God.

In the context of the history of religion and thought as a whole, Jesus was clearly a man with a prophetic vision and a highly developed consciousness of vocation, sufficient to tear away a skilled craftsman from his home, his family and his calling and to provoke the understandable distress and astonishment of his own relations. Consequently, since some of his statements, for example those beginning 'But I say to you', reveal a consciousness that contradicts all human experience, we have to take seriously the question of whether or not we are dealing with the words and actions of an enthusiast who is enigmatic and uncanny, unhealthy and confused. This would point directly to a psychiatric view of Jesus's person. This would not advance and confirm our understanding of Jesus's ministry, but would demolish everything we have already established. We do much better in this case to abandon the discussion and consideration of Jesus's self-consciousness, and to stick to the principle that in the case of the great men of history our concern should be not for their person but for their works. But Jesus did not belong to the context of religious and intellectual history in general, in which context only a very unsatisfactory evaluation can be given, but worked against the very

special background of the Jewish people, with their claim
to be the people of God, the 'Church'. This means that
it can be virtually taken for granted that Jesus of Nazareth regarded himself as the *Messiah*, even though we have
no information about the origin and the stages in the
development of his messianic consciousness.

1. The 'Church'

According to Matt. 16.18 Jesus the Messiah founded the
Church. This is a genuine saying of Jesus; there is nothing
in textual criticism to challenge its authenticity, very
little from the point of view of literary criticism, and little
more in the argument against the appropriateness of its
content. We get a proper picture of the whole saying and
its detailed interpretation, when we realize the significance of the Semitic original of the Greek word ἐκκλησία;
qāhāl (or any word which in the first place means a
community, but regards an individual community as
representative of the *qāhāl*) is the people of God in the
context of eschatology, which is a characteristic feature
of all statements concerning the people of God from the
prophets on; the community which consisted of Jesus
and his disciples is Israel, specifically Israel, the remnant
of Israel, the Israel of the final phase of time. This eschatological idea at first sight contradicts the different implications of the idea that what God is doing with Jesus
and his disciples is to be built up by Jesus. Perhaps this
building—though we cannot reconstruct the original
Semitic text with certainty—had had to be abandoned so
that the meaning of the saying would be as follows: You,
Simon, who are called the Rock, are the rock of the
Church of God, the people of God which you constitute
as the true Israel; and this people of God shall not perish.
This would not be an isolated procedure in the life of
Jesus. Jesus separated a small group from the mass of
the Jewish people, a group which contrasted sharply

with the Pharisees and scribes, and ultimately with the whole people, who were stubborn and impenitent. It is true that as it is presented in the gospel, this circle of disciples is somewhat indefinite—one has only to think of the variations in the list of their names; and individual details about those who formed it are lacking in the tradition. But the same is true of the primitive community where, at the latest, the college of twelve disciples must have been formed. In the words and acts of Jesus, the eschatological conception that the kingdom of God which was imminent was the destiny of the remnant and élite of the people of God reaches its climax. The claim of the kingdom of God is present in Jesus himself. Jesus acted as Messiah the moment he uttered to his Jewish audience a single word that laid a real obligation upon them. He pointed to the *setting up of the community of Jesus the Messiah*, that is the Church. On the one hand, he tried to win over the people, all Israel; on the other hand, he fell back on his disciples and a few faithful followers, a remnant which ultimately included the whole of Israel. The special status of Simon Peter in this remnant is a riddle which must be accepted as such. In fact, we are also unable to answer the question why God should have made the people of Israel his own people, his Church. Peter was chosen, then failed, but remained chosen as the *fundamentum ecclesiae*. Israel was also chosen and failed, but remained chosen because a remnant repented. This is the promise and fulfilment spoken of in the Old and New Covenants.

2. The Suffering and Death of Jesus

This view, concentrated on the person of Jesus as the Messiah, became the reason for his *passion and death*. What Jesus carried out in secret at the moment of his last meal with his disciples (*cf. Eucharist I*, 1 p. 341 below) had become, with the distinctive honour accorded him by the people, a claim of which the Jewish authorities were fully aware. Jesus was condemned by the Jewish ecclesiastical authorities as a blasphemous pretender to the office of Messiah (Mark 14.61 and parallels), and was executed by the Procurator Pontius Pilate as a claimant to the throne who was a danger to the state (Mark 15.26 and parallels). We have already mentioned the messianic act carried out in the cleansing of the temple (*cf.* IV 2 above). The entry of Jesus into Jerusalem amidst the jubilation of the people (Mark 11.1-10 and parallels) implies a similar claim. Jesus entered the city of God not as a prophet, but as the future ruler of the kingdom of God. He permitted the acclamation of the crowd, which greeted him as Messiah. And he encouraged this belief, not by his words, but by all that he did during the period of his passion in Jerusalem. Not only did the crowd gather about the Messiah, later to betray him. The same was true of those who were closest to him, his disciples. When the sons of Zebedee sought from Jesus the Messiah places of honour in the kingdom of God, Jesus referred them to the necessity of suffering, the baptism of death (Mark 10.35-45 = Matt. 20.20-8). Peter confessed Jesus as the Messiah (Mark 8.27-30 and parallels), and was immediately reminded of the suffering that was facing him; yet the next thing Peter did was to deny him, that is, to betray him whom he had acknowledged as Messiah. Judas Iscariot betrayed his master.

3. *Jesus's Messianic Secret*

It is a paradox worth further thought, that a jubilant people and the disciples who acknowledged Jesus betrayed him. This is associated with the contradictions, the glaring duality of the Jewish messianic hope. The so-called *messianic secret* is also associated with it. His appropriation of the messianic ideas was both a step forward and a burden to Jesus. The words he uttered from authority, together with the acts he carried out with the same authority, forced him to accept openly the messianic office which was hidden and concealed in his words and deeds. If he had not done this, his hearers would have had to look forward to someone else, and so indeed would Jesus, just like John the Baptist. On the other hand, his claim to be Messiah meant a constant conflict with human claims opposed to the purposes of God. Even those who were closest to Jesus were not free from such a self-seeking outlook. Thus he had constantly to instruct his disciples in the meaning of the messianic office (*cf.* for example, his words on the subject of service, Mark 10.42-5 and parallels). And Jesus had to face this conflict on his own account, as we learn from the story of the temptation (Matt. 4.1-11=Luke 4.1-13; *cf.* Mark 1.12 f.) in association with the story of his baptism, which precedes it (Mark 1.9-11 and parallels).

There is no need to describe in detail how as Messiah Jesus saw everything in the light of a complete obedience in the sight of God, such as is expounded in his preaching of the kingdom of God. It is from this point of view that Jesus spoke of the title of *Son of David* (Mark 12.35-7 and parallels; *cf.* Vol. II *Christology* I, 1). He did not apply to himself the quite frequently occurring messianic title *Son of God* (*cf.* Vol. II *Christology* I, 1). In two sayings in which he speaks of himself as the Son (Matt. 11.25-7= Luke 10.21 f.; Mark 13.22=Matt. 24.36) there is no real messianic significance. But these words, in which Jesus sees himself as the Son who is obedient to the Father, who is related to God in a unique way, and who is therefore the bearer of God's revelation (*cf.* the gospel of John), show clearly the nature of the messianic office as Jesus desired and presented it. According to the gospel account, Jesus constantly called himself the *Son of Man.* In the Aramaic which he spoke this term means 'human being'. The title comes from Daniel 7.13 f., which speaks

of the heavenly and pre-existent man who is one day
to come on the clouds of heaven (*cf. Eschatology* II, 7
p. 242 below). At the same time, a *direct messianic emphasis* is not clearly expressed in the passage in Daniel.
It is quite possible that Jesus himself made the expression
'Son of Man' into a messianic title (*cf.* Mark 14.62).
An essential feature of this messianic title is that the
Messiah comes from heaven, and that the glory that is to
come is concealed, latent and unobtrusive. Certainly this
is the view implied by what Jesus said of himself as Son
of Man, that his daily life was less certain than that of the
foxes and the birds (Matt. 8.20=Luke 9.58). The Son of
Man here is entirely dependent upon God, whose
anointed he is; he is obedient in that he is concerned not
for his own status, but for the act of God; he does not
take the kingdom of God, but has it given to him. On
the day of the last judgement he will come to those who
have confessed him as the Son of Man. 'Everyone who
acknowledges me before men, the Son of Man also will
acknowledge before the angels of God; but he who denies
me before men will be denied before the angels of God'
(Luke 12.8 f.; *cf.* Matt. 10.32 f.). The division brought
about by the kingdom of God is effected by Jesus, the
Son of Man, as the Messiah of the kingdom of God:
'Blessed is he who takes no offence at me' (Matt. 11.6=
Luke 7.23). 'He who is not with me is against me, and
he who does not gather with me scatters' (Matt. 12.30=
Luke 11.23). Why is this? and how? 'The Son of Man
has authority on earth to forgive sins' (Mark 2.10 and
parallels). Thus Jesus places himself on the same level
as his brethren, and at the same time as unique and over
them. Man looks forward to the kingdom of God, which
is already a reality in Jesus the Messiah, but in him alone.
Thus our hope is directed towards the Messiah, who,
being unique in his relationship to his Father, has torn
down the veil woven by obstinacy, disobedience and self-

assertion. The kingdom of God lies behind this veil. But Jesus, who fulfils the promise, says to men, '*Today, this scripture has been fulfilled in your hearing*' (Luke 4.21).

VI. CONCLUSION

It required a new and special act of God to make all this clear to Jesus's disciples: not until after the *events of Easter Day* did they understand and proclaim in new tongues what Jesus had done in his lifetime, what Christ had carried out in his earthly existence. In the light of the Easter experience the evangelists clarified and heightened their christology. At the same time, the evangelists let us see the difficulty of the first followers of Jesus, a difficulty which could not simply be resolved by a doctrinal statement concerning the work and person of Jesus, something which had first to be accepted and only then could be grasped and understood.

The confession of himself as *messianic Son of God* which Jesus demanded, preserves christology from the perversion found in docetism (*cf.* Vol. II *Christology* I, 4; II, 2*b*.), and the watering down that is implied by venerating him as an heroic figure. What is at issue is not a speculation concerning a Christ myth or an ideal represented by Christ, nor the search for the dominant attributes of a religious genius; we are concerned with something unique which forms more than simply a part of world history, but which is derived from the context of the scriptures: the task and calling of Jesus Christ as seen in his words and deeds.

Karl Ludwig Schmidt

5
Paul[1]

I. SOURCES

The sources for a historical knowledge of Paul are essentially his genuine letters; these include Romans, 1 and 2 Corinthians, Galatians, Philippians, 1 Thessalonians, and Philemon. These letters come from a limited period in his life and, as occasional writings, contain only a few notices and intimations about his life; on the other hand, they give a rich picture of his views and intentions. So far as the outer course of his life is concerned, Acts provides much good material in its sources, even if alongside of these it also provides legendary tradition. As far as possible, its information must be controlled by Paul's own letters. The later Christian tradition, to which the spurious Pauline letters in the New Testament already belong, contains only a few reliable statements in addition to legendary information. Paul is not mentioned at all in heathen literature, although he is perhaps referred to in certain Jewish writings.[2]

[1] 'Paulus,' Religion in Geschichte und Gegenwart, IV (2nd ed.; Tübingen: J. C. B. Mohr, 1930), 1019-45. Translated by Schubert M. Ogden and reprinted from EXISTENCE AND FAITH: Shorter Writings of Rudolf Bultmann, with the permission of Hodder and Stoughton Ltd., London, and World Publishing Co., Cleveland and New York. Also published in The Fontana Library, 1964, London, pp. 130-172.
[2] Cf. G. Kittel, Rabbinica (1920); Hans Lietzmann, Petrus and Paulus in Rom (2nd ed., 1927).

II. LIFE

1. Background and Training

Paul was the child of a true Jewish family of the tribe of Benjamin (Rom. 11.1; 2 Cor. 11.22; Gal. 2.15; Phil. 3.5). According to Acts 22.3 (*cf.* 9.11,21.39), he was born and raised in Tarsus in Cilicia and thus came from a hellenistic city in which there was a mingling of Oriental and Greek populations. Tarsus was significant as a commercial city and was also a place where Greek science (and especially Stoic philosophy) was carried on. If Paul speaks of himself in Phil. 3.5 as a 'Hebrew of Hebrews', this can be taken to suggest that his family had strictly preserved its Palestinian character (especially the Aramaic language) in the Diaspora. Whether his parents actually migrated to Tarsus from Gischala in Judaea —and, indeed, whether he himself was born in Gischala (Hieronymus)—is uncertain and is hardly confirmed simply because in Acts 23.16 ff. the son of his sister appears in Jerusalem. In fact, it seems rather improbable, if Acts (22.28, *cf.* 16.37) is correct in handing down that he was born a Roman citizen and had the civic rights of a citizen of Tarsus (21.39). If he was born a Roman citizen, then he had the name Paul (the only name he ever uses in his letters) from birth, while his Jewish name was Saul. Moreover, this means that he cannot have belonged to the lower social classes. In any case, his letters show that he was a hellenistic Jew, i.e., that in his training Jewish tradition and Greek culture were combined. And if his scientific development was not anywhere near as comprehensive as that, say, of Philo, he still had mastered the Greek language to a high degree; not only are many of the techniques of rhetoric and of popular philosophy ('diatribe') familiar to him, but he is also acquainted with certain concepts and ideas of Stoic philosophy (e.g., the concepts of 'conscience', 'freedom', and 'duty'). He obviously had enjoyed a systematic training in Jewish scribism, as is evident not only from his having belonged to the company of the Pharisees (Phil. 3.5; *cf.* Gal. 1.14), but especially from the style of his thinking, his argumentation, and his exegesis. According to Acts 22.3, he had studied in Jerusalem with Gamaliel the elder. But this is hardly correct, since one must surely conclude from Gal. 1.22 that prior to his conversion he had never resided for any length of time in Jerusalem (although this naturally would not exclude occasional trips for religious festivals). As a rabbi Paul practised a trade (according to Acts 18.3, he was a tent-maker), for he frequently makes reference to his work (1 Thess. 2.9; 1 Cor. 9.6 ff.; 2 Cor. 11.12). His world of ideas gives evidence of an acquaintance with heathen cults and with Oriental and Gnostic mythology. To what extent this stems from the views that he acquired in his youth or from his later travels cannot be said; it would have been mediated to him in part through his Jewish connections, among whom, in addition to scribism, apocalyptic and mythological speculations were also carried on. In any case, his christology did not grow entirely from Christian ideas, but rather presupposes the concepts of a mythological-apocalyptic expectation of Messiah and redeemer in which he already lived as a Jew.

2. *Conversion*

So far as the pre-Christian period of Paul's life is concerned, we know for certain only that as a Pharisee he was a zealous champion of the law and of the scribal tradition (Gal. 1.13 f.; Phil. 3.6). It appears likely from Gal. 5.11 that even as a Jew he engaged in missionary activity among the heathen, apparently with the point

of view that is characterized in Rom. 2.19 f. In his zeal
he became a persecutor of the Christian community
(Gal. 1.13;1.23; Phil. 3.6; *cf.* Acts 9.1 ff.;22.4 f.;26.9 ff.).
Since he cannot have resided in Jerusalem prior to his
conversion (see above, II., 1.), this persecution cannot
have taken place in Judaea; and his participation in the
death of Stephen is a legend—a judgement that is also
confirmed by a literary-critical investigation of Acts
7.58-8.3. From Gal. 1.17 one must infer that the scene
of the persecution was either in or around Damascus.
Moreover, the character of the persecution is considerably exaggerated in the account in Acts; for what was
involved could not have been a carrying out of sentences
of death, but only beating with rods and expulsion from
the synagogue—or, in other words, the same kind of
persecution that Paul himself subsequently experienced
as a Christian missionary (2 Cor. 11.24). But why did
Paul persecute the church? Naturally, for him also it
was scandalous that Christians proclaimed a crucified
one as the Messiah (1 Cor. 1.18 ff.) and claimed that the
time of salvation was already breaking in. But while in
the judgement of Jews this would indeed be madness,
it would not be a crime that was deserving of punishment.
The Christian message first became a crime when, with
the preaching of the crucified one, the validity of the
law was also called in question. Thus when Paul characterizes himself in Gal. 1.13 f. as a persecutor of the church
and at the same time as one who was zealous for the law,
he shows that he had come to know Christianity in a form
in which it already stood over against the law in a critical
way and to some extent had actually overcome it. This is
also evident because for him the question concerning the
acceptance of the Christian message is identical with the
Either/Or decision between the law and Jesus Christ. And
it is further confirmed because we know of different forms
of hellenistic Christianity, all of which to some degree

pose this either/or and yet are not determined by Paul's characteristic teaching concerning the law. Therefore, Paul first came to know Christianity in its hellenistic form; and he became a persecutor because he could not help seeing it as an attack on the law that was the holy will of God and 'the embodiment of knowledge and truth' (Rom. 2.20).

It was as a persecutor that Paul experienced his conversion; and to be sure, as a psychic process this conversion was a vision of Christ (Gal. 1.15; 1 Cor. 9.1;15.8; there is very likely an allusion also in 2 Cor. 4.6), which has been coloured over with legendary features by Acts (9.1 ff.; 22.4 ff.; 26.9 ff.). In view of the complete lack of biographical reports, nothing at all can be said about how this process is to be made psychologically understandable and thus how it was prepared by Paul's inner development. In particular, it is nothing other than sheer fantasy when one depicts the impression that was made on him by the persecuted Christians; and that he even saw Jesus and was impressed by him is also to be read out of 2 Cor. 5.16 only by fantasy. Paul himself had no interest in his personal development, but only in the theological meaning of his conversion; and it is solely the latter that we are in a position to know. Especially may one not understand Rom. 7.7-25 as a biographical document of Paul's inner development; for the 'I' of these verses is as little the individual 'I' of Paul as is, for example, the 'I' of 1 Cor. 13.11. On the contrary, Paul is there presenting the situation of the Jew under the law in the light of the real meaning of that situation as it is disclosed to the eye of faith. Moreover, the phrase 'kicking against the goads', in Acts 26.14 does not refer to an inner struggle, but rather is a widespread proverbial expression that means that man cannot withstand the divine. It is completely clear from Paul's letters that his 'conversion' was not a conversion of 'repentance', in which after long suffering under an afflicted conscience and inner resistance he finally succeeded in confessing his guilt before God and thereby inwardly set himself free. For as one who has been converted, he does not look back on his past with a feeling of shame, as though it had been a time in which he was sunk in guilt, but rather views it with a feeling of pride (Gal. 1.13 f.; Phil. 3.6). He has not been freed from a burden, but rather has sacrificed a proud past (Phil. 3.6 ff.). That he was a persecutor does not impress him as guilt, but merely provides a measure of the grace of the God who has called him (1 Cor. 15.9 f.). His conversion also does not appear to him as an enlightenment that emancipates him from an illusion, from the unbearable burden of works of the law and a false idea of God. For he never doubts that up to the time of 'fulfilment', the way of the law was commanded by God and was meaningful (Gal. 3.23 ff.; even Rom. 7.7 ff. is a defence of the law, not an attack on it!). Thus he knows nothing about the law's being a burden from the standpoint of the Jew's subjective experience; and at no time in his Christian polemic against the law does he represent faith as an emancipation from such a burden. Nor is what is meant by the 'anxiety' in which man exists prior to faith the subjective feeling of anxiety that is caused by false religious ideas (see below, III., 2). Faith is not the emancipation of a man who is yearning for freedom from chains that he himself experiences as oppressive; rather it is the resolution to surrender all that was man's pride, all self-glorification, all 'boasting'. This means, however, that Paul's conversion was the resolve to surrender his whole previous self-understanding, which was called in question by the Christian message, and to understand his existence anew. If God had already permitted the time of salvation to break in by sending the Messiah, then the way whereby man himself sought to achieve righteousness by means of works of

the law was called in question. If God himself had introduced salvation by sending the Messiah and permitting
him to be crucified, then he had destroyed the Jewish way
of salvation and had thereby passed judgement against
everything human, which had reached its highest point
in Judaism. Thus what Paul was asked by the Christian
proclamation was whether he was willing to see in a historical fact like the person and destiny of Jesus the
breaking in of the time of salvation, the new creation that
was being introduced by God. He was asked whether he
was willing to acknowledge in the cross of Jesus the
judgement against the previous self-understanding of the
pious Jew and whether he was thus willing to understand
himself anew and to accept the judgement of 'sin and
death' against his previous life. And this he affirmed in
his conversion.

3. Career as Apostle

a. Paul apparently knew himself called to be an apostle by
his conversion (Gal. 1.15 f.) and immediately engaged in
missionary activity in Damascus and Arabia. After a
brief visit to Jerusalem, he then worked in Syria and
Cilicia (Gal. 1.21) and resided for a time in Tarsus, in
order thence to be fetched by Barnabas to Antioch,
where hellenistic Jewish Christians who had been driven
from Jerusalem had already established a congregation
(Acts 11.19 ff.). Since as a result of this hellenistic mission
there arose a gentile Christianity that did not accept the
law and specifically did not accept circumcision, a discussion with the primitive community, which remained
faithful to the law, became inevitable. This took place
at the so-called Apostolic Council, for which Paul and
Barnabas went up to Jerusalem. They sought to see to it
that the gentile Christians' freedom from the law was
acknowledged and thus were able to preserve the unity
of the two early Christian groups; this was especially

expressed by the determination that there should be a collection taken in the gentile Christian congregations for the 'poor' at Jerusalem (Gal. 2.1-10; the presentation in Acts 15 is legendary). Since, however, the question concerning the intercourse in mixed congregations (especially at table) of Jewish Christians who were faithful to the law and gentile Christians who were free from it was apparently left undiscussed, there subsequently arose a conflict between Paul and Peter in Antioch, which also led to Paul's falling out with Barnabas (Gal. 2.11 ff.). Later on, also, Paul's mission was occasionally interfered with by 'Judaizers', i.e., by Jewish Christian missionaries who demanded from converted gentiles an acceptance of the law or, at least, of circumcision. Paul struggled against such 'Judaizers' in Galatia. However, the opinion, which has been influential ever since F. C. Baur, that throughout the whole field of Paul's missionary activity there was a constant struggle between Paulinism and Judaizing Christianity is false. To be sure, in 2 Corinthians also, Paul has to struggle with Jewish Christian adversaries; however, they clearly are not preachers of the law; and whether he is fighting against 'Judaizers' or rather against Jews in Phil. 3.2 ff. is disputed. In any case, his polemic in Romans is not directed against 'Judaizers', but rather takes issue in principle with the Jewish position of legalistic piety.

The mission field that Paul undertook to serve after the Apostolic Council can be determined from Acts, which is frequently confirmed by statements in the letters. He first preached in Cyprus and in Pamphylia, Lycaonia, and Pisidia in Asia Minor (Acts 13 and 14, which are falsely placed before the Apostolic Council in ch. 15). Then, a subsequent journey led him from Syria-Cilicia clear across Asia Minor (the Galatian congregations were founded at that time; Acts 16) to Troas and thence to Macedonia (Philippi and Thessalonica) and back to

Achaia. In Corinth, then, he tarried for a longer period
and from there also established other congregations (Acts
15.40-18.22). After what seems to have been a short return trip to Antioch (Acts 18.22 f.), he once again undertook a large-scale mission for which Ephesus was his
headquarters. From there, after a trip through Macedonia to Corinth, he again went up to Jerusalem to
deliver a collection (Acts 18.23-21.16). There, at the in-
stigation of the Jews, he was arrested by the Romans
because of a riot and then (the record is not clear) was
brought to Rome for sentencing (Acts 21.17-28.31).
Acts closes with the statement that he was imprisoned in
Rome for two years. So far as the outcome of his trial is
concerned, nothing certain is known; however, it is
firmly fixed in the tradition that he died the death of a
martyr. This is evidenced already by the intimations in
Acts (especially 20.22 ff.; 21.10 ff.), and it is specifically
narrated in I Clement (ch. 5), which is apparently of
the opinion that Paul, like Peter, was executed under
Nero. According to I Clem. 5.7, before he died, Paul also
preached in Spain, just as he says he had planned to do
in Rom. 15.24 f. Whether he actually did so, however
(to do so he would have had to be freed from the Roman
imprisonment that is reported by Acts), or whether the
Spanish journey is a legend that has grown out of Rom.
15.24 f. is a matter of dispute. It is certain, however, that
he did not do any further work in the East, as is assumed
by those scholars who argue for the Pauline authorship
of the Pastorals in order to be able to maintain the statements that are contained in these letters concerning
journeys that cannot be assigned to his career prior to
his (first) Roman imprisonment.[3]

b. Paul was not the first nor was he the only missionary of

[3] For the chronology of Paul's life, *cf. Christianity, 1, 6 c*, in Volume
III of this series.

the apostolic age. Already before him, hellenistic Jewish Christians, among them especially Barnabas, had engaged in missions to the gentiles (Acts 11.19 ff.), and in Damascus as well as in Antioch there existed Christian communities. Moreover, Paul did not found the congregation at Rome, any more than he established the Christianity of Alexandria, whose origins are in general unknown to us. Thus in addition to him and his fellow workers, there were both before and alongside of him a whole host of missionaries who are now forgotten. Whether some one of them envisaged the missionary task in the same way that Paul did, to carry the gospel to the ends of the earth until Christ returns (Rom. 15.17 ff.), we do not know. In any case, Paul himself was sustained by a consciousness of this task; and he supposed that he was fulfilling it by founding congregations in the important cities, whence the faith might then be spread to the surrounding countrysides. His work as a missionary was his 'boast', which, to be sure, was wrought by Christ; and he was proud of having only preached the gospel where it had not as yet been heard (Rom. 15.20; 2 Cor. 10.15 f.), and also proud that he had renounced the right of the apostle to be supported by the congregations (1 Cor. 9.15 ff.; 2 Cor. 11.7 ff.). All the same, however much he looked upon his work as a missionary as his life-task and however certain he was that the results of his mission had been prodigious—in his own conviction, the greatest of all (1 Cor. 15.10)—it is not in his accomplishments as a missionary that his real significance lies. Nor does it lie in the fact that he not only won the gentiles to the faith, but also organized viable congregations and inwardly and outwardly strengthened them by his letters and visits. In this respect, there may well have been others who were his equal. Moreover, his real historical accomplishment is not that he fought for and won freedom from the law for gentile Christianity, even if his part in this was a prominent one. For there is little doubt that this also would have happened without him, even as it had been prepared for before him and was actually carried out alongside of him. Writings like Hebrews, Barnabas, and 1 Clement, which in one sense or another, although in an un-Pauline sense, are free from the law, show that in this connection there were several possibilities; indeed, this is even shown by the so-called 'Apostolic decree', which was not concluded by Paul and the earliest apostles at the Apostolic Council, as Acts reports, but rather was afterwards agreed upon by the Jerusalem community and the hellenistic Christians and then subsequently communicated to Paul (Acts 21.25). In this respect, the way had also been prepared by hellenistic Judaism through reinterpreting the law and easing its requirements for proselytes. Thus there was hardly a danger that the Christian communities in the Greco-Roman world would become legalistic Jewish sects. However, there was considerable danger that they would become a passing phenomenon of hellenistic syncretism, like the other religious communities that grouped themselves around the cult of some oriental redeemer-deity. An essential part of Paul's accomplishment consists in his having joined the Christian communities into a firm unity and in seeing to it that there was no break with the mother community in Jerusalem. By teaching the individual churches to understand themselves as members of the one ecclesia, and by helping those who had faith in Jesus Christ to see themselves as the true Israel, he gave the new religion a historical consciousness of itself as a church and also endowed it with the power that indwells such a consciousness. The Christian congregations were not only bound together, like the mystery congregations, by the same cult, and the same theological or mythological ideas, but rather by the conviction that they stood at the end of a closed and unified history and thus also by a strong feeling that they belonged together and to Jerusalem. It is for this reason that Paul puts so much importance on what seems to be the most trivial stipulation of the Apostolic Council—namely, the collection; hence also his endeavour to bind the congregations together, not only by exchanging news and greetings between them, but also by impressing upon them their ties with Jerusalem (Gal. 2.10; 1 Cor. 16.1 ff.; 2 Cor. 8 and 9; Rom. 15.25 ff.). Thus, to a high degree, Paul's significance consists in his having given to Christianity not the consciousness of being a new 'religion', but rather the consciousness of being a 'church' in a sense that was unknown in the hellenistic world. Nevertheless, this consciousness of being a church is but a recasting of the Jewish inheritance; for in Judaism also the idea of the church as the people of God was very much alive. And there undoubtedly were other Christian missionaries of hellenistic-Jewish background who were also sustained by such a church consciousness (*cf.* again Hebrews, Barnabas, and I Clement), so that here, too, it is impossible to speak of an exclusive accomplishment of Paul. If, however, his accomplishment actually does tower above that of others, this is not only because the idea of the church was determinative in his work, but especially because as a writer he surpassed everyone else in quality and influence. Even if his letters are only occasional writings, still, in form as well as content, they are the surpassing monuments of early Christian literature (with the sole exception of John), which almost immediately were read in the church way beyond the congregations for which they were written, were subsequently collected together, and were also frequently imitated. However, even with this we still have not spoken of Paul's real significance. For this lies in the fact that as a *theologian* he gave to the Christian faith an adequate understanding of itself. However much his thought still moved within the mythological ideas of antiquity, still, on the one hand, he extricated Christian thinking from the realm of mythology and speculation and made it into an unfolding of the understanding of man, the world, and God that is given in faith itself; he based Christian knowing on our being known by God and defined its proper object as that which has been 'bestowed' on us by God through grace (1 Cor. 2.12); thus he understood knowing in its unity with the whole Christian life, so that knowing proves its legitimacy by realizing itself in unity with the obedience of faith and love as *existential* thinking. On the other hand, he also demonstrated the indispensability of such thinking for the life of faith and love, by showing that it preserves for this life a correct self-understanding, so that the latter does not fall away and is not led astray, whether by Jewish legalism or by the speculations of pneumatics and Gnostics. Paul finally performed the greatest service, for the freeing of faith from the law and for uniting the congregations into a church, because he gave a firm conceptual expression to the necessities that others also had more or less clearly recognized. This expression gave strength to the self-understanding and self-consciousness of the Christian community and determined Christian theological thinking forever after, again and again saving it from falling away into a false understanding of faith. And Paul's theology acquired such significance even where its propositions were passed on without their meaning's really being understood in its fullness, as was in fact immediately the case with his disciples and imitators; even as truths that were only half or badly understood they carried their corrective in themselves.

III. THEOLOGY

1. Presuppositions

a. PAUL'S PERSONALITY AND CONVERSION. If we are concerned to inquire about the actual content of Paul's theology, then it would be wrong to go back to his 'personality' in order on that basis to understand his theology. For in the first place, a picture of his personality and his character can only be obtained by reconstructing it on the basis of having first understood his theological and non-theological statements; and so one deceives oneself if one imagines that one can understand what Paul says by understanding his personality. In the second place, however, what one customarily refers to as the 'character' of a man is not something outside of his work to which one can refer it in order to explain it; his 'character' is as little this as, conversely, his work is something that is detached from his 'character'. Rather a man first acquires his 'character' in his work, and his work is a presentation of his 'character'. Thus it is certainly correct to say that the prominent features in a picture of Paul are his concern with his subject and his passion, which together combine to make for a radicalism in thought and judgement. However, in saying this, one is not speaking about presuppositions from which his work has grown, but rather is characterizing that work itself. If, on the other hand, one means by the question concerning Paul's character the natural dispositions that were a given condition of his work, then indeed it is possible to say something about these on the basis of his letters; but what is said can never be of any use in making the content of his work understandable. For that Paul was temperamental, was given to brooding, had a sensitive feeling for life, was touchy, etc. are all things that he shared in common with countless other men. Therefore, while to draw this kind of a picture of his character can offer an aesthetic fascination, it is of no consequence whatever in understanding the subject matter with which he was concerned.

Likewise, it is a popular error to try to derive Paul's theology from his conversion experience. For this experience also can only be reconstructed by having first understood what he says. Thus the question about the actual content of his conversion is a question about his theology itself. His conversion was neither a conversion of repentance nor one of enlightenment (*cf.* above, II., 2). And if one, by viewing it from the standpoint of the psychic course of his life, can speak of it in general as 'a break in his development', this still does not say anything about its meaning. For what happened when Paul was changed from a persecutor into a faithful man was, in his view, only an extreme instance of what happens in principle whenever a man is smitten by the 'word' and resolves to believe it, surrendering his old self and obediently placing himself under the grace of God. This is clearly shown by Phil. 3.4-16 and 2 Cor. 4.3-6. Indeed, Paul demands such a 'break' from every man, although it is characteristic of him, in contradistinction to hellenistic mysticism and pietistic and Methodist religiousness, that he says nothing about the psychic conditions of the 'break' or about the forms of experience in which it takes place.

The presuppositions of Paul's theology which must be considered in order to understand it all have to do with the *actual subject matter* of his thought. Whoever would understand him must, on the one hand, become acquainted with the understanding that he had of himself (and thus also of God and the world) as a Jew under the law, and likewise with the word of the Christian proclamation that encountered him and constrained him to a yes or no decision. On the other hand, one must acquaint oneself with the world-views and the traditional modes of thinking and forming concepts in which Paul lived and in terms of which (or in opposition to which) he developed his new understanding of faith. It is only in this way that one can translate his statements into a modern conceptuality and yet at the same time avoid modernizing reinterpretations. In fact, of course, both types of presuppositions overlap; for the Jewish faith in God as well as the Christian kerygma were naturally expressed in a specific contemporary conceptuality.

b. THE EARLY COMMUNITY AND JESUS. It is impossible here to present the Jewish faith in God and the Christian kerygma (*cf.* above, II., 2). However, the one thing that must be emphasized is that Paul's theology cannot be understood as a further development in the 'history of ideas' of the preaching of Jesus. It is not with the preaching of Jesus that he begins, but rather with the kerygma of the early community, the content of which is not Jesus's proclamation, but Jesus himself. It is the message that Jesus of Nazareth, the rabbi and prophet, the one who was crucified, has been raised by God and made Messiah; that he will shortly come as the 'Son of Man' in order to hold judgement and to bring salvation. At the same time, it says that the community of his followers knows itself to be the congregation of saints of the end-time, the elected Israel, which is in possession of the spirit, the promised gift of the last days. Therefore, the early community did not detach itself from the ordinances of life of Israel but rather continued to move in them in the way that had been taught by Jesus, whose sayings it preserved. To be sure, it did define itself as a unique congregation within Judaism (without, however, segregating itself from the cult of the temple) by baptism, which it understood as the purifying bath for the penitent and those who were sanctified for the breaking in of the time of salvation. It also met together for common meals, although there was as yet no talk of cultic veneration of Jesus Christ. It is this community and its kerygma that is a basic presupposition of the theology of Paul. On the other hand, the preaching of Jesus is such a presupposition only insofar as it signified radical Judaism in the spirit of the old prophetic proclamation. Paul neither heard Jesus's preaching itself, nor did he permit it to be mediated to him by the first disciples, in relation to whom he knew himself to be completely independent (Gal. 1.1,1.11 ff.). To be sure, he did take over some of the sayings of Jesus (whether genuine sayings, or sayings created by the community) from the Palestinian tradition, namely, bits of regulation having to do with congregational order (1 Cor. 7.10 f.; 9.14), which he, of course, regarded as words not of the 'historical Jesus', but of the exalted Lord (*cf.* 1 Cor. 7.25). Perhaps 1 Thess. 4.15-17 also stems from traditional sayings of Jesus; but this is hardly true of 1 Cor. 11.23-5. It is also possible that certain sayings of the Lord are echoed in Paul's moral instruction (e.g., Rom. 12.4; 13.9 f.; 16.19; 1 Cor. 13.2); however, what is involved here is precisely a type of moral instruction which, with Jesus as well as with Paul, to some extent came from Jewish tradition or the Jewish spirit. In any case, Paul's real doctrine of salvation, with its anthropological and soteriological ideas, is not a continuation of the preaching of Jesus. This is clear for example, from the fact that he never once appeals to a saying of Jesus in support of his teaching about freedom from the law. And if in his letters he never makes reference to the tradition concerning Jesus's life (outside of 1 Cor. 11.23, where what is really involved is the basing of a cultic feast in the destiny of the cult deity), then one may not say that he must have proceeded very differently from this in his missionary preaching and must have told a good deal about Jesus's life. (Nor may one appeal in support of such a statement to Gal. 3.1; for what is meant there is the preaching of the cross, as is indicated in Gal. 3.10 ff.; 1 Cor. 1.18 ff., and elsewhere.) Whether Paul knew much òr little of the tradition about Jesus's life, the content of that life as that of a teacher, a prophet, a miracle-worker, or one who had been crowned with thorns plays absolutely no role in his preaching of salvation. For him, the significance of Jesus's person lies in the latter's having been sent as the Son of God in human form in order through his death and resurrection to free men from the law and sin (Gal. 4.4 f., etc.).

However, just as little as one may say that Paul's theology represents a development in the history of ideas of Jesus's preaching, so little, of course, may one say that, from the standpoint of the history of ideas, it stands in opposition to Jesus's message—as though the latter's piety, say, was a joyous faith in God the Father, whereas Paul's religion is to be characterized as an austere faith in redemption. Looked at in terms of the history of ideas, the proclamation of Jesus and that of Paul are essentially the same. Thus their idea of God is the same: God is the Judge and also the God of grace; and similar also is their view of man, who is obligated to obey the will of God and as a sinner is dependent on God's grace—who can exhibit no merit before God and also can make no claims on him. Neither for Jesus nor for Paul is God the immanent law of the world or the hypostatization of an eternal Idea of the Good. Rather he is the one who stands before man as he who comes in judgement and grace; and for both men God deals with man in history. The difference, however, is that Jesus proclaims a final and decisive act of God, the Reign of God, as coming or, indeed, as now breaking in, while Paul affirms that the turn of the aeon has already taken place and, to be sure, with the coming, the death and the resurrection of Jesus. Thus, for Paul, it is Jesus's cross and resurrection that are the decisive event of salvation through which the forgiveness of sins, the reconciliation of man with God is effected, and with which, therefore, the new creation is introduced. Consequently, while the person and history of Jesus do indeed constitute a presupposition of his theology, they do not do so from the standpoint of their historical or ideal content, but rather as the act of God, as the occurrence of the revelation of salvation. Paul does not teach other and new *ideas* from those that Jesus teaches, but rather teaches us to understand an *event* in a new way. This he does by saying that the world is new since and because Jesus has come; now the reconciliation between God and man is established and the word that proclaims this reconciliation is instituted.

c. THE GENERAL CONDITIONS IN THE HISTORY OF RELIGION. Outside of Paul's rabbinic training (*cf.* above, II., 1.), the presuppositions from the history of religion that must be considered in relation to the formation of his theological concepts and his explication of the kerygma are the following: (1) *The preaching of the one God and his judgement* that was characteristic of the propaganda both of hellenistic Judaism and of pre-Pauline Christianity. Under the influence of the Greek enlightenment, there had taken place in hellenistic Judaism a new conceptual formulation of monotheistic faith, together with a total interpretation of the world in the manner of the philosophy of religion, and a critique of polytheism and its cult as well as the moral life of the gentiles. This tradition was directly taken over by Christianity; and Paul also stands within it when he makes use of the Stoic theory of a natural knowledge of God (Rom. 1.18 ff.), or varies somewhat a Stoic formula concerning the divine omnipotence (Rom. 11.36; 1 Cor. 8.6), or when he applies the concepts of 'conscience' (Rom. 2.15, etc.), 'duty' (Rom. 1.28), 'virtue' (Phil. 4.8), 'nature' (1 Cor. 11.14, etc.), or even when he interprets the heathen gods as demons (1 Cor. 10.10) or as 'elemental spirits of the world' (Gal. 4.3; 4.9). In all probability such ideas played an even larger role in his actual missionary preaching; thus they are presented also in Acts 14.17; 17.23 ff. (2) *The discussion concerning the law* in hellenistic Judaism and in pre-Pauline hellenistic Christianity. Here, too, there is a unified tradition running from the former to the latter, which attempts to demonstrate the moral character and universal scope of the divine demand. Insofar as this tradition practised allegorical reinterpretation of the narratives and laws of the Old Testament, Paul also stands in it (*cf.*, e.g., 1 Cor. 9.9 f.; 10.6 ff.); however, insofar as it made a distinction between moral demands and cultic-ritual ones, he has left it behind, although he is still affected by it, as is shown by 1 Cor. 7.19. (This is probably a saying that Paul quotes and then modifies in his own sense in Gal. 5.6; 6.15.) (3) *The Kyrios-cult and the sacraments* in pre-Pauline hellenistic Christianity. If the early Palestinian community had expected Jesus the risen one as the coming Son of Man and if, accordingly, its messianic faith was essentially eschatological, there had already developed prior to Paul in the hellenistic Christian communities in Syria (which did not participate in the Jewish temple cult and the ordinances of life that emanated from it) a cultic veneration of Christ as the 'Lord'. He was known to be present in the congregation's worship, dispensing supernatural powers to those who belonged to him. Baptism was understood in the sense of the hellenistic mysteries as a sacrament that mysteriously unites the baptized person with Christ and thus grants him a share in the latter's death and resurrection. And the common meals of the early community became the 'Lord's Supper', which likewise brings about sacramental communion with Christ. Naturally, the form of the kerygma corresponded to this, and already prior to Paul there were represented different interpretations of Jesus's death, which in part expressed the ideas of an atoning or covenantal sacrifice and in part the ideas of a cosmic process and a sacramental *communio*. This can be learned from the remarks concerning baptism in Rom. 6.3 ff. and the saying concerning the Lord's Supper in 1 Cor. 11.23-5, which already combine different interpretations, as well as from the tradition to which Paul refers in 1 Cor. 15.3 and, likewise, for example, from the theology of Mark. For the rest, we can no longer prove which of the concepts that Paul uses to interpret Christ's death and resurrection were already in use prior to his time; it is clear, however, that the frequently encountered ideas of 'for us', of an atoning sacrifice (Rom. 3.25), of reconciliation (Rom. 5.11; 2 Cor. 5.18 ff.), of a ransom (Gal. 3.13; 4.4 f.; 1 Cor. 6.20; 7.23), and of substitution (Gal. 3.13; 2 Cor. 5.14 f.) all stem from this sphere in which the Jewish ideas of sacrifice and the notions of the hellenistic mysteries were combined and from which Paul's formulations came to him. (4) *Gnosticism and pneumaticism.* In the syncretism of the hellenistic-oriental world and, of course, hardly ever sharply separated from the mystery cults (which, having originally been vegetation cults, celebrated the dying and rising of a deity in which the faithful were vouchsafed a share), there was a religion of redemption which had migrated to the West from Iran, combined itself with certain astrological ideas, and found its historically significant expressions in 'Gnosticism'. The cosmological and soteriological ideas of this religion give expression to a dualistic understanding of human existence. They teach, first of all, the heavenly origin of the soul, which has been banished to the body and the world of the senses, and then, second, the soul's redemption by a divine being, who disguised himself in human form, took upon himself all the misery of earthly life, thereby deceiving the demonic rulers of the world, and then after having brought revelation to 'his own' through doctrines and rites, once again was exalted to the heavenly world, whither his own will subsequently follow him. According to the Gnostic or the pneumatic, whoever believes this revelation has knowledge and freedom. Hence his intense self-consciousness and peculiar way of life, which could lead either to asceticism or to libertinism. That such Gnosticism and pneumaticism had already prior to Paul or contemporaneously with him penetrated the Christian congregations is shown by his struggle against the pneumatics in Corinth. With them, apparently, such Gnosticism had been combined with Jewish theology, very much as also happened with Philo. But these Gnostic ideas had already influenced Jewish apocalypticism and in this way had also influenced Paul. For as much as he fights against the consequences of such pneumaticism, he still appropriates Gnosticism's concepts (e.g., the contrast between 'spiritual' and 'psychic', the concepts 'knowledge', 'freedom', or 'authority') and makes use of its mythology in his own doctrines. Thence stem the ideas of 'this aeon' and the 'coming aeon', the idea of Satan as the 'god of this aeon' (2 Cor. 4.3 f.), of the 'rulers' (1 Cor. 2.6) and other spiritual powers. Thence also the notions of Adam as the first, and Christ as the new 'man' (Rom. 5.12 ff.; 1 Cor. 15.21 f.; 15.44 ff.), of the giving of the law by angels (Gal. 3.19), of Christ's descent in the disguise of a man (1 Cor. 2.6 ff.; Phil. 2.6 ff.; 2 Cor. 8.9), and of redemption as a mighty cosmic drama (1 Cor. 15.24 f.; Rom. 8.18 ff.).

2. *Content*

a. THEOLOGY AND ANTHROPOLOGY. For Paul, *God* is not a metaphysical being and thus is not an object of speculation, but rather is the God whose action does not take place primarily in cosmic occurrences, but in relation to man in history. On the other hand, he does not understand *man* as an isolated being within the world, but rather always sees him in his relation to God. Therefore it follows that what God and man mean for Paul can only be understood together as a unity and that his 'theology' can be presented as anthropology.

And the same thing is true of his 'christology'; for he also does not understand Christ primarily as a metaphysical being about whose 'natures' he speculates, but rather understands him and his work as God's act of salvation in relation to man. Of course, one may not make a division between a 'physical' anthropology that describes how man is 'in himself' and an 'ethical' anthropology that expresses how he stands in relation to God. For as Paul understands him, man is never what he is outside of his relation to God; and even general anthropological concepts like 'body' and 'soul' are decisively determined for Paul by man's standing before God. However, there *is* a division that arises because man has acquired a new possibility for relation with God through the revelation in Christ, namely, faith. Therefore, the arrangement must be as follows: (1) man prior to the revelation of faith; and (2) man under faith. It must be noted, however, that the being of man prior to faith first becomes visible in its true lineaments only from the standpoint of faith itself and that it is from this perspective alone that it can be understood.

b. MAN PRIOR TO THE REVELATION OF FAITH. (i) With the word 'man' Paul can, of course, occasionally refer to one being in the world among others (e.g., angels; *cf.* 1 Cor. 4.9;15.36 ff.); but his more precise use of language is such that the title 'man' characterizes man in his relation to God and, indeed, in such a way that before God all the differences and advantages of which individuals could boast disappear (Rom. 3.28 f.; 1 Cor. 1.25; Gal. 1.1). 'Man' designates man in his humanity before God. And this God before whom he stands is not a cosmic being that is separate from him; to be sure, there may also be such a being, but insofar as *God*'s being is spoken about, it is not a being that is merely on hand, but rather a 'being for us', so that in a precise sense God alone 'is' (1 Cor. 8.4-6). Man's being in relation to God is primarily a being claimed by God as the Creator. When Paul makes use of the Stoic theory of a natural knowledge of God (Rom. 1.20 ff.), it does not serve him in order to conclude to God's being *in* the world and to the divinity of the world and the security of man by reason of divine providence, but rather in order to conclude to God's being *beyond* the world, to the world's creatureliness and to God's claim to be honoured by man. Correspondingly, 'world' for Paul means 'creation' (Rom. 1.20; 1 Cor. 3.22). And, to be sure, it can mean the totality of what is created by God as that which surrounds man and concerns him; but it especially refers to the world of man himself (Rom. 3.19; 11.12; 2 Cor. 5.19, etc.), although not in the sense of a total class of being on hand within the world, but rather as a community of creatures who are responsible to God. Insofar as men have withdrawn from this responsibility, have denied their creatureliness, and have made themselves independent of God, they are called 'this world'. This world (or 'this aeon', as Paul can also say in order to express the notion that it is provisional) is at enmity with God and seeks its own glory; therefore, it stands under God's wrath and will be judged by him. That this 'dualism', which is several times expressed in Gnostic terminology, is not meant in the cosmological sense of Gnosticism is shown by the counter-concept 'new creation', with which Paul refers to the men who are reconciled and are faithful (2 Cor. 5.17; Gal. 6.15). Thus 'world' does not refer to men as a 'what', but rather as a 'how', as a 'how' of their life and, to be sure, as a 'how' that they themselves have created by turning away from God. As such it is a power that always already encompasses each individual, encountering him and taking him along with it, so that he cannot isolate himself from it (by believing, say, in his soul that has tragically fallen from the world of light and is imprisoned in 'this world' or by imagining his free spiritual personality). And this 'how' manifests itself in the 'care' (1 Cor. 7.29 ff.) in which each man takes his life in his own hands and wills to secure it. From 'care', then, grow 'boasting' and confidence', which base themselves on anything that, by man's estimation or accomplishment, passes for a work. Precisely this pride, whether it is based on national or social advantages, or on wisdom or works of the laws is rebellion against God, before whom no man may boast (Rom. 2.17; 2.23; 3.27; 1 Cor. 1.29; 3.21; 4.7). The height of illusion is that man thinks he can separate himself from the 'world' and bring himself to a being beyond it. The Jew who wills to earn 'righteousness' before God is fallen under this illusion, even as is the pneumatic who imagines that he can become a 'perfect one' by means of his 'wisdom'. The counterpart of such boasting and confidence is 'anxiety' (Rom. 8.15); such a man is in fact a slave. For in his care and putting confidence in worldly values and accomplishments he lets these become lord over him, and because they are all transitory (1 Cor. 7.31), he himself falls under death; by understanding himself in terms of the transitory and the provisional, his being is not authentic, but rather has fallen subject to what is passing away. In the mythological way of thinking of his time, Paul sees such an existence as an enslavement to spiritual powers, Satan and his hosts. Indeed, he can even speak of the law as having been given by such spiritual powers, insofar as man understands the law as a pretext for his own accomplishments; and he can also speak of the service of worship as a veneration of the 'elemental spirits of the world'

(Gal. 3.19 ff.; 4.8 ff.). Nevertheless, how little these mythological notions have a speculative character, how little Paul wants to 'explain' something by them, but rather makes use of them simply in order to express a certain understanding of human existence, is shown, for example, by his not tracing sin back to Satan (Rom. 5.12 ff.; 7.7 ff.) and by his saying that such powers are no longer really of any concern to the man of faith because for him they no longer even 'are' (1 Cor. 8.4 ff.); i.e., they no longer mean for him the lordship over the world under which he is fallen, but simply the quality of the world to tempt him; Satan is the 'tempter' (1 Cor. 7.5; 1 Thess. 3.5).

(ii) It is on this basis that the individual anthropological concepts, like 'body', 'soul', and others, are also to be understood. They do not refer to *parts* of man, individual members or organs, but rather always mean *man as a whole* with respect to some specific possibility of his being. For this reason, Paul can also use almost every one of these concepts in the sense of 'I' (*cf.*, e.g., 1 Cor. 6.15 with 12.27; or 1 Cor. 13.3 with 2 Cor. 1.23; 12.15), and so also, the concepts can many times seem to flow into one another. One may not, for example, permit oneself to be misled by 1 Cor. 15.35 and attempt to understand 'body' as the form of man and 'flesh' as his matter. In this passage, this meaning is of course present; but it is a mistake to take this passage as one's starting point because Paul here lets himself be misled by his adversary into speaking apologetically. Passages in which he speaks calmly, like Rom. 1.24; 6.12; 12.1; 1 Cor. 13.3, all clearly show that 'body' for him does not mean 'form' but rather refers to the whole man and, to be sure, insofar as, for others as well as for himself, man can be the object of observation and action. 'Body' designates man insofar as something can be done to him or can happen to him, indeed, insofar as he is always exposed to such happenings and never freely has himself at his own disposal—and thus, for example, can become ill and die. Man is 'body' in his temporality and historicity. That 'body' is not thought of 'dualistically' is made especially evident when Paul affirms the resurrection of the body; i.e., to have a body for him is something that belongs to man as such, and he is as anxious about the prospect of being without a body as if it meant nothingness (2 Cor. 5.1 ff.). Thus the body is not some part of man in which the soul or the real I is stuck. And if man yearns to be free from 'this body of death' (Rom. 7.24), he yearns to be freed from himself as he now is, to be transformed', as Paul elsewhere puts it (2 Cor. 3.18; Phil. 3.21; Rom. 8.29). The extent to which Paul has at the same time formulated this thought in terms of mythological ideas is unimportant, if one sees what the understanding of existence is that is hereby expressed.

So also 'soul' is not a something *in* man—say, his better self—but rather is the whole man himself insofar as he is alive, is a living being (1 Cor. 15.45). Therefore, 'soul' for Paul is neither the bearer of spiritual life in the Greek sense nor our immortal self, the heavenly stranger in a darksome body, in the sense of Gnosticism; rather it is the vitality, the 'life' (Rom. 11.3; 16.4; Phil. 2.30), which also belongs to animals in contradistinction to lifeless instruments (1 Cor. 14.7). Precisely as such a vitality, however, the soul is not immortal, but mortal; it does not at all signify man's authentic being. But, of course, 'soul' can also be the 'I', for man is a living being (2 Cor. 1.23; 12.15; 1 Thess. 2.8). As in the Old Testament, 'every soul' means 'every man' (Rom. 2.9; 13.1).

Insofar as the life of man is a conscious life, Paul can occasionally refer to it as 'spirit' (1 Cor. 2.11; Rom. 8.16; to be distinguished, of course, from the Spirit of God, the Holy Spirit, that is also referred to alongside of it!). And once again 'spirit' also can mean simply 'man',

or 'I' (Rom. 1.9; 1 Cor. 16.18; 2 Cor. 2.13; and in formulas of greeting). But the real word that Paul uses to
refer to man as conscious is 'mind'; it designates man
insofar as he understands or knows something and, to be
sure, insofar as he knows about his own possibilities and
understands himself (e.g., Rom. 14.5). Since, however,
man's being is a being before God, the knowledge about
his own possibilities is at the same time the knowledge
of the claim of God, of what man ought to do (Rom.
1.20; 7.23). And, further, since the specifically human
knowing about oneself does not have the character of a
theoretical, neutral confirmation that something is so,
but rather also has the character of laying hold of a
possibility, of willing (Rom. 7.15 ff.), it follows that 'mind'
can be either a correct or a false self-understanding. The
mind of the heathen is base (Rom. 1.28 f.); their minds
are blinded (2 Cor. 4.4); on the other hand, the mind of
Christians is renewed (Rom. 12.2). Paul can also speak
of the mind as the 'inner man' (Rom. 7.22; however, one
may not draw on 2 Cor. 4.16 to explain this, for what is
spoken of there is the man of faith!). But what is meant
by this is not something like a better self 'in' man; for
in Rom. 7.13 ff. the 'mind' or the 'inner man' is as much
the 'I' or self as is 'flesh' (*cf.* below, III., 2., b., iii.).
The wretchedness of man that is presented here does not
consist in his better self's standing over against his worse
material corporeality, but rather in his self's being split,
in I standing over against I. Indeed, the essence of the
unredeemed man is to be thus split.

In order to refer to man as one who has knowledge of
himself, i.e., of his possibilities before God, and thus a
knowledge that can also go astray, Paul likewise makes
use of the Old Testament expression 'heart' (e.g., Rom.
2.5; 8.27; 2 Cor. 4.6) and the Greek expression 'conscience' (Rom. 2.15; 1 Cor. 8.7 ff.; 10.25 ff., etc.).

What has been given now by this clarification of Paul's

basic concepts is not anything like a 'physical' anthropology; for the concepts 'body' and 'soul' refer to man in respect of his creatureliness, while the concepts 'mind', 'heart', and 'conscience' speak of him in his responsibility before God.

(iii) If man as having a body is withdrawn from his own disposal and always stands in the context of a history, then, for Paul, there is only a twofold possibility for the determination of this history—by God or by sin. He expresses this either/or by means of the contrast between flesh and Spirit. And, to be sure, the being of man prior to faith is determined by the 'flesh'. This word means, first of all, the animated flesh of the body. But, then, just as 'body' refers to man himself as object of an action or as subject of a happening, so also 'flesh' refers to him in his pure being on hand in which he can become an object. Hence the concepts body and flesh can to a certain degree mean the same thing (2 Cor. 4.10 f.; 1 Cor. 6.16); illnesses and marks are in the body as well as in the flesh (Gal. 4.13 f.; 6.17; 2 Cor. 12.7). And as 'body' can be the 'I' or self, so also can 'flesh' (2 Cor. 7.5). Thus flesh is not a part of man, but man himself as he is actually found—as well or ill, as belonging to a nation or to a family. Abraham is the father of the Jews 'according to the flesh', while Christ 'according to the flesh' is a descendant of David(Rom. 4.1; 1.3; 9.5). The natural life of man is a life 'in the flesh' (2 Cor. 10.3; Gal. 2.20; Phil. 1.21 ff.), and whatever belongs to such a life, like food or means, is called 'fleshly' (Rom. 15.27; 1 Cor. 9.11). But in close connection with this, 'flesh' acquires yet another meaning, which becomes clear when it is said that the man of faith no longer exists 'in the flesh' or 'according to the flesh'. As the characteristic of a certain type of demeanour (boasting, knowing, walking, etc., 1 Cor. 11.18; 5.16; 10.2), 'according to the flesh' does not designate man as he appears to others, but as he understands himself, namely, on the basis of what he is found to be, of what is immediately evident (Rom. 2.28). 'To be according to the flesh' means 'to be intent on what is fleshly' (Rom. 8.5). This does not mean to be determined by what is fleshly in the sense of the life of impulse or of the senses, but rather to be determined by anything in the entire sphere of what is immediately evident, whether this be national advantage, legal correctness, the accomplishments of the man who exists under the law, or human wisdom. All of this is 'flesh' (Phil. 3.4 ff.; Gal. 3.3; 1 Cor. 1.26); therefore, works righteousness is included under the concept as surely as are vices. No man can get out of the flesh as existence in what is immediately evident; but the question with which he is faced is whether he will understand himself in terms of it and put his 'confidence' in it—whether as one who is situated in the flesh he also wants to walk according to it (2 Cor. 10.3). To understand oneself in terms of the 'flesh', however, is 'sin'; for sin is the care, boasting, and confidence of the man who forgets his creatureliness and tries to secure his own existence. It reaches its acme in the Jew; for to pursue one's own righteousness means precisely to put one's confidence in the flesh (Phil. 3.4-9); it is similar, however, with those who are 'wise according to the flesh'; for they, too, do not honour God, but boast of themselves (1 Cor. 1.18-31). Sin is falsely wanting to be oneself; and there is the deep connection between the flesh and sin that the man who thus wills to be himself can only do so by understanding his existence in terms of what is on hand, what has been accomplished, what can be grasped and proven—in short, in terms of the 'flesh'. And so also there is a connection between flesh and sin *and* 'death'; for each man understands himself in terms of what is transitory, what is fallen under death, and so death is already at work in him (Rom. 7.5). For everyone, on the other hand, who no longer understands himself on the basis of the flesh, or of what is visible, but rather understands himself on the basis of the invisible, and walks accordingly, flesh, sin, and death have come to an end (Rom. 8.9; 6.2; 6.10 f.; Gal. 5.24; 1 Cor. 15.56 f.). Thus, for Paul, flesh is neither matter in the Greek sense, i.e., the material that has to be given shape by spirit as the power of form, or the life of the sense that must be educated, nor is it matter in the sense of Gnosticism (even if he is influenced by the latter's terminology), i.e., the inferior, evil realm of the senses, which is opposed to the soul. Rather it is the world of what is on hand, which first becomes the sphere of sin through the attitude of man, just as the creation only becomes 'this world' through men's falling away from God.

But now Paul does not look upon sin as something accidental, which is present here and there or even in most places; rather he views it as the attitude that man necessarily has since the first sin of Adam; i.e., he sees that every man is already guided by a false understanding of human existence and that the man who wants to free himself from this world only becomes the more entrapped in it because he but repeats the primal sin of wanting to be himself. In order to illustrate this fact of sin's sovereignty, Paul makes use of the Gnostic myth of the primal man and interprets it in terms of the contrast between Adam and Christ (Rom. 5.12 ff.; 1 Cor. 15.20 ff.; 15.44 ff.). And from the crossing of his own ideas with the notions of the myth there arise confusions that cannot be considered here. The one thing that we must note, however, is that he never traces sin back to something that is not yet sin; rather sin has come into the world through sin, although it has thereby become an absolute and all-dominating power (Rom. 5.12). Even in Rom. 7.7 ff. sin is not referred to the flesh as matter or as a mythical power, but rather to the sinner, to the man who lives according to the flesh. What Paul means becomes clear when it is recognized that for him the sole way of becoming free from sin is forgiveness; i.e., if man has sinned, then he is a sinner. What has happened in his past is not an individual fact that has now been left behind, but rather is present in that it qualifies him as guilty before God. Neither man nor mankind can become free from the past by their own self-will; on the contrary, they bring the past with them into every present. However, because sin is guilt before God there is also the possibility that God will free man from the past, that man will become new. But this can only become clear when the final factor that determines the existence of man prior to faith has been taken into consideration.

(iv) The 'law' means that there is a fact in the existence of the sinful man that, in spite of his false understanding of himself, again and again makes audible to him the claim of God. This fact is given in the concrete demands that always encounter man and point out to him that he does not belong to himself. From the standpoint of his Christian understanding of the law, Paul sees that these concrete demands actually grow out of man's constantly being bound together with other men at whose disposal he ought to place himself. For it seems to him that the final meaning of all of the specific requirements of the law is that man should love his neighbour as himself (Rom. 13.8 ff.; Gal. 5.14; *cf.* 6.2). That the gentiles also hear such demands is indicated by Paul in the letters that we have only in Rom. 2.14 f. Thus it is with reference to the Jews that he develops his detailed consideration of man's situation under the law, because being himself a Jew, he naturally assumes that the true embodiment of the law is the law of Moses. From this it becomes clear, first of all, that for him the law of God is not the eternal moral law, not the Idea of the Good that springs from the human spirit as the idea of its perfection and at the same time is its norm. Rather the law is the whole complex of concrete, historically given moral and ritual demands that encounter the Jew in his actual historical community. It is characteristic of Paul that, unlike the prophets and Jesus, he does not distinguish between cultic-ritual demands, formal-legal demands, and moral demands; for man prior to faith, the law is the 'letter' that kills (2 Cor. 3.6) even in its moral demands. Paul does not criticize the law from the standpoint of its *content*, but with respect to its *significance* for man, i.e., he criticizes it as it appears from the standpoint of the Jewish understanding. In the law, man is confronted by the demand of God, obedience to which would bring life, for God is the Judge (Gal. 3.12; Rom. 2.10; 2.13; 10.5). Moreover, the demand of the law is also valid for the Christian, for it is once again taken up in the commandment to love; and for the Christian also God is the Judge (1 Cor. 1.8; 3.12 ff.; 2 Cor. 5.10, etc.). Therefore, the situation of man prior to faith is not so frightful because the law is inferior, but because man does not fulfil it, because at best he wills it, but does not do it (Rom. 7.11 f.). Nevertheless, Paul says that man not only *can* not be made righteous by the law, but also *should* not be made righteous by it. And he also says that although the law is indeed the holy will of God, which is valid also for Christians, it still is something provisional that is done away with for the man of faith (Rom. 7.1-6; 10.4). The apparent contradiction is simply resolved. Since in fact every man is a sinner (Rom. 3.9-20), it is an illusion to want to earn righteousness by works of the law, as the Jews suppose they can do. For what is evident in such a supposition is not only that they regard sin as an individual work that can also be abstained from or, in any case, can be compensated for, but also that they understand obedience to the law as the accomplishment of individual works of which they can boast before God. In other words, they are not obedient at all in the genuine sense; and the law ought not to meet men in the way in which it meets them. The way of the law, when it is understood as a means for earning righteousness, is false. Thus the sin of the Jews is the failure to appreciate that man owes God an absolute obedience and therefore is dependent on him, on his forgiving grace; the real sin is 'boasting'. And insofar as it is precisely the law that provokes this extreme possibility in the man who has a false self-understanding, the law is what allows him thus to founder, so that he can understand what grace is in case it encounters him. So the law becomes the 'taskmaster to bring us to Christ' (Gal. 3.24) and finds its end in him (Rom. 10.4). So also, in accordance with God's plan, sin has increased so that grace might increase all the more (Rom. 5.20; Gal. 3.19). Precisely because under the law man is driven to his most extreme possibility, there also develops under it an understanding for Christ. Therefore, the unity of man in the history that leads through his sin and redemption is clear. Redemption is as little a magical transformation of his 'nature', or his endowment with a higher 'nature', as it is enlightenment. It is forgiveness, through which he is brought from bondage to freedom, from anxiety to joy, and from disobedience to obedience. And equally clear is the unity of the will of God that encounters man in law and grace; for just as the law demands obedience, so also does the message of God's gracious act (*cf.* below, III., 2., *c.*).

However much Paul's doctrine of the law is polemic in character, it is by no means something occasional and secondary, but rather contains his central thoughts. This becomes especially evident when he struggles against the Gnostic pneumatics in Corinth on the basis of the same fundamental ideas. As the Jews use the law in order to boast, so also do the pneumatics use the gospel and imagine that they are able thereby to lift themselves above the ranks of a sinful humanity. They forget that man himself does not build his life, but that everything that he has has been received as a gift (1 Cor. 4.7) and that he may boast of nothing save of the Lord (1 Cor. 1.31). Jews and pneumatics alike repeat the world's primal sin of not honouring God as God (Rom. 1.21).

c. MAN UNDER FAITH. (i) Like every man, Paul knows that human life is governed by the image of salvation, by an ideal, a state or a condition in which all of man's questions and grievances and anxiety have ceased—or, in purely formal terms, that it is governed by the image of man's authenticity. And he fully agrees with Judaism in understanding this authenticity as 'righteousness'. Man ought and wants to be 'righteous'; as righteous he can stand before God, and the pious Jew hungers and thirsts for the day in which God will pronounce him righteous in the judgement. As for Judaism, 'righteousness' for Paul is primarily a forensic and eschatological concept; i.e., it does not mean, first of all, man's moral uprightness, a human quality, but rather the position that he has in his relations with and before others, and preeminently before God in the judgement. His righteousness is his 'acceptance', which is granted to him by others and especially by God. Paul entirely agrees with Judaism that man can finally receive this acceptance only from God in the last judgement (Rom. 2.13; 3.20; 4.3; 4.6, etc.). However, he differs from Judaism at two points: (1) He says that God's eschatological sentence of judgement *has already been passed*, namely, in the death and resurrection of Christ; we are already righteous if we have faith in this act of salvation (Rom. 4.25; 5.1; 5.17, etc.). This does not mean that the faithful have a new quality, that they are ethically perfect, or that, their guilt having been cancelled, they must now take care for themselves. Rather it simply means that God accepts them as they are. On the other hand, this does not mean that God merely regards the faithful man 'as if' he were righteous; on the contrary, by accepting me, God takes me to be a different person than I am; and if I (in faith) let go of what I am in myself, if I affirm God's judgement and understand myself in terms of him, then I really *am* a different person, namely, the one that he takes me to be. (2) Judaism regarded fulfilment of the law as the condition of God's eschatological verdict; according to Paul, however, God pronounces the faithful man righteous entirely without conditions (Rom. 3.21 ff.; 10.4 ff.; Gal. 2.16 ff., etc.). Thus, for him, righteousness is not something that is merited, but rather is utterly the gift of God. Consequently, he refers to it in contrast to one's 'own' righteousness, i.e., the acceptance merited by one's own accomplishments, as the 'righteousness of God', i.e., the acceptance that God freely gives. Its sole basis is in God's freedom and grace, and so Paul can also speak of the 'reconciliation' that God has established (Rom. 5.10 f.; 2 Cor. 5.18 ff.).

(ii) The meaning of the saving act of God through which he actualizes righteousness for men is forgiveness. However, according to Paul, this forgiveness is carried out by God in the death and resurrection of Jesus Christ as the Son of God who became man (1 Cor. 1.18 ff.; 15.3; Gal. 3.1; Phil. 2.6 ff.; Rom. 3.24 f.; 4.24 f., etc.). Thus, for Paul, Christ is significant neither as teacher and prophet nor as example and hero. His humanity and his destiny come into question only insofar as in them he realizes his obedience, *and*, to be sure, this is the obedience of the pre-existent Son of God (Phil. 2.6 ff.; Rom. 5.18 f.). However, the idea of pre-existence for Paul is not a speculative theory about a divine being, nor does it stand in the context of a cosmological mythology, as it does in Gnosticism (even if materially this is whence it stems). Rather it has the significance of saying that what has happened in Christ is not a human or earthly event in the continuum of such earthly occurrences, but, rather is the act of God. In what has happened in Christ *God* has acted, God's act of love has taken place. This act, however, is completely unapparent, and it also is not made apparent by the different images, drawn from cult and myth, in which Paul describes it (*cf.* above, III., 1., c.). These all say only one thing, that the historical fact of the cross is God's judgement against sin and the world and that therefore whoever accepts this judgement in faith is free from sin (Rom. 6.10 f.; Gal. 6.14). And so also can one believe in Christ's resurrection; for however much Paul thinks of the latter also as a cosmic event, he still endeavours to understand it as an occurrence in which the believer himself participates. He tries to understand it as the making possible of a new humanity that is not caught in what is provisional and in death, but rather has the future and *life* (1 Cor. 15.20-2; Rom. 5.12 ff.; 8.29).

In actual fact, faith does not relate itself to historical or cosmic processes that could be established as free from doubt, but rather to the *preaching* behind which faith cannot go and which says to man that he must understand the cross as God's act of salvation and believe in the resurrection. Only in preaching is the cross God's saving act, and therefore the preaching that is based on the cross is itself God's act of salvation and revelation. Faith comes from preaching (Rom. 10.10-17), and God's act of salvation is the institution of the 'word' of reconciliation (2 Cor. 5.18 f.). It is in the preaching of the gospel that the righteousness of God is revealed (Rom. 1.17); and in the preaching of the apostle, what is encountered is the word of God itself (2 Cor. 5.20) or the actual speaking of Christ (Rom. 15.18). This preaching of God's saving act, however, is not a communication about events that one can also establish outside of faith;

rather in speaking of God's act of salvation, it at the same time addresses the conscience of the hearer and asks him whether he is willing to understand the occurrence that it proclaims as occurring to him himself and thereby to understand his existence in its light. For this reason, preaching has the possibility of working death as well as life (2 Cor. 2.14-16; 4.1-6). Thus the event of preaching is itself the eschatological event of salvation (2 Cor. 6.1 f.).

As the preaching has its basis in what has happened in Christ, so also does the 'church'. For Paul, 'church' is the community of the faithful, the central point in the life of which is the worshipping congregation; and, to be sure, it is the community of all those who are called by God, which is represented in each individual congregation. As the community of those who are called, it is constituted by the 'word', and likewise by the sacraments of baptism and the Lord's Supper, which, like preaching, make the salvation-event something present and thus are also a kind of proclamation (*cf.* 1 Cor. 11.26). Therefore, the church is neither an association that constitutes itself nor a crowd of pneumatic individuals. As established by Christ and the word, it is itself an eschatological fact; those who belong to it are the 'saints' of the last days who are already taken out of 'this world'. Since the last days have been introduced by Christ, the church is nothing other than the continuation of the Christ-event. It is his 'body' (1 Cor. 12.12 ff.), and he is its 'Lord', i.e., the one to whom the individual comes to belong in baptism (1 Cor. 6.11; 12.13 f.; Gal. 3.27 f.), at whose table one eats the 'Lord's Supper' (1 Cor. 10.21; 11.20), and who is present with all his power in the congregation (1 Cor. 5.4). The congregation is 'in him' (Rom. 12.5; Gal. 3.28); it acknowledges him as its Lord and at the same time as the Lord of all (Rom. 10.9; 1 Cor. 12.3; Phil. 2.11). So also, then, does each individual belong to Christ, since

he is baptized in him (Rom. 6.3; 1 Cor. 12.13; Gal.
3.27); he is 'in him', i.e., he belongs to him (Gal. 3.28 f.;
5.24; Rom. 8.9; 14.7 ff.), he belongs to the new world
as a 'new creation' (2 Cor. 5.17). Thus the meaning of
the salvation-occurrence is that the act of God that takes
place in Christ continues in preaching and in the church,
that the 'world' has come to an end, and that the time
of salvation has already become a reality for faith. Just
how what is wrought by this occurrence can actually be
understood as the possibility of a new human existence
must now be made clear by an elucidation of the concept
of faith.

(iii) 'Faith', first of all, is the obedient hearing of the
word of proclamation. It is 'obedience' because it is the
subjection of oneself to the act of God that is proclaimed
and realized in the word (Rom. 1.15;10.3;11.30; *cf.* Rom.
1.8 and 1 Thess. 1.8 with Rom. 15.18; 16.19; further,
2 Cor. 10.5 f. with 10.15, etc.). As obedience, faith is the
exact opposite of a 'work', and Paul takes great pains to
show that faith is not a 'condition' of salvation in the
sense of an accomplishment (Rom. 3.28; 4.5 f.; 9.31 f.;
Gal. 2.16; 3.2, etc.). But although it is not an accomplishment, it is an *act* of genuine obedience, in which man
radically renounces his own existence and gives glory
to God alone (Rom. 3.27; 4.20 f.). Therefore, faith for
Paul is not a psychic state or a spiritual attitude, as it is
for Philo. Nor is it trust in God in general. Rather it is
obedience toward a specific act of God that is proclaimed
to man. It is faith *in* . . ., namely, in Jesus Christ, i.e., in
the saving act of God that has occurred in Christ. Thus
it is not 'piety', but rather a specific 'confession' (Rom.
10.9). And since the righteousness that is awarded to it
(*cf.* above, III., 2., c., i.) is not an individual attribute,
which the believer obtains and possesses, but rather is
the acceptance that is awarded to it by the judgement of
God, faith is never closed, but is always simultaneously

'hope'. Indeed, the proclamation does not say that the image of God's wrath is false, but rather that whoever believes escapes from his wrath. But the wrath itself abides (Rom. 2.5; 2.8; 5.9; 1 Thess. 1.10); for it is not God's 'attribute' or his 'affect', but his rule as Judge; and God's grace has its character precisely in that he is and remains the Judge. It is the grace of the Judge, i.e., it is forgiveness; and it can only be understood as grace where God's verdict as judge is simultaneously seen with it. If for the faithful, anxiety is a thing of the past, this is not so with the 'fear of God', which rather belongs to faith itself (Rom. 11.20 f.; 2 Cor. 5.10 f.; Phil. 2.12 f.). Only so is the 'trust' that also belongs to faith (Rom. 4.5; 4.17; 4.20; 6.8) genuine trust, in which man utterly looks away from himself and completely surrenders himself to God (2 Cor. 1.9). Faith is also a 'knowledge' in that it knows about the saving act of God that is proclaimed to it. However, it is not knowledge in the sense of speculation about some historical or cosmic event, but rather a knowledge in which the man of faith also knows about himself and understands himself anew, in that he understands the saving act as a gift and himself as one to whom it has been given (1 Cor. 3.12). God's revelation in Christ is not the communication of knowledge as such, but rather an occurrence for man and in man that places him in a new situation and thereby also opens up to him a new understanding of himself (*cf.* especially 2 Cor. 2.14-4.6). Thus his knowing has its basis in his being known by God (1 Cor. 8.2 f.; 13.12; Gal. 4.9). So it is that faith is the new possibility for existence before God; it is created by God's saving act, is laid hold of in obedience, and manifests itself as confession and hope, as fear and trust—in short, as a new understanding of oneself. That faith actually is such a new possibility of existence comes to expression when Paul can say not only that the righteousness of God was revealed (Rom. 1.17; 3.21), but also that faith was revealed (Gal. 3.23-5).

In its unity of obedience, confession and hope, of fear and trust, faith as a new self-understanding is not the once for all resolve to join the Christian religion or a once accepted world-view. Rather it has reality only as the *obedience of faith that is always new*. However much such faith may begin with a foundational resolve and confession, the existence of the faithful man is not at all the simple state that is thereby established or the natural development that is thus begun. For if it were, faith as an act would become a process in the past and would be understood as a 'work', which by its very essence it is not. It is only faith if it always remains faith, i.e., if the individual with his entire existence always realizes his obedience anew. This comes to expression (1) when Paul again and again admonishes his hearers to examine themselves and to stand fast in faith (1 Cor. 10.12; 11.28; 16.13; 2 Cor. 13.5; Rom. 14.4; 14.22; Gal. 5.1; 6.3 f., etc.), inasmuch as fear of God belongs to faith (Rom. 11.20 f.; Phil. 2.12, etc.); (2) in the statements concerning the individual possibilities of faith; i.e., faith can be weak or strong (Rom. 14.11; 5.13 f.; 1 Thess. 3.10; 2 Cor. 10.15, etc.), and from it can arise both this judgement and that (Rom. 14.2; 22 f.). Thus the man of faith also still stands in a life in which it is necessary to judge and to act, and all this should be determined by faith (Rom. 12.6), for otherwise it is sin (Rom. 14.23). So, then, faith also 'abides' (1 Cor. 13.13); for no future can be imagined in which the Christian could understand himself otherwise than as having his basis in the saving act of God; the same thing follows (3) from the fact that the relation to the Lord that is acquired through faith and baptism is also thought of as a determination of one's entire life (Gal. 2.20). To die with Christ in baptism means a life-long crucifixion with him (Rom. 6.6; *cf.* Gal. 5.24; 6.14), so that henceforth his life and sufferings are at work in the ministry and sufferings of the man of faith (Rom. 8.17; 2 Cor. 1.5; 4.7 ff., 13.3 f.; Phil. 3.10). If this consciousness of being bound to the Lord occasionally found expression with Paul himself in mystic or ecstatic experiences (2 Cor. 12.12 ff.), still being 'in Christ' is in principle not mysticism, but rather precisely life in the new historical possibility that is determined by Christ. One 'stands fast' in the Lord just as he 'stands fast' in faith (1 Thess. 3.8; Phil. 4.1), and as there are levels of faith, so also are there levels of being in Christ (Rom. 16.10; 1 Cor. 3.1; 4.10) and individually different ways of manifesting one's life in him (1 Thess. 5.12; Rom. 16.2; 16.8; 16.12; 16.22; 1 Cor. 15.58; 16.19; 16.24; Phil. 1.13; 2.1; 2.5; 4.2; 2 Cor. 2.17; 12.19; Philem. 8). In life and in death, the man of faith belongs to Christ (Rom. 14.7-9; 1 Cor. 15.18; 1 Thess. 4.16), and this communion, which can also be designated as Christ's being in the believer (Rom. 8.10; 2 Cor. 13.3; 13.5; Gal. 2.20; 4.19), is never completed, but is a constant striving forward; it is the determination of a life that is free from the past and open for the future (Phil. 3.12-14) because it is no longer dominated by the will to be oneself (Gal. 2.19 f.).

(iv) Paul can designate this new life in still a different way and thereby further describe it by the concept of the 'Spirit'. Just as 'flesh' signifies the determination of life by what is on hand (*cf.* above, III., 2., *b.*, iii), so 'Spirit' signifies its determination by what is *not* on hand, not produced, not disposable—by what is invisible, miraculous, and solely the object of faith. In the popular image of the Spirit with which Paul makes contact, the idea of 'miracle' as a power that determines man's existence is already laid out, although it is thought of somewhat primitively in that remarkable phenomena, and especially psychic ones, are understood as miraculous and

wrought by the Spirit. Paul radicalizes this idea by showing that all the phenomena that can be grasped on the
plane of what is on hand are ambiguous and as such do
not attest the Spirit of God. This they do only when they
stand within a specific life-context (1 Cor. 12.) The only
miracle is that which transforms man in his entire existence and, of course, also attests itself in all of the concrete expressions of his life. Therefore, for Paul, Spirit is
the 'how', the determination of the new life, which is not
produced by man himself, but is given to him. Thus,
on the one hand, Paul speaks of the Spirit as the gift that
is given to the faithful man (Rom. 5.5; 1 Cor. 2.12; 2
Cor. 1.22, etc.), the gift of the last days in which the final
consummation is already guaranteed (Rom. 8.23; 2
Cor. 1.22; 5.5); on the other hand, he speaks of it as the
determination of the new life, which must be laid hold of
in faith and which proves itself in the concrete way in
which one leads one's life (Gal. 5.25; Rom. 8.13-14).
Spirit is the determination of heart and conscience, of
walking and striving, of joy and of love (Rom. 5.5; Gal.
4.6; Rom. 9.1; 8.4-11; Gal. 5.16; Rom. 14.17; 15.30). The
life of the man of faith is one of being led by the Spirit
(Rom. 8.14), a constant bearing of fruit and being transformed (Gal. 5.22 f.; 2 Cor. 3.18). Since this new possibility of life that is designated by 'Spirit' must be expressly laid hold of, and since, further, it is faith that is
the laying hold of it, Paul also does not refer faith to the
activity of the Spirit, but rather, conversely, refers the
reception of the Spirit to faith or to baptism. This clearly
shows that he has no need of the wonderful or the miraculous for the purpose of explanation (Gal. 3.2; 3.5; 3.14;
2 Cor. 1.21 f.). Insofar, however, as the resolve of faith
must maintain itself as the determination of one's entire
life, a life in the Spirit and a life in faith are one and the
same. And as faith brings one into communion with the
Lord, so this communion with the *Lord* is nothing other

than being determined by the *Spirit*. Hence Paul can say that where in the Old Testament 'Lord' is spoken of, what is meant is the 'Spirit' (2 Cor. 3.17). Lord and Spirit almost coincide (2 Cor. 3.17 f.; Rom. 8.9-11; 9.1; 15.18; *cf.* Rom. 8.8 f. with 1 Cor. 15.5; Phil. 2.6, etc.); both terms designate the new eschatological mode of existence in which the faithful stand.

Both designate the 'freedom' of the faithful (2 Cor. 3.17; Gal. 5.1). This freedom is (1) *freedom from sin* (Rom. 6.18; 6.22; 8.2), i.e., not a sinless state, but rather the opening up of the possibility of new life through forgiveness; it is freedom for God's claim, for the imperative (Rom. 6.11 ff.; Gal. 5.13 f.; 1 Cor. 5.7 f.), which did not exist before (Rom. 7.13 ff.), but exists now (Rom. 7.4 ff.). Thereby it is also (2) *freedom from the law* (Gal. 2.4; 5.18; 5.23; Rom. 6.14; 7.1 ff.; 2 Cor. 3.7-18, etc.) and (3) *freedom from men* and their standards (1 Cor. 7.21-23; 9.1; 9.19; 10.29; Gal. 3.28) and, finally, (4) *freedom from death* (Rom. 8.2), which receives its power precisely through sin and the law (1 Cor. 15.56).

The new covenant is the covenant of 'life' (2 Cor. 3.7-18), and Romans 5 seeks to establish, in face of the claim of Judaism, that faith actually has the righteousness that is the substance of eschatological salvation because it has life, because it can live in hope. Faith has life not as a state in which dying has ceased, but as hope (Rom. 8.18-39), so that precisely every distress must serve as a confirmation of faith because it brings to mind that everything here and now, all that is simply on hand, is provisional (Rom. 5.3 f.; 8.19 ff.; 2 Cor. 5.1 ff.). Thus the believer who actually puts his hope in God alone (2 Cor. 1.8 f.) is raised above all the powers of natural life, yes, even above life and death themselves (2 Cor. 5.6-9; Rom. 14.7-9; 1 Cor. 3.21 f.). This never means, however, that he has salvation as a possession that is at his disposal or that he is perfected and can boast. On the contrary, he can boast solely of God and of what God gives him (1 Cor. 1.29; 3.21; Rom. 5.11; 11.17 f.) and, in a paradoxical way, of the cross of Christ and of his own nothingness (Gal. 6.14; Rom. 5.3; 2 Cor. 11.16-12. 13); for in this he becomes certain of the power of the Lord, which is made perfect in weakness (2 Cor. 12.9 f., 4.7). Indeed, he is not his own lord, but rather has his freedom precisely in that he no longer belongs to himself, but to another (1 Cor. 6.19; 7.22; Rom. 7.4-6; 14.17-19; 2 Cor. 5.14 f.; Gal. 2.19 f.), that he obediently stands at the disposal of God (Rom. 6.13). Everything belongs to him because he belongs to Christ (1 Cor. 3.22 f.). Therefore, his freedom is not the right to indulge every caprice; for precisely such capriciousness would once again make him a slave to what is on hand, from which he has now become free.

If for the believer everything worldly and on hand that he encounters turns out to be radically indifferent, inasmuch as nothing can be held against him, this indifference nevertheless immediately disappears before the question of the individual's concrete responsibility (1 Cor. 6.12; 8.1 ff.; 10.23). Service of Christ realizes itself in actual life as *service to the neighbour* of whom precisely the man who is free, and only he, should and can make himself a genuine servant (1 Cor. 9.19-22, *cf.* 8.9; Rom. 14.13 ff.; 15.1 ff.; Gal. 5.13). Such service is the fulfilment of the 'law of Christ' (Gal. 6.2); it is 'love', which is the fulfilment of the law (Gal. 5.14; Rom. 13.8 ff.), the love in which faith manifests itself as the determination of one's life (Gal. 5.6) and in which knowledge has the criterion of its genuineness (1 Cor. 8.1 ff.); the love that is higher than all of the other Spirit-wrought phenomena of the Christian life (1 Cor. 12.31; 13.1 ff.); the love in which the new creation becomes a reality (*cf.* Gal. 5.6 with 6.15) and which therefore never ends (1 Cor. 13.8 ff.). Naturally, for one who stands in love, an 'ethic' is no longer necessary, however much brotherly admonition, such as Paul himself practises, can point out to another his responsibility and show him what he has to do (1 Thess. 5.11 f.; Rom. 12.8; 15.14).

All this, this life in the Spirit, in freedom and love, which is based in the faith that no longer seeks itself, but gives all glory to God, remains understandable and realizable only to him for whom the 'glory of God' is indeed the final motive and the final goal. It is to the glory of God that Christ is confessed as Lord (Phil. 2.11); and the same thing is true of the life of the congregation (Rom. 15.6; 1 Cor. 1.20), our eating and drinking (1 Cor. 10.31), the work of the apostle (2 Cor. 4.15), and the works of love of the faithful (2 Cor. 9.11-13). To God's glory, Christ accomplished his work (Rom. 15.7); for even as we belong to him, so also does he belong to God (1 Cor. 3.23), and in the end he will relinquish his reign to God so that God may be all in all (1 Cor. 15.28).

Rudolf Bultmann

6
Eschatology

I. ESCHATOLOGY IN THE HISTORY OF RELIGION

Eschatology, the doctrine of the last things, usually means both the *final destiny of the individual* and also the *future of the universe*. This article is principally limited to the second meaning.

1. Origin and Dispersal

a. The habits and thought of primitive man, who lived mainly for the present moment, meant in general that it was rare that he gave much thought to what was to come; it was sufficient for him that each day brought its own troubles. But even in this limited sphere there were events powerful and disturbing enough to shake man out of the routine of his everyday life and raise before his mind the fearful question, whether all this might not suddenly come to a terrifying *end*; in fact even in very advanced cultures we meet from time to time evidence of the powerful sentiments which an eschatological expectation (of course already present) is capable of bringing to the surface—as for example in the early centuries of the Christian Middle Ages (*cf.* IV, 2 below). And one must also remember that primitive thought is completely lacking in the idea of continuity: what we take for granted as persisting and unchanged, on the basis of our concepts of the conformity of the course of nature to fixed laws, appears to primitive man as something constantly new: even the return of quite ordinary phenomena such as the rising of the heavenly bodies. Of course primitive man also knows of forces of nature. But he considers that wherever possible new force must be added to them in order to increase their effectiveness or simply to maintain it: thus the Lapps kill a reindeer and rub the blood into the support of the altar, in order to make the pillars of the world strong, to prevent the heavens falling in. And in such circumstances what could guarantee the continued existence of the world forever? When the skies resound with a thunderstorm, when the sun or the moon grow dark, when the ground shakes under one's feet in an earthquake, when fire rages through forest and steppe, when floods cover the country, does this not mean that one day is going to be the last? And in fact it is the *impression formed by such natural catastrophes* which form the *original basis of ideas of the end of the world,* and from which all eschatology must therefore be derived.

b. There is a second point which must be mentioned. Primitive thought sees in the world the effect not only of natural forces, but of living beings. The rumbling of thunder is the loud roaring of a being with a mighty voice, sometimes regarded as a kind of animal, sometimes more as a human being; the sun or the moon grow dark because a monster is trying to swallow them; there is an earthquake because a being dwelling within the earth is shaking it by its movements; water floods over the earth because a water or sea demon is raging against the earth in order to swallow it, etc. Eschatology has inherited numerous themes from this mythical way of looking at natural events; for the monster or the demon has only to achieve a final victory to bring about the end of the world (no real distinction is made between the two at first). Thus the Kai from the Eastern part of the north coast of the former German part of New Guinea tell of Mâlengfung, who once upon a time created the world in its entirety, and set the first man to live in it, but now no longer interferes in its history: he lies at the end of the earth on the horizon and sleeps a long, long sleep. Only when he turns over on to the other side can men notice by the movement of the earth that he is still there. But at the end of time he will rise up from his dwelling place 'at the edge of the red light of dawn' and break the sky into pieces, so that it falls down upon the earth and brings an end to all life.

c. As gods properly speaking are raised to a higher level and replace the demons, so that the gods come to be regarded as the original cause of eschatological events, the religious element begins to be of importance. A classical example of this is Parseeism, which possessed an eschatology that influenced that of Judaism (*cf.* II, 7,8 below), through Judaism that of Christianity (*cf.* III, IV below), and through both that of Islam, which has an eschatology very highly developed in religious terms. In Indian religions, moral points of view at least have affected ideas of the end of the world. In a similar way, in Burma and Cambodia the differences in the coming final catastrophe correspond to the different kinds of moral evil: for wickedness there will be fire, for anger water, and for ignorance a storm. But that eschatology was originally neutral from the religious point of view, is shown by the fact that in Nordic conceptions the gods themselves are drawn into the process of the final world catastrophe. Nevertheless, the triumph of religion over eschatology is also visible here, since in the battle with the wolf Fenrir, in which Odin is defeated, Odin's son Widar is victorious. Through this victory 'the concept of divinity is saved and with the victory the values are preserved which were associated with the gods' (Olrik).

d. The end of the world is not the last word in eschatology. The end of the world leads to the *renewal of the world.* Different themes underlie this idea. First of all, man could not permanently abandon his belief in the continued existence of the circumstances and environment in which he lived. There is also a powerful feeling of self-assertion, reaching out beyond a negative conclusion. But finally, there is the inextinguishable urge for happiness which makes it impossible for man to look forward merely to decline and extermination. And this urge is nourished and strengthened by his experience of nature, which after its death in the winter is restored to new life in the spring. After the end of the world, ought there not to be a universal spring? And just as the sun and stars of heaven go down and rise again, ought not a new sun to shine upon a world made young again? This point can sometimes give rise to reflection, leading to the idea of a succession of world catastrophes and world renewals occurring in strict rotation at the end of each epoch (especially in India). Another favourite theme of eschatology, giving it a distinctive direction, is that of national ambition, especially in the expectation of a future ideal kingdom. Thus amongst the American Indians we find the belief proclaimed by the chief and shaman of the Paiute Tavibo. When his tribe had to retreat before the coming of the white men, he went into the mountains to receive a revelation. He came back with the message that the earth would swallow the white men up; all their possessions would fall to the Red Indians. When this seemed unbelievable to them, he received a second revelation, according to which every one would be swallowed up, but the Red Indians would be restored to new life. When his adherents were possessed by doubt, he proclaimed that only those who believed his message would rise again. The idea is often that of a king who brings salvation, and who inaugurates this future kingdom; when these conceptions are transferred into the spiritual sphere, such a figure can develop more and more into a universal saviour (*cf.* II below). It is also possible for the introduction of moral ideas to have a decisive effect on the form taken by the concepts of the renewed world, and to lead to a differentiation between heaven and hell, while in the original picture of what is to come it may perhaps have been thought sufficient to present a mere continuation of the present conditions of life upon earth, though in a more exalted and more pleasant form. At the same time, however, the differentiation in the world to come also corresponds to a natural desire for moral rewards, and at this point an act of judgement may be introduced to make a decision on this, either immediately after the death of an individual or in a general judgement which assumes the resurrection at the end of time. Finally, eschatology can culminate in a belief in the ultimate conquest of all evil (*apocatastasis*, the restoration of all things) as in Parseéism.

e. Where eschatology exists amongst primitive people, one must ask in some cases whether, or to what degree, conceptions from a higher religion, either from Islam, Buddhism or in particular from Christianity, perhaps through the teaching of missionaries, may perhaps have influenced it. Nevertheless there is no lack of *traces of indigenous eschatological belief even amongst primitive peoples* (see above). The example of this usually given is that of the Andaman Islanders, who believe that their dead, dwelling in the gloomy underworld, will one day shake the palm tree that supports the earth, until the earth is overturned, when they will take the place of the living, and live again without sickness and death. In itself the growth of an eschatological belief of this kind is possible anywhere where natural catastrophes can inspire the imagination to a similar degree. In fact such conceptions can arise in complete independence from one another, because the same spiritual forces are at work in different parts of the world. But there still remains the possibility of the borrowing of ideas, either the general conception of a future end of the world, or of the eventual renewal of the world, or else of individual themes. The study of these matters has barely begun. With regard to the Nordic conceptions of the end of the world (*ragnarök*), Axel Olrik has already carried out a detailed analysis. He is led to the conclusion that they are partly of heathen and partly of Christian origin, and contain a mixture of genuine Nordic and foreign conceptions: a Western Celtic group (the struggle between the gods) and an Eastern-German, Finnish, Caucasian, Tartar, and Persian group (the *fimbul*-winter, the setting loose of the monster). A much disputed question is that of the dependence of Israelite and Jewish eschatology on that of the ancient East, either Babylonian or Egyptian eschatology on the one hand, and Persian on the other.

In the sections that follow we shall attempt to give a brief thematic summary of the principal non-biblical eschatological conceptions.

2. *Signs of the End*

If it is accepted that the origin of eschatology lies in the experience of terrifying natural catastrophes, then it is inevitable that natural events of this sort be regarded as *signs of the approaching end*. But they form only one part of a general belief in omens prophesying disaster, so that wherever any kind of eschatological belief existed, other things, such as disorder in human life, and also startling occurrences in the animal world, could be seen as pointing to the approach of the end of the world. Thus we hear of inhabitants of Greenland who expected it after an eclipse of the moon, or on an occasion when the sun did not shine brightly and the sea was disturbed, and because in addition they had seen geese flying north at an unusual time of the year. Indians feared the extinguishing of the eternal fire which sustained them. In an almost systematic way a belief in an ominous decline in the power of the earth and of man was developed in India. Thus the *Viṣṇu Purāṇa* (VI, 3 f.) tells us that at the end of a thousand periods of four eras each the life force of the earth will be almost exhausted. There will then be a complete failure of crops, which will last one hundred years. All living beings will grow weak from lack of nourishment and finally die. Then the eternal *Viṣṇu* will take on the form of Rudra the destroyer, and climb down 'to unite all creatures with himself'. This weakening of the human race is portrayed in many countries and in many different ways. People become only a yard high (Mongolia) or only an inch high, or so small that two men can stand together in a wooden shoe and thresh corn (Denmark), while horses are no bigger than hares. Men live a bare ten years (Mongolia). This physical decline is accompanied by a moral decline. Thus the Indian *Mahābhārata* reads: 'Men mostly speak falsehood; there is only a trace left of sacrifice, generosity and pious vows ... the twice born, that is the Brahmans, take gifts from princes who are unjust and tainted with the murder of Brahmans; fathers of families are thieves; the disciples of Brahmans lead a wicked life in the hermitages and fornicate with their master's wives. The hermitages are filled with many heretics'. Similarly in Persia we find the following statement: 'All men become deceivers, good friends take up quarrels against each other; respect, love and care for the soul will leave the world; the love of the father will turn away from the son, and that of the brother from his brother, and the mother will be estranged from the daughter' (*Bahman Yasht*). In the *Völuspá* it is not so much the increasing wrongdoing of mankind as that of the gods which directly precedes the end. The signs familiar from the gospels (Matt. 24.10 ff.; Luke 21.16 ff.) of increasing disorder and civil conflict seem, for example, to have influenced Circassian sagas.

Islam reckoned nine 'signs of the last judgement', while medieval Christianity reckoned fifteen.

3. The End of the World as a Result of Natural Catastrophes
a. EARTHQUAKE. We have already mentioned above that the Andaman Islanders held this belief (*cf.* 1*e.* above). It naturally occurs in areas where earthquakes are very common, such as Mexico, Peru, amongst the Indians of the Sierra Nevada in California, where the idea of a volcanic eruption is associated with it, and amongst the Lapps and the Eskimoes. Where the idea of the overturning of the earth as a result of an earthquake exists, this goes back to the experience of people living on the sea coast, who conceive of the earth as a boat floating upon the primitive oceans.

b. More frequently, however, coast dwellers expect the end of the world in the form of a *catastrophic flood*, either by the sea sweeping over the land, or by the land sinking into the sea, which both amount to the same thing; this belief is found amongst the inhabitants of Greenland, on the coast of the North Sea, in Denmark and in Iceland (in the *Völuspá*), amongst the Celts, but also amongst the Greeks (Heraclitus and the Stoics), and the Indians. According to Berosus the Babylonians expected the overwhelming of the world in a flood when the stars gathered together in Capricorn. From coast dwellers similar conceptions of the end of the world also reached those who lived inland (e.g. the inhabitants of Southern Germany). In southern lands the idea of an endless downfall of rain, causing a flood, is widespread. But even in Greenland the Angekuts say that there is a great water in heaven held back by a dam, and that this water sometimes runs over and rains down upon the earth, but that if the dam breaks the whole sky would fall in. Here this conception is linked with another widespread idea of the end of the world—see *c.*

c. This idea of *the falling in of the sky* is found not only among the Eskimoes, but also the Lapps and the Celts; according to the Lapps, the Pole Star, which holds the sky up, will be struck by an arrow, so that the sky collapses. Strabo (VIII, 3,8) tells that the ambassadors of the Celts answered a question by Alexander the Great about what they most feared, by saying that the only thing they feared was that the sky should fall in.

d. A related idea is that of *the falling of the stars.* Thus the *Völuspá* says: 'The bright stars fall from heaven', while the Persian *Bundahish* (XIII, 17 ff.) states: 'When Gocihar (probably a meteor) falls from a ray of the moon on to the earth, the earth will be as afraid as a sheep when a wolf falls upon it. Then the fire will melt the metal', etc., *cf.* Matt. 24.29. Perhaps it is in fact the moon which falls upon earth: this is the Persian belief.

e. The Persians also believed in *the darkening of the moon and sun*, or else their disappearance, and there is evidence of a similar belief amongst the Indians, Lithuanians, and the people of Southern Germany, etc.

f. A particularly frequent belief is that of the end of the world as the result of a *fire*. Perhaps it is in fact a fallen star (*cf. d.* above), which kindles this fire. Belief in a fire burning up the world is also found amongst North American tribes, in Peru and Mexico, but principally in Asia and Europe. Berosus testifies to the belief in Babylon that the earth will burn when all the stars, which now follow different courses, come together in Cancer. Besides the *Mahābhārata* a principal source for this belief is the *Viṣṇu Purāṇa* (VI 3 f.) *Viṣṇu*, taking on the form of the destroyer Rudra, descends (*cf.* 2. above); he enters the seven rays of light, drinks up all the water and causes all the moisture on the earth, in living creatures and in the ground to evaporate. Nourished thus by his help with abundant moisture, the seven rays of the sun increase to become seven suns, whose rays shine from every direction

and set on fire the three worlds, together with the underworld . . . the destroyer of all things becomes the burning
breath of the world-serpent *Seṣa* and thereby reduces the
underworld to ashes. But when the mighty fire has burnt
up every part of the underworld, it moves on to the earth
and destroys the earth as well. A further whirlwind of
flame then spreads through the realm of the air and up
into the heaven where the gods dwell. Perhaps independently of the Indians, to whom the fire kindled by the
sun must be attributed as a theme drawn from nature,
the Persians held the conception of a glowing stream of
metal flowing out from a volcano and burning up the
earth. The Parsees transformed this into the idea of the
mighty fire of ordeal through which the judgement between the pious and the godless would be carried out
at the last day (for a Jewish parallel *cf.* Mal. 3.2 ff. 19;
Enoch 1.6 f.; 102.1 f.), while later on this became increasingly to be regarded as a fire of purification, bringing about the renewal of the whole world. Amongst the
Greeks the world-conflagration seems more to have been
a doctrine of the philosophers (Heraclitus, the Stoics)
than a popular belief. Thus in the *Timaeus* of Plato we
read: 'The story is told amongst you (the Greeks) that
there was once a certain Phaeton, the son of Helios,
who harnessed his father's chariot, but because he did
not understand how to drive along the path his father
followed, burned up everything on the earth and himself
was struck down by the blaze. This story itself sounds
like a myth, but the truth that lies behind it is that after
the elapse of certain long periods a change will take place
in the movement of the heavenly bodies surrounding the
earth, with the destruction of everything upon earth by
an enormous fire. Then all who live on mountains, and
in elevated and dry places, will be destroyed to a greater
extent than the dwellers in the rivers and the sea'. The
Celts may have obtained similar conceptions of the end of

the world from the Greeks. In Nordic countries only the
Völuspá speaks of a universal conflagration; but apart
from this there is the fire of Surt, which burns down the
dwelling of the Ases. In the South German *Muspilli* we
already find a variation on Judaeo-Christian ideas of the
end of the world: 'When the blood of Elias drops upon
the earth, the mountains burn up, the trees do not stand
any longer upon earth. Water dries up, the swamp is
swallowed up, the sky burns up in fire, the moon falls,
the round earth burns', etc.

g. By contrast, in regions which suffer severely from the
cold of the winter, the idea of *destruction by cold* occurs.
'When the world grows old, the summers become cold',
is a proverb found in the Upper Palatinate. The classic
expression of this idea is the *fimbul*-winter of the Nordic
peoples, to which the cold of ancient times is regarded as
a parallel (*cf.* the *Vafthrudnismál*: 'As the ice-cold drops
of the sea grew hard in the cold, the first form took shape'),
and this theme also occurs in Iranian literature, where
the second millennium of world history includes a great
winter: 'Thus out of a thousand people in the world,
only one will remain, trees and bushes will all grow dry
and every four-footed animal will die.' This corresponds
to the order of Ahura Mazda to Yima in the earliest
age, to build a fold to protect his followers against the
onset of winter (though in fact in the Yima saga this
theme seems to have belonged to the final expectation).

4. The End of the World Brought about by Living Agents
This follows quite naturally from the preceding ideas, insofar as it is a habit of mythical thought to conceive of
purely natural events as the actions of living beings (*cf.*
1*b.* above). Thus a being to which the earthquake (3*a.*),
the darkness of the sun and the moon (3*e.*), or any other
of the catastrophes mentioned above were attributed,
only needed to attain freedom and power in order to

bring about the ultimate end of the world. Beings of this nature are the serpent *Śeṣa* of the Indians, mentioned in 3*f.* above, but especially the serpent *Azhi Dahak* of the Persians, which sleeps in the Demawend, is awakened and freed from its chains by Angro Mainyu, until it falls in the battle against the good god or his heroes, and also the dragon called the *Lindwurm* in the North, which came out of the mountains to destroy mankind, the cow *Urko* in Sweden, the wolf *Fenrir* of Nordic mythology, the seven dogs of the Tartars, at whose barking 'the end draws near to all men, animals and birds' (*cf.* the dog *Garm* of the ancient Germans). Often the monster appears in human form like the Australian *Buddai*, the giant of the Caucasus, the South Arabian volcano giant *Chikk*, and *Typhon*, of whom it was said that Sicily would be destroyed when he broke out. In *Pegu* (Burma) the sixty foot long image of a sleeping deity is displayed. The natives believe that he has lain there for six thousand years; but once he awakes, the end of the world will come. Amongst the Germans it was *Loki* who would one day lead vast armies out to the battle of Ragnarök. And this leads on to the idea of great *battles* at the end of the world, fought either by men, by gods, or by both together, as in Nordic mythology, which tells of the fall of the king of the gods and his avenging, in Celtic mythology, but especially in that of Persia, where the decisive battle between the powers of good and of evil leads to the final victory of the good god Ahura Mazda.

5. *The Renewal of the World*

That belief in a time of future happiness exists even amongst primitive peoples can be seen from the example of the *Andaman Islanders* mentioned above (*1e.*). We meet it again in the form in which one man or several succeed in escaping the catastrophe, to become the fathers of a race which lives on under much happier conditions. This of course must be distinguished from ideas about the state of the individual after death, which in general has always been the subject of a much more lively concern. It is natural that at first the eschatological future should be seen as taking place under purely earthly conditions. Thus in India, the *Mahābhārata* describes it as follows: When the sun, the moon, Jupiter and a star meet in Cancer, the *Krtayuga* returns. The thunder clouds give rain at the right time, the stars shine, the planets move in their right courses and fruitfulness and prosperity reign. A Brahman called *Viṣnuyaśas* appears, and rules over the earth as a just and victorious king, exterminating the hordes of the barbarians. And after he has destroyed all robbers, he hands the earth over to the Brahmans, and when everything has been brought within the bounds laid down by the Creator he goes back to live the life of a hermit in the forest. A new golden age begins, and all the four castes fulfil their own tasks. *Buddhism* presents a similar picture of the renewal of the world in its doctrine of the world eras (*kalpas*), which alternate with one another. In *Persia*, as in Nordic countries, we meet the idea that the destruction of the world which is taking place is prevented by the intervention of a great champion, which prepares the way for the development of a new world and a new humanity. Amongst the Persians it is *Saoshyant* who with his assistants restores all the dead to life and gives to everyone the reward he has deserved, according to his acts. Then, after the great battle and victory of Ahura Mazda, there takes place according to his will the renewal of the worlds, and the purified universe becomes immortal and eternal, and the earth becomes a plain without ice, and without hills and valleys (*Bundahish* 30,32 f.). The expectation of this renewal of the world, to be brought about through a great ordeal of fire, obviously alternated with the idea found in the saga of Yima (*cf.* 3g. above), which still maintained its influence, of a universal spring following a universal winter. In a similar way to Saoshyant, in the *Manichaeism* the return of the Friend of Light, the 'Third Ancient', sets in motion the process which leads to the gathering together of all the elements of light in the highest sphere. Modern *Bahai* religion looks forward to a new age characterized by the universal love of all mankind. In Nordic religion, after the *fimbul*-winter, the earth is cleansed by the cold, the sun shines on it, and it is ready to receive new inhabitants. These come out of the forests, where they have found shelter during the terrible winter. A new race, descended from the single human pair Líf and Leifthrasir, populates the earth. The world of the gods is renewed just as completely on the same basis as before.

There is much dispute as to how far *Babylon* and *Egypt* possessed any hope of salvation which may possibly have influenced Israelite ideas. For Babylon Berosus describes the alternation of the decline and renewal of the world in the alternation of the ages. Apart from this, it is the omen literature which provides the principal evidence for the idea of a time of blessedness in contrast to an accursed period, and it seems to have been a favourite practice to make use of the description of this period of blessedness when a new king came to the throne, in order to greet him as a redeemer who would prepare the way for a new age, while the description of the accursed time must have been used to remind the king of the misfortune which would face him if his rule was bad. From *Egypt* we have prophecies by a priest under King Snefru (ca. 2950), from the period 2000-1800; the prophecies of a lamb under King Bokchoris (ca. 720), the prophecies of a potter under King Amenophis from the third century A.D., going back perhaps in their substance to the eighteenth dynasty. The first of these, for example, describes the time of distress, and goes on to tell of a redeemer king coming from the South, or of a (Nubian) woman (?), who unites the separated Egyptian kingdoms, puts all his enemies to shame and quietens all unrest. The people at the time of this 'son of a man' will be glad to recall his name for all eternity. Truth will once again return to its dwelling places, while deceit will be cast out. Those in misery will be relieved, etc. The second, which is unfortunately very fragmentary, begins in the same way with a description of the wretched condition of Egypt, to be followed by a great transformation, as a result of a successful campaign by the men of Egypt against Assyria. The fragments of the first half of the third text likewise speak of 'unhappy Egypt'. But then the beloved king appears, and the city of 'those who wear girdles' (?) is made desolate because of the lawlessness they have practised against Egypt. The blessedness that comes to Egypt is so great that those who survive wish that those who have already died could rise again to share in it. The calendar, which has fallen into disorder is put right again. The sun, which has grown dark, shines bright once again, etc. It is particularly noteworthy that here the cosmic powers share in the catastrophe. The 'messianic' interpretation of a fourth text: '*The Warnings of a Wise Man of Egypt to a King*', from about 1300 B.C., is at the moment too uncertain to permit any extended conclusions to be drawn from it. In general, the fragmentary character of the texts we possess means that great care has to be exercised in interpreting and applying them; but the importance which they may have in the rise of Israelite eschatology leads us on to the particular study of the eschatology of the Old Testament.

Alfred Bertholet

II. ESCHATOLOGY IN THE OLD TESTAMENT AND JUDAISM

1. The Beginning and the End of History

Eschatology deals with the last things. Like the accounts of the earliest times and the creation, the conceptions of eschatology are not meant to be judged by the standards of earthly reality. Rather, both groups of ideas belong to the world of faith; the roots of both lie in religion. Thus there are similarities between the description of the *beginning of history* (*cf.* Gen. 1.1; Isa. 46.10) and the *end of history* (*cf.* Gen. 49.1; Isa. 2.1; etc.) in the Old Testament. But in Hebrew accounts of the beginning of history and of eschatology, the observation of nature and the observation of history play a different role. In the accounts of creation and the beginning of history, the question of the origin of man is of course dealt with, rather from the natural than from the historical point of view. By contrast, the principal theme of eschatology is the destiny of Israel; the historical idea far outweighs mythical features, even though the final phase of historical time is portrayed in images drawn from nature. This is due to the fact that the description of the beginning draws its figures and images almost entirely from non-Israelite conceptions, amongst which Babylonian and Aryan elements can be clearly distinguished, while the final phase of history, as it is described in the Old Testament, is very much a peculiarly Israelite conception, to which any foreign material (*cf.* I above) has been fully assimilated. The eschatology of the Old Testament is therefore a distinctively Israelite creation. The Hebrew mind was seized from the first by the future hope, just as the prophetic impulse was peculiar to Israel. Thus it is a false approach to attempt to interpret Hebrew eschatology on the basis of foreign conceptions; any analogies that may exist in neighbouring countries are not to be regarded as giving rise to the Israelite view. The only decisive outside contribution to the form later taken by Hebrew eschatology was that of the Persians; Canaanite or Accadian eschatology can scarcely be said to come into the question (*cf.* I above).

2. *The elements of Israelite Eschatology*

The reign of David was a decisive moment in the development of eschatology. With regard to the future king, the *messianic element* was understood at that time in a different sense. It is true that the messianic king only appears in Judaean prophecies, and is unknown in the prophecy of the Northern Kingdom; for David *redivivus*, who is to return to Israel, is a later interpolation in Hosea 3.5. But in Judaea David provided the original pattern for the messianic king. This expectation probably goes back to David himself; for his 'last words' (2 Sam. 23.1-7) seem to be very ancient in origin and consequently can be ascribed to him. They are complemented by the well-known prophecy that David should not build a house for Yahweh, but Yahweh for David (2 Sam. 7.11*b*.,27), which in its present context is uttered by Nathan, but in the original version was regarded as being uttered by David himself (2 Sam. 7.4*a*,5*b*.,11*b*β,12,14,18, 19,27*a*.). From David there is to descend a royal line which is guaranteed by an eternal covenant (2 Sam. 23.5). The king at any time is regarded as the adopted son of Yahweh, and calls Yahweh his father, even if he suffers the chastisement of God (2 Sam. 7,14). But the perfect king whom David describes in his last words seems to be the last member of this line of kings. He is just in the sight of men, because he is guided by the fear of God, and he brings the light of morning to the country like the rising sun (2 Sam. 23.4). The origin of the royal oracles of the prophets, which became the centre of the future hope in Jewish prophecy, is to be sought in this Davidic picture of the Messiah.

The expectation of the *promised land* by the people of God is even older than the idea of the messianic king. As early as the work of Moses, with his unwavering vision of the land where 'milk and honey flows', and his plan to lead Israel to Canaan, which, in spite of what Wellhausen says, must be regarded as part of the original substance of the Mosaic tradition, an eschatological idea can be perceived. But a view of history with an increasing emphasis upon a vision of the future seems to be less a heritage of the Israel-Leah tribes, from which Moses was descended, than of the Jacob-Rachel tribes, of which the principal representative was Joseph. For the patriarchal saga has its origin amongst the Rachel tribes, as is clear from the material common both to the Yahwist and the Elohist. In this patriarchal saga, especially in its Elohist version, faith in the future constantly reappears as a fixed and basic part of the tradition from Abraham (Gen. 15) to Isaac (Gen. 27), Jacob (Gen. 28) and Joseph (Gen. 37); while in the oracles of Balaam it is referred to all Israel (Num. 23 f.). The patriarch looks forward to a flourishing future for his tribe in a land of blessedness (Gen. 27; 28 f.; 48.21 f.; 49.22 ff.; Deut. 33.13 ff.), and Joseph is distinguished from his brothers as the one consecrated to lead his people's holy war. These Elohistic visions of the future can still be traced in Hosea (Hosea 2.23 ff.); they had made a deep impression upon the mind of the northern Israelites. One can also see from them that the principal theme of the earliest Hebrew eschatology was *happiness*, not misfortune. It was the great prophets who first added the idea of judgement, by conceiving of the necessity of the fall of the historical Israel before the new age could begin.

Eschatology

While the second Yahwist oracle of Balaam (Num. 24.16 f.) can present the Davidic kingdom as the climax of the national development, the Yahwist oracle of Jacob concerning Judah (Gen. 49.8-12) looks towards a wider future. For beyond the period of Judah's hegemony over his brothers, which came about when David and Solomon ruled, there can be seen a future in which a messianic ruler will reign. His rule will be extended over the nations, while Judaea will flow with wine and milk. After the division of the kingdom, the greatest national misfortune (Isa. 7.17), the hope of the perfect restoration of the nation retreated more and more into the messianic future (Amos 9.11 f.; Isa. 9.5 f.; 16.5; Ezek. 37.15 ff.). But besides this, the question of the opposition between natural law and the law of God was raised in the course of the conflict between the kings and the prophets, and the people as a whole were involved in this dispute from the time of Elijah on. Thus even at the period of the earliest prophets *the idea of judgement* came to form part of the vision of the future. From now on this theme dominates the idea of the future held by the great prophets both in northern Israel and in Judah, up to the time of the destruction of Samaria and Jerusalem. Eschatology now takes on the moral and religious feeling which gives it its compelling force. The *day of the Lord* (Amos 5.18), which according to popular belief brings the victory of Yahweh in a judgement upon his enemies, is not light but darkness. For Israel had made itself the enemy of God and had consequently fallen under the judgement of God. This coming judgement is portrayed in numerous images from nature and from history, so that the prophesying of salvation threatens to disappear behind the disaster which is imminent. The people as a whole will be destroyed in God's judgement and only a *remnant* will be saved. In this remnant, for which the judgement will

233

bring not destruction but purification, the people of God, to whom the messianic age is to be revealed, grow towards the future.

3. Hosea and Amos

In *classical prophecy before the exile* these three themes, the messianic king, the blessed nation in the promised land, and the judgement, are clearly the principal concern of the prophets, though not every one presents them all with equal force. The most ancient vision of the future is that of *Hosea*, where the ideas of the Messiah and the remnant are lacking, so that it is the nation as a whole which receives judgement and salvation. He is concerned of course not with the final destiny of Judah (*cf.* 4.15; 5.10; 12; 6.11), but only with that of the northern kingdom of Israel. Nevertheless, the personality of the nation is portrayed with an astonishing passion and intensity. There is in Yahweh's encounter with Israel a tragedy of love, which as the result of Israel's breach of faith has brought about her downfall, and from which she is finally rescued by the infinitely merciful and unconquerable love of Yahweh. Everything is referred here to the communion of love between God and his people, and because this communion of love has been broken, every sorrow and suffering is brought down upon the guilty people, so that we find visions of judgement portrayed in terms of a powerful pathos, and telling of the downfall of Israel. But the repentance to which the nation eventually attains after its judgement (2.9; 3.5; 6.1; 14.2), makes possible their redemption. The future communion of love between God and Israel is likened to an everlasting betrothal (2.21 ff.), from which all sensuous features have been removed. The end will come in a flourishing land, blessed by heaven and earth with corn and wine—we see the recurrence of the Elohist images of the future; or else Israel is likened to the garden of Paradise, in the midst of which Yahweh stands as the tree of life (14.6 ff., 9.). The Messiah is missing from this picture; for the idea of King David (3.5) as a ruler during the final age is taken from Ezekiel, and did not belong to the original version of Hosea. The vision which concludes the book of *Amos*, on the other hand, is that of the restoration of the fallen tabernacle of David, that is, the royal dynasty of Judah, ruling over the whole area of David's original kingdom, including Edom and the neighbouring peoples (9.11 f.). There is to be a great 'turning again' of all things (9.14), in which everything will return to its original condition, Israel will once again be established in her land, the mountains will flow with wine, the fields will bear fruit and the gardens will flourish (9.13 ff.). This ancient series of visions is similar to the Judah oracle from the time of Solomon (Gen. 49.8-12); there is no reason for not attributing it to Amos. It is true that this great restoration is not to take place until after the judgement of Israel to which the whole prophecy of Amos is devoted. This judgement, which also affects the neighbouring peoples, who are thus also subjected to the unwritten laws of God, falls hardest upon Israel; for Israel's special relationship to God as his chosen people means that their guilt is all the greater (3.2). In visions and images Amos repeatedly describes how the fall of Israel is inevitable. However, he still considers as a possibility that God may have mercy on the remnant of Joseph (5.15); thus the idea of the remnant is also found in his work. By the promise of life as a reward to those who seek God and try to do good (5.4; 6.15), he means by life not merely the preservation of their existence but the experience of inner blessedness which flows from piety and morality, an experience which the prophet himself has known. A small group of the living will escape the fate of death, from which the people will grow up towards the final salvation that will appear at the end of time (9.11 ff.).

4. Isaiah

The fundamental themes of eschatology are found in their most forceful and frequent expression in *Isaiah*. The kingdom, the nation and the judgement appear in his writings in many different relationships. Whereas after the vision in which he was called to prophesy (Ch. 6), with its fundamental distinction between the holiness and glory of God and human guilt and insignificance, the principal emphasis is on the idea of judgement, it is accompanied and modified after his encounter with Ahaz in the year 735 by the idea of salvation, which serves to preserve the balance. In order to bring the young king back to the faith which is the sole basis of his historical and religious existence, he offers him a miracle from heaven or from hell (7.10 ff.). When the king refuses the miracle, God threatens him through the prophet with the miracle of *Emmanuel* (7.14). 'God with us' is a king raised up in opposition to Ahaz, inaugurating the messianic kingdom, while Judah disappears as a political entity. As his name signifies, he brings a communion with God to the small group of the faithful. Of course his birth will follow a period of profound national suffering, in which he will decide for the good in the conflict between good and evil. Thus this figure is a hopeful promise to the faithful, but a threat to the king and the state, at a time when the national independence was being bartered away to Assyria. The Emmanuel oracle is accompanied by the nativity oracle (9.1-6), and the Jesse oracle (11.1-9), which were probably composed not much later. In these passages the figure of the Messiah appears out of a period of gloom, either in the form of the light which suddenly shines out in the darkness, when Yahweh has struck his blow against Assyria, at night, and away from human eyes (9.1 ff.), or else when the king springs up as a young shoot from the stump of the fallen royal tree (11.1 ff.), or else when he founds from David's throne the kingdom of righteousness, after the destruction of unrighteousness and violence (16.4*b*,5). His supernatural nature is characterized in the nativity oracle by the names 'Wonderful Counsellor, Mighty God, Everlasting Father, Prince of Peace' (9.5); in the Jesse oracle his being is indwelt by the spirit of Yawheh, which expresses itself in the three groups of double qualities, wisdom and understanding, counsel and might, knowledge and the fear of the Lord, so that supernatural and spiritual effects proceed from him (11.1 ff.). His rule will extend through the throne of David to the whole of Israel (9.5 f.; 16.5), so that he is the fulfilment of the Davidic oracle (2 Sam. 23.1 ff.). Then comes the inauguration of the kingdom of righteousness and justice which David longed for, and the powers of evil sink into the abyss, their mission fulfilled.

But besides the image of the Messiah, the *image of the temple* also occurs in Isaiah's eschatology. In the vision in which his calling took place Isaiah saw Yahweh in the temple of Jerusalem, where the darkness grew light to him. The consciousness remained with him that this was the earthly dwelling-place of Yahweh (8.18). From the beginning he nursed the hope that a part of the people, however small, would be saved, as is shown by the name of his son Shearjashub, 'a remnant shall return' (7.3). Only a remnant will return, but a remnant there will be. The starting point of this new development lay in his own family, in which a living seed was being separated from the chaff of the dying nation. When he withdrew into silence after his breach with Ahaz and built up a community of disciples, who were to be the pledge of the future people of God, the temple seems to have been the place around which this community of believers gathered (8.16-18). The poor of the people of God shall find refuge upon Mount Zion (11.5;14.32). At a later period this idea was developed into the well-known oracle concerning the corner-stone upon Zion (28.16). Yahweh is building there a new, invisible temple, which we are to think of as growing out of the forms of the visible temple. From the slogan that the believer shall not be in haste, we may conclude that the idea is of a community of believers built up inwardly according to the rule and standard of justice and righteousness (28.17*a*.). In this temple community there is built up a people of God which will survive even in the judgement, while the policy of the opponents of the prophet will be confounded. But just as the temple is the centre of the community of believers, so it is also to become the central point of all nations. The oracle to the Ethiopians (ca. 715) already expresses the hope that when the victory of God has come about they will bring presents to the temple, to express their allegiance (18.7). Even more profound is the temple oracle 2.2-5, which probably forms part of Isaiah's last revelations. According to this, at the end of the ages the temple of Yahweh will be lifted up on high from its mountain, so that from the mountain of God it will shine far out into all countries. Foreign nations will come as pilgrims to it from every direction, in order to receive there the law of God as the basis for their own way of life. This law of God will finally bring about peace amongst nations. While the image of the Messiah is purely national, the image of the temple enshrines a message for the whole of world history.

5. *The Seventh Century*

As the historical struggle died down *in the seventh century*, after Judah had become an Assyrian vassal state, the eschatological tension also grew less. It is still very strong in *Micah* about the turn of the century; it is here that the historical themes of the time of Isaiah are still most clearly recognizable. The messianic king from the family of Ephrahthah from which David was also descended (1 Sam. 17.12), appears as the redeemer of Israel after a time of the utmost distress, in which the temple of Jerusalem is destroyed (Micah 5.1-4*a*,5*b*; *cf.* 3.12). Like Solomon, he brings with him salvation (v. 4*a*), after he has saved Israel from Assyria (v. 5*b*). In his peaceful kingdom, which is to extend to the horizon (5.3), neither earthly nor supernatural powers will avail any more (5.9-13). Three quarters of a century later (ca. 625) in Zephaniah, the day of Yahweh's wrath, of which the hordes of the Scythians are regarded as being a preparation, is associated with elements which form a threat to the whole world as part of the judgement of God (Zeph. 1.2 f., 14 ff.). While the messianic king is missing from the portrayal of the future, the pious remnant enshrines the future hope. As in Isaiah it is the meek who are called to follow righteousness and humility, and again as in Isaiah the heathen nations will call upon Yahweh in the future with consecrated lips, while in Jerusalem a poor and lowly remnant of the people will survive the judgement, and, as the people of God, do no more evil (3.12 f.), and Yahweh will rule in the midst of them as king (3.16). Nor does the Messiah play any notable part in *Jeremiah*, the Hosea of Judah (23.5 f.; 30.21); instead, it is the people as a whole who are destined to rise again in the end after the fall, which is now to overwhelm Judah as well, and is portrayed in powerful images (Ch. 4-6); and this is true both of the northern kingdom of Israel (3.19 ff.; 31.1-5,14 ff.) and of Judah (30.10 ff., 17 ff.; 32-1 ff.). Meanwhile, the ancient Mosaic idea of the covenant had been brought into circulation again by Deuteronomy (Deut. 17.2; *cf.* 2 Kings 23.2 f., 21), and by the renewed unity given to the nation by the reform of *Josiah*. Jeremiah took the idea of the covenant into his picture of the future; for he proclaims that after the downfall of the old covenant there will be a new covenant, not written upon tables of stone but on the heart, and that Yahweh will be the God of Israel, and Israel the people of God (31.31-

3; *cf.* Hosea 2.25). The will of God is to be realized in the nation not through outward force, but by an inner compulsion, and the people will consist henceforth of active individuals each attaining spontaneously to the knowledge of God (31.34).

6. Deutero-Isaiah

The climax of classical prophecy is found in *Deutero-Isaiah* (Isa. 40-55; 57.14 ff.; 60-6). In his original eschatology, which takes the whole of world history into its scope, it is Cyrus of Persia who is regarded as the Messiah (Isa. 45.1), since as ruler of the world-empire he breaks the bonds and allows the kingdom of God to develop freely within it. In this world-wide vision the special relationship between Yahweh and Israel is maintained. It can in fact be seen from the history of the shattered nation of Israel, that Yahweh has shown himself to be the true God, for his prophecy has come true; he is the God who rules throughout space and time. His holiness and righteousness demand a judgement upon wrongdoing. But this God who rules over the whole world as the holy one, who alone is God (44.6), and the righteous one, whose victory maintains the balance of the universe, is also the redeemer of Israel (Isa. 41.14; 43.1, 14; 44.6.22 f., 24 etc.). It is Deutero-Isaiah who first made the concept of *redemption* the central theme of the future of Israel. The redemption out of Egypt is compared to the redemption from Babylon, on which is based the divine ordinance of freedom as the basis of the eternal covenant of peace (54.10; 50.5; 55.3; 61.8). Jeremiah's oracle of the new covenant reappears again here; in the new covenant the promises of grace made to David are fulfilled in the whole nation (55.3 f.). This eschatology was later expanded and made more profound in the poems concerning the pious *servant of Yahweh* (42.1-7; 49.1-7; 50.4-10; 52.13 f.; 53.1 ff.; 61.1-3). The servant of God, related to the figure of Jeremiah as a work of art to its model, is certainly a messianic figure (42.1; 61.1), but is not so much a king as a prophet, working as a preacher and pastor amongst Israelites and the heathen (42.1-4). It is his destiny to be both an incarnation of the covenant of God with Israel (42.6) and to be a light to the heathen (49.6). His death has an atoning significance (Ch. 53); when he is risen from the dead he proclaims the redemption and the onset of the acceptable year of the Lord (61.1 ff.).

The principal effects of the work of Deutero-Isaiah can be seen in the *Psalms*, which draw in part on his language and his spirit. The *enthronement hymns* (Pss. 47.93 ff.) in which Yahweh is celebrated as king over the whole world, can be regarded as eschatological psalms. It is possible that they may have been sung at the New Year, forming a parallel to the songs of the Babylonian New Year feast; but they are set in an eschatological context, for they celebrate Yahweh 'when he comes to judge the earth'. In this context can also be placed some of the *royal* psalms, especially Ps. 2, which assumes the rule of God over all the nations of the earth. At the last day, when the troubles of the end are taking place, the son of God appears as king upon Mount Zion, and power over the world is given to him. By contrast, Ps. 72 places an earthly king in an eschatological context; in Ps. 110 he does not bear the title of king, but that of priest (v. 4), and therefore he must presumably be the high priest whose princely function culminates in the final victory at the last day over the enemies. But in the psalms the messianic age does not ordinarily depend upon a king who is to rule in the last days, but upon the great 'return' of all things, when Yahweh shall bring about the redemption of his people, and for which Ps. 126 is the classic example.

7. *Canonical Apocalyptic*

With Ezekiel, whose work was carried out in exile, begins the *apocalyptic period of eschatology*. The historical outlines grow faded; an abyss appears between this world and the next; above this earth there appears a transcendental world which in the course of time becomes filled with numerous historical figures. As Ezekiel himself was a priest, this apocalyptic eschatology seems to have its roots in priestly circles; they were more open to foreign influence than classical prophecy. Ezekiel's first period (up to 586) is almost entirely taken up by visions of judgement in which Judaea perishes. There are only rare mentions of the hope that the messianic prince will come (21.32), like the young cedar shoot from an ancient trunk, planted upon the mountains of Israel to grow up into a tree spreading wide its branches (17.22 ff.). But after the destruction of Jerusalem, when everything lay in hopeless ruins, he prophesied the return of David in the messianic kingdom (34.23 ff.; 37.22 ff.). Then, as in Jeremiah and Deutero-Isaiah, the divine covenant of peace will persist as an eternal covenant (34.25; 37.26); Israel will live in a fruitful land (34.26 f.), a free and united people (37.15 ff.), after she has been cleansed from her sins and has received a new heart and a new spirit (36. 22 ff.). That it is David himself who is to reign, and not a descendant of his, follows from Ezekiel's belief in the resurrection, according to which all Israel will rise from the grave (37.1-14); this brings a completely new element into eschatology. The vision of the temple (Ch. 40-48) and its cult, which still includes sin and guilt offerings (44.29), must be regarded as a preliminary to this final condition, unless the two series of images are to be seen as independent and parallel. The influence of Ezekiel's thought can be widely traced throughout the post-exilic period.

In *Haggai* the messianic hope is associated with the

appearance of Zerubbabel (2.20 ff.), the true descendant of David (*cf.* Ezek. 17.22 ff.), but is also closely linked with the restoration of the temple (1.1 ff.) as the seat of the majesty of Yahweh (1.15*b*; 2.1 ff.), with whose entry into the temple the time of salvation begins (Ezek. 43.1 ff.). This is also of importance for the heathen world outside Israel. The building of the temple, with Zerubbabel as the chief builder (4.6-10), and Joshua as its priest (Ch. 3), is also of importance in Zachariah; both are presented as the anointed of Yahweh (4.1-6*a*,10*b* ff.), and so are of equal rank. Though there seems to be an expectation here of the immediate commencement of the final age after Jeremiah's seventy years (Zach. 1.12 f.; Jer. 29.10), after the abdication of Zerubbabel this vanishes into the distant future, so that the high priest Joshua, with the priesthood as a whole, is now regarded as the pattern and pledge of the Messiah (3.8-10; 6.9 ff.). When guilt and wickedness have been removed from Canaan (Ch. 5), then Yahweh's spirit will extend as a pentecostal spirit over the whole earth (6.1-8), so that the heathen world can also have a part in the religion of Yahweh (8.18 ff.).

In *Malachi* the call to repentance in face of the approaching end grows more urgent. The messenger of the covenant (3.1), who is perhaps to be identified with Moses (3.22) or Elijah (3.23), goes before Yahweh himself to purify the priesthood (3.3), before Yahweh appears for the final judgement (3.5 f.). While the godless are burned up, the sun of righteousness, that is, of salvation, will then rise upon those who fear God (3.19 ff.). The later the texts, the more historical features vanish from apocalyptic, while natural phenomena increase. In *Joel*, a plague of locusts (1.1-17) becomes a presage of a people descending like locusts from the north (2.18), after whose destruction salvation will begin (2.13 ff.); or again, the stars grow dark, fearful visions increase, (3.1 ff.) and the time of the spirit prepares for the end. The raging of the people against Jerusalem is brought to ruin under the judgement of Yahweh (4.9 ff.).

Whereas the prophecy of Joel, with its many obscure images, still belongs to the Persian period, Habakkuk takes up a new theme of world history with the new nation of horsemen (Hab. 1.5-11), which according to Duhm represent the Macedonians. The *world conqueror* (2.5 ff.) whose downfall is finally brought about as the result of his arrogance before God, is probably Alexander the Great. The theophany at the judgement is painted in colours recalling the storm of Sinai raging down from the south, in order to unleash itself upon the conqueror in God's promised land; similarly, in Isaiah, Ezekiel and Joel, the world power suffers judgement in Judaea (Hab. 3). But at the end of the ages there is raised up out of the judgement the Righteous One, who will live by virtue of his faithfulness (2.1-4), so that the central theme is the redemption of the devout of Israel. The same is true of Deutero-Zechariah (Zech. 9-13), an apocalypse probably from the time of the early Diadochi, in which the messianic king sets up the kingdom of peace (9.9 f.), and in which Judah and Ephraim are once again united as a single people in the struggle against the Greeks (9.11 ff., *cf.* Ch. 10). On the other hand the parable of the shepherds (11.4-14; 13.7-9, 11.15 ff.) seems to have its historical model in Josiah and Jehoiakim.

The *apocalypse of Isaiah* (Isa. 24-7) can best be understood if it is set in the period of the Diadochi. An important conception here is that of the cosmic world judgement (Ch. 24), in which the astral powers are included in the judgement, as is also the common meal eaten by the gentiles on Mount Zion (25.6-8), in the course of which the veil is taken away from their eyes and death is swallowed up. There is an explicit promise of the resurrection of Israel's dead (26.19), so that we are now approaching, albeit with uncertain and tentative steps, the apocalypse of Daniel (*cf.* Dan. 12.1). with which Old Testament eschatology comes to an end.

In the vast conception of the *Book of Daniel*, characterized by a powerful eschatological tension as a result of the approaching end of the four thousand year world epoch (cf. 9 below), world history since the time of the exile is divided into four periods, those of Babylon, Medea, Persia and Macedonia (Ch. 2; 7); the Macedonian empire is further sub-divided into the states of the Diadochi, amongst whom Egypt and Syria stand out as antagonists (Ch. 10. f.). This world-empire is opposed to the kingdom of God, which is not of earthly but of heavenly origin (2.34 ff., 44 ff.; 7.13 ff.). When it comes into being the world-empire is overcome; its realm is taken over by the kingdom of God. Israel is involved in this struggle; as long as the world-empire rules, she is oppressed; when the kingdom of God is set up, she becomes free. Those whose names are written in the book of life are saved from the messianic woes; the grandiose vision is concluded by the resurrection of the dead, a double resurrection, to eternal life and to eternal suffering. Israel is by no means identical with the kingdom of God, the origin of which is in heaven; the 'saints under the heights' or 'the saints of the Most High' are angels and not men (7,18.25 ff.); their representative is certainly formed like a Son of Man, but because he comes forth out of the depths of heaven, he is a heavenly being who will not be revealed until the last day.

8. Extra-canonical Apocalyptic

This follows the example of Daniel in making figures from previous history prophets of the future. As a result, the whole of Israel's past history is increasingly drawn into the eschatological picture, which as a result of this immediately loses its proper meaning. In addition, the historical element in eschatological imagery becomes increasingly overgrown by mythological features, which in classical prophecy had a purely ornamental function. Thus the *Book of Enoch*, with its various distinct parts, is more a mythological compilation than a prophecy. Apart from its very brief messianic conclusion (Enoch 90.37 ff.), the historical vision (Enoch 85-90) contains no eschatological material; and the Apocalypse of Weeks (Ch. 93; 91.12-17) contains in the last three 'works' eschatological ideas concerning the new temple (92.12 f.), the triumph of righteousness (v. 14), and the world judgement (v. 15 ff.), but these are wholly unoriginal. In the visions (Ch. 37-71), which in spite of all arguments to the contrary must be regarded as pre-Christian, the figure of the Son of Man is drawn from Daniel; the eschatology here does not refer to history as a whole, but to the destiny of the pious and the godless in the world to come. In the *Assumption of Moses* the persecution of the Jews by the Roman Emperors after the death of Herod the Great and his sons (Ch. 6) is awaited as a preliminary to the end (Ch. 7 f.), to continue until the last day comes, on which Israel is to be lifted aloft on eagles' wings (Ch. 9 f.). In the meantime, the beginning of Roman rule under Pompey once again aroused a longing for the Messiah of the house of David, who is looked forward to in the *Psalms of Solomon* (17.21 ff.; 18) and who also plays a part, assimilated with the Son of Man from Daniel, in the Syriac *Apocalypse of Baruch* and in the *Apocalypse of Ezra* (4 Ezra). The destruction of Jerusalem (70 A.D.) led the leaders of the unhappy nation to look forward to the end of all things. Forceful expression was given to the feeling that the youthful power of the world had decayed (*Apoc. of Baruch* 20.1 ff.; 85.10) and the end was approaching. At the end of history the Messiah will bring about the period of splendour upon earth (*Apoc. of Baruch* 29 f.), at the end of which he will return to heaven, while the resurrection of the dead will divide the righteous from the godless (30.1 ff.). In the messianic age the world-empire will be destroyed (Ch. 30-40), and the devout will live in joy (Ch. 72 f.). For Ezra is a profound work in which the first half (Ch. 3-9; 25) deals with theological problems from the point of view of eschatology, while the second part (1 f.; 9.25-13) portrays the destiny of Jerusalem (9.25-10) and the history of the Roman Empire (Ch. 11 f.). The rule of the Roman eagle is to be brought to an end by the appearance of the messianic lion from the tribe of David (12.1 ff.). But the Son of Man, who rises up out of the depths of the sea to rule the whole world after the final battle is over (Ch. 13), is the pre-existent Son of God (13.25 ff.; 32.52), who is destined to redeem creation at the end of time. Alexandrian Judaism tried to compete, in the Sybilline Books, with the heathen oracles of the same name, but never succeeded in producing anything of equal value to Palestinian Judaism.

9. The Calculation of the Date of the End
We must add a word about the calculation of the *date of the end* in the Old Testament. In view of the eschatological character of the Old Testament view of the world, we need not be surprised at the attempt to calculate the date of the end of the world. But the origin of this attempt is not to be found in the ancient prophets, who expected the ultimate destiny of Israel in a final judgement to take place at an unspecified time in the immediate future, but lies in the priestly concept of a world era of four thousand years. According to Alfred von Gutschmid we first find evidence of this in the Massoretic priestly writing (P), where the exodus from Egypt falls in the year 2666 from the creation of the world, thereby dividing a world period of four thousand years in the proportion of 2:1. From the year of the Flood (1656) to the birth of

Abraham was 290 years; adding the years to the birth of Isaac (+100) and Jacob (+60), Jacob's entry into Egypt (+130), and Israel's exodus (+430) we reach a sum of 2,666 years. This calculation, with which the Samaritan and Greek texts disagree, cannot have been made before the end of the exile (537 B.C.). Here the Deuteronomic chronology intervenes; it reckons the fourth year of Solomon's reign as the time of the foundation of the temple (1 Kings 6.1). This year is 480 years after the end of Israel's servitude in Egypt, and 480 years before the end of the Babylonian exile, which was set in motion at the end of the first year of Cyrus's reign, and brought to a conclusion with the refounding of the temple in the second year of his reign (537 B.C.—Ezra 3.1 ff.). This second year is taken to be the 480th year after the foundation of the temple, since according to the Deuteronomic era Jerusalem was destroyed in the 430th year after the foundation of the temple (587 B.C.); thus the year 537 B.C. comes in the year 3626 since the creation of the world. The missing 374 years lead to the year 136 B.C. as the four thousandth year of the world era. About this period Daniel (*cf.* 7 above) actually expected the end of the world, with the resurrection of the dead, after the fall of Antiochus IV (164/63). Daniel himself reckons the final period of Israel's history from the destruction of Jerusalem (9.24). In this calculation he makes use of the oracle of Jeremiah concerning the seventy years (Jer. 29.10) up to the end of the exile. But while Zachariah took these seventy years literally and regarded them as ending with the year 517/16 B.C., so that he urged the rebuilding of the temple in view of the onset of the new era (Zach. 1.12), Daniel interprets them as seventy weeks of years, that is $70 \times 7 = 490$ years (9.24 ff.), after the lapse of which the last day will occur. The seven first weeks (7×7 years) cover the Babylonian exile; the next 62 periods ($62 \times 7 = 434$ years), to which the future is fitted as to a Procrustean bed, extend to the deposition of the last legitimate High Priest Jason (171 B.C.); the final week of years is meant to end with the death of Antiochus IV, which according to 2 Macc. 11.16 ff. took place early in 164 B.C., and according to 1 Macc. 6.16 early in 163 B.C. This last week of years has been halved by the ending of the sacrifices of the Jerusalem temple by Antiochus IV in the year 168 B.C.; an altar of Zeus, the βδέλυγμα ἐρημώσεως ('abomination of desolation', Mark 13.14), was set up over the altar of burnt offerings. When the last half-week of years, with its three and a half years, is multiplied out as 1290 days (Dan. 12.11), and shortly afterwards as 1335 days (Dan. 12.12), the round figure $1260 = 360 \times 3\frac{1}{2}$ days seems to have been increased, as a result of the delay in the final period of time, first by a 'time' (12.11), and the second time by two 'times' and half a 'time' (12.12); while the oldest *Apocalypse of John* resolved the half week of years into $42 = 12 \times 3\frac{1}{2}$ months, giving 1260 days (Rev. 11.2 f.; 12.6; 13.5).

Otto Procksch

III. THE ESCHATOLOGY OF PRIMITIVE CHRISTIANITY

1. Significance

It is impossible to over-estimate the *significance of eschatology* for the religious faith and the whole conceptual system of primitive Christianity. The eschatological character of *Jesus's* preaching is immediately obvious from one of his principal concepts, that of the kingdom of God. The more the transcendental and eschatological features of the kingdom of God in Jesus's preaching are recognized, the more clearly we see how his words and ministry are all conditioned by eschatology. His teaching, which begins with the words, 'Repent, for the kingdom of heaven is at hand' (Matt. 4.17), immediately directs the attention of the listener to the approaching end. And the conclusion of his preaching takes the form of a promise of his return upon the clouds of heaven (Mark 14.62). When in connection with his proclamation of the last things, Jesus impresses upon the minds of his disciples that their golden rule must be to watch and to pray (Mark 13.33; Matt. 24.42; 25.13; Luke 12.35 ff.; 21.36), he has at once established the principle which underlies the eschatological hope of the *earliest Christians*. They were of course inspired by a longing for the final and everlasting consummation, but this was not a longing of the conventional apocalyptic sort; their whole will, and all their ethical thinking, was directed towards the one end of standing unblemished in the sight of God when the great day should come: 'We make it our aim to please him' (2 Cor. 5.9; 1 Cor. 15.58). Thus the expectation of the end of the world, and the certainty associated with it: 'The Lord is at hand!', not only meant that there was a powerful compulsion behind their faith and their ethical teaching, but also lent a distinctive note of tension to their whole religious experience; the close presence of the Lord impressed upon them a profound sense of judgement and repentance, and at the same time filled their hearts with comfort and joyful assurance (e.g. Phil. 4.4 ff.). For the believers, Christ who was to come again was both judge and redeemer in one. Thus we can see not only from the Revelation of John, but from the whole body of New Testament writing, that their whole attention was riveted on the imminent onset of eternity, whether we look at the exultation of the eighth chapter of Romans, or the sober warning of James (5.7) or at Hebrews 13.14, in which all transitory things are merely a shadow of the reality that is to come. The influence of the eschatological hope touches the very heart of devotion, the life of prayer itself: apart from Matt. 6.10, there

is also the invocation of 1 Cor. 16.22, which like Rev.
22.20 contains a prayer for the return of the Lord (*Maranatha*), and also the eucharistic prayers in the *Didache*
(9.4 and 10.6; *cf. Eucharist* IV, 1B. p. 386 below). That
eschatology also influenced the form taken by the earliest
theology can be seen, for example, from Paul's doctrine
of justification, which is inconceivable without its eschatological orientation. In the missionary preaching of
primitive Christianity which, in fact, enshrined the
fundamental truths of the faith, eschatology played a
particularly important part (1 Thess. 1.10). Even the
good things of this world were regarded from an eschatological point of view, and were consequently seen as being
of only relative importance (1 Cor. 7.29 ff.; Matt. 6.19
ff.). Of course one cannot thereby conclude that this
was an 'interim ethic' which was only so rigorous in its
form because of the short time before the end of the world.
A similar relative value is placed upon worldly goods and
relationships, not merely where there is a belief in the
imminent coming of the end of the world, but wherever
the longing for eternity is present with the same force as
in primitive Christianity.

2. *Old and New Material*

a. The roots of the eschatology of Jesus and of the earliest
Christians can be found in the eschatological expectations of the Old Testament and contemporary Judaism
(*cf.* II above), and especially in that of apocalyptic. We
encounter *ancient material in a new form* not only in the
general pattern of primitive Christian eschatology, but
also in individual concepts, images and turns of phrase.
The figure of the Messiah, the coming kingdom of God,
the doctrine of the different aeons of world history, the
'day of the Lord', the destruction of the satanic powers of
the Devil and of Anti-Christ, the resurrection and the
judgement of the world are all present. All these elements

could already be found in the popular or apocalyptic expectation of the end, and had been elaborated in great detail in the piety of apocalyptic groups. We need only mention the figure of the Son of Man in Dan. 7.13 f., which was in Jesus's mind when he looked forward to his return in glory and the resultant establishment of the kingdom of God (Matt. 26.64 and parallels), or 4 Ezra 7.50 (the two aeons) and Dan. 12.2 f.; Enoch 38.3 f.; 51.1 ff.; *Apoc. of Baruch* 49 ff.; 4 Ezra 7.32 (the resurrection of the dead and the judgement). On the other hand, we must not underestimate the importance of the earlier Old Testament prophecies which are clearly taken up in the New Testament (Jer. 31.31 ff. in Matt. 26.28 and parallels and in Heb. 8.8 ff.; 10.16 ff.; and Joel 3.1 ff. in Acts 2.16 ff.). Nor is it difficult to show that even certain national and what one might call 'earthly' features of the popular and apocalyptic hope have been carried over into the vision of the events of the last days accepted by Jesus and the earliest Christians. An example of this is not so much Jesus's status as a son of David, but rather turns of phrase like 'the kingdom of our father David', (Mark 11.10; *cf.* also Matt. 5.35), or the expectation of the gathering-in of those who have been dispersed (Mark 13.27), while in the promise given to the twelve disciples (Matt. 19.28) we meet a final fragment of the ancient national hope. The question put by the disciples in Acts 1.6 belongs to the same realm of thought. There is no need here to point out in detail the great weight which these elements carry in the Revelation of John, in which national longings are united with apocalyptic fervour; we only mention Rev. 17.5 f. (Babylon=Rome), and 11.2 and 20.9 (Jerusalem the Holy City). It must likewise be admitted that Jesus himself portrays the future life in the eternal kingdom of God in forms and images drawn from the earthly life of this present world. He sometimes speaks of 'eating and drinking' and of 'sitting at table⁹ in the coming kingdom of God (Luke 14.15; 22.30; Mark 14.25; Matt. 8.11; Luke 13.29).

b. But all this is of little significance by contrast with the *new ideas* which can be clearly perceived in the content and the form of primitive Christian eschatology. The most profound difference between this eschatology and the Jewish future hope is found in the fact that primitive Christianity already represents a partial *fulfilment* of the future hope, and that on the central issue the decision in the great struggle between the forces of good and evil in the final phase of time has already been made. This note of victory breaks through not merely in the faith of the disciples, who can look back to the Messiah's appearance on earth, but also in the consciousness of Jesus himself. The eschatological drama, which consists in essence of a struggle between divine and demonic powers, *has now begun to reach its conclusion*: the demonic powers are driven out and deprived of their rule; the victory is being won by the kingdom of God and those who are fighting for it. For with the appearance of the Messiah, who overthrows the satanic powers and their princes, their downfall has begun, and this brings the onset of the kingdom of God, even though the *final* annihilation of Satan and his servants is still to come (Luke 10.17 ff.; Matt. 12. 25-8; Luke 11.15-20; *cf.* also the account of the temptations of Jesus). The disciples and the earliest Christian communities are now able to look forward to the end of all things with such assurance, by the very fact that they are already able to look back upon one stage in the divine events which prophecy foretold would take place at the crisis in world history; in these events they possess a certain pledge of the realization of their ultimate hope. Their main guarantee of this is their faith in the resurrection of Jesus; for with the resurrection of Christ, who rose from the dead as 'the first fruits of those who have fallen asleep' (1 Cor. 15.20,23), the resurrection of all

Christians has already begun. Such a certainty as received its loftiest expression in Romans 8.38 f., is only possible on the basis of the conviction that all the powers enumerated here are already mortally stricken (*cf.* also Col. 2.12-15). The same is implied by the fact that the disciples know that they possess the Holy Spirit, which has been promised from the last days (Acts 2.16 ff.). Their hope of being preserved from the coming judgement of wrath is based upon what God has already done (Rom. 5.6-10). Even the Revelation of John, which apparently only looks to the future, is only inspired by so powerful a spirit of victory because the appearance and exaltation of Christ have already decided in essence the outcome of the final struggles which are just beginning; this also follows from the titles which Jesus bears in this book (*cf.* esp. 1.5 f.; 3.21; 7.17).

It is also noteworthy that in spite of the national and earthly elements which still persist, Christian eschatology, by contrast with the future hope of Judaism, rejects on principle *all political and eudaemonist elements, so decisively* that the world to come is genuinely *God's* world, all man's earthly and sensuous desires grow silent, and *God's* will alone is triumphant. How decisively Jesus contrasts the coming kingdom of God with the earthly world and this present life! The explanation of 'Thy kingdom come' is found in the phrase that follows, 'Thy will be done' (Matt. 6.10). A new order of all things is inaugurated (*cf.* the Beatitudes and Matt. 20.25 ff.). The answer Jesus gives to the Sadducees is particularly characteristic (Matt. 22.30 and parallels). Thus the Johannine phrase of John 18.36 reflects the true opinion of Jesus. The 'earthly' elements which still remain are to be explained in the first place by the fact that we are able to speak of eternal things only in parables borrowed from earthly reality, and secondly by the fact that throughout the New Testament the conception of the eternal world of

God is that of a living organism which can never be completely 'spiritualized' along the lines of Greek thought. *Paul* is completely in accord with Jesus when he regards the essence of the kingdom of God as 'righteousness and peace and joy in the Holy Spirit' (Rom. 14.17); when, in the very places where an extended description of the glory to come would have been appropriate, he describes the object of religious longing briefly and with restraint as that of personal communion with the Lord (1 Thess. 4.17; 2 Cor. 5.8; Phil. 1.23); and when he says of the climax of the whole course of history that God will be 'all in all' (1 Cor. 15.28). The contrast between this world and the world to come is clearly expressed in 1 Cor. 15.50, where he takes issue against materialist expectations of the future. Even in Christian apocalypse, where the events of the last days are painted in rich colours, the final and most sublime outcome of the events of the last days is the *presence of God* (Acts 21.1-4). It is true of course that even Jewish conceptions of the world to come did not merely have earthly aims in mind; in particular, the psalms of Solomon (17.32 ff.; 18.6-9), Enoch (10.16) and Jubilees (1.15 ff.) regard righteousness and union with God as of the essence of the new age. But just as it is primitive Christian eschatology which places these elements in the foreground, fundamentally rejecting all earthly and sensuous conceptions so it is the gospel of Jesus which is the first to reject the idea that the Messiah will pass judgement upon the political enemies of the Jewish nation and triumph over them.

A further characteristic of primitive Christian eschatology is that the fate of the individual in the last judgement no longer depends upon his belonging to the people of Israel, but upon the fulfilment of the divine will. The judgement also extends to those who do not believe amongst the people of Israel (Matt. 8.11 ff.; Luke 13.28

f.), as had already been proclaimed by the ancient prophets and also by John the Baptist (Matt. 3.9 f.). Thus God in his judgement applies only one standard to all men and nations (Matt. 7.21; 25.31 ff.; Rom. 2.5 ff., 11 ff.). This is the real reason for the disappearance of nationalist tendencies and the presence of *universalism* in the future hope of Jesus and the earliest Christians. Paul also holds firmly to this universalist view, although passages like Rom. 3.1-3; 9.4 f.; 11.16 ff.; 25 f. have caused this to be doubted on occasion. But these passages can be explained in part by the structure of the Christian community in Rome, which Paul had to warn against an attitude of presumptuous arrogance with regard to Jews (11.18-21); and indeed when Paul has to explain the significance of the saving acts of God in the past history of his people, the only judgement open to him is that of Rom. 3.1-3; 9.4 f. But he is not thinking here of the restoration of the ancient privileges of Israel, as can be seen not only from the whole tone of the Epistle to the Romans, but from Rom. 11.25 itself, which states that the fullness of the gentiles will enter the kingdom of God *before* the people of Israel. In the Gospel of John the universalist idea finds a ready expression in the title 'Saviour of the world' (4.42), as well as in the statement that the worship of God will no longer have a fixed association with Jerusalem in the future (4.21 ff.).

3. Basic Features
In the *structure of the eschatological drama* the following stage can be distinguished: the *parousia* of Jesus, the resurrection of the dead, the judgement of God over the world, and the final establishment of the new kingdom of God. In Revelation (20.3-6) the general resurrection of the dead is still preceded by the intermediate messianic kingdom: Christ reigns for a thousand years with the martyrs who have already been restored to life. There is a hint

of the same idea in Paul (1 Cor. 15.24 ff.), but he does not give a clear exposition of it.

The original view of the earliest Christians was that the *return of Christ was imminent*, and to be expected in their own lifetime. Jesus himself had thought the same (Mark 13.30 and parallels; Mark 9.1; Matt. 10.23); Paul expected at least at first to see the *parousia* while still in his earthly body (1 Thess. 4.15,17; 1 Cor. 15.52; Phil. 3.20 f.; *cf.* Rom. 13.12). On the other hand, we already encounter in the New Testament a generation which is lamenting the delay of the *parousia*, and must be exhorted to be patient (2 Peter 3.4 ff.). Although the morning light of eternity can already be seen in the distance, there is never any attempt made to calculate the time of the end of the world, as was normal in contemporary apocalyptic. Jesus himself admitted (Matt. 24.36; *cf.* Acts 1.7), that he did not know the day nor the hour of his return; this knowledge was reserved to God the Father alone. The onset of the end of the world, the 'day of the Lord', would be entirely *unexpected*, like a 'thief in the night' (Matt. 24.36-42; Mark 13.35; Luke 12.39; 1 Thess. 5.2-4; 2 Peter 3.10; Rev. 3.3; 16.15). This, however, appears to be contradicted by numerous passages (in the gospels, in Paul and in Revelation) which list a number of *preparatory events* which must take place before the end of the world can begin. Mark 13 and the parallel chapters in other gospels, for example, describe the beginning of the 'woes', consisting of wars, earthquakes, and famine (v. 8), and the appearance of 'the abomination of desolation' (v. 14; *cf.* Dan. 11.31) and of false messiahs and prophets (v. 21 f.), and the final disintegration of the whole world through great catastrophes of nature (v. 24 ff.), which leave the way open for the arrival of the Son of Man (v. 26 f.); there is also the description in 2 Thess. 2.1 ff., where the end of the world is preceded by the 'falling away', and the 'son of perdition' (Dan. 11.36), the Anti-Christ must come. Finally, there are the many plagues and catastrophes which Revelation (5 ff.) enumerates in great detail as preliminaries to the end. All these passages, which also reproduce regular features of Jewish apocalyptic, such as 'messianic woes', and the 'abomination of desolation' (Anti-Christ), do in fact seem to lead to the conclusion that there was a calculation of the end of the world in the style of the apocalyptic writings, and apparently contradict those which prophesy the sudden onset of the last things, though they probably also imply the imminent return of Christ. But when we remember that certain inconsistencies can be found in all apocalyptic descriptions, and that both sets of ideas can be encountered in one and the same passage (e.g. Mark 13), we have to explain the differences not as contradictions but as variations upon a single eschatological idea which is adapted to the eternal circumstances of a particular audience, or to the situation envisaged by a letter. In this way, for example, the eschatological picture presented by Paul in 2 Thess. 2.1 ff. can be entirely reconciled with 1 Thess. 4.13-15,17. Each must be interpreted according to the different situation of his readers: it is essential to be ready, for the end will come when it is not expected (1 Thess.); but this is no reason to become fanatical, or to let oneself be 'troubled'; for much has still to take place before the day of the Lord dawns (2 Thess.). Furthermore, the descriptions of the preparatory events are never concerned with calculating the time at which the *parousia* is to take place; a veil is drawn over the actual date of the return, even when it is described as 'near' (Mark 13.29 and parallels). Like the passages proclaiming the sudden coming of the end of the world, these descriptions are inspired by one message: 'Watch and pray' (Mark 13.33 ff.).

As for the conception of the *apocatastasis* (the restoration

of all things), we can only note here that even passages
like 1 Cor. 15.24 ff. or Romans 11.32 are not to be interpreted in terms of the restoration to life and salvation
of all men, and also that many sayings referring to a
judgement or to eternal damnation can be quoted against
this idea.

4. Realistic Eschatology and the Future Hope of the Individual
The question of whether and to what extent the *'realistic'*
eschatology set out in the previous paragraphs existed side
by side with a more *'individualistic'* tendency, in virtue of
which the believers expected eternal life and communion
with God or Christ *immediately after death*, becomes particularly acute with regard to the Pauline and Johannine
theology. But the gospels also think in terms of a decision
on the fate of the individual immediately after death
(Luke 16.22 ff.; 23.43; *cf.* also Matt. 22.31 f.), as do Heb.
12.23 and Rev. 6.9 ff. But in none of these passages have
we to look for special impulses from popular belief or
hellenistic modes of thought; they can all be explained
on the basis of the reality found in the Christian faith,
the experience of the living God, from whom even death
was unable to separate the believer (Rom. 8.38 f.). If the
risen Christ was for the believer an already present reality
of the world to come, then Christians were bound to
share the hope expressed by Paul in 2 Cor. 5.8 and Phil.
1.23 of 'being with Christ' immediately after death. But
the old eschatology was neither shaken nor weakened in
Paul by this hope. It is true that in the Gospel of John
the conviction of the *present possession of eternal life* (3.36;
5.24; *cf.* 11.25 f.) and the belief that the judgement has
already been carried out at the present time (3.18; 5.24)
overshadow specifically eschatological ideas. The original
expectation of the *parousia* is also transformed by the
evangelist, when he describes the coming of Jesus to the
disciples as being brought about by the sending of the

Holy Spirit (14.18 ff.; 16.16 ff.). But passages such as John 5.28 f.; 12.48, etc. show nevertheless that the eschatological events (resurrection and judgement) were by no means without significance for the evangelists. It must therefore be accepted that even in John the eternal life that begins at the present time and continues immediately after death calls for a development and perfection which does not take place until the last day.

Kurt Deissner

IV. CHRISTIAN ESCHATOLOGY AND THE HISTORY OF DOCTRINE

1. The Eschatology of the Early Church
a. The primitive Christian preaching from which the Church came into being was an eschatological message of judgement and salvation (*cf.* III above). Christianity entered the world as the hope of the *parousia* of Jesus Christ the Lord and the inauguration by him of the kingdom of God. The Christian faith was building on its own original foundations when it developed an eschatological dogma. But from the very first, Christian eschatology was burdened by extraneous material, and had its treasure in the vessel of *Jewish apocalyptic*. This powerfully influenced its destiny, for both good and ill. It helped early Christianity to avoid the danger of absorption by the world of the Greek and Oriental mysteries, and to maintain the primitive Christian expectation of the end and the kingdom—whenever the Church rejected or watered down Jewish eschatology this hope invariably grew weak. But at the same time it has burdened the Church, right down to the present day, with ideas and problems which are remote, alien and even contradictory to faith in Christ, so that it has repeatedly prevented the development of a genuinely theological eschatology.

Eschatology

As a result of hellenistic influence, the eschatology of the Judaism of the Diaspora was to a large degree spiritualized, as in Philo: the resurrection came to be of lesser importance. But even in Greek-speaking areas the Church did not follow this line. Belief in the resurrection of the Lord meant that the assurance of eternal life took the unwavering form of *hope in the resurrection* (*cf.* III, 2*b* above). The 'resurrection of the flesh' became a fixed article of belief (*cf.* I Clem. 26.3 and the Roman [Apostolic] Creed). The imminent expectation of the end found in the New Testament was still present in the post-apostolic period. In the manner of late Jewish apocalyptic, the Epistle of Barnabas speculates upon the time the world is to last; the world is said to last for a week of seven days, each consisting of a thousand years, and the sabbath is the thousand year kingdom. Thus Christian eschatology had taken over the idea of an intermediate messianic kingdom between the first and the second resurrection, which in late Jewish eschatology maintained the balance between a future hope based on nationalist ideas centred on the present world, and universalist and cosmological ideas looking towards the world to come, that is, between 'messianism' and 'apocalyptic'. As a result of the calculation of a week of days each consisting of one thousand years (*cf.* above II, 9), this idea took on the form of *chiliasm* (the thousand years are probably first mentioned in the Slavonic Enoch, and also in Rev. 20.1 ff.), that is, the expectation of a thousand year kingdom of Christ on earth before the end of the world. Papias closely follows Jewish originals (Enoch, *Apoc. of Baruch*) in describing the intermediate kingdom in purely material terms. Even the *apologists* retain this realistic understanding of eschatology, a proof of the degree to which it was an automatic assumption for them. Nothing in primitive Christian eschatology was given up: the hope of the resurrection of the body is evidence of the way in which the gospel took precedence over philosophy, while Justin regarded the expectation of a thousand year kingdom in Jerusalem as part of orthodox belief.

b. The breakdown of Jewish and primitive Christian eschatology began with gnosticism. The dualism of spirit and matter made impossible a realistic belief in the resurrection and in chiliasm. The drama of the end of history was replaced by the journey of the soul to heaven. In gnosticism only the soul possesses eternal life, when it attains to the knowledge of the truth through Christ; this means that its 'resurrection' has already taken place (an idea already implied in 2 Tim. 2.17 f.); it then ascends into the *pleroma*. In opposition to gnosticism the *anti-gnostic Fathers* lay a strong emphasis on traditional eschatology, even where it cannot be reconciled with their own hellenistic conception of the doctrine of salvation and view of history. Eschatology is particularly prominent in Hippolytus, who follows Daniel and Revelation in his discussion of the four world-empires, and, like Irenaeus, develops a theology of history. But in spite of all the dogmatic emphasis it received, the chiliastic hope no longer possesses its early force, and it may be noted that the Church of that period did not make the drama of the end of history into an explicit dogma. Not only the gnostics, but Christians who were faithful to the Church, were already rejecting chiliasm as early as the second century. At that time they formed a minority. Resistance to Jewish elements in eschatology first became a powerful force in the Church in *Alexandrine theology*. The dualism and spiritualism maintained by gnosticism was introduced by Origen into the Church's theology itself. His system actually deals with the 'fall' of souls and the 'ascent' to God by which this fall is reversed. The only theme of his eschatology is therefore the progressive purification and transfiguration of souls. In this process—as in the teaching of the gnostics—the Church's doctrine of the last things is transmuted. The eternal fire of judgement becomes a fire of purification. The less material the souls become, the higher the knowledge to which they *all* attain—Origen teaches that after endless ages all, even the demons and the Devil, will be restored by the *Logos*-Christ to God. All this is worked out in hellenistic and gnostic terms; it is not surprising that the primitive eschatology of the Church ceased to be of account for Origen: for him it is merely the product of a perversely literalist faith, which interpreted the prophecies *judaico sensu*. Nevertheless, Origen maintained the 'resurrection of the flesh' in the face of the heretics and heathen, but in a strongly spiritualized sense based on 1 Cor. 15.44. He also retains the *parousia*.

The Alexandrine theology decided the fate of chiliasm in the East. Wherever philosophical theology gained ground, chiliasm disappeared. Up to the sixth century no further commentary on Revelation seems to have been produced; the book is absent from the canon of many Oriental theologians. The decline and retreat of chiliasm was of great significance: it meant the watering down of the living hope of the imminence of God's kingdom, and the disappearance of the eschatological outlook of primitive Christianity. In the *West*, the traditional eschatological picture of the end of history, including chiliasm, survived for a longer period. The Church was engaged in a severe struggle with the 'world' and armed itself for and in the course of this struggle; and the Book of Revelation, with its military imagery, had an immediate message at this time, and the apocalyptic eschatology, itself the expression of a life and death struggle on the part of Judaism, once again became of direct relevance to a generation locked in conflict—as it did so often later.

2. *Augustine and the Middle Ages*

a. The victory of the Church in the *fourth century* brought with it the *great turning point* in eschatology. The end of the persecution, peace with the state, and the establishment of the great Imperial Church inevitably had a profound influence on the Christian view of history. This influence can be seen in someone like Eusebius of Caesarea. In his great thanksgiving oration after the victory (*Hist. Eccles.* 10.4), he rejoices that the promises of Isa. 35 and 54 are now fulfilled, that the Church is now partaking in the resurrection of Christ, and that a new day has dawned. It is obvious that this victory of God within history would overshadow the picture of the conflict at the end of history and that the future would be altogether dominated by the present. The weakening of the eschatology of the early Church was made easier by a change that took place in the fourth century in the interpretation of Revelation. The Donatist Ticonius, in his commentary on Revelation (before 380), transferred the first resurrection, the binding of the Devil (equated with the overcoming of the strong man in Matt. 12.29 by Christ's first appearance), and the thousand year kingdom, from the future into the past and present: according to him the millenium of Rev. 20 is the period of the Church from the first coming of the Lord until his return. Ticonius' commentary exercised great influence everywhere. Of particular significance was the fact that *Augustine*, who at first placed this period at the end of history, later followed Ticonius. He regarded the first resurrection as the lifting of sinful mankind into the state of grace through Christ and the Church. As a result 'the millenium was changed from an eschatological fact to a period of Church history' (H. Reuter). Like others before him (besides Ticonius, Paulinus of Nola), and in spite of his predestinarian and eschatological idea of the Church, he frequently equated the *Catholic Church* with the *kingdom of God*. Previously the teaching of the west had been that the Church was earthly, and the kingdom of God heavenly, belonging to the world to come; now this eschatological entity had become the universal Church, and chiliasm was replaced by the hierarchical conception that Christ was exercising the kingly rule described in Rev. 20 through the Church. This of course relaxed the eschatological tension completely. Otherwise, Augustine maintained the idea of the drama at the end of history: the final struggle is in accord with the dualism of the *De civitate Dei*. But eschatology had now lost its characteristic note; a change taking place in the historical consciousness of Christianity. Augustine also had a vital influence on *individual eschatology*. He maintained and strengthened the cosmic pessimism and other-worldliness of Christian piety. He gave to the Middle Ages its two classical terms for the description of blessedness; *Visio* and *fruitio Dei*, two concepts which, in spite of biblical parallels and reminiscences, implied the taking over by Greek intellectualism and the concept of the mystical enjoyment of God, of the principal teleological doctrines of the faith. Finally, Augustine introduced to dogmatic theology the concept of *purgatory*, which came from Orphic religion, though it had also influenced Judaism, and had probably long been wide-spread as a popular Christian belief.

b. The *Middle Ages* followed in the steps of Augustine. This meant that the Church's eschatology was almost exclusively concerned with the fate of the individual; the only development took place here. Gregory the Great took up the concept of purgatory and associated it with the idea of the propitiatory sacrifice of the Mass. The hierarchical authority of the Church was regarded as extending even into the world to come. In other respects, there was no significant eschatological development in theology. This is true of dogmatic Catholic theology up to the present day. Thomas Aquinas took over the formulas of Augustine for eternal blessedness, and Catholic theology retains them right up to the present.

The eschatological tension persisted under the surface in the Middle Ages. From the tenth century on eschatological and apocalyptic ideas were increasingly expressed in the Church. The expectation of the end reappeared with renewed force. With Joachim of Floris the hidden stream of chiliast eschatology came to the surface. Joachim was certain that he was living in the final age; he regarded the Book of Revelation as being written essentially for his own time. The age of the Holy Spirit was at hand, in which Christ would return in person. This prophecy, the new view of history it contained, and its vision of the final age, exercised a powerful influence throughout the whole of the late Middle Ages and even in recent times. The Joachimites sharply criticized Rome in the light of the imminent end of time. One element amongst the Franciscans, the *spirituales*, accepted Joachimism, and saw the Babylon of Revelation in the Church, the power of Anti-Christ in the hierarchy, and the Messiah of the Devil in the Pope. Joachimism persisted amongst the Hussites and the Anabaptists; the new eschatological tension was relieved in Christian revolution, a radical movement for reform. How far this was from Augustine!

3. The Reformation and Protestant Orthodoxy
a. The *Reformation* is also of decisive importance in the history of eschatology.

i. By contrast with the Roman idea of the glory present in the Church on earth, *Luther's theologia crucis* lays the utmost emphasis on the concealment of the Church of God, the form of a servant in which the rule of Christ is exercised, and the power of Satan upon earth. This provides a new basis for the eschatological tension, the expectation of the 'blessed last day', in which Satan will be vanquished and the believers led from the struggle of faith to the vision of the power of Christ. Chiliasm, however, was rejected by the Reformers; their dominant interpretation of the millenium continued to be in terms of Church history. The chiliasm of the Anabaptists so revolted them that the Reformation Churches rejected any form of it, along with the caricature of chiliasm condemned in the *Confessio Augustana* (17), and the *Confessio Helvetica* (11). Nevertheless, the Reformers had an acutely eschatological consciousness of history; the end was imminent, the Pope was Anti-Christ, and the new preaching of the gospel was a direct sign of the end.

ii. The reform of the concept of the essence of religion brought with it a purification of the ideas of blessedness and eternal life, which were cleansed of their mystical and eudaemonist features, and restored to their biblical clarity. The ideas of *visio* and *fruitio Dei* became less prominent, and were replaced by the idea that 'to be blessed means that God rules within us and we are his kingdom' (Luther, Weimar ed., p. 98).

iii. This eternal life is already possessed by the faith which has seized hold upon justification. A certain assurance of salvation overcomes the fear of the end. Purgatory, as a place of atoning satisfaction, disappears with the righteousness of works. Luther replaced this by a theology of death which takes it more seriously than ever before: death and purgatory are regarded as one. Death fulfils the promise of justification and perfects the work of sanctification; by destroying the old man, it is a rebirth to eternal life, judgement and grace in one.

b. *The orthodox theology of early Protestantism* dealt in its doctrine of the last things with death, resurrection, judgement, the destruction of the world, eternal death and eternal life. The entire emphasis is placed upon *individual eschatology.* Death is regarded with full seriousness as the final struggle with Satan, the ultimate decision. Consequently, pastoral care in Lutheran regions shows a predominant emphasis upon a good death. The soul undergoes judgement immediately after death; the faithful receive at once, with God and with Christ, a perfect and blessed life, to describe which the medieval terms (*visio, fruitio*) are brought back into use. The idea that the blessedness of the individual is unthinkable without or before the victory of the kingdom of God, is not expressed. The only significance of the end of the world for the dead is that the soul takes on again its transfigured body. It is only then, however, that the full experience of eternal blessedness or damnation becomes possible. The insoluble difficulty of the 'intermediate' stage is also present here. The expectation of the *kingdom* withers away. The emphasis is entirely on the desire for a personal assurance of salvation. The eschatology of the end of history is maintained in theory, but has lost its force. Not only is chiliasm excluded in every form, however crude or sophisticated, but the whole of history, the victory and the consummation of the kingdom, and the *parousia* itself, fall into the background behind the problems of personal consummation. Christian hope is also largely individualistic and directed towards the world to come. Lutheran theologians were united in teaching the complete annihilation of this world—J. Gerhard is the only one to regard the theory of its transformation as even possible. Since the place of the blessed both before the resurrection, in the intermediate condition, and after, is heaven, the *new earth* is of no significance. Protestant orthodoxy differs here from Luther, who, although his statements on the subject were made in the language of popular belief, was serious in according to the lower creation, freed from the curse, a place in eternity. The orthodox view is all the more striking in that with regard to man, it continued

to teach the resurrection of the body or the transfiguration of those who were still alive at the end. No one
realized that the fate of the world and that of the body
were inseparably related, and that the two questions
were one and the same, and could only have the same
answer. The new body would be in substance the old,
whereas in substance the former world would be destroyed. Thus the Jewish realism of belief in the resurrection remained isolated and out of context in what was
otherwise an entirely spiritualized picture of the future.
This contradiction is the most serious theological weakness of orthodox Protestant eschatology (Reformed
Church dogmatic theology tended in part more towards
the idea of the transformation, rather than the annihilation of the world). Its practical attitude to the world and
to history followed from this dogmatic belief. Both were
considered only as the place in which faith was exercised,
tried and tested. Lutheran orthodoxy never developed
a real interest in the historical future of the Church, and
saw no eschatological significance in the task of changing
the condition of the world. Thus a heavy price was paid
for the rejection of chiliasm. In the German Lutheran
Church, an individualistic and other-worldly eschatology, and a lack of interest in missionary work and the
future of the Church are closely related.

4. *From Pietism to the Present Day*
a. During the period of Lutheran orthodoxy, *chiliastic
apocalyptic* at first only remained a living force amongst
the Anabaptists and sectaries, and varied very much in
detail from one group to another. Significant figures
such as Comenius and the Reformed theologian Alsted
regarded it with favour. Chiliasm first came to be of
theological significance in the Churches through the
scripture commentaries of *Cocceius* and his attempt to set
out a 'theology of the kingdom' in terms of the history

of salvation. Two disciples of Cocceius who belonged to the Lutheran Church, Vitringa and F. A. Lampe, introduced these new ideas to German *pietism*. Once again, they placed the apocalyptic a thousand years in the future, and made this idea, which previously had been held almost exclusively by separatist sects, once again acceptable to the Church. Spener, von Labadie, and English eschatological thinkers, all of them, however, clearly influenced by Cocceius, argued for the 'hope of better times in the future', in conscious disagreement with the view of Luther. Other leaders of pietism favoured chiliasm. They expected the conversion of the Jews, the fall of 'Babylon', and the glorious establishment of the kingdom of God upon earth at the end of time. The Church once again had a future, and therefore a goal for its work. The renewal of chiliasm and the turning of the Church to new activity, to missionary work and to internal reform are closely associated, and depend one upon the other. The vision of the end of history fully restored history to theology and the Church, enabling them to deal with history and to understand history. In the *'theology of the kingdom'* of the Württemberg theologians Bengel and Oetinger, the movement reached its peak. The ancient idea of 'economy' once again attracted attention; the history of the world and the Church was systematized from an eschatological point of view, and the drama of the end of history was portrayed in the terms of Daniel and Revelation. The element of fantasy in interpreting the scripture, and the artificiality and presumption of the calculation of the date of the end, must not be allowed to obscure the outstanding features of this theology. These apocalyptic theoreticians were theologians of history, who broke through the individualist limits of the orthodox doctrine of salvation to achieve a magnificent conception of world history, in the assurance that the Bible casts light on everything and offers a comprehensive vision of history. Through the influence of Bengel chiliasm also obtained recognition and respect in the Lutheran Church. The indifference of orthodox Lutheranism to history was replaced by the idea of the 'history of salvation', and individualism, spiritualism and otherworldliness by the expectation of the kingdom upon earth.

b. But the biblical theologians and their followers by no means commanded the assent of the whole Church, let alone of all the intellectual circles of their time. Here forces had long been at work which threatened the disintegration of eschatology. But theology, so far as it had not itself succumbed to these forces, was too biblicist and narrowly pietistic to have the strength and flexibility to overcome its opponents. The *Enlightenment* secularized and watered down the Christian faith in eternal life to the idea of immortality based on metaphysical or ethical principles, and reduced the expectation of the kingdom to the idea of progress. Philosophical considerations and the historical criticism of the Bible, particularly in association with the study of comparative religion, shook belief in biblical prophecy. All its concrete features (the resurrection, the judgement of the world, eternal punishment in hell) seemed to be very much the product of a particular time, or else an accommodation on the part of Jesus and the apostles to the understanding of their own age. The result was that immortality and infinite progress were even more jealously defended.

The philosophy of *German idealism* shared with the Enlightenment a critical attitude towards the Church's eschatology. The expectation of the end grew faint. The resurrection, the judgement, the destruction and renewal of the world were transferred 'from the world to come into this world, from the future into the present', and transformed from objective ideas into states of mind. There was a precedent for this in mysticism (e.g. Angelus

Silesius), and those who took this view felt that they were guarding the pure truth of the gospel, purged of all the false ideas that had overlaid it. Students of the philosophy of history also regarded themselves as the heirs of Christian thought. In fact idealism from Lessing to Hegel produced in its picture of history a secularized version of theological chiliasm. There is no doubt about the relationship. The dualism of the Church's portrayal of history and its vision of the end was abandoned, and the chiliastic miracle was replaced by the outcome of an *imminent development*. But when the conception of the goal of historical development is the 'kingdom of God' or the ultimate community of the spirit upon earth, the relationship to chiliastic theology, with its emphasis on the end of history, is obvious. The general outline of this idealistic evolutionism has dominated European thought right through the periods of materialism and pessimism up to the recent past. In America, given a wider basis, and reduced to a eudaemonist theory of social development in conjunction with the scientific and sociological theories of Darwin and Spencer respectively, it has been the guiding principle up to the present day not only of the secular historical and cultural consciousness but also of theology and the active life of the Church. Finally, through the heir and antithesis of Hegel, Karl Marx, the socialist movement received the burning imminent and chiliastic expectation which has persisted in present day Communism and Bolshevism.

This imminent chiliasm took the place of the Christian hope of the *parousia*. But in *individual eschatology* idealism was unable to prevent the disintegration of the Christian tradition in the face of the materialism of 'scientific thought'. Kant, Fichte, and Goethe had all laid great emphasis on their own conviction of personal immortality, although Fichte also disputed the conventional eudaemonist hope of the future life with ideas reminiscent of Luther (*cf.* Fichte, *Sämtliche Werke* V, p. 519 ff. with Luther, Weimar Ed. II, p. 97 ff.). But the principal influences of idealism tended in the opposite direction. Both its mystical element and objective idealism either regarded the survival of the individual after death as a matter of indifference, or rejected it. Hegel's 'eloquent silence' on this subject was ultimately better understood by the left wing amongst his followers than by the apologists who believed in the possibility of a synthesis. F. Richter, (1843-1844), D. F. Strauss and Feuerbach correctly regarded themselves as heirs of the hidden legacy of idealism, when in the name of a pantheistic immanence they rejected the world to come and personal immortality as the 'last enemy': 'we must replace the world to come beyond the grave in heaven by the world to come beyond the grave on earth, the historical future, the future of humanity' (Feuerbach, *Sämtliche Werke* VIII, p. 364). Even those whose theoretical thinking was opposed to these radicals, found themselves in practical agreement. The century of natural science, technology, history and socialism was preoccupied with the present world.

c. Nor was *theology* able to alter this, least of all a theology which had come under the influence of the idealist conception of development. In *Schleiermacher* there is a constant struggle between the Christian and the philosopher, an evolutionary philosophy of civilization and the word of Jesus Christ. He attempted to base on the latter alone his certainty of personal survival, which on other grounds he regarded as far from certain; he expected the consummation of the Church to come about by an act of the kingly power of Christ. But these features, which must not be overlooked in the whole picture of Schleiermacher's theology, make no difference to the complete

273

lack of any tension in his expectation of the redemption. The dualism of primitive Christianity is weakened, to say the least, by the idea of development. Schleiermacher's Christianity is certain of the progressive 'realization' of redemption within time and lives confidently in the present. The eschatology of his *Doctrine of Faith in Christian Belief* is ultimately little more than a masterly analysis of the insoluble philosophical problem of 'perfection'. R. Rothex linked an immanent and evolutionary view of civilization with a supernatural chiliasm, and in this respect his 'secular Christianity' has experienced a contemporary revival on the part of some advocates of religious socialism. But immanence and an optimistic theory of development were of much greater importance to him than his belief in the miracle of the *parousia*—in spite of everything, the spell of idealism had not been broken. The expectation of the kingdom was given theological expression with far greater force by the heirs of Württemberg biblicism, Menken, J. T. Beck, Blumhardt, Auberlen, and in the Erlangen theology of history represented by *von Hofmann*. The 'biblical philosophy of history', including chiliasm and the distinctive hope of Israel, were vigorously defended by them. The realistic drama of the end of history was regarded as a necessary conclusion to the divine 'history of salvation' that was there for all to see. These theologians of the missionary century sought in the scriptures not only 'the solution of the riddle of individual life', but also 'the solution of the riddle of the universe', the riddles of history. They were conscious of filling a gap in orthodox dogmatic theology. But this 'biblical' theology of history and eschatology, however much more imaginative it was, nevertheless possessed serious weaknesses. It was based on the theory of the Bible as a complete and infallible 'organism', comprehending the whole of history in its historical accounts and prophecies. It had therefore to ignore the established conclusions of the scientific study of the context and interpretation of the scriptures. The questions of the proper place of Jewish apocalyptic in Christianity, and the relation of the 'prophecy' of the Old Testament to its 'fulfilment', were not taken as seriously, nor asked as critically, as they should have been. Consequently, the clear distinction between theology and the popular biblicist eschatology of pietistic circles was lost, and the only effective weapon against the Judaistic expectation of such sects as the Adventists was blunted. Nor must one forget that while theologians defended and maintained eschatological doctrine, the basic elements of devotion and of the understanding of history, even within the Church, were almost without exception anything but 'eschatological'. The fervent expectation of the end, the serious posing of eschatological problems, as well as a deluded calculation of the date of the end, principally survived amongst the pietistic 'brotherhoods', and also amongst the sects, who added numerous and weird ideas of their own. The basic outlook of the ordinary member of the Lutheran Church was far better represented by the completely uneschatological theology of *A. Ritschl* than the dogmatic eschatology of the chiliast school.

d. Since then, however, there has been a *return to eschatology*, not only in theoretical thinking, but at the heart of a general attitude to life, not only in the Church, but far beyond it. The war was a fearful revelation of the demonic elements in our civilization, and a shattering blow to evolutionary optimism in Europe at least. The experience of an 'end' and a profound impression of the intrinsic meaninglessness of history has made the present time ripe for eschatology. The growing power of Bolshevist Communism and its claims for the future have meant that Christianity has once again been directly faced with the chiliast problem; the question of the kingdom of God upon earth and the genuine contribution of chiliasm has once again been brought to the fore, most consciously by the 'religious socialism' which attempts to understand and explain socialism in primitive Christian and chiliast terms. Dialectic theology, in its emphasis on death, on the radical distinction between time and eternity, and on the transcendence of salvation and redemption, is calling for a new eschatological attitude on the part of the *whole* of dogmatic theology and ethics, and of the entire thought and activity of the Church. The result of all this is that theology is once again faced with the task of constructing an eschatology.

Paul Althaus

V. ESCHATOLOGY IN THE PHILOSOPHY OF RELIGION AND DOGMATIC THEOLOGY

1. The Concept of Eschatology
Eschatology is the theological or philosophical doctrine of the 'last things' (Ecclus. 7.36), that is of the conclusion and goal of human life, human history and the universe. It is distinguished from hypotheses about the end of the universe based on natural science or scientific historical study, in formal respects by its categorical character, and with regard to its content by the fact that it is based on the experience of the absolute in history; thus the statements of eschatology, even of philosophical eschatology, are religious in nature. As such, it is now an unimportant supplement to a given philosophy or theology, but, purporting as it does to describe the consummation of all things, it is the consummation and conclusion of the whole of the system of thought to which it belongs, determining and influencing the meaning of everything else in that system.

2. The Origin of Eschatology

The purpose of examining eschatology from the point of view of the *philosophy of religion* is to demonstrate that *the origin of all eschatology lies in the certainty of God.*

a. Not every concept of God provides a basis for eschatology. Every value-judgement depends on the certainty of the absolute. This of course assumes the idea of the 'eternal' but does not necessarily an eschatology. The 'eternal' is the 'ultimate' here only in the sense of what is absolutely valid or essentially real within, beyond and above the data of perception. Time signifies the change *beyond* which, or the fullness, *within* which the eternal lives, is reflected, or becomes incarnate. There is no realization of the progress of time, of time as the form of becoming, of history. Thus the future presents no problem. It is swallowed up in the present moment of the eternally present, wholly valid and essentially absolute, which in its timelessness and changelessness gives meaning to the world. Any attempt to speak of eschatology here must simply identify it with theology: God is the 'ultimate'. The form of religion which corresponds to this hellenistic idealism is *mysticism* in its various forms. It is not important here whether the eternal is thought of as immanent, present in all temporal things, or as transcendent and outside the world—even in the latter case the life of God is immediately present as a higher world which on principle is always accessible to mystical experience, and is therefore not strictly transcendent at all. The tension displayed by this pattern of devotion is not directed towards the future, but is so to speak vertical, directed towards the 'depths' or the 'heights'. In the midst of time it seeks peace in 'the present moment of eternity' (to use the words of Angelus Silesius).

b. This static doctrine of two distinct worlds is based on an incomplete understanding of the problem of the universe. It breaks down the moment there is a decisive recognition, as in the prophetic religions, of God as the sacred will, as the Lord. The description of the problem of the universe as that of the relation of the essential to the contingent and changing then ceases to be adequate, and it is understood in a more profound sense as the conflict between God and the will of forces opposed to God, and is expounded on this basis. The world is a battlefield in which the object of the battle is God's dominion over the universe. God intends his will and power to be triumphant, and this must be so because he is God. But at the moment he is not triumphant. Where this conflict is genuinely experienced the flight into the eternal world of being is no longer an acceptable answer. God's will is made known to the created historical world, and it is here that it must be carried out. This gives rise to the certainty that God, because he is God, will *come* to rule. The attention is directed not towards the peace of the *world above*, but towards the *future* which is drawing near; the eternal is the 'ultimate' no longer simply in the sense of the essential present, beyond and outside time, but in the sense of the final end of time. This is the religion not of a higher world, but of the coming kingdom of God; not of the co-existence within or alongside each other of natural and supernatural worlds, symbolized in spatial terms; it presents a temporal distinction, implying a strict transcendence, between this and the coming 'aeon'. This gives a completely new meaning to time and the temporal world. It is not merely an alternation, from which one may flee, or a fullness, in which one may lose oneself, but a progress towards what is to come, the approach of the 'end', the kingdom of God. The world becomes a place of conflict, of purposeful action in the light of the coming kingdom; and in the light of the future which brings judgement, time is transformed into the 'hour', the moment of responsibility for every decision and action.

c. Up to the present time this eschatology has been the decisive influence on our view of the world and of history. Its force is seen even in *German idealism*, though at its height, idealism deprived eschatology of its original force by bringing it into a synthesis with the non-eschatological view of the world (*cf.* 2*a*. above). The divine present takes the historical process into itself, and it is regarded as the continuous development of the life of God. History is of course a conflict, but a conflict of the spirit with itself, and thus a conflict within a unity. Conflict and peace, death and life are regarded as one. The process has a goal, but the way to it is as important and as valuable as the goal. The transcendence explicit in the distinction between the two aeons disappears in the face of an immanence expressed in these terms. The eschatological tension is relaxed, since in a development that follows creative laws accessible to the understanding, the reality of what is to come exists already potentially in the present. Consequently, the existential seriousness of decision and conflict are absent; this too has given way to the calm assurance of contemplation. The prophetic vision of history is deprived of its force, and eschatology is deprived of its emphasis and seriousness. The 'ultimate' itself is in fact already present within the whole process.

d. The eschatology of the *gospel* also implies a transformation of prophetic eschatology, for it too places the 'ultimate' in the present, but in a quite different way from idealist evolutionism. There is no prophetic eschatology in which the coming aeon is not already looming up in the present in the form of the revealed will of God, or of the community which has received his call. But the eschatology of the gospel is clearly distinguished from all prophecies by the assertion that the kingdom of God is there in the presence of Jesus Christ (*cf.* III, 2*b*. above). The temporal succession of the aeons, one following and excluding the other, is modified without being done away with. A decisive *kairos* lies not only in the future, but in the past: the decision has been taken. The emphasis is not only on the future, but on the *present existence of what has already been achieved.* It is Christ, the historical and present Christ, who is to 'return'. But this relationship between what has been achieved in time and what is to come has nothing to do with the idealist synthesis, let alone with the mystical presence of the eternal. For what has already been achieved is not an historical or psychological reality, an empirical datum, but 'the word', certain and accessible only to faith as the presence of the world to come. Strictly speaking, the relation of the future to the present is not that of the fruit to the seed, but that of direct vision to faith. The kingdom of God does not develop—it is present in its entirety, and in its entirety is not yet present. Thus the present reality of what has already been achieved by no means weakens the tension of the longing for the future, but raises it to the highest pitch of intensity. The certainty of the victory that has been won is a compelling call to take part in the struggle —for in this world such a certainty is not possible except by taking part in the struggle. Those who have been redeemed long for redemption. Peace and conflict, rest and disturbance, present joy and longing for consummation are inextricably mingled.

3. Christian Eschatology (Methods and Principles)

With this, we have already begun to describe Christian eschatology. The *method* to be followed can be seen from what we have already said:

a. Like all theology, eschatology is also a mode of thought exercised in obedience to the *word of God.* But the word of God is the *promissio*, bringing about faith, and in which we are seized hold of by the kingdom that is to come, as by a present reality. Of course, dogmatic theology will always give serious attention to the promises and the apocalyptic sayings of the Bible. But they can only be evaluated theologically insofar as their words lead on to 'the word', that is, insofar as the 'prophecies' take their proper place within the unity and wholeness of the one 'prophecy' which is given by the presence of the kingdom in Christ himself. Thus the testing and sifting of biblical eschatology is a task that must constantly be renewed.

b. Eschatology must not forget that it is a mode of thought which takes place in *faith*. It is faith which gives this thought the impulse and direction. But the point is, that as a mode of thought conducted in faith eschatology cannot give a fixed and detailed picture of the outcome of human history. The believer, the Church and humanity are constantly faced by a fresh decision, and this means that neither the two-fold destiny of man nor the idea of the *apocatastasis* can be accorded a place in their own right in the picture of the end. Thus by contrast with an idealist system eschatology must remain 'open-ended'.

c. Eschatology deals with what 'has never entered the heart of man'. This leads to the problem of the *language* used to describe the last things. The consummation, life without the pain and dignity of decision, and the presence of Christ in glory are beyond the power of our words and concepts to describe. Consequently, we are unable to speak of them, and yet we must. The way in which we speak of the end must make use of *parables*—this, for example, is the justification for the traditional picture of the *parousia*—but theology must also remain conscious of the fact that it does speak here in parables.

The basis of the certainty of Christian eschatology, and its *content*, are drawn from revelation of God in Christ, on which the Church is based. The act of God is visibly proleptic in its nature; consequently, it has intro-

duced a *contradiction in the life of the Church*. As a result of
God's calling, the characteristics of the Church are unity,
sanctity, its universal claim extended to the entire world
and the whole of human life and its power to proclaim
the truth—and yet it is divided and sundered, a Church
of sinners, and sinful as a whole, separate from the world
both in its composition and its purpose, and yet able to
fall prey to worldliness. As the body of Christ, the Church
is hidden.

This contradiction calls the Church to action. It has
to struggle for sanctification and unity, and pursue the
conflict involved in missionary work, and the battle
against the demonic wilfulness of the forces manifest in
human life, and of the means man uses to maintain life.
But whatever may be achieved as the result of this
struggle, the contradiction cannot be removed. Progress
in missionary work is constantly faced by the painful
riddle of the closed door, and progress in sanctification
inexorably reveals the hidden power of sin even in the
Church, while zealous Christian activity in the social
sphere soon finds stiff barriers placed in its way. The removal of this contradiction cannot be looked for from
developments within the history of the Church. The contradiction cries out to be resolved by him whose word of
revelation in Christ brought it into being, Faith cannot
believe in God's acceptance of mankind, proclaimed in
this revelation, nor in his establishment of Christ as
Lord, if this acceptance does not lead to the hope of the
fulfilment of what God has already achieved prolep-
tically.

This hope is for one thing alone: that by the exercise
of God's power in Christ, the Church may become what
she is. But this means the emergence of Christ from the
concealment in which he lives, the realization of the
universal claim to which the Church bears witness, and

therefore the revelation of Christ to all men as the Lord—
the *parousia*. The revelation of the Lord in glory is a
judgement upon all who have heard his claim; not merely
a judgement dividing between one man and another,
but also, for the Church of believers, a judgement of
consummation, overcoming *death* and bringing to reality
the *eternal communion* of God. How God will set about the
redemption of those who have 'passed on' in the course
of history is hidden from us. But it is certain that the
removal of the contradiction that is in the Church will
include the passing away and the new creation of the
whole cosmos. It will pass away, because the law of sin
and death in the life of the Church is profoundly associated with the basic pattern of our present world and its
history; it will be recreated because the Church is not
exiled in the world, but intimately involved with it
through the creation, and by sharing in the curse which
is on it. The Church looks forward to a redemption not
out of the world, but with the world.

4. The Criticism of the Eschatology of the Final Phase of Time
This basic outline contains the premises necessary for an
answer to the most urgent problem of eschatology at
the present day: that of the relationship between *history*
and its *consummation*, or the *justification of an eschatology
which looks for an end within history*.

The traditional eschatology of the Church is concerned
not merely with the fact that history is finite, but with
the nature of the end of history. The *parousia*, the resurrection and the judgement are the final phase of history. The end is a goal. Consequently, history is regarded
as moving and maturing in an essentially progressive
process, in preparation for this end. Not that the *parousia*
and the consummation are brought about by, or consist
of, any development in history itself; but history pro-

gresses towards the 'fullness of time' before the *parousia*, and becomes ripe for this conclusion: first of all by the completion of the Church's mission to the world, the growing unity of mankind, and the gathering in of the Church, and secondly by the intensification of human sin and the increasingly acute opposition this produces between the kingdom of God and the world (Anti-Christ). Thus the final age consummates and draws to a conclusion the whole of history, and so brings to a head within history the great struggle which is the theme of history. If history comes to maturity in this way, is there any point in asking when the end will come, or in looking for signs of the end?

This view can of course claim the authority of biblical prophecy and apocalyptic. The eschatological statements of the New Testament prophesy the drama of the end of history, and look forward to the victory of Christ upon earth. But over and above its positive use of biblical and theological tradition, this theory is advanced in full con-sciousness of its practical necessity. An eschatology which looks forward to a consummation within history corres-ponds to a positive relationship to history on the part of God. God's activity in the history of salvation is through-out an acceptance of history—how can he deny it in the end? Mankind fell in history, and will be judged and redeemed in history. Through sin the curse of death fell upon the whole creation and it will be lifted at the end. The same history which saw the struggle and humiliation of Jesus, will also see his victory and a consummation within glory. Only an eschatology which proclaims a consummation within history can take seriously the his-torical character of the revelation and the redemption of God, the historical Church, the Church's history, its progress, and the work that goes on within it to achieve its goal. Without an eschatology looking to a consumma-tion within history, there can be no true theology of history, nor any thinking in terms of the Church's history in the theological sense.

Nevertheless, this theory is not theologically tenable. Our *criticism* is based not on some theology of history; it is a theological criticism and goes back to first principles. What is at issue is the fundamental question of the true theological understanding of revelation and its relationship to history. It is the will of God to lead men to communion with himself. This is why he has given us the way of decision and faith: God conceals his glory, and his revelation takes the form merely of a 'word', that is, a claim which demands a response of faith and allegiance. Because this is the way God desires to redeem man and bring him to communion with himself, he sets history free as a life of decision, defined and limited only by death—this is a *kenosis* on the part of God. He does not exercise this *kenosis within* history, but *by means of* history, which he has brought into being for the sake of his love. History *means kenosis*. The sudden revelation of the unveiled glory of God is not conceivable within history. For history is not merely the temporal condition under which we live our life, but life lived under the limitations imposed by death, and therefore under the law of conflict, God being concealed from us. History, death and faith belong together. Death cannot be treated as an accidental feature which might be removed from history. Death is not merely the external limit but also the inner form of all life lived within history: like history itself, *everything* within history is subject to death. Death forms part of the concept of history. This means that the 'original state of innocence' cannot refer to any historical moment. The concept of the state of innocence is essentially an aspect of man's consciousness of guilt, and cannot be made an objective feature of an historical world without sin and death. Such a picture is only of value for the sake of comparison. The same is true of the end. The state of innocence and the consummation, Paradise and the millennium all belong together. The direct and evident vision of the glory of God in Christ—that is, the *parousia*—means *the ending of history*. In the *kenosis*, which is implied by God's intervention in history, his glory is 'contemplated' only by faith. Anyone who doubts this is transgressing against the 'word of the cross' and ends up with the Jewish or pagan concept of revelation and of God. This is also true with regard to the miracles and resurrection of Jesus. Because the crucified Christ was glorified on Easter Day, he was taken away from the world of our perceptions. Even for the witnesses of the resurrection the glory of the living Christ was 'hidden in God'; it is only evident to faith. Jesus's miracles, on the other hand, are in no sense a real onset of the new age, the beginning of the conquest of death by life within history—both Christ who healed and those healed by him were going on to face death—and are merely prophetic signs of the conquest of death that is to come. Thus an appeal to the history of revelation cannot refute our principal thesis. The *parousia* signifies the limit of history, and chiliasm in any form, as a theoretical picture of the end, is an impossible concept in theology. Even at the end, the kingdom of Christ is not of this world.

Furthermore, this theory does not take death seriously as a dividing line between history and its consummation, between the 'world' and glory. Consummation and glory lie beyond death; this was revealed in Christ himself, and is the basic law of the Christian life. But the history of the individual and the history of the Church are similar in nature. Both have an end. But the end (even if there is in addition to death the other possibility of a 'change' without death, *cf.* I Cor. 15.51) in both cases signifies a real ending and abrogation of history. The goal lies beyond the end.

The correspondence between the life of the individual

and the history of the world leads to a further point. Time moves towards the end. To this extent history progresses; later periods are nearer to the end than those which preceded them (Rom. 13.11). This is also true of the life of the individual. But is it true that the last period before death is really the consummation and critical climax of life, the harvest time of the whole period? The spiritual movement of a life is not orientated towards death; from this point of view the time of death is arbitrary and incomprehensible. With this in mind, it is clearly a questionable procedure to designate the final phase of history as a whole as the climax and the time of maturity. History might very well come to an end as the result of the weakness of old age in humanity, just like the life of an individual. Or else a cosmic catastrophe might bring it to an end, without regard for its empirical 'ripeness' for the end. One cannot even say that a life comes to an end only as soon as it has developed and exhausted all its possibilities. And even if this were true of history, the exhaustion of its possibilities could not mean that they had been raised to their highest pitch. Thus history is progressing towards the end chronologically, but not necessarily with respect to its content or maturity, nor in such a way that one might conclude from the signs that the end is near.

Perhaps future history will see an even more fearsome manifestation of the demonic forces of Anti-Christ in Church and state. But such speculations must be carefully distinguished from the certain expectation of faith. And when the final phase of time is presented as a direct encounter between the gathered and purified Church and the 'world', this pietistic and judaising view must face the question of whether the Church can ever in the course of history be a distinct and perceptible entity, or whether it will remain the Church of faith to the very end. Even a Church tried and purified by persecutions cannot simply be equated with the Church of God, and is never merely opposed to the world. There can be no historical moment in which the Church would not have, and would not have to have, great solidarity with its opponents. The image of the final struggle has only a regulative significance for the Church: it expresses the severity of the struggle, and the Either-Or of the kingdom of God and the world, with which we are always faced, and therefore has a serious existential significance—but it cannot be turned into an objective theory of the final phase of history.

Nor is such a view demanded by the acceptance of biblical prophecy, properly understood. The true attitude to this is that biblical eschatology is always the *imminent expectation* of the end. But this means that prophecy has an entirely *pastoral significance*; it is meant to serve the needs of the present moment, it provides a basis for responsibility here and now, and it interprets the struggle that is under way in terms of its suprahistorical significance. It is true that Jesus makes use of apocalyptic material, but in his dramatic portrayal of the end, he falls behind his contemporaries, and the most chacteristic feature of the language he used about the end is that it is apocalyptic, but that everything serves as the basis of a call to decision, faithfulness and vigilance. The same is true of the Revelation of John: whether or not its individual images can be interpreted as references to contemporary events, the whole work is meant to be interpreted 'existentially' as a serious call and proclamation of consolation to its audience, the final generation. But this means that biblical prophecy is being misused when its concepts and images are isolated from the existential attitude of the imminent expectation of the end, and the certainty of the hour of decision which faces us at the present moment, and is turned into a dogmatic theory of the final period of history in the vague and distant future. One must not forget that all serious and living eschatology has taken the form of the imminent expectation of the end and saw the signs of the *parousia* in its own time. To take biblical prophecy as the word of God means to use its interpretation of the time in which it was written to interpret one's own present existence in the light of the ultimate decision. The 'signs of the time' point directly to the present moment. Biblical prophecy helps us to see the profundity and the limits of history, and in this, and in no other way, to foretell its future.

The rejection of an eschatology looking forward to a final phase of history by no means implies that history is regarded as a matter of indifference. Neither the consciousness of the approach in time of the end and the kingdom of God, nor a responsible attitude to the transitory moment and its unique claim, has anything to do with apocalyptic eschatology. Neither the course of history, nor the unity of the Church through the ages become matters of indifference—for it is the course and condition of our life as such which provides the basis for serious and mutual responsibility as the end draws near. The Church must arm itself not for the final battle, which may be far off but for the battle it is facing now, which must be fought as though it were the last.

5. *The Truth contained in Chiliasm*

At the same time, we must take note of the fact that in early Protestant theology the rejection of chiliasm, and the lack of emphasis on an eschatology looking forward to a consummation within history, was associated with indifference to missionary work and with practical inactivity on the part of the Church, whereas the return of *chiliasm* has brought with it an increased understanding of the history of salvation in a Church alive to its missionary task and to the need for Christian action. Thus our objection to chiliastic theology must not mean that we accept an anti-chiliastic view. The early Protestant rejection of chiliasm failed to recognize the *truth concealed in it*: the certainty of the eschatological significance of the activity of the Church within its own life and in the world.

We sanctify ourselves because we possess the hope of eternal life; we sanctify ourselves that we may become the new men whom it is God's will to create. But our action is directed not merely towards ourselves, but also towards specific commands and tasks. It is possible for these to mean more than merely the material on which men destined for eternity carry out their duty, more than merely the instruments of the faithful exercise of a particular individual service, more than just necessities for the maintenance of our own lives. If we take up our practical tasks with love, we do so in the certainty of their eschatological value, their relevance to the 'new world'. The sanctification of the body is carried out in the hope of the resurrection; for the resurrection signifies a connection between the present state of our mind and body, and its heavenly form. But the body is a part of the world, and the world, an extension of our reality; thus the service we carry out towards the world is related to our hope of resurrection. Even in this world we acknowledge this relationship. Thus all earthly attempts to build up the 'city of God' and the whole medical struggle against death point to the eternal victory; all our wrestling with refractory material in coming to understand the world and in our social formation, points to our eternal freedom in a world wholly filled and formed by the spirit. Our service to the Church, to civilization and to the ordering of the life of society does not create the new world, any more than our work of sanctification creates a perfect man. In both cases, the gospel excludes a teleology in which perfection is obtained by ethical means.

What we build, even as members of the Church, is subject to death. It is not true that the 'history of Christian civilization', guided by the power of God, will lead on into the kingdom of God. Here the pessimism of Lutheranism is completely justified. *God* creates the new world from the death of this world of ours, including all its 'imperishable values'. But although Christian action does not lead directly to the consummation, it does so indirectly. In this world we act in the certainty that God has set up a relationship between the new world and our service. Just as the consequence of our personal hope is not a pessimistic tolerance of sin, but a serious devotion to the task of sanctification—even though we remain in sin until the end—so the hope of the world to come is expressed in action in this world. Insofar as the relationship is 'metaphysical' it is hidden to us, insofar as it is ethical it is clear. We must bear testimony to our faith in the resurrection not by theosophical speculation, but by our ethical responsibility. We fight against death—as people who nevertheless must die—as a witness to our hope of life. We struggle with the demonic elements in social life to bring about a better social order, and with chaos to bring about a genuine coherence, although we are constantly defeated and disappointed—but the question is not one of optimism or pessimism, nor of the degree of our success, but of our testimony to the promised consummation of the whole world. The unity of the Church is a confession of our hope. Our service to the Church, to civilization and to the world is a petition for our consummation.

This is the truth that is contained in chiliasm. As an objective vision of the future of the *homo otiosus*, as a piece of wishful thinking and a Utopia, it must be rejected. But as an expression of the relationship between concrete historical service and the world to come, or of the responsibility of orientating everything here and now upon earth towards the kingdom that is to come, it has a real and obvious value as a parable. Thus even chiliasm has a contemporary and existential use and interpretation. It preserves the genuine realism of our hope and responsibility in the face of every mystical and spiritualizing abandonment of this world. It proclaims the truth that contradicts all the empty promises of other-worldly consolation. Chiliasm means to be true to this world, even in the certainty of death, for the sake of the hope of the resurrection; it means to fight for the victory of God through Christ even within the historical reality of this world, and to realize that it is in this world, and in concrete activity, that we must bear witness to the kingdom that is to come.

Our criticism of the eschatology looking to a consummation within history, insofar as it is intended to be an objective description, is not a simple negation. Its purpose is also to preserve the 'contemporary' truth of this eschatology.

6. *Eschatology and Ethics*

Like death in the life of the individual, the *parousia* is both the end and the consummation of history. Of course if these two statements are both asserted simultaneously, they do not make possible any theoretical portrayal of what is to come, nor do they permit an unambiguous metaphysical explanation of the co-existence of the total breach and the continuity between this world and the next. But both are necessary principles for the attitude of faith. Eschatology completely fulfils its purpose, when it brings to faith responsibility and joyfulness in *action*. It has nothing to do with the thirst for speculative knowledge, peaceful contemplation, or pleasurable fantasy. It is always actuality. *Eschatology and ethics* belong together. One without the other is futile. To hope is to labour; the Church hopes by struggling earnestly for the gathering in of the Church and the conquest of the demonic powers. But as we work we must renew the sober and humble attitude of expectation, for our victories are never true, perfect or pure victories. Within our actions there sounds the prayer: Thy kingdom come. But this prayer goes far *beyond* our actions and what they achieve.

Paul Althaus

7
Baptism

I. BAPTISM IN PRIMITIVE CHRISTIANITY

1. Pre-Christian Baptismal Practices
a. THE MYSTERY RELIGIONS. *Baptismal practices* are found in innumerable forms throughout the ancient East. *In Egypt* the water of the Nile, from which life and fertility flows out over the whole land every year, was regarded as having magic power. Washings in the temple had a sacramental significance from the earliest times. At later periods such rites seem to have been even more highly valued and more widespread. The dead passed through a baptism into the next world. But even in this life those who desired salvation were consecrated by sprinkling or dipping, as in the mysteries of Isis; by this means they were made partakers of the life of the goddess, and received purity, and new and incorruptible life. In the countries along the Euphrates we hear much from the earliest times of penitential and purification ceremonies, and also of the magical power of water, but very little of washings or immersions. But it seems to be the case that sacramental baths of purification played an important part in the *mysteries* of Mithras. The same is true of the elaborate and esoteric mysteries of Greece and Asia Minor. Those who took part in the mysteries of the Phrygian Attis were incorporated by a baptism in blood into the death and life of their god. They climbed down into a dark pit, just as the god had once descended into the grave. But there they received new life through the

blood of a sacrifice, which poured down upon them, and climbed out, 'born again unto eternity'. This is the most extreme expression of a theme which underlies the meaning of all the various baptismal practices of the Near East; those who seek salvation are longing for a life which is stronger than sin, the world, and death. Penitential prayers and efforts of the will fail to lead them to their goal. They find their salvation in baths of purification, which wash away their old sins with a magic power, that is, in the *sacrament* of baptism. They were raised above the world, and their lives were united with that of God through the *mystery* of baptism. In fact they are not content with one consecration and one mystery. By undergoing one 'baptism' after another, they hoped that in the end all their corruptible nature would wither away and ultimately be replaced by the life of God. For this is the basic principle which is increasingly evident in these baptismal usages; *the analogy between baptism and death.*

b. JUDAISM. *Ancient Israel* was also acquainted with ritual washings and sprinklings, the meaning and purpose of which was the restoration of cultic purity (2 Sam. 12.20; Pss. 26.6; 51.9; Ezek. 36.25). The later *law* made numerous purification ceremonies an obligation on the devout Israelite (Lev. 11 ff.; Num. 19). Baptismal baths became more and more widespread. For centuries the 'bath' formed part of the Jewish synagogue. Amongst the *Pharisees* particularly strict purification regulations were developed (*cf.* Mark 7.1 ff.) as also amongst other groups which separated themselves from the mass of the people in order, in a small and restricted community, to fulfil the law of God down to the last detail and to realize the ideal of the true congregation of God (*cf.* e.g. *The Damascus Text* 12). We also hear of purification rites in the syncretistic sects which sprang up in colourful profusion wherever the Jews were, especially amongst the *Essenes* and the various *baptist sects* of the land east of the Jordan (*cf.* 2c. below). Here, in addition to the daily baths, particular baptisms on special occasions possessed an enhanced significance. It appears that the high value placed on such customs considerably increased during the first century of the Christian era, (*cf.* the 'Baptists' in Justin, *Dialogue* 80 and the Hemerobaptists described by Hegesippus, in Eusebius, *Hist. Eccle.* IV, 22.7). The desert saint Banus mentioned by Josephus (*Vita* II), whose zeal for sanctification was expressed in continuous washings, must have been a typical phenomenon at that period. It is clear that the repetition of these washings was not merely optional, but obligatory, and the more they were repeated ('by day and night') the more it was a sign of the utmost piety. On the other hand, an immersion carried out once only later became the custom at the reception of proselytes into the congregation of the Jewish covenant. It is true that this *proselyte baptism* is not recorded before the first century of the Christian era; but it was probably adopted earlier. Anyone who underwent it had for the first time, and in a decisive way, attained to the ritual purity without which it was not possible to belong to the people of God. From then on he was a new creation—or rather, he was regarded as such; the baptismal customs practised in ordinary Judaism were not intended to make the magical power of the water available to the person baptized in the sense of the mysteries, or to carry out any sort of consecration. There was no renewal of man apart from God. The washing, the bath of baptism, is in the strictest sense a sign *ordained by God*, a legal condition for acceptance under the law. Anyone who fulfils these conditions with knowledge and a right intention, is regarded from henceforth as purified and renewed in the sight of God and his law. In the groups which produced the Jewish Sibyllines this strictly Jewish conception of baptism took on an apocalyptic element; in a decisive *moment of history* the bath of baptism is the last means of salvation for a humanity which is subject to the wrath of God that is about to break forth. 'Turn away from your acts, . . . bathe your whole body in the ever flowing streams and . . . beg for forgiveness for your previous works' (*Sibyllines* IV, 162 ff.; *cf. The Life of Adam and Eve* 4 ff., and also Apuleius, *Metam.* 11.1). The atmosphere and ideas which form the background to the appearance of the Baptist are obviously of a similar nature.

c. THE BAPTIST. The career of *John the Baptist* recalls in many respects (Mark 1.6; 6.17 ff.; *cf.* Luke 1.15,80) the ideal of the ancient Rechabites and Nazarenes, and the figure of Banus sketched for us by Josephus. But the Baptist was not a hermit, but a prophet (*cf.* Luke 1.76 f.; 3.19 f.), an apocalyptic preacher who interpreted to his people the threatening signs of their time and communicated his passionate concern to a growing circle of disciples (*cf.* Mark 6.29; John 3.25 f.; 4.1). He preached that it was no longer of any value to belong to the people of Abraham, that the only thing that was of any worth was repentance, the abandonment of one's previous practices, and a return to a new and righteous life (Luke 3.7 ff.; Matt. 21.32; Acts 13.24). Those who were ready to repent in this way underwent baptism in the Jordan (Mark 1.4 f.; *cf.* Acts 13.24; 19.4) and were thereby sealed as members of the new and true people of God (*cf.* Luke 1.17), who would survive the coming catastrophe and receive the spirit who was to come upon them. The promise of the forgiveness of sins (Mark 1.4; Luke 3.3) is unlikely to be a later addition, *cf.* Josephus, *Antiquities* XVIII, 5.2 (?), but should be understood on the analogy of the words in the Sibylline Oracles (*cf.* also the theme of the prayer in Luke 3.21). In any case, the Jewish *apocalyptic* character of John the Baptist, by contrast with anything resembling the mysteries, is quite clear (*cf.* for the terminology Mark 7.1 ff.; Luke 11.38; Acts

9.37; John 3.25; 13.10; Heb. 6.1 f.). In this baptism the status of man with regard to God and his own history is decided (*cf.* Mark 11.30; Luke 7.30; Josephus *loc. cit.*), as well as his destiny in the coming aeon (but *cf.* Luke 3.7 ff.). The Baptist and his 'baptism' evidently made a powerful impression on the people: Josephus, *loc. cit.*, Mark 11.30; Luke 7.29 ff.; Matt. 14.5; 21.32. Even in Ephesus, as late as the middle of the first century, there were still disciples of John the Baptist who practised the baptism of John, Acts 18.24 ff.; 19.1 ff. (*cf.* also John 1.19ff.; *Ps.-Clem. Hom.* 2.23). In the later strata of Mandaean literature John appears as the highest revelation of Anosh Uthras, the final ambassador of the heavenly world (*cf.* also *Ps.-Clem. Hom.* 1 ff.), who renews the original revelation and brought the first baptism (*cf.* 2*c.* below). But the movement begun by the Baptist is important in world history on account of its effect on Christianity.

2. The Beginnings of Christian Baptism

a. JESUS. The Baptist prepared the way for *Jesus* (*cf.* Acts 1.22; 10.37 f.; 13.24). Jesus himself received the *baptism of John*—as one of many (Mark 1.9); this in itself was a considerable scandal to later Christianity (Matt. 3.14), which makes it all the more certain that the incident is historical. Perhaps Jesus worked for a period east of the Jordan, alongside John and in a similar way to him (John 3.26; 10.40 f.), proclaiming the imminence of the Kingdom and gathering a circle of disciples about himself, and also—though there is some doubt about this—baptizing (John 3.22; 4.1 ff.). The gospels describe and portray this, like all other events, in terms of the ultimate purpose of God (*cf.* Luke 1.17; 7.26 ff.; Mark 1.7 f.; Matt. 11.12 ff.; Acts 19.4), and the teleological emphasis is the strongest in John. According to him the only significance of the baptism of Jesus was that of a testimony to the Son (1.31 ff.), and the purpose of the baptism with water is fulfilled by its pointing beyond itself; the true power to baptize lies in the hands of the Messiah, who brings the water of life (3.5; 7.37 ff.; 15.26; 19.34 f.; 1 John 5.6 ff.; *cf.* Rev. 22.1,17; *Odes of Solomon* 6; 11; 30; *Poimandres* 4.4; *Right Ginza*) and baptism with the spirit (1.25 ff.; *cf.* 20.21 ff.). The Baptist himself had fulfilled his mission when he had led the first disciples to him who was greater than himself (1.19 ff., 35 ff.; 3.29). From the moment when the Baptist disappears we hear nothing more in any of the gospels about baptizing. Even in the missionary discourses, which go into so many individual details, Jesus says nothing about baptizing. Jesus apparently did not continue the baptism of John, nor did he replace it by some other baptismal practice. Even in the mind of the Baptist, baptism was merely a sign foretelling, as though in a parable, the baptism with spirit and fire. When Jesus speaks of 'baptism' he is using it as an image for what he was truly sent to do, his *death*. This passage through the world of death is the ultimate and fundamental realization of what is meant in every baptism. Only when this passage has been carried out is the consummation of his work possible—the casting of fire upon the earth (Luke 12.49 ff.; *cf.* also Mark 14. 36). Is it a coincidence that here the old analogy of baptism in death reappears, although in a new form? The East understood baptism as an image of death, whereas Jesus presented his death as a baptism! The relationship between a visible and an invisible reality is completely reversed. The same is true of the saying in the synoptic gospels concerning the sons of Zebedee (Mark 10.35 ff.; *cf.* also Rev. 3.21). Here again 'baptism' is a metaphor for the final demand that Christ has to make upon the disciples who wish one day to be exalted to the right and left hand of his throne—death as martyrs.

b. THE EARLY CHURCH. Just as suddenly as the baptism of John disappears from the purview of the gospels as soon as the Baptist is imprisoned, so in the same way *the practice of Christian baptism* seems to have begun immediately after the resurrection. It is not easy to draw a reliable picture of its earliest form, especially since the description given in Acts is not altogether unambiguous or disinterested. But it is clear enough from the Epistles of Paul (Rom. 6.3) that baptism was practised amongst the Christian churches before Paul began his work. And we can probably draw some conclusions about the nature and meaning of baptism in the early years from the saying of Peter in Acts 2.38: 'Repent, and be baptized every one of you in the name of Jesus Christ for the forgiveness of your sins; and you shall receive the gift of the Holy Spirit'. It was preceded by the call to repentance (*cf.* Acts 8.12). Even the way baptism was carried out may have been borrowed, in its basic pattern, from the baptism of John (8.38). There was not much concern as to the person who carried the baptism out; he did not need to be an apostle (8.16; 9.18); in fact sometimes it actually seems as though the apostles held back from so doing (10.48). The decisive point is that the baptism was carried out '*in the name of Jesus Christ*'—and this implies a fundamental difference from the baptism of John (19.5). The name was probably spoken (frequently as an exorcism; *cf.* also Mark 16.16 f.) over the person being baptized as he was immersed (10.48; 8.16). But it also seems as though the baptized person himself had called on this name immediately before baptism in a prayer which took the form of a *confession of faith* (22.16; the later and more detailed description—8.37—gives a different picture). This shows that the person to be baptized must have learnt this name and known what it signified (2.36; 8.35; 19.15,33; 18.8; *cf.* Matt. 28.18 f.). The preaching of the kingdom and the name deeply affected those who had heard it, and they accepted baptism as a confession of repentance and faith in Christ. This explains the *double effect* of baptism; the forgiveness of sins and the bestowal of the spirit. What in the baptism of John was still only a promise and a hope of the mercy of God, had now, through what Jesus had done, become a fact, to which the believer became subject in baptism (22.16). Through the forgiveness of sins, the baptism of primitive Christianity became a sacrament. The old life was taken away. But this is not all: a new life entered the believer in the form of the spirit—and this was an event which surpassed everything. This is what finally replaced John's baptism of repentance (19.1 ff.). But even this event does not seem to have been invariably and absolutely dependent on the (previous) carrying out of the rite of baptism. This must be the reason why the baptism practised by the early Church was not called a mystery. Baptism is a human provision, a visible pointer to an act of creation carried out by God. But this act of God can precede the human ceremony (9.17 f.; 10.48). God remains free with respect to men, and even free with respect to his own ordinance; the spirit is not bound by this external form. Thus by comparison with the baptism of the spirit the rite of baptism was a subsidiary feature; and this explains why in early Christianity the rite was far from having the same central position as in the baptist sects, and why, furthermore, it was administered in such a free and unpedantic fashion, far different from any baptismal practice in the heathen world. Nevertheless, when a person was filled with the spirit, this normally demanded that the act of baptism precede or follow it. And in all circumstances baptism retained its fixed and immovable place in the life of the early Church—as an act of acceptance into the covenant of the new and true people of God. To be baptized, and to be incorporated into the people of God are synonymous (2.41; *cf.* also John 4; Matt. 28.18 f.). Mass baptisms as in the case of John and related manifestations, seem to have been quite frequent.

Acts in particular mentions huge numbers especially at the early baptisms. Even later whole 'houses' were received (16.15,33; *cf.* 1 Cor. 1.16; for the terminology compare the parallel passage Ignatius *ad Polyc.* 8.2). The baptism of infants is not mentioned.

The *origin of early Christian baptism* remains a problem. It is a problem when we look at the comparable baptismal usages in the Near East; it is even more of a problem when we look again at the baptism of John. At the beginning there is the Baptist, and the baptism of Jesus; then during the actual period of Jesus's ministry baptism is an image for his passion (and for martyrdom); in the early Church, a new kind of baptism appears as an established usage. What is the connection between all this? Each of the three synoptics suggests by their own particular presentation a solution of the problem, an understanding of the matter which once again is based on the state of affairs that ultimately prevailed. On the day on which Christ was baptized the spirit brooded over the water as it had done on the first day of creation. What took place in the Jordan is in truth the baptism of the spirit and the calling of the Son, it is a consecration for his work (*cf.* Acts 10.38). It is superseded in importance (*cf.* Mark 1.11 with 9.7) by the transfiguration and the proclamation of the Son, the consecration for his suffering (*cf.* Matt. 17.12 f.). It must be consummated (*cf.* also Ignatius *ad. Eph.* 18.2) in the death of the Son, the baptism by death which now looms over the whole story—and is at the same time a pattern for the martyrdom of the disciples. Thus Mark sees the course of events as proceeding from one baptism to another 'baptism'. The Marcan ending goes a step further (16.15 ff.). The same is true of Matthew, whose gospel reaches its climax in the institution of Christian baptism. In both cases it is a saying of the risen Christ which founds the new practice. The words of Matt. 28.19 do not give the impression of being original. But this tradition must go back to a fact, and behind the fact there must stand the exalted Lord. This is the only way in which the origin of Christian baptism can be understood. Luke also understood it in this way. The line he traces reveals the clearest unity; his account leads from the baptism of John and the promise of him who is to come to baptize with the Spirit and with fire, through the baptism of Jesus with the Spirit, and the saying concerning the baptism of suffering and the fire that is to break out over the earth, back to the promise of the Spirit (Acts 1.5,8). It ends, not with the command to baptize (but compare also Luke 24.47) but with the baptism from heaven through the Spirit, who descends in tongues of fire upon the disciples, and from then on pursues his course through the world through the chosen bearers of the Spirit, through the bearing of witness, baptism and the laying on of hands (Acts 11.11 f.).

It is difficult to trace the early origins of primitive Christian baptism. But its *basic character* is clear. It is not related only to God and to history like the baptism of John; its distinctive nature is decided by a third factor, its relationship to the act of Jesus. This is what is assumed when the name of Jesus is spoken over the newly baptized. The baptized person is drawn into a new story of creation, which has begun with Christ, who is the divine act of creation. This is the basic idea which can be traced through the descriptions of the gospels. But the principle which gives shape to this cosmic history is the Spirit, who now takes possession of the believer himself. Thus there is a deep significance in the later administration of baptism in the name of the Father and the Son and the Spirit.

c. SYNCRETISTIC BAPTIST COMMUNITIES. What, then, is the *relationship between early Christian baptism and later baptismal usages*? However highly baptism in the name of Jesus may have been regarded, the strict observance of the *first church of Jerusalem* would naturally still include the washings prescribed by the law (*cf.* Acts 21.23 ff.). In the same way those who may have joined it from the new Jewish baptizing movement, or came under the influence of these movements, would have brought their devout practices with them into Christianity. But our sources are silent on the matter (*cf.* however Mark 7.1 ff.), and it is not likely that these earlier usages played any important part in the new Church—so long as, and insofar as there was still a living awareness of the link between the act of baptism and a history understood in an apocalyptic sense. But in the Palestinian churches the law soon triumphed once again over Christ, and it was also very early that the gospel of Christ was accepted by groups with a gnostic tendency and assimilated by them (*cf.* Acts 8.9 ff.). Thus in the wide field of *Judaeo-Christian syncretism*, in spite of a great deal of profound speculation concerning baptism (*cf.* the Nazarene gospel, the Ebionite gospel, the Pseudo-Clementines, etc.), the understanding of the unique and creative character of the act of baptism was increasingly forgotten. As this went on, the high value placed on baptism and the freedom of usage in its administration, which is so characteristic of the early Church, was naturally also lost. Christian baptism became one custom alongside others, and was elaborated and degraded by numerous ancient and alien baptismal practices which had to be scrupulously observed down to the last detail (*cf.* also *Ps.-Clem. Hom.* X, f., *et passim*). This is particularly true of the baptizing sects which maintained themselves for a long time east and south-east of the Jordan, the country where the Baptist had worked (e.g. the Ebionites; *cf.* also the mention of the Jordan in the *Life of Adam and Eve* 6 f.). This is the region in which it appears that about 100 A.D. the prophet Elchasai attempted to found a syncretistic 'universal religion', which proclaimed a new forgiveness of sins, a baptism that could be repeated, and a large number of religious washings. From such movements the baptizing community of the Mandaeans seems to have adopted numerous elements. In their writings the Baptist is opposed to Jesus (*cf.* also the *Pseudo-Clementine Recognitions* 1.54 ff.). The name Nazarene reappears; 'Jordan' is a technical term in their baptismal ritual, which has close connections with the later Nestorian baptismal liturgies. In all these communities, and often even in their names, baptism plays a predominant part, more in a sense than in Christianity. But the distinctive nature of primitive Christian baptism—both in theory and in practice—has been lost. The early history of Christian baptism goes from Jesus through the primitive Church and is continued by Paul.

3. Paul

a. BAPTISMAL PRACTICE. In the *baptismal practice of the Pauline churches* the tradition of the primitive Church seems at first to have been continued, even in the fact that baptism could easily be left to subordinate assistants (1 Cor. 1.11 ff.; *cf.* John 4.2; Acts 10.48). As before, the name of Jesus is of decisive importance. It appears that Paul himself did not interfere in the traditional practice or in its continuing development. He apparently has no knowledge of the baptism of infants; what he writes in 1 Cor. 7.14 concerning the sanctifying of children by their parents does not imply this. He did not oppose the baptism for the dead practised by the Corinthians. It was only occasionally or indirectly that he dealt with such matters at all. This was not on account of a *disciplina arcani* such as that of the mysteries, but a deliberate attempt to reject any over-estimation of the value of external cultic acts. He was not sent to baptize, but to proclaim the gospel (1 Cor. 1.17). But Paul certainly did not despise the event which was manifested and consummated in the human action of baptism.

b. PAUL'S CONCEPTION OF BAPTISM. Rather, he saw and evaluated it in a completely new and profound context. Paul's thought spans the centuries. At the time of the very origin of the ancient people of God the Baptism that is to come was foreshadowed (1 Cor. 10.1 ff.). But the basic premise on which Christian baptism rests is *the reality of Christ*, the fact of the life and death of Jesus and his new life in heaven. The Christian is cleansed, sanctified and justified in the name of the Lord (1 Cor. 6.11); he is founded upon Christ (1 Cor. 1.21 f.), anointed and—the ancient apocalyptic term for the signing with the sign of salvation and the covenant—sealed (*cf.* also Rom. 4.11). All these phrases probably refer to baptism. The rite of baptism is the visible act through which the existence of a Christian is founded upon the fact of Jesus. A baptized person is taken up into the living unity of the body of Christ (1 Cor. 12.13); he puts off the old man and puts on Christ (Gal. 3.27). Baptism into Christ looks back in particular to the death of Jesus (*cf.* 1 Cor. 1.13) and is in fact a baptism into his death. What originally happened in Christ as a pattern for others, is now repeated in the Christian; he is buried with Christ in baptism and resurrected with him 'through faith' (Rom. 6.3 ff.; Col. 2.12). Thus the old expression, the baptism of death, once again takes on a real meaning. Jesus called his death a baptism. Paul calls baptism a death. The relationship of Paul to the primitive Church is clear. For him also, the nature of baptism is given by three basic themes: God, history and the fact of Jesus. But for the Apostle, here as elsewhere, the decisive element in the fact of Jesus is the *cross*. Baptism stands under the sign of the cross. Thus it is the Pauline understanding of baptism which gives a due place to the final and most profound insights of Jesus. A comparison with the mystery religions surrounding the Pauline churches shows even more clearly the distinctive nature of his baptism. For Paul baptism is neither a magical mechanism nor a symbol full of meaning but a mythical fact which is accomplished in moral action; if it is not carried through to its consummation it ceases to be of value (1 Cor. 10.2 ff.). Thus in its entirety it points beyond itself. It is the point through which man passes to a new existence, which can now begin, and must begin. He who has been baptized has risen from the dead. But this mythical fact only takes shape and effect in this world in the way he 'walks'. At the same time, however, even this form of life, which is lived entirely under the sign of faith, points beyond itself to a consummation, to the visible resurrection and future life with Christ. The rite of baptism consists of this: that God places man at the heart of a history that embraces the whole universe, which began at the cross and ends in glory.

4. *Post-Pauline Churches*

a. BAPTISMAL CUSTOMS. We have little knowledge of the baptismal usages of the *gentile Christian churches* after Paul. *Didache* 7 is the first indication we possess (*cf.* IV, 1 below): the stress is placed on the Trinitarian formula (*cf.* Matt. 28.19; Justin, *Apol.* I, 61), which clearly became more and more widespread (*cf.* 1 John 5.8). In accordance with this, the baptismal confession of faith which precedes the act of baptism also takes a three-fold form. But the relating of baptism to Christ alone and to his name was not immediately abandoned (Hermas *Sim.* IX, 16.3; Acts 8.37). The sign of the cross was made numerous times over the person to be baptized. A wide freedom of usage still obtained; the ideal was immersion (*cf.* Hermas *Mand.* 3.1), but this was not obligatory; there was a choice between running and still water, and between cold and warm water; and we soon hear of the laying on of hands (Heb. 6.2) and of the witness of the baptism (*Didache* 7.4); sometimes there is no mention of who carried the baptism out, and sometimes there is the instruction that there was to be no baptism without the bishop (Ignatius *ad. Smyrn.* 8.2). And we scarcely ever know over how wide a region an individual rule or custom was in force. We find an occasional mention of anointing, renunciation, exorcism and other practices; in Eph. 5.14 we seem to possess a baptismal hymn; the Acts of Thomas suggest that the form taken by the celebration of baptism in gnostic and syncretistic circles was much more complicated (as can also be seen from gnostic formulae of baptism). In the early Church not much importance seems to have been placed on the way in which baptism was carried out (Tertullian *de baptismo* 2). The day of baptism was distinguished more and more as the decisive turning point in the life of the newly baptized. Baptism formed the conclusion of an impressive period of preparation (*Didache* 7.1; *cf.* Hermas *Sim.* III, 7.3); it signified entry into the congregation (*cf.* Eph. 4.5); it was the only way to obtain admission to the Eucharist (*Didache* 9.5; *cf. Ps.-Clem. Hom.* 11.36). A baptism of this sort is exclusively intended for adults. The presuppositions and motives for the baptism of infants can be understood, and the early stages of this practice gradually become visible, but no account is taken of it in the rite (against this *cf.* Tertullian *de baptismo* 18). Baptism was meant to be an ending and a new beginning. It was a penitential confession—and there practical problems are powerfully evident (Heb. 6.4 ff.; Hermas *Mand.* IV; Tertullian *de baptismo* 18)—a vow to observe purity of life (2 Clem. 6.9; *Acta Pauli et Theclae* 6). This it was able to be because the sternness of the demand is transfigured by the glory of the gift of God, for in the insignificant human act of baptism the great *creative event of baptism* is made visible.

b. THEIR CONCEPTION OF BAPTISM. However impoverished the act of baptism was at that period in external ceremony, the *ideas* that at the same period gathered around the event of baptism were numerous and profound. The typological 'pre-history' of Christian baptism is traced back even beyond Moses (*cf.* 3*b*. above) to Noah (1 Peter 3.20 f.; Heb. 9.10,19; 10.22, *cf.* Mark 4.7; *Barn.* 11). The baptism of Jesus once again becomes a problem (*cf.* Ignatius *ad Smyrn.* 1.1); Jesus was baptized in order to purify the water through his sufferings (*ad Eph.* 18.2). Baptism and death belong together and together they provide the prerequisite for Christian baptism: the death of Christ must first cleanse the water of sin (*cf.* III *Enoch* 42; *Right Ginza* 140.3; 163 ff.), if the water of baptism is to have the power to take away sin (*cf.* with Melito *Fragm.* VIII, the analogy between the king's bath of purification and that of the sun god Re in the Pyramid texts). It is natural that an event which was foreshadowed and prepared in such a way should be accorded the highest significance. Without baptism there is no salvation (*cf.* *Ps.-Clem. Hom.* 13.21; *Recogn.* 6). Baptism '*redeems*'! This is the word which occurs again and again with the most varied meanings. To what extent does baptism redeem? It cleanses the inner man and brings about the forgiveness of the sins he has previously committed (Eph. 5.26; Heb. 10.22; *Barn.* 11; Hermas *Mand.* 3.1; 1 Peter 3.21; *cf. Sybillines* 4.167 f.). The demons flee. Their power is broken. In the midst of the night of death the dawn of a new day in the life of the baptized and the world shines on him (Eph. 5.14; Heb. 6.4). He is armed with the spirit (Eph. 4.5; 1 John 5.6 ff.; Ignatius *ad Polyc.* 6.2), and is 'upheld by the angelic powers'. But the spirit is the seal and pledge of his redemption at the end of time. Thus baptism still has its original significance of acceptance as one of the heirs of the world to come (Eph. 1.13; 4.30).

This apocalyptic idea is found again in the Epistle to Titus, but the other conception, of the death of the old man and the resurrection of the new in baptism, is developed and forced into a formula drawn from a language of the mysteries: baptism is a bath of rebirth (Titus 3.5; *cf.* Justin *Apol.* I 61; *Barn.* 16.8). Both ideas, of baptism as a passage to new life and as a precondition of the future life, can in fact scarcely be separated from each other (*cf.* also the heavenly baptism in the *Apocalypse of Peter* 14). Originally and in essence they belong together, and both are still prominent in the same elementary unity in Hermas (*Sim.* IX, 16). In the descent (*katabasis*) into the water the death of the old man takes place. The rising (*anabasis*) out of the water is the entry to new life. And at the same time the passage through the water is the sealing of those who enter into the kingdom that is to come. But the water of which the parable speaks is described under many images; sometimes that of the baptismal water (*Sim.* IX 3.3; 4.4; 15.4; 16.4; *cf.* *Vis.* III, 3.5), sometimes the water of Hades (*Sim.* IX, 16.5; *cf.* *Vis.* III, 2.2) and the water of death (Syrian *Apoc. Baruch* 53 ff.)—and sometimes both together (*Sim.* IX, 16.6 f.; *cf.* *Vis.* III, 5.5 f.). Once again we meet the basic *analogy between baptism and death*.

It was also possible to understand the death of martyrdom in terms of the same analogy, and this was bound to happen. Just as the believer saves his life through the water (*Vis.* III, 3.5; *cf.* I Peter 3.20), so the martyr saves his true life through death (*Sim.* VIII, 2.1; 3.6; *cf.* I Peter 4.1; *Ps.-Clem. Hom.* 13.20). As baptism cleanses from sin (*Mand.* IV, 3.1), so martyrdom renews and brings to a conclusion this purification (*Sim.* IX, 28.3,5 f.). Melito of Sardes (*Fragm.* XII) makes this point even clearer: 'There are two means which bring us the forgiveness of sins, suffering for Christ's sake and baptism' (*cf. Acta Pauli et Theclae* 34). In the *Martyrdom of Perpetua and Felicitas* (18.2; 21.2) the death of those who bear witness by their blood is described and portrayed as a 'second baptism', and Tertullian brings his treaties *de baptismo* to a climax in a chapter (16) about the baptism which replaces and renews the baptism of water, the 'baptism of blood'. The development of the Church can be seen in this. But martyrdom is still seen as Jesus saw it, as a baptism. Baptism still stands where Paul set it, under the sign of the cross.

Ethelbert Stauffer

II. THE HISTORY OF THE DOCTRINE OF BAPTISM

1. The Earliest Period

From the very beginning (*cf.* I, 2-4 above) baptism was regarded as the form of acceptance into the Church of Christ, ordained by Christ himself, and as such not to be repeated. At the same time, however, it was easy for gentile churches to think of it also as a sealing or illumination, on the lines of the ceremonies of initiation into the mysteries, although it was by no means as strongly exposed to the influence of the mysteries as the Eucharist (*cf. Eucharist* I, 3-4 p. 352 f., below). As a sacred custom which derived from the will of Christ it had to be observed, but was far less subject to fanciful notions picked up by individuals from their environment. Because the stimulus of this kind of speculation was relatively less, the adaptation of baptism did not develop far along these lines even in Greek theology. When the newly baptized Christians were accepted into the congregation, they entered into the possession of all the spiritual heritage of that congregation. There was no absolutely fixed theory as to what was essential in the rite and what was merely an addition (e.g. immersion, the naming of the holy name, the laying on of hands, or anointing). There was equally little agreement as to whether any particular element was of special value and which were to be regarded as the peculiar gifts of baptism. The formula 'in the name of Christ' remained, although the Pauline idea of incorporation into Christ became less prominent. But the Church, which possessed his body and his spirit, offered through them a fullness of individual gifts. Examples of this development can be found in the *Apostolic and early Catholic Fathers*. The *Didache* emphasizes the name of God; *Barnabas* makes a connection between the purifying bath of water and the atoning cross; Hermas speaks of the uniqueness of baptism; Ignatius of Antioch sees in it a weapon against the devil (*cf.* I, 4*b*. above). Justin compares it to a rebirth. Irenaeus regards it as indispensable to the union of Christ and the Church. Melito (of whose work only fragments were known at the time this article was written; a fairly complete text has since been discovered—Translator) and Tertullian (*de baptismo*) wrote at length concerning baptism. The latter emphasizes the absolute necessity of baptism according to the will of Christ, justifies the simplicity of the rite by pointing out that this was appropriate to the simplicity of God, and speaks of the secret power of the water, which, together with the prayer to God, makes it the vehicle of the sacrament. Of course faith and the confession of faith also form part of baptism; anointing (with chrism) and the laying on of hands are similarly of importance; but it is the water that procures life. Baptism is indispensable, only to be administered once, and a sure source of salvation. Defilement of it by lapsing can only be atoned for by martyrdom. Because it is such a heavy burden, it should not be administered too early, and certainly not to children. The same danger exists for the sponsors (god-parents). On the other hand there is no clear opinion as to whether baptism works naturally or with the co-operation of the will, and whether what takes place should be understood symbolically or as a real experience.

The *fourth century* goes i ito greater detail. According to Cyril of Jerusalem, the soul is espoused in baptism to its heavenly bride-groom. This obliges the candidate for baptism to prepare himself worthily for the reception of the spiritual gifts associated with the water, which alone are able to bring him who has been sealed to the kingdom of heaven. Baptism and martyrdom belong together, like the water and blood which flowed from the wound in Christ's side. Cyril also seeks to corroborate what is already accepted in baptism by allegorical proofs from the scriptures. Gregory Nazianzen (*Orat. Catech.* 40) offers more rhetoric than new ideas. Baptism is a beginning, which is followed by an increase in the moral powers. Consequently it should not be delayed. Without baptism blessedness cannot be attained. Gregory of Nyssa also demands that the life that follows baptism should be in accordance with the spirit which has been received, and that baptism should not be deferred. *The baptism of infants* is actually attested by Irenaeus; according to Origen this removes a stain inherent from birth, and also the sin and guilt brought with us from a previous life. The Cappadocians, on the other hand, are thinking principally of the life that is to follow baptism, for which children ought to be sealed no later than their third year, in order not to die without being sealed and consecrated.

2. *Augustine*

The dispute of *Augustine* with Donatism (*Seven Books on Baptism*, 400 A.D.) and against Pelagianism were of vital importance for the doctrine of baptism. He made a distinction between the sacrament and its content (*res*). It is possible he says, to receive the sacrament without the *res*; but only he who belongs to the Church as the body of Christ, can be a member of Christ and partake in re-birth. For baptism is the sacrament of rebirth, or in fact, of the forgiveness of sins. If concupiscence is regarded as culpable in men before baptism, this is no longer the case after baptism. Besides this, baptism has the positive effect of restoring the natural powers, which have been damaged by the Fall. But since not only baptism but also repentance are necessary for rebirth, baptism is of no use to someone who has not repented, nor to a heretic or schismatic, or to someone baptized by such a person. For all these, baptism remains merely a symbol, and therefore without effect. It is true that even they have received baptism, and have irrevocably become members of the body of Christ, so that if they repent they ought not to be baptized a second time, but only endowed with the spirit who forgives sins and the love which covers sins, through the laying on of hands. Augustine was always in favour of the baptism of infants. For since even a child shares in the guilt of Adam, it must be born again once for all through baptism. For the Holy Spirit rules as the spirit of unity and fraternity both in the parents who bring their child for baptism and in the child itself. Behind the parents there also stands the Church, the mother of all. Baptism makes the child a believer in the sense that when it attains to reason it understands the sacrament and accepts its truth; but until then the child is at least protected by baptism from hostile powers. The struggle with Pelagius then provided Augustine with the opportunity to develop his teaching along more rigorous lines, and to relate baptism particularly closely to original sin.

3. The Doctrine of the Catholic Church
Scholastic theology up to the *Council of Trent* simply elaborated the ideas of Augustine into a system. As the first sacrament, baptism gives the right and the ability to

receive the others. The sacrament consists essentially of baptism with water. Consecrated water forms the material of the sacrament, and the words: 'I baptize you in the name of the Father and of the Son and of the Holy Ghost' its form. For the sake of greater solemnity, the Church has added numerous ceremonies which are not in themselves necessary. In its basic outline baptism was ordained by Christ; as a result of his own baptism the sacrament received the power to convey grace (*cf.* Vol. II, *Grace* IV, 2*b*.). The ultimate effect of baptism is justification or rebirth. All sins and guilt are done away by baptism (*cf.* Vol. II, *Sin* IV, 7*c*.), although original sin continues to assert itself in the form of base desires. But baptism also takes away the punishment of the sinner in the future life, although his punishments in this life remain, in order that we may suffer with Christ and struggle against sinful desire. The positive effects of baptism consist of the grace of God and the powers which make possible a new life, and finally, the removal of all hindrances and the opening of heaven to a baptized Christian as to Christ. But all these effects depend on the candidate for baptism firmly desiring to receive the sacrament, and not resisting it through unbelief, contempt, carelessness, or lack of reverence. Thus for all who come to baptism, the outward purification is linked to an inner effect; it is in this that the spiritual character of baptism consists. This character imprinted upon the soul brings the baptized person into such a relationship with Christ that he partakes of the stream of grace which flows from Christ. This character is printed indelibly upon the soul for all time and eternity, either for glory or for punishment. This is why baptism cannot be repeated, even for a heretic who is returning to the Church, in the same way as a heretic, if he is baptized, remains under the jurisdiction of the Pope. The baptism of infants presents a difficulty, insofar as immature children

lack *fides formata*, and consequently cannot attain to justi-
fying grace, but are only able to accept the faith of the
Church with whom they are united as members. The
Council of Trent clings to the view that in baptism the
habitus of faith, love and hope are infused into them, and
that in consequence they themselves possess faith.

In the *Greek Church* of the Middle Ages the doctrine of
baptism was only of minor significance. There was some
discussion of the ceremonies of baptism as part of mystagogic theology. Rebirth and illumination by baptism
gave rise to philosophical speculations about matter and
image, darkness and light. But there is a strong element
of rhetoric in these discussions.

4. Protestantism
a. *Luther* regarded baptism as necessary because Christ
himself had ordained it. Because in baptism Christ himself acts on the child and promises his grace to it, it is
comparable to the word, which conveys the impression of
the person and work of Christ and sets Christ in his
mercy before the eyes of men. The effect of baptism is
unlimited; it can be hindered by unbelief, but can also
be restored by renewed faith. At first Luther distinguished between the 'sign' (immersion) and what the
sign signified (new birth, in which we die to our sins).
But from 1520 on he emphasized the material and actions
of the sacrament as signs and seals associated by God
with his works and his promise in order to strengthen
faith. And finally, he added to the sign and the word the
command and ordinance of God, through which both
sign and word were joined together, so that the natural,
earthly element of water became a divine, heavenly,
holy and blessed element. His followers meanwhile had
repudiated this rather rhetorical turn of thought. For
Melanchthon and his disciples the important thing was
the practice itself and the trust in the grace of God,

which went with it. Brenz sees in baptism a seal set upon the promise given in the word, that sins are already and truly forgiven. Urbanus Rhegius emphasized that in baptism the Holy Spirit was invisibly and inwardly taking possession of man. Bugenhagen and Sarcerius are inclined to see in the water only an outward sign, which has nothing to add to the word. It was held that even infants require baptism and must be justified through it, especially as they have little faith, so that God acts on them by changing them. This is the view held by Melanchthon and Brenz, whereas Selnecker considers that the child of Christian parents, already privileged by his birth, possesses in essence what baptism can give him, even without being baptized. It was *Lutheran orthodoxy* (e.g. Quenstedt) which first markedly externalized the idea of baptism, by regarding word and sacrament as prescribed ordinances, by which God was not of course bound, but man was, as a result of God's command.

b. Before this, *Zwingli* had adopted a different view from all Lutherans, by rejecting the idea that baptism conveyed anything in itself, and by understanding God's action upon man in predominantly spiritual terms. It is true that in contrast to the Anabaptists he continued like Luther to accept the baptism of children, and saw in it a distinguishing mark and a sign of their duty. Consequently, he did not deny that baptism stimulated and strengthened faith. According to *Calvin* baptism is the sign of our acceptance into the visible Church. It assists our faith, as a sealed document attesting the forgiveness of our sins, as a sign of our rebirth, and as an attestation of our incorporation into the death and life of Christ. At the same time, we make in baptism a public confession of the fact that we belong to the people of God. By showing that we receive only insofar as we believe, Calvin comes very close to Luther. But Calvin is even less able to deal with the difficulties associated with infant baptism. For all the blessings of baptism can only be of use to those infants who are of the elect, and are consequently assured without more ado of blessedness. Consequently baptism cannot really be regarded as necessary to salvation. For the elect it is only the sealing of their election; even baptism is not able to save those who are not of the elect.

c. An even lower value was set on baptism by the Socinians and Arminians, and also by pietism, and in the rationalism and supernaturalism of the end of the eighteenth century and the beginning of the nineteenth century. Here there is an emphasis either on revival or on the moral attitude, and the only significance that prevails for baptism is that of an edifying action carried out by the congregation, an act of acceptance. Schleiermacher associated himself with this view, although he and the theologians influenced by him, and even more those who advanced the confessional theology, sought to find a deeper value in baptism (*cf.* III, below).

Friedrich Wiegand

III. THE DOGMATIC THEOLOGY OF BAPTISM

1. It is particularly difficult to produce a dogmatic description of baptism which is adequate to it, which does not contradict or water down the tradition of the Church, and at the same time does not demand a slavish acceptance of the value put on it by primitive Christianity and the Church. The reason for this is not only the complete remoteness from the modern mind of the sacramental mysticism of the ancient world and of the Church, but especially the problem of infant baptism, which is our main concern nowadays, but had no effect on the

earliest baptismal practice and doctrinal ideas (*cf.* I, 2-4 above).

The Reformers were already aware of this difficulty, and arrived at no certain solution (*cf.* II, 4 above). It was pietism which first found a real stumbling block in the fact that the rebirth, the beginning of a true Christian life, should be related to the baptism of an infant. Rationalism was content with the idea of a solemn acceptance into the congregation. Even Schleiermacher accepted this view; but he placed so high a value on belonging to the Christian fellowship, that he regarded fellowship with Christ, perfection and blessedness as being only possible within it; it is only here that the individual can attain to understanding and make his own assent, so that the act of confirmation and the confession of faith associated with it can make up what is lacking in the baptism of an infant. Albrecht Ritschl held that baptism was effective insofar as the congregation had a real effect on its members; but the assertion that baptism had the power to bring about rebirth was explained by Wilhelm Herrmann as a relic of scholastic thought, since in fact rebirth signifies a genuine life of faith. R. A. Lipsius speaks in a similar way; but for him, baptism, as the acceptance of a child into the congregation, is not merely a symbolic act, but also a confession of faith by the congregation, and both to itself and to the parents and the god-parents a pledge and assurance that the spirit is still at work within the congregation, which is then able to arouse and strengthen this faith in the baptized child as it grows up. M. Kähler and Scheel also stress here that the sacrament is a 'visible' word; thus the only thing which distinguishes baptism from the assurance of grace in the word is its concrete form, and it likewise needs to be followed by the acceptance of faith. It was along these lines that the explanation came to be accepted that baptism, and the baptism of children in particular, should be everywhere maintained but was not *necessary to salvation*: Lipsius regards emergency baptism as superstition. Scheel would in fact abandon the idea of baptism as a sacrament.

A different approach is followed by the Confessional Lutheran theology of the nineteenth century, where in direct reaction to this there was an attempt to maintain *the indispensable necessity of baptism for eternal life*, and its nature as a miraculous sacrament, which brings about a change in the spiritual and bodily nature of man. This takes place in a process similar to those of nature but of supernatural origin (G. Thomasius, Von Oettingen); the later conversion is only the appropriation of this grace (Kalweit). A somewhat less extreme version of this view is widespread amongst modern Lutheran theologians, who see in baptism at least the seed of rebirth, a spiritual potentiality placed in man (R. Frank), though this is by no means a 'Lutheran' doctrine. There is another way of asserting the objectivity and necessity of baptism which is closer to Luther; according to this view, baptism promises and confers, even on a child, justification, the forgiveness of sins and redemption (H. Cremer, P. Althaus Snr.); together with the exorcism, it carries the baptized child out of the realm of sin and the devil into the kingdom of grace (this view is found in the Lutheran baptismal services).

2. The assurance with which infant baptism was introduced and defended everywhere in spite of all resistance, shows that there lies behind it a popular psychological need; through it (as in confirmation and betrothal, Christmas and the New Year) there is provided a consecration of each new departure in life. Thus primitive Christian baptism itself was a consecration of the neophyte who had just left the impure world, hostile to God, and entered the holy Church, the world of divine grace and of eternity. It is in no way a perversion of this, but

follows naturally, that Christian parents should wish to place their children from the very beginning in the care of God and to make them his own; the Church answers this wish in the name of God by receiving the child into the fellowship of those who belong to God. At the same time, by this action the parents confess their faith in the God of Jesus Christ and pledge themselves to him; I and my house wish to serve the Lord. But what gift does baptism give, or what use is it? It is certain that it cannot bring about rebirth as though by magic; that it confers the forgiveness of sins is true insofar as it places us in the care of our God and Father, by whose grace we all live. That baptism does not protect us from wickedness, unbelief and depravity, is all too clear; but it is still a 'sign' which constantly points to the fact that we belong to God, and to which parents (and god-parents) should constantly make reference; it is a pledge and consolation in every temptation. Even in the case of *adult baptism* we have no guarantee that the baptized are truly converted, nor that they will remain constant in the faith; but again, they are shown by their baptism to whom they belong, and they show this in themselves by being baptized; it is the visible gospel of the eternal life to which they too are called.

Arnold Meyer

IV. THE LITURGICAL HISTORY OF BAPTISM

1. The Formation of the Rite of Baptism

Since in the gentile Christian Church baptism was regarded as a mystery, the actions which formed part of it were bound to grow more elaborate like those of all mysteries. It was the natural result of such growth, that certain individual features should become independent and be regarded as sacraments themselves. The state of our present knowledge, and the way the actual historical development took place, do not permit a clear historical picture to be drawn. In fact all it is possible to do is to sketch the *formation of a basic pattern of baptism*. In various different places and at different periods in the history of the Church, this form of baptism underwent different developments.

1. The point of origin of baptism itself in the New Testament is obscure (*cf.* I, 2-4 above). In accordance with the meaning of baptism as an act of acceptance into the Christian congregation, by which at the same time the sins of the baptized were blotted out, the elaboration of the rite of baptism was bound to give rise to a *period of preparation*. Justin (*Apology* I, 62.2; 65.1) and *Didache* 7, which are major sources for the second century rite in Rome and Syria, tell of a preparatory period of fasting, which both the candidate for baptism and also members of the congregation who were personally concerned had to take on. According to Justin this was concluded with a *confession of sin* and a *promise* to conduct oneself according to the 'truths of our doctrines and sayings' which were acknowledged to be correct. The *act of baptism* itself was a *bath*, that is, a genuine immersion in the open air in flowing 'living water'. The *Didache* also permits—evidently having regard to the conditions of the Syrian landscape—the use of other water: still and cold water; and if this was lacking, then warm water; and in case of need, sprinkling alone was sufficient. In the course of the immersion the *Trinitarian formula of baptism* was pronounced (see I, 4*a*. above). Neither Justin nor the *Didache* make any mention of a custom for which there is evidence in the New Testament (Heb. 6.2), *the laying on of hands*. But this does not necessarily imply that it disappeared completely, particularly as it can frequently

be seen in pictures of baptism in the catacombs. The conclusion of the celebration of baptism was provided by acceptance into the circle of 'brethren' and participation in the Eucharist.

2. The Further, Formal Development of Baptism

The continued development of baptism can be traced in the writings of Tertullian, who devoted his treatise *de baptismo* to the subject. Baptism was preceded by a long period of *preparation* which was taken up by many prayers, frequent fasts, and services of genuflection and prayer; it was concluded by a confession of sin. An essentially new liturgical element appeared in the form of an *epiclesis* over the baptismal waters (Ch. 4). *The act of baptism* fell into three parts: the public and solemn *renunciation*, in which the candidate for baptism rejected the devil, the *baptismal confession of faith*, in answer to the question put by the person carrying out the baptism, and the three-fold immersion in the name of the Father, the Son and the Holy Spirit. All these formulae already had a strict liturgical form. The actual ceremony of baptism concluded with the *anointing* and the *laying on of hands* with prayer. The newly baptized immediately took part in the Eucharist. Finally they were given a mixture of milk and honey, a usage which had its origin in Greek mythology, but which in Christianity was given a symbolic meaning in which it referred to the milk and honey of Canaan, or to the duties of a Christian, according to I Peter 2.2.

This basic pattern, which had grown up and taken shape in a quite natural way, was elaborated by different churches in the course of the centuries that followed. The sources that are available mostly tell us only the order of events in the different forms of baptism which developed as a result of this process, and very rarely contain the texts of the prayers. There is a clear distinction between the development in the East and in the West.

3A. Baptism in the East

In the *East* a long series of individual acts of preparation was introduced. A series of ceremonies or exorcisms was carried out on those who presented themselves for the preparation for baptism, the *catechumenate*: σφραγίς, signing with the cross on the brow and the breast, and the laying on of hands with an intercessory prayer, were intended to snatch the catechumens from paganism and out of the power of the demons. The assumption in the case of these *exorcisms*, of which the oldest example we possess is in the *Acts of Thomas*, is the idea that the evil spirit actually dwells in the unbaptized, in the same way as the Holy Spirit really comes to dwell in them at baptism. The catechumens were expected to be present at the Mass of the Catechumens, and to submit to the Church's penitential discipline. At the end of a period, usually three years, as catechumens, they were allowed to present themselves for baptism and thereby became *competentes*, φωτιζόμενοι. At special instructions (*cf.* the *Mystagogic Catecheses* of Cyril of Jerusalem) they were introduced to the mysteries of the sacrament. In addition to this there were fasts and prayers for exorcizing, night vigils and sexual continence, which were understood as scrutinies (tests) to prove the seriousness of their repentance. Further exorcisms (signing with the cross, laying on of hands, and breathings) were provided to support their earnest desire. The conclusion of this series of preparations was the making known and learning of the Creed (*traditio symboli*), in the East the Nicene Creed, and the Our Father.

The *baptism* began with an act of exorcism, in which in an ante-chamber of the baptistery on the previous evening or early in the morning of the day of baptism, the bishop called down the power of God on to the candidates in eloquent terms. The preparation was as it were gone over again on the day of baptism in a three-fold ceremony surrounded with prayers, genuflections, the laying on of hands, breathing and anointing: the renunciation of the devil (ἀποταγή), the pledge to Christ (συνταγή) and the solemn confession of faith (*reditio symboli*) took place before the whole congregation. The ceremony in the baptistery began with the consecration of the water. After this, or in some liturgies before, the bishop consecrated the two oils, the *oleum exorcismi* needed before the baptism and the *oleum eucharistiae* used after the baptism. The candidate, anointed with oil and dressed only in a χίτων, now underwent the *interrogatio de fide*. After each answer was given the bishop laid his hand on the candidate's head and immersed him. The conclusion was provided by an anointing with μύρον or τὸ τῆς τελειώσεως χρίσμα on the forehead, ears and breast.

Apart from differences in the order in which individual ceremonies took place, the description of baptism in sources of the fourth and fifth centuries (*Apostolic Constitutions* 7; the *Catecheses* of Cyril of Jerusalem for Syria, and the prayers of Bishop Serapion of Thmuis for Egypt) are in agreement with each other. A decisive factor in the liturgical development was the *influence of the mysteries*, from which the clothing with white garments, the crowning, the burning candle and the tasting of milk and honey were borrowed, though with this limitation, that only customs which could in some way be based upon the Bible were adopted. As *infant baptism* came into use, the ceremonies of baptism were shortened and cut down. The acts of acceptance originally meant for the *competentes* were attached directly to the baptism itself. Their significance was made greater by several repetitions of the renunciation and the confession of faith. Finally, however, certain particularly important parts of the ceremony became separated from baptism and developed—for reasons connected with the development of the ministry—into separate ceremonies.

3B. *Distinctive Features Found in the West*

In the *West* baptism developed in a simpler form, going back to that attested for *Africa* by Tertullian (*cf.* 2. above), and in a more or less fixed form with very minor changes by Cyprian, Optatus of Milevis and Augustine. Since the Synod of Carthage (256 A.D.) assumes that the *baptismal exorcism* is already known, one can suppose that it came into use about this period; Tertullian at least was not acquainted with it, since he ascribes the ability of 'drowning' the devil to the baptismal water. There were some features peculiar to individual regions. According to the *Pseudo-Ambrosian* writings *de mysteriis* and *de sacramentis,* in Milan and North Italy there was a special anointing of the candidate on the ears and nose, associated with a vow, before the renunciation of the devil. According to the *Missale Gothicum* and the *Missale Gallicanum vetus,* in Gaul what is obviously a very ancient exorcism of the water was used, and also a preface from the Mass at the consecration of the baptismal water. According to the canons of the Council of Elvira (*ca.* 300 A.D.) and the work *de officiis ecclesiasticis* of Isidore of Seville, *de cognitione baptismi* of Ildefonsus and *de correctione rusticorum* of Martin of Braga, a particularly elaborate consecration of the water was in use in *Spain,* in which the bishop dipped a wooden cross into the water, and which in fact contradicted the significance of the epiclesis; there was also both a single and a three-fold *immersio in nominibus* introduced in opposition to the Arians, a formula of renunciation which did not consist of question and answer, and a washing of the feet after baptism. But in place of these comparatively ancient customs, a decision of the Synod of Braga of 561 (can. 5) introduced the Roman baptismal rite which Pope Vigilius had sent in 538 to Bishop Prosoturus of Braga.

4. Roman Catholic Baptism

This Roman baptismal *Ordo* is preserved as the Seventh of the Roman *Ordines*, in the Gelasian sacramentary, and in some of its details, also in the Gregorian sacramentary, although the Gelasian sacramentary and *Ordo* VII both originate in their present form in the Frankish region, so one has to keep a careful watch for Gallican influence in the first place, and Mozarabic influence in the second. One must also note that the form of baptism that is presented there has adults in mind in its prayers, in spite of the fact that it must ordinarily have been used for the baptism of infants. Thus it is possible to conclude that a very much older basic form lies behind it, and we have some further evidence of this in the writings of Leo I. The distinctive feature of the Roman baptismal *Ordo*, which distinguished it from the eastern baptismal rites, and from the present day Roman rite, is that the preparation for baptism in the strict sense is not all gathered together on to the day of baptism, but is spread out, as a highly developed *rite of scrutiny*, over the whole of Lent, and incorporated into the liturgy of the Mass, with the twofold purpose of giving the candidates for baptism a thorough preparation, and also of presenting them to the congregation, so that if the need arose an unsuitable candidate could be rejected. Consequently, scrutinies took place in every week of the Lenten fast, beginning with the announcement of the names of the candidates, and always with this double aim in mind: to drive out the devil by signing with the cross, genuflections and prayers, and to call upon the help of God. The task was shared out amongst the officiating clergy in such a way that it was the work of the exorcists to drive out the devil with prayers, while the priests appealed to God for the illumination, purification and sanctification of the candidates. These scrutinies are all similar, but those of the third week (*apertio aurium*, the opening of the ears) and the seventh week (*Ephpheta*) are particularly interesting. In the *apertio aurium* the knowledge of the gospel, the Creed and the Lord's Prayer were solemnly and officially made known to the candidate. A number of deacons each carried a gospel book in a solemn procession from the sacristy to the altar. A priest explained the meaning and content of the gospel; then a deacon read the beginning of the gospel of Matthew, of which the priest gave a short explanation. Then the opening passages of the other gospels, and the Creed and the Lord's Prayer, were made known to the candidates; in the case of the Creed regard was had to the fact that both Greek and Latin were spoken in Rome. In the rite of *Ephpheta*, the last scrutiny, the priest attacked the devil for the last time in the strongest terms. Then, using a practice which is an analogy to Mark 7.31 ff. and also a borrowing from the Roman *dies lustricus*, the priest moistened the nose and ears of each candidate with his spittle. This is followed by an anointing on the forehead and the breast, the three-fold *abrenuntiatio Satanae* and the *reditio symboli*.

For the Church, the ceremony of baptism was preceded by the consecration of the chrism on Maunday Thursday, a Mass provided with a typical epiclesis. The candidates for baptism took part in a celebration of the Easter Vigil, where the readings were so chosen as to provide a summary of God's historical dealings with men, as a final instruction for them. The Pope carried out the baptism early on Easter morning (*cf.* 6*b*. below). A collect and a preface, interrupted by the three-fold dipping of the cross into the water, and concluded by the pouring of the chrism into the baptismal water in the form of a cross, introduced the baptism. The three-fold baptismal interrogation was followed by a three-fold immersion or sprinkling, and finally by the anointing of the back. Then the newly baptized, dressed in white, proceeded into the *consignatorium*, where the Pope carried out the rite of confirmation or consignation, the signing of the forehead with chrism in the form of a cross. During the baptism, the *schola cantorum* sang litanies in the church. The newly baptized took part in the Easter Mass which followed and communicated for the first time. They wore their white clothing throughout the Octave of Easter.

There are two main features in the *further development of this rite of baptism*: the attempt to join the rites of scrutiny directly to the acts of baptism, a necessity brought about by infant baptism, and the desire, based on the development of the ministry, to reserve an essential part of baptism, confirmation, to the bishop. Both these changes took place: the *ordines ad catechumenum faciendum* gathered together into one ceremony, by contrast with the baptism itself, all the actions which make up the catechumanate. Confirmation becomes entirely separate from baptism, and is henceforth only administered by the bishop. The amalgamation of this *Ordo* for the catechumenate and the baptismal *Ordo* gave rise to the *present day Roman baptismal rite*, which goes back to Paul V (1614). In its shortest form, the present day Roman ritual of baptism (*Ordo baptismi parvulorum. Rituale Romanum tit. II. c. 2*) consists of: *a.* the ceremonies at the church door, including the giving of a 'Christian' name, for preference that of a saint who will be an example, intercessor and protector of the child; and a short instruction on the two great commandments of Christianity, a symbolic banishment of the unclean spirit (*exsufflatio*), and finally the acceptance of the child into the protection of the Church by the signing of the cross, the laying on of hands and the giving of salt. *b.* The ceremonies of illumination, in three stages, further exorcisms at the church door, then the authoritative leading into the church, including on the way to the font the recitation of the Creed and the Lord's Prayer, and before the font a final exorcism and the *apertio aurium*. *c.* The act of baptism itself; this follows a solemn *abrenuntatio* and symbolic anointing against the devil and a short interrogation concerning the Christian faith and the candidate's intention in seeking baptism; it takes the form of a threefold pouring of water in the form of a cross, in the course of which each person of the Holy Trinity is named in turn. *d.* The ceremonies following baptism, consisting of anointing with chrism as a sign of the fullness of grace, and of the likeness of the newly baptized to Christ the anointed; the putting on of a white garment as a sign of baptismal innocence; and the giving of a burning candle as a sign of the duty to practise the Christian faith. The conclusion consists of a blessing to the newly baptized and an exhortation to the godparents.

5. Different Types of Protestant Baptism

Apart from the earliest stages, represented by a translation into German of the existing Catholic formulary (Thomas Münzer's *Ordnung und Berechnunge des Deutschen Amptes zu Alstedt,* 1523; Luther's *Taufbüchlein verdeutscht,* 1523), the baptismal rites produced by the *Protestant Churches at the Reformation* can clearly be seen to follow three distinct lines.

a. Luther had already removed some of the exorcisms from the *Taufbüchlein* of 1523, and perhaps added the prayer which refers to the Flood, but on the whole limited himself to increasing the participation of the congregation—the Lord's prayer is prayed and not merely recited by the priest. The new version, the *Taufbüchlein verdeutscht, aufs Neue zugerichtet* of 1526, is an abbreviation of the version of 1523, and the rite consists of the following stages: a. Outside the church door: a brief exorcism ('Come out, thou unclean spirit, and give place to the Holy Spirit'); a signing with the cross on the forehead and breast; a prayer over the candidate; the prayer referring to the flood; a longer exorcism ('I abjure thee, unclean spirit, to come out and go away from this servant of Christ. Amen'); a reading of Mark 10.13; the laying on of hands and the Lord's Prayer, in which all join. b. Then the child is led to the font, and greeted with the words of Psalm 121.8. The god-parents answer for the child the three questions of the renunciation, the three questions concerning belief, and finally, the question: 'Do you wish to be baptized?', to which they answer 'Yes'. The priest carries out the baptism with a three-fold immersion, and as he does so, pronounces the baptismal formula. Then, while the god-parents hold the child, he puts on it the baptismal garment, the *Westerhemd* (from the word *vestis*, clothing; it usually consists of a little cap or a handkerchief), and recites the concluding prayer. The distinctive elements of this baptism are clearly influenced by the Catholic model. However, an essential emphasis is provided by the words from the introduction to the *Taufbüchlein*, in which Luther explains the necessity of an earnest struggle with the devil in prayer on behalf of the 'poor little child', and also treats an earnest intercessory prayer as of greater importance than all the external ceremonies of baptism.

b. The second Protestant baptismal rite is that which appeared in *Strasbourg* under the influence of *Bucer* in his work *Grund und Ursach aus göttlicher Schrift*, 1525. It is distinguished by the absence of all exorcisms and of the renunciation, by the question to the god-parents, which takes account of the character of the rite as one for the baptism of infants, and asks whether they intend to bring the children up as Christians, by the 'pouring of water' as the means of carrying out the baptism, and, in the form it took from 1537, on by the introduction of the Apostles' Creed directly after the reading and before the baptismal interrogation; the reason for this change in position is given by the interpretation of the meaning of baptism; the children are to be 'baptized into the communion of this faith'.

c. Similar to the rite of Strasbourg is the third Protestant baptismal rite, that drawn up for *Zürich* by *Zwingli* in 1525, published as *Form des toufs, wie man die jetzt zu Zürich brucht*. It likewise lacks any exorcisms and renunciations, but is distinguished from the rite of Strasbourg by the question put to the god-parents on two occasions, at the entry into the Church and after the reading of the gospel, whether the child is to be baptized and what its name is.

d. In the Church Orders of the Protestant provincial churches, these three rites of baptism underwent many alterations, in the form of variations in detail, the inclusion of baptismal hymns, and the introduction of admonitions, etc. The form provided by Luther remained the basic pattern in all Lutheran provincial churches. The influence of Strasbourg extended to the West and the South of Germany: Cologne, Strasbourg, Württemberg, and the Palatinate. The rites used in the regions of Switzerland which came under the influence of Calvin also show the basic outlines of the Strasbourg rite in their baptismal services. The Zwinglian form is in use in German-speaking Switzerland. *Pietism* and the *Enlightenment* removed the exorcisms and the renunciation of the Lutheran formularies; the former is in use at the present day only in the Old Lutheran Church, and even there it is optional, while the renunciation is still quite widely used. The rationalists altered the traditional liturgies according to their taste, especially in numerous private orders of service; they were intended not merely to satisfy the requirements of individual taste, but also to accommodate the act of baptism to the particular social and family circumstances of a particular case. These formularies were certainly personal in their conception, but were lacking in genuine Protestant thought, so that they did not prove satisfactory over any length of time. But even the reforms in the orders of service which took place in the *nineteenth century* did not produce really satisfactory baptismal liturgies. The questions to the child, and in some of them, the renunciation, based on Luther's *Taufbüchlein*, were restored in them, and several parallel formulae were offered for use. In the order in which the various acts take place, they frequently lack any unifying idea. In general it can be said that in a Protestant baptismal liturgy there can be found the biblical passages Matt. 28.16 ff. and Mark 10.13 ff., the Lord's Prayer, a confession of faith (the Apostles' Creed), an explanation to the god-parents of their duty to bring up the child in the Christian Faith, and the Trinitarian baptismal formula; the baptism is carried out by the sprinkling or pouring of water over the child's head. The rites of baptism practised by the Protestant provincial churches in Germany show marked differences in form, and a considerable lack of unity in their underlying ideas; this is due to a large degree to different views of the sacrament of infant baptism (*cf.* III above), and not least to the practical difficulties which occur in the circumstances of the congregation (see V below).

6. Baptismal Customs

a. THE RIGHT TO BAPTIZE. Every Christian originally had the *right to baptize*. Tertullian is the first to claim that the bishop must carry out baptism; but this claim is limited by the right which even lay-people possessed to baptize when no bishop was present. The view that only a bishop might baptize quickly spread through the Church; baptisteries were only constructed in episcopal sees. Although it later came about that bishops entrusted the celebration of baptism to subordinate clergy, their basic right with regard to baptism was not removed, but rather was maintained in their special privilege of consecrating the objects necessary for baptism. The scholastic view of the right to baptize is the same as that in the *Rituale Romanum*: 'the legitimate minister of baptism is the parish priest or another priest delegated by the parish priest or the Ordinary of the place'. (see VI, 1 below). The Protestant churches similarly grant the right to baptize to the duly appointed minister of a parish, part of whose office is the *ministerium verbi et sacramenti* (*cf.* VI, 2 below). But the idea of the right of any and every Christian to baptize is still conceded in the teaching both of the Protestant and the Catholic Churches, in the sense that both Churches allow a lay-person and even a woman to baptize in case of necessity.

b. THE TIME AND PLACE OF BAPTISM. The *day of baptism* does not seem to have been limited to any particular day of the year in the post-apostolic period, but as early as the time of Victor I Easter had become the only occasion for baptism. The practice of having a long period of preparation made it necessary to gather numbers of candidates for baptism together to be prepared, and to accept them into the fellowship of the faithful through baptism and participation in the Eucharist at what was, from the liturgical and religious point of view, the most solemn period of the Church year. In addition to Easter, it soon became the practice to baptize at Pentecost. This custom, particularly advocated by Rome, was augmented in the East by the addition of baptisms at Epiphany, and in Jerusalem, also on the feast of the consecration of the church of Calvary. These customs also found their imitators in the West; Leo I tells that more baptisms took place at Epiphany than at Easter. As early as the sixth century, baptisms also took place at Christmas. Finally, popular superstition forced the introduction of baptism on the feasts of the apostles, saints and martyrs. Since children and the sick had to be baptized as soon as possible, from the time of scholasticism on there was no regulation about the day of baptism in the Catholic Church, except that 'the Church has always observed the feasts of Easter and Pentecost, on which the baptismal water is to be consecrated, with great devotion', *Catechismus Rom. p. II cap. II quaest. XLVII.* The Protestant church does not place any limitation on the day of baptism. The normal *place of baptism* is the parish church. But under the influence of class distinctions baptism at home has also been permitted, a concession which, considering the nature of baptism as a celebration for the whole congregation, should be as far as possible restricted or removed (*cf.* V, 1 below).

Hans Hohlwein

V. PRESENT DAY LITURGICAL PRACTICE

1. The Presence of the Congregation
Every baptism, except in cases of emergency, should take place as far as possible *when the whole congregation is together*, as takes place at present among the Moravian Brethren, in Reformed Church districts, in the extensive region where the Lüneburg and Lauenburg Church Orders are in use, and also in East Friesia, where it is still carried out at the Sunday service before or after the sermon. In *private baptisms* at home, the aspects which concern the Christian congregation are all too often over-

shadowed by those that concern the family. Modern service books are right to demand that where it is feasible baptism should be carried out within the ordinary service, or at least in the course of a children's service or instruction. The least that can be expected is that not only the god-parents (and nurse) should come with the mother, but that both parents should be present and that the questions (*cf.* IV, 5 above) should be put not only to the god-parents, but above all to the parents themselves.

2. Baptism in Emergency

The cases of necessity where this demand cannot be met include that of *emergency baptism*, whether carried out by a minister or by a lay-person. The very simple form used on occasions of urgent necessity consists of the vow, the baptism and a prayer. But these provisions vary in different places. Where this is so, a *ratification* by the minister has to take place later. Since the Reformed Churches do not practise this emergency baptism, the question as to how far it is justified must not be overlooked, in particular since it is frequently associated with false or even superstitious beliefs.

3. The Baptism of Adults and Re-Baptism

For the *baptism of adults* (occurring so rarely in the past that they were known in Germany as 'Jewish 'or 'Moorish' baptisms) are provided for in even quite early service books. Almost all new service books make provision for it, because, apart from *foreign missions*, since the obligation of baptism was removed, and the movement away from the Church has grown stronger, such cases have increased. In general they are able to follow the pattern of infant baptism in use up to the present, but their special nature is marked by a different choice of scripture readings and prayers. Naturally, the questions are answered by the candidate himself, and of course there is less hesitation, for example in the case of a change of religion, in including some form of renunciation (ethical decision). Many orders of service, e.g. Hanover, Hesse-Kassel, and Bavaria, require the presence of god-parents as 'witnesses of the baptism'. In the case of conversion to a Protestant church, there is no requirement of *re-baptism*, by contrast to the occasional Roman Catholic practice of re-baptizing (*cf.* VI, 1 below), which rests on the assumption that one cannot know whether the baptism has been correctly carried out in the Protestant Church.

4. *Present-day Needs*

The baptismal formularies found in present-day service books satisfy only a few of the requirements which we shall mention here. It is certainly possible to express a great deal in the *hymns, instructions*—both of which should be related as far as possible to the season of the Church year—and admonitions, which are always of course optional, and in spite of every emphasis on what concerns the whole Christian congregation, are bound to deal with personal circumstances (one of the difficulties in mass baptisms). There should also be an *account of the institution of baptism* (at the beginning, or in a similar way to the Eucharist, immediately before the actual baptism takes place) and a reading of the *gospel of the little children*, Mark 10.13 ff., the *Lord's Prayer* and the *laying on of hands*, in spite of the hesitation of those who prefer to follow the Reformed pattern (*cf.* IV, 5*b*—*c* above), and also the *divine promise* of Psalm 121.8, accompanying the movement from the church door to the font (but only where this actually takes place); this can often be a very beautiful symbol. But the profession of faith itself, and the *act of baptism*, both need to be reformed. The use of the Apostles' Creed is provided for everywhere, except in Gotha, Württemberg (1912), Baden (in the provisional order of service of 1912, it is only one amongst several confessions of faith, but in the provisional service book of 1930, there is only the Apostles' Creed, which is used as a summary); *cf.* the removal of the minister at Bayreuth, Knote, for failing to use the Creed in 1929. From the purely liturgical point of view, the question of the retention of the Apostles' Creed is far from being the greatest difficulty in the present-day orders of service, for a justification can be found for this in the promises given by the god-parents on behalf of the child. But there is no good reason for the form of the question as to whether the child is to be baptized 'into this faith'; for this question is obscure, and Rietschel, Thümmel, and Smend, etc., have long ago tried to replace it by a better. There is less difficulty in the conclusion with its prayer of thanksgiving and blessing, so long as *the churching of the mother* is not introduced at this point.

Paul Graff

VI. BAPTISM IN CANON LAW

1. According to Catholic doctrine (*Codex Juris Canonici* 737-779), baptism is the *sacramentorum janua ac fundamentum*, necessary for salvation. Consequently, if there is danger of death even a child who is not yet fully born should be baptized; in such a case, if a part of the body other than the head has appeared it is to be baptized *sub conditione*; in some circumstances even the *foetus in utero* (*Can.* 746) is to be baptized. Baptism is only valid when it is carried out *per ablutionem aquae verae et naturalis cum praescripta verborum forma* (*Can.* 737,1). The use of

any substance other than water to replace it is consequently not allowed. The word *ablutio* can be understood as *infusio*, *immersio* or *aspersio* (*Can.* 758). The person who has the right to administer baptism (*cf.* IV, 6 above) is normally the parish priest, or with his permission, or the permission of the bishop who is the ordinary, another priest, or a deacon under the same conditions; and in case of emergency anyone (*quivis*), but better a deacon than a sub-deacon, a sub-deacon than a lay-person, or a man than a woman; and the parents only in the last resort (*Can.* 741-742). Consequently, if the conditions of *Can.* 737 (*cf.* above) are fulfilled, the validity of baptism carried out in other Christian Churches is not disputed on principle, but in practice doubt is cast on the validity of these baptisms. Where there is doubt as to the validity of a baptism, because the condition of *Can.* 737 (*cf.* above) may not have been fulfilled. baptism has to be repeated *sub conditione* (conditionally). This frequently leads to the re-baptism of those who have been baptized by non-Catholics; the custom of re-baptizing Protestant converts to the Catholic Church seems at the present time to be widespread. Two *god-parents*, one of either sex, are required.

2. The Protestant churches recognize every validly administered baptism as the acceptance of the baptized into Christianity; even baptism carried out in a non-Protestant Church, if it is followed by the Protestant upbringing and confirmation of the child, is sufficient for acceptance into the Protestant Church. This corresponds to the legal view of the state, which bases the obligation of paying the church tax on baptism carried out according to a Protestant rite, and followed by a Protestant upbringing. In addition to the minister (in the first place, the minister in charge of the parish), all who have been confirmed have the right to carry out baptism in

case of necessity; such emergency baptisms (*cf.* V, 2 above) must be followed by a ratification by the minister. In many parts of the country a period of six weeks must elapse before baptism, but this is not strictly enforced. The regulations of individual churches or parishes decide whether the baptism should take place in the church or at home.

Martin Schian

8

The Eucharist

I. THE EUCHARIST IN THE NEW TESTAMENT AND THE PRIMITIVE CHURCH

The Scriptures of the New Testament and the other writings of the primitive Church, which are not particularly fruitful sources of information, have very little to say about one of the most important manifestations of primitive Christianity, the Eucharist or 'Lord's Supper'. From this point of view alone, the question of the primitive Christian Eucharist presents many difficulties; the sources are to say the least too defective for us to build up a wholly certain and complete picture of the early development and meaning of the Eucharist. But the principal difficulties concern the question of the origin or what is called the institution of the Eucharist, a question that cannot be separated from that of the form taken by its celebration within the primitive Christian Church. Since, apart from Paul who in fact clearly represents a 'sacramental' point of view in the narrower sense of the word (*cf.* 3 below), the three synoptic gospels also record the 'institution' of the Eucharist, the problem of the Eucharist in the early Christian Church must be dealt with from the point of view both of the history of religion and of literary criticism.

1. Jesus and the Eucharist
In order to have a more or less firm basis on which to begin, it is best first to approach the problem of *literary criticism*. More than almost anywhere else, the problem

is complicated here, and also simplified, by the fact that we possess several gospels, of which three are very closely related to each other, and at the same time different from each other. The complications occur because the question of the original form of the narrative grows more involved, the more differing parallel accounts there are; but it is made easier by the possibility of comparing one account with another, distinguishing different stages in their composition, and understanding more fully the question of the form taken by the original narrative, than would be possible if only one account existed. In the present case, we have to deal not only with the narrative of the synoptic gospels but also with that of Paul. John gives no account of the institution, but presents his view of the Eucharist in a discourse of Jesus (6.51 ff.). Paul's narrative (1 Cor. 11.23 ff.) is therefore particularly' valuable, because it was the first to be committed to writing; it comes from the period shortly after A.D. 50, while the synoptic gospels in their present form are unlikely to have been composed before A.D. 70. Paul comes to discuss the Eucharist in 1 Cor. because abuses had arisen in the way it was celebrated by the church at Corinth, and he wished to remove them. He points out what is unworthy in what ought to be worthily celebrated, and emphasizes his point by laying great stress on a tradition received by him from the Lord Jesus himself concerning the first such supper, celebrated by Jesus with his disciples. 1 Cor. 11.23-5 reads: 'I received from the Lord what I also delivered to you, that the Lord Jesus on the night when he was betrayed took bread, and when he had given thanks, he broke it, and said, "This is my body which is for you. Do this in remembrance of me". In the same way also the cup, after supper, saying, "This cup is the new covenant in my blood. Do this, as often as you drink it, in remembrance of me".'

In the course of their account of Jesus's passion, the

synoptic gospels relate that Jesus celebrated a passover meal as his last meal with his disciples, i.e. on the 14th Nisan, after sunset. Mark (the oldest evangelist) 14.22-5 reads: 'And as they were eating, he took bread, and blessed, and broke it, and gave it to them, and said, "Take; this is my body." And he took a cup, and when he had given thanks he gave it to them, and they all drank of it. And he said to them, "This is my blood of the covenant, which is poured out for many. Truly, I say to you, I shall not drink again of the fruit of the vine until that day when I drink it new in the kingdom of God".' The parallel passage in Matthew 26.26-9 is almost identical with Mark's account; after the words 'which is poured out for many' in v. 28 he adds 'for the forgiveness of sins', but this is merely an addition to bring out the meaning and implies no contradiction. Luke 22.15-20 reads: 'And he said to them, "I have earnestly desired to eat this passover with you before I suffer; for I tell you I shall not eat it until it is fulfilled in the kingdom of God." (And he took a cup, and when he had given thanks he said, "Take this, and divide it among yourselves); for I tell you that from now on I shall not drink of the fruit of the vine until the kingdom of God comes." (And he took bread, and when he had given thanks he broke it and gave it to them, saying, "This is my body) [which is given for you. Do this in remembrance of me." And likewise the cup after supper, saying, "This cup which is poured out for you is the new covenant in my blood"].'

These four accounts fall into two groups: (a) Mark, Matthew and Luke, and (b) Paul. But Luke follows such a different direction that one is inclined to treat his account apart from the others. We are supported in this by the fact that in vv. 19*b* and 20 Luke's account contains verses which from the point of view of textual criticism are uncertain: the words above in square brackets are lacking in one ancient and widely disseminated textual tradition. It is at least possible that they were interpolated later in order to assimilate them to Paul (1 Cor. 11.24) or to Mark. If the original text of Luke is reduced in this way to vv. 15-19*a*, it is clear that we must distinguish *three different traditions*: (a) Mark-Matthew, (b) Paul, and (c) Luke. Of these, the traditions of Mark and Matthew on the one hand, and of Paul on the other are relatively close, except that Paul stresses more explicitly the character of the Last Supper as the institution of a sacramental rite meant to be repeated ('Do this . . . in remembrance of me'). Luke, however, presents a completely different tradition of his own. That there is also something odd about this shorter version can be seen from the large number of individual variations in the oldest manuscripts and translations: the official Syriac translation of the Bible, the so-called Peshitta, which in fact contains the longer text, lacks vv. 17 and 18; the old Syriac translation of the Bible and some manuscripts of the Old Latin translation present the interpolated verses in a different order. The state of the text (which can best be seen in A. Huck's *Synopsis of the First Three Gospels*) show that attempts were made to improve the unusual text of Luke. It can also be seen, besides this, that in the early Christian Church, even at the very earliest period, the whole rite and the words of administration at the centre of it varied greatly (*cf.* IV below). That the words of administration themselves did not have one single fixed form seems also to be shown by the fact that Paul set out in full what he held to be correct, instead of restricting himself, when talking to one Christian Church, to reminding them of a formula that they would already have known. On the whole, however, all the traditions are largely in agreement by contrast with what we have just argued was the original text of Luke.

The peculiarities of the text described above are not
the only things that should be mentioned in Luke.
Neither the long text (vv. 15-20) nor the shorter text
(vv. 15-19*a*) form a unity in themselves. In the longer version there is the obvious fact that in the order it presents
—the cup (v. 17), the bread (v. 19), the cup (v. 20)—
the cup occurs twice. In the shorter version (without
vv. 19*a* and 20) this difficulty is removed. But it is then
obvious that in contrast to the usage found elsewhere,
Luke places the cup before the bread and only gives the
words of administration in connection with the bread.
This difficulty is removed if v. 19*a* is also regarded as a
later interpolation into one ancient tradition of the text
in imitation of Mark and Paul (by Luke himself?).
But in this case, v. 17, which likewise assimilates the
text of Luke to the rest of the tradition and causes a break
in the style, should perhaps also be regarded as a later
addition. The oldest tradition we can trace probably
consists only of vv. 15, 16 and 18 and therefore did not
contain either vv. 19*b* and 20 (the words in square
brackets in the quotation above, which have already been
disregarded on the grounds of textual criticism), nor vv.
17 and 19*a* (in round brackets above; these verses, in
addition to 19*b* and 20, are uncertain on the grounds of
literary criticism and style). The verses that remain describe how at his last meal amongst his disciples Jesus
expressed the certainty that he would celebrate his next
meal with his brethren in the kingdom of God. This
attitude, typical of Jewish eschatology, characterizes the
primitive Palestinian Church (cf. 2 below) as opposed to
the hellenistic and sacramental outlook of the hellenistic
Church (cf. 3 below) and presumably goes back to Jesus
himself. Only a hint of this is retained by Mark and
Matthew: the words which Luke 22.18 places in a context of eschatological sayings both in the preceding and
following verses are simply added to the words of ad-

ministration in Mark 14.24 and Matt. 26.29, while they are completely absent from Paul's account.

The accounts of the institution of the Eucharist, of which the only form available to us consists of liturgical accounts based on the celebration of the Eucharist of the hellenistic Church, have therefore replaced an *older account* of which only traces remain in Mark 14.25 and Matt. 26.29, and which is probably preserved in the account of Luke 22.15 f., 18 given above. Thus we have stumbled upon a text which in fact probably had its place in the earliest Christian worship, but which we do not possess in a strictly liturgical and cultic version. And the older account in Luke, which we have recovered with a reasonable degree of probability, shows indirectly, in a somewhat negative way, that the version which we have separated from this account, and which appears most clearly in St. Paul, but also in Mark and Matthew, and has then been introduced into the text of Luke, is not originally an historical account of the first Eucharist. In the more extended account of the institution of the Eucharist we possess a part of the tradition which in the context of the history of religion in general could be called an *aetiological cult-legend*, a ἱερὸς λόγος, providing an explanation of a cultic action in use in the Church. Even without separating from it an older and contradictory account, the careful critic would in any case accept that all accounts of the institution of the Eucharist are in the first place evidence only for the content and understanding of the rite of the time of Paul and the evangelists or of their predecessors.

In this context, we must also make a closer examination of the short text of Luke. The fact that it is the oldest version available to us does not necessarily prove its historicity. In Mark, Matthew and Paul, Jesus interprets his *death as an act bringing salvation*, and by the reference to his entry into the kingdom of God (Mark 14.25,

Matt. 26.29) he also treats his resurrection as a saving act in the same way; and this is likewise intended in Paul's version. Luke 22.15 speaks only of Jesus's knowledge that he is to suffer, and his readiness to suffer. It is not certain whether the meaning of this account in Luke is that Jesus referred to his suffering as redemptive suffering, and therefore as a saving act. In this particular case, Luke must be treated with caution, for in the parallel passage to Mark 10.45 (=Matt. 20.28) according to which the Son of Man is to offer his life as a ransom for many, he has preserved what is clearly an older version of this saying which contains no reference to his vicarious and atoning death: Luke 22.27. And Mark 10.45 may correspond to what is perhaps intended in Luke's account of the Eucharist, and which is clearly expressed in Mark, Matthew and Paul: the body of Christ is given for Christ's adherents, and the blood of the covenant is shed for them and for many for the forgiveness of sins. Apart from the saying concerning the ransom, the tradition of which is not completely unanimous, and the sayings at the institution of the Eucharist, which are similarly disputed—and these two passages are the clearest utterances of Jesus on the subject of the interpretation of his death as an act of salvation (*cf. Jesus Christ*, page 93ff above)—the remaining comparable sayings of Jesus are not sufficiently explicit to compel the conclusion that Jesus spoke of his death as an act of salvation.

Further, the question whether and in what way Jesus spoke of his death at the last supper, is related to the important problem of when this meal took place. Paul says simply, 'on the night when he was betrayed' (1 Cor. 11.23); the setting in which Mark and Matthew place the Last Supper show that they considered it to be a *passover meal*. A study of the framework in which the passages Mark 14.12-16; 17-21; 22-6 and the corresponding passages in Matthew are set show that each individual pericope is in fact independent, so that the reference to the passover meal, so far as it concerns the account of the institution of the Eucharist, depends in fact on the setting in which the evangelists chose to place it. All that is certain, therefore, is that at the time of the evangelists the first Eucharist had been related to the Jewish passover. It was probably Luke who introduced the reference to the passover into Jesus's words: Luke 22.15. The saying concerning the cup which follows, however, only refers to the kingdom of God which is to come. Further, it is unlikely that Jesus died on the 15th of Nisan, as in the synoptic chronology, but on the 14th of Nisan (as in the Johannine chronology; *cf. Jesus Christ*): the meal on the 13th of Nisan was not a passover meal, for this took place on the 14th of Nisan.

Accordingly, the *oldest extant account is that of Luke 22.15 f., 18,* and in its earliest version it spoke only of eating and drinking together in the kingdom of God, and did not mention any interpretation of the death of Jesus as an act of salvation or of the linking of this conviction to the Jewish passover.

Nevertheless—and this qualification must be strongly emphasized—Jesus's own point of view, so far as we can know and understand it, does not make it improper for others to speak of the death of Jesus as an act of salvation on the grounds that through it they themselves have been assured of divine forgiveness. From this point of view, we see the peculiar and essential nature of the much discussed problem of the 'institution of the Eucharist' Jesus did not in fact institute the Eucharist with the words of administration as they are commonly used, any more than he instituted the rite of baptism (*cf. Baptism* I, page 294 ff, above) or founded the Church. But just as the primitive Church administered baptism in a meaningful sense in the name of Jesus, because it regarded itself as the Church or congregation of God and the body of Christ, so the remembrance of the last meal of Jesus with his disciples became for the Church a repeated and enduring reminder of the suffering, crucifixion and resurrection of the Lord, thus establishing its connection with this act of salvation.

The much disputed questions concerning the origin and the meaning of the 'elements' *bread and wine* are not as important as has been made out. Just as in baptism, as a rite of purification, water is the usual element (*cf. Baptism*), bread and wine, and in the first place bread even without wine, formed the natural elements of a common meal. It was only because they were conscious of being gathered together as the Church of Christ that those who took part in the meal came to regard it as the Lord's Supper, and connected the ordinary food and drink of which they partook with the Lord Jesus Christ. This does not yet amount to a sacrament in the hellenistic sense, in which the inferiority inherent in human nature could be removed by the inherent quality of the holiness of God. Such a view, which is peculiar to the ancient hellenistic world, leads to the idea that man can obtain an assurance of God's forgiveness from something which is there for everyone to experience. But Jesus did not point to the objectively perceived occurrence of a visible event in which the forgiveness of God should be clearly manifested; he proclaimed that forgiveness. The decisive factor is his *word*. To this extent the early Christian Church, like Jesus, gave a closer definition to the act of salvation it encountered in the Eucharist, in a sense which can only be stated in the context of a view of the preaching of Jesus as a whole (*cf. Jesus Christ*, above). This is the one decisive anticipation of the sacramental outlook which was constantly becoming more strongly established.

2. The Eucharist in the Church of Jerusalem (and Palestine)
The celebration and the meaning of the Eucharist (on
this and the two following paragraphs *cf.* IV below,
'The Liturgical History of the Eucharist') in the primitive Church of Jerusalem, with which a few other Palestinian churches of which we have no detailed knowledge
are connected, give no indication that the bread and
wine were regarded in a sacramental sense as the food
and drink of immortality. The common meals of the
primitive Church, at which, according to Jewish custom,
bread was broken (*cf.* IV, 1 below) took on a special
character through the fact that the tiny group formed
by the first adherents of Jesus regarded itself as *the Church*,
that is, the Church of God referred to in the promises of
the Old Testament. Since the crucified and risen Lord
Jesus Christ was the concrete fulfilment of these promises, every gathering in which the members of the
Church were united was a 'supper of the Lord'. At these,
the remembrance of the Lord, and especially of the last
meal he had taken with his disciples, was always present,
because Jesus himself had lived in a table fellowship with
his disciples, who now formed the basis of the first church,
and had particularly emphasized this community and
companionship on the occasion of their last meal. The
particular stress laid on the expression 'the breaking of
bread' clearly shows that wine was absent at first. Indirect evidence of this is provided by the story of the
disciples at Emmaus (*cf.* Luke 24.30,35) and the story of
the feasting of the five thousand or four thousand (*cf.*
the description of the behaviour of Jesus in these stories:
he took the bread, pronounced the prayer of thanksgiving, broke the bread and gave it to the disciples; Mark
6.41; 8.6, and the parallel passages). Later Judaeo-
Christian sects celebrated the Eucharist without wine.
It was celebrated with water instead of wine as late as
the third century in North Africa. This provides a reason

why the text Luke 22.15-19*a* contains words of administration for the bread alone. And the remarkable emphasis laid on the words: 'And they all drank of it' in Mark 14.23 (*cf.* Matt. 26.27), may perhaps be aimed against the disregard of the cup elsewhere. And it is the words which go with the cup which in every account of the 'institution' of the Eucharist interpret the death of Jesus as a covenant sacrifice. Even if, as was also customary, *wine* was sometimes taken as well as bread, this finally becoming the custom in order to give greater solemnity, it did not at first make any difference to the nature of the rite, nor to its meaning. According to the text which we have shown was the original text of Luke, these common meals are *a pledge of the great messianic meal*. Those who partook of them did so with 'glad hearts' (Acts 2.46). We would be able to add to this if we knew more about the prayers which preceded and followed the meal. The Eucharistic prayers in Ch. 9 f. of the *Didache* (*cf.* IV, 1 below) are entirely in agreement on one point with the reference to rejoicing in Acts 2.46: there is no allusion to the flesh and blood of Christ, nor to his death or to any partaking in that death. It appears as if this rite, in which the cup comes first according to the Jewish custom, preserved the substance of a very ancient rite which goes back beyond Paul. On the other hand, there are also clear allusions to concepts of the hellenistic mystery religions, such as are found in particular in the Fourth gospel. In the ancient liturgies this duality, the interweaving of the eschatological parousia and the cultic epiphany (that is, the 'return' of Christ as a figure of the future, at the end of time, and the 'appearance', coming about within the act of worship, of Christ present here and now), is even more marked. But there is no mention of the sacrificial death of Christ. The primitive Palestinian Church, influenced as it was by Judaism, set the death of Christ on one side as a painful enigma. For the Jews, the death, and especially the judicial execution of the Messiah, was a stumbling block (*cf.* I Cor. 1.23). In the speeches of Acts, with their very ancient Christology (*cf.* Vol. II *Christology*, I) it is not the death of Jesus which is the act of salvation, but the resurrection, brought about by God in spite of his shameful death. A true understanding of the death of Jesus, in the sense that Jesus gave to us, without needing to make or in fact making a statement about his saving death, was not attained by the first disciples.

3. The Eucharist in St. Paul and in the Hellenistic Churches

A deeper understanding of the death of Jesus in relation to the Eucharist is found in *Paul*. He belonged to *hellenistic Christianity* (*cf. Paul* p. 173 above) and his most pointed comments on the subject of the Eucharist occur in I Cor. 11.20 ff.; this polemic passage is the most likely to contain Paul's true view. Going beyond what is given in the hellenistic tradition of Mark and Matthew, Paul stresses that Eucharist *celebrates the remembrance of the Lord's death*, (*cf.* I above). This in no way contradicts Mark and Matthew, but emphasizes the point that they make. This emphasis is most clear in v. 26, 'For as often as you eat this bread and drink the cup, you proclaim the Lord's death until he comes'. The expression 'the Lord' shows that this verse does not form part of the words of Jesus given in the previous verses. In addition, in contrast to Mark and Matthew, Paul expands certain passages, and abbreviates others, and is clearly attempting to make the two actions (bread and wine) parallel parts of a unified and balanced liturgical formula. The broken and blessed bread represents the body of Christ, which was given for his disciples, and the cup represents the new covenant, which was founded in his blood shed on the cross. A parallel is being drawn to the sacrificial death of Jesus and to the making of the covenant of Sinai

(Exod. 24.3-8). The atoning sacrifice is elevated to become a *new messianic covenant* (*cf.* Heb. 8.13; 9.15). That this is the fulfilment of the promise of God in the Old Testament is more important than the fact that in the records of the founding of ancient cultic fraternities we find almost exact verbal parallels to the formula 'in remembrance of me'. In this one turn of phrase Paul may be borrowing from such a document. But when he interprets the Eucharist as a *celebration of the death of Jesus* he was not developing his whole conception from the meals in memory of the dead celebrated in the ancient world. The cause of the abuses censured by Paul in I Cor. 11.20 ff. was probably that the members of the hellenistic churches themselves were constantly being tempted back by the spell of the ancient cult. The decisive thing for Paul himself is the preaching of the cross of Christ, which is also proclaimed in the Eucharist when the disciples of Christ are united in it as the body of Christ. If this is the case, we are concerned not with what was later the source of constant dispute (*cf.* II below), the relation between the elements and the reality of the Eucharist, but with the action as such. Those who took part in it were demonstrating, or were intending to demonstrate, that they recognized their Lord, who, though he was outwardly invisible, was as truly present as the bread and the wine. But this Lord was still only the crucified Lord who was to come again at the end of time. This *theologia crucis* (theology of the cross) was probably responsible for the form taken by the whole tradition of the 'institution' of the Eucharist, including the form it later took in Mark and Matthew. At the same time, however, we must not forget that with his words 'I received from the Lord what I also delivered to you' (I Cor. 11.23) Paul was pointing away from himself and from his own Pauline theology.

Apart from this direct concentration on the cross, the

Eucharist is *a meal of the community with Jesus Christ.* The way in which Paul speaks on this theme in 1 Cor. 10.1 ff. shows that he takes for granted the existence of this point of view in the Church of Corinth. In fact what he says about 'communion' must have been a widely held view within any hellenistic Church. Paul here compares the Eucharist with the sacrificial meals of the Jews, and of the heathens in particular, 10.16 ff. The latter, he says, is 'the table of demons', but the bread that is broken is the 'table of the Lord' and the cup that is blessed is 'the cup of the Lord'. The sacrificial meals bring about a partnership with demons, while the Lord's Supper brings about a communion with the exalted Lord. In 10.3 ff. Paul relates the bread and the cup to the manna and the water from the rock which nourished the children of Israel in the desert. This is presumably to be interpreted as meaning that the Lord's supper represents a spiritual food and a spiritual drink, and that both are given in Jesus Christ, vv. 4-5. Thus the meal is a supernatural, spiritual and bodily eating and drinking with Jesus Christ. This is made particularly clear in v. 16: 'The cup of blessing which we bless, is it not a participation in the blood of Christ? The bread which we break, is it not a participation in the body of Christ?'

But since, as Paul tells us elsewhere, the body of Christ can be identified with the Church, the concrete effect of this communion with the exalted Lord is *the communion of the faithful with one another.* Vv. 17 f. read: 'Because there is one bread, we who are many are one body, for we all partake of the one bread. Consider the practice of Israel; are not those who eat the sacrifices partners in the altar?

Here Paul himself draws our attention to the *analogies with the history of religion* as a whole. In ancient sacramental meals one of the main means of achieving union with the God was that of eating and drinking. Numerous examples exist in primitive religion, which continued as an active force in the hellenistic mysteries themselves, as for example in those of Mithras and Attis. The relation between Christian and heathen practice is in fact so great that Justin Martyr (*Apology* I 54,66) stigmatized the meal of the worshippers of Mithras as a diabolical imitation and anticipation of the Eucharist. Why then should Paul not have come to hold the ancient belief in unity with God by eating and drinking, under the influence of the prevailing sacramental conceptions of this pagan environment? Could he not have taken over such views from the churches he set up? This possibility exists. What must be said is this: that just as the hellenistic churches felt the need to interpret baptism (*cf. Baptism,* I p. 294, above) which was originally an eschatological sacrament, as a hellenistic mystery, so the same may have taken place in the case of the Eucharist. Now the more Paul makes clear how the sacral meals of the pagans are to be regarded, the more obvious it must have been that he was defining his own view in contrast to that of the pagans. The mystery of the Eucharist is concerned with the death of Christ as a bloody reality, and not with a mythical drama, so that however many hellenistic expressions and concepts are used, he is saying *something quite different:* the mystery is the cross, and this mystery of the cross is not exclusively linked either to the rite of baptism nor to the rite of the Eucharist. The relationship to the hellenistic mysteries would have been very close if the cross had been merely a symbol. But this cross (the gallows of the ancient world!) is a cruel paradox which God permitted and ordained. By the fact that the Christian brethren claimed of themselves that they were the congregation of God described in the Old Testament, they were something different from a hellenistic fraternity. And the death of Christ is not something which is acted out in an exciting and tragic fashion like the drama of one of the mysteries, but is a real event which transforms, judges, and brings blessing to our own very being, if we are crucified with Christ.

In spite of all this it was possible for Paul to think *sacramentally* in the narrower sense of the word. Besides I Cor. 10.I ff., a sacramental outlook is notably obvious in 11.29 f.: the unworthy partaking of the meal causes sickness. There is no question with Paul of explaining away this sacramental point of view (*cf.* I Cor. 15.29: vicarious baptism on behalf of the dead; *cf. Baptism*, I).

Paul's view of the Eucharist, and his sacramental outlook as a whole, shows features both of acceptance and rejection. The hellenistic Christianity of Paul accepts material from the *hellenistic mysteries*, but draws an immediate contrast with them. If this hellenistic visualization and concretization (the encapsulating of spiritual reality in visible objects) is traced back and reduced to its content, without regard to its form or the cultic apparatus with which it is related, there remains a kernel, which, however undramatic it may be, is characteristic of the rest. It is not possible to explain everything in terms of what is called Christ-mysticism (*cf.* Vol. II *Mysticism*, IV), though this also required no cultic apparatus. We must rather point to the fact that in his sacramental teaching, the apostle of 'justification of faith', the former Jew who for all his Christ-mysticism remained true to the biblical God of his fathers, *must* ultimately have implied something different from the corresponding doctrines of the hellenistic mysteries: for Paul the act of salvation, that is, the cross of Christ, and the communion with Christ and with one another, based on that saving act, of those who have been crucified with Christ, is represented and made visible in the sacrament of the Eucharist; and the cross and this communion form the content of the word of God which judges and brings his grace.

4. The Eucharist in the Post-apostolic Churches and in the Fourth Gospel

In the *post-apostolic* period, the few statements on the Eucharist that are to be found in early Christian writings show on the whole the continued effect of Paul's views, except that there is a greater stress on the hellenistic mystical and sacramental aspect. Whereas in the circles in which Mark and Matthew originated, the meal was maintained as a celebration of the death of Christ in the Pauline sense, and is related to the Jewish passover, there is no trace of this in other churches. From one of these comes the *Didache*; the passages discussed above (*cf.* 2 above; *cf.* also IV, 1 below) show how powerful was the effect of the hellenistic outlook even where any reference to the death of Christ was absent. Eucharistic language and doctrine become constantly more *realistic*. With the influence of the cultic accounts of the institution, even more powerful *liturgical* formulae came into being: 'To eat the flesh of Christ, to drink the blood of Christ' (John 6.51 ff.). There is evidence that these expressions sometimes gave offence (6.60). But the Fourth Evangelist clings firmly to them in his polemic. John 6.51 ff., in fact, probably represents the view of practically the whole of Christianity in the post-apostolic period. For John himself, rather than for this universal Christian view, it is significant that he sets crude material and terminology in a context where the idea of the spirit is specifically stressed. What that period was most concerned with was realism: Ignatius of Antioch calls the bread of the Eucharist 'a medicine of immortality, a means of avoiding death, and of living in Jesus Christ forever' (*Epistle to the Ephesians* 20.2). Even Justin Martyr (*Apology* I 66) stresses this realism. The Fourth Evangelist himself intended to oppose such a view of the sacrament, and presented a different account of its content from that of Paul, attempting to reduce it to its essential significance in the way described above.

Within Catholicism the idea of the *sacrament in isolation*, with its natural and mystical elements, was the one that prevailed. The Pauline *protest* against any materialization of the Eucharist being accepted as inevitable or natural ceased to be an active force, but has constantly reappeared wherever the voice of the Pauline protest as a whole has been raised.

Karl Ludwig Schmidt

II. THE HISTORY OF THE DOCTRINE OF THE EUCHARIST

1. The Earliest Period

The violent quarrels provoked by the doctrine of the Eucharist since the early Middle Ages, and especially since the Reformation, form a notable contrast to the silence of the early Church concerning the Eucharist. The material from the first thousand years is so slight, and so indefinite in its terms, that every side in the disputes of the present day can find its own view reflected there. There is, of course, from the early Church a great deal concerning the celebration of the Eucharist (*cf.* IV below) and the practical questions related to it, but very little is said about the religious meaning that underlay it.

a. The *Didache* contains in Ch. 9, 10 and 14 a series of eucharistic prayers which present the Eucharist as an act of thanksgiving, and portray to those who took part in it a future in which the division and fragmentation of the present time would come to an end in the all-embracing unity of the kingdom of Christ. But the church concerned does not seem to have given any thought to the question of what the spiritual food for eternal life, received with thanksgiving, the 'Eucharist', really was.

At least these impressive prayers are silent on the subject. The indications contained in *Ignatius* of Antioch (*To the Smyrnans* 7.1; *To the Ephesians* 20.2) are somewhat fuller. But they are too short and ambiguous to be of value in describing the doctrine of the Eucharist in the second century. What Ignatius says about the Eucharist is reminiscent of liturgical formulae. It is perhaps possible to read into his words some suggestion of the real presence of the flesh and blood of Christ in the elements of the Eucharist: but it is open to dispute how far one can go in this. One characteristic thought is clear, that just as Christ himself died in the body and rose again in the body, so he confers incorruptibility (ἀφθαρσία) upon his Church. His flesh, which had overcome death, becomes a means of immortality, a medicine (φάρμακον) against death for all in his Church who partake of the Eucharist. In relation with faith in the death of him who died for us, the Eucharist unites us both spiritually and bodily with Christ. In this communion with him we possess to the highest degree of perfection what the true worshippers of the old covenant already looked forward to in hope. Neither do the *Apologists* of the second century give us any clear answer. For them the goal of salvation was immortality with God, in which both body and soul would take part; and it was the Eucharist which so nourished our flesh and blood that it underwent a transformation into the state of immortality. Justin (*Apology* I 66) also in some sense sees the flesh and blood of Christ in the Eucharist. The Logos unites himself to the bread; by the word of command proceeding from him the bread becomes his flesh and the wine his blood, in order to be a food for immortality.

These very early Christian churches in fact regarded the bread and wine of the Eucharist as *the body and blood of Christ*. They were acquainted, after all, with the words of institution, referring to the body and blood of Christ (*cf.* I, 1 above) which were repeated and heard again and again. The false teachers whom Ignatius opposed (*To the Smyrnans* 7) and who did not believe in the 'flesh of Christ', disassociated themselves in consequence from the Eucharist. Where on the other hand the elements were conceived of as the body and blood of Christ, they were treated with scrupulous reverence, great care was taken to avoid letting a particle of the Lord's body fall to the ground (Tertullian, *de corona* 3; Origen, *in Exodum* XIII 3), and miraculous stories were told concerning the sacred elements (Cyprian *de lapsis* 25-6). The pagans very early reviled the Eucharist as a 'thyestean meal', and this likewise implies that the Christian churches saw in the Eucharist the body and blood of Christ. The theologians too presupposed this as a fact, without asking in what way this was so, and without going into detail. The early Christians, even in the West, thought in images, not in abstractions. They lived in a world of *mysteries*. It was a perfectly natural idea to them that by an act of consecration earthly elements could become something more unearthly, something divine, without in any way changing their nature. Even the expression 'food of immortality' in Ignatius is best explained as a result of the influence of the mysteries (*cf.* I, 3 above). Even Christians and gnostics were acquainted and familiar with the religion of the mysteries. But, being a matter of religious emotion, it was not distinctly or clearly defined; it lay rather in an obscurity which individuals understood and interpreted very differently. In the atmosphere of the mysteries of the ancient world there was no liking for precisely framed questions and answers. Symbols were taken in a real sense, and reality in a symbolic sense, according to the level of religious understanding which each individual possessed.

The less it was possible to construct a precisely articulated doctrine of the Eucharist, the more alien teachings and concepts crept into the Eucharist at this early period. *b.* The most important of these was the concept of *sacrifice.* At first it remained entirely within the limits of New Testament thought. The prayers of thanksgiving at the celebration of the Eucharist (*cf.* IV, 1 below) and the charitable gifts, which, insofar as they were not used at the *agape* itself, were used for needy members of the Church, did not permit the Eucharist to be regarded as anything more than a *thank-offering* to God. But almost simultaneously, the rite developed into what was considered simply as the particular sacrifice practised by the Christian Church. At first it consisted of a true meal, and of the prayers of the members of the congregation. But when the prayers recited over the elements which were offered became an official task of the leader of the congregation, the relationship to a *cultic sacrifice*, very remote from the gatherings for edification of the Church of the earliest period, became more obvious; at the same time, the Eucharist became separated from the 'love-feast' or *agape*, and was joined to the meeting for instruction. This process was complete by the middle of the second century, somewhat earlier in Asia Minor, and later in Egypt. Justin still recognizes in essence only the sacrifice of prayer in the primitive Christian sense, and in his view all Christians were still priests. But by this time he too saw in the elements the object of the sacrificial action; the bishop already had something in his hand which he could offer to God (*Dialogue* 41, 70). And it was above all the priest who bestowed on the elements their true significance by his prayer. What was already a matter of experience, *Cyprian* took and defined precisely, making it a conscious belief, although his view did not immediately prevail everywhere. According to him (*Ep.* 63.14,17), the priest repeats what Christ did, by offering a perfect sacrifice to God. Thus within a hundred years from the time of Justin the sacrifice of thanksgiving of all Christians had become a *propitiatory sacrifice offered by the priest*; this change has no basis in the New Testament, but is explained by the Greek and Roman environment. Soon prayer was offered for those who gave the gifts; and gifts were offered for the dead, which were tacitly regarded as propitiatory in nature. For although even according to Tertullian (*de exhort. castit.* 11) a member of the congregation offered his sacrifice for the dead, this soon became no longer possible except through the priest. The concept of sacrifice and that of priesthood depended on each other, and strengthened each other.

2. The Greek Development

Without there ever being a dispute or a conscious conflict over what the Eucharist was, nevertheless, under the influence of the cult and of popular feeling, and largely in connection with other dogmatic statements, theological ideas concerning the Eucharist begin to appear.

a. Irenaeus (*adversus haereses* IV 18.5) sees in the Eucharist the body of Christ, an entity within which there is both an earthly and heavenly part. The heavenly, however, is the spirit of God, which is called down upon the elements. Through the invocation this heavenly part is added to the elements; as a result they become something which they were not before, a food through which flesh receives into itself the powers of immortality, and which is a pledge to the body that it will become a partaker of eternal life. This is the current Christian view of the body and blood of Christ; but Irenaeus elaborates it, makes it more precise, and seeks to explain it by the concept of a *consecration* of the elements. *Origen* (*cf.* Vol. III *Origen*) gives a much clearer picture. When Jesus nourished his disciples with the bread of the Eucharist, it is his own body (*in Matthaeum ser.* 86, Lommatzsch IV, p. 419; *in psalmos hom.* II 6, Lommatzsch XII, p. 268). Thus whoever comes to the Eucharist partakes of the body of Christ. It is evident that Origen is seeing this universal Christian idea in the light of the consecration offered by the mysteries, when one of the demands he makes for participation in the rite is the purity of him who receives the mystical body of Jesus. It is true that all Origen's teaching is in spiritual terms, and his words must be interpreted accordingly. Everything that is material belongs to this world alone, and passes away with it. Thus the eating itself has nothing to do with immortality; the resurrection does away with everything material. Even the food in the Eucharist is material in nature; consequently it has no relationship to the spiritual life. The risen Lord no longer has a body and blood in the accepted sense; he has ceased to be human. Consequently, Origen takes the word 'body' in the Eucharist in a symbolic sense, as a sign of the true food of the soul, the living word, the Logos. Although those who are beginners in Christianity accept the common view, those who are more mature cannot doubt that by the bread which Christ calls his body he does not mean the visible bread which he holds in his hands, but a mystical bread and a mystical drink which gladdens the heart. We drink his blood when we hear his preaching and come to life through it. All that distinguishes the Eucharist from any other hearing of the word is that in it a symbol is added to the word. The idea of a previous consecration, and the concept of the eating and drinking of the body and blood of Christ, fall into the background behind that of the hearing of his word.

Thus as early as the beginning of the third century there is a clear division of opinion. On the one hand there is the *realism* of Irenaeus, who considers that as a result of the priestly blessing something supernatural is truly present and effective in the elements, and consequently describes the elements themselves as the body and blood of Christ. On the other hand there is the *spiritualizing view* of Origen, from which any thought of the real body and real blood of Christ is absent. The first is a specifically Greek conception and it is related to the mystery religions of the Imperial period. In the same way, the gnosticism of that period sanctified not only oil for anointing, but also baptismal water and bread, by a formula of consecration. It is a popular view which would have been understood outside the Christian churches in the Greek world as a whole. By contrast, Origen, who saw in the Eucharist only something spiritual, a food for the soul, was rejected both by the Church and by the gnostics, but is approved by theologians such as Eusebius of Caesarea and Gregory Nazianzen. Athanasius also comes close to this symbolic conception.

It would be remarkable if the *Antiochene School* had not produced their own interpretation of the meaning of the Eucharist. Typical of their thinking is the expression which describes the elements as the 'representations' (*antitypes*) of the real historical body of Christ; not, moreover, insofar as these elements are consumed, but insofar as they are offered. This expression refers to the eucharistic meal, but within a new and distinctive conception of the Eucharist as a whole, in which the principal feature is the idea of a sacrifice. As symbols of the sacrificed body and blood of Christ, the elements which are consumed convey what as an objective fact has been gained by the sacrificial death of Christ, that is, the forgiveness of sins and eternal life. The characteristic expression 'antitype' is also found in Eusebius of Caesarea and Gregory Nazianzen. They too make a clear connection between the Eucharist and the body and blood of Christ; not merely with the Logos in Christ, like Origen, and not merely with the incorruptibility of his flesh like Irenaeus. *b*. That these three conceptions gradually became widespread was due in part to the influence of the Christological disputes of the fourth and fifth centuries (*cf.* Vol. II

Christology, II), without much advance having been made in the meantime. *Cyril* of Jerusalem puts forward a formal doctrine of the Eucharist in his fourth and fifth *Mystagogic Catecheses* (347/8). But it is only natural that in them he reflected the popular point of view. The Eucharist is a sacrifice in which we offer Christ who was slain for our sins. But insofar as we receive a food in the Eucharist, Jesus himself said of it: 'This is my body'. For if he was able to change water into wine, why should he not change wine into blood? We pray to God, and he sends his Holy Spirit upon the elements, in order to make the bread his body and the wine his blood. Although the elements look and taste like bread and wine, yet in reality they are the body and blood of Christ. But it is emphasized that although the elements are sanctified, and although they are more than ordinary bread and wine, yet they are merely an image of the body and blood of Christ. Even the invocation of the Holy Spirit signifies in the first place no more than a sanctification of the material elements. For the powerful influence of the symbolic conception had first to be overcome, before the idea of *conversion* could prevail. Whether Gregory of Nyssa (*catech.* 37, *PG* 45, 93 ff.) went beyond what Justin had said, and whether it is possible to speak of a conscious theory of the conversion of the elements in what is certainly a very detailed discussion of the subject, is to say the least very questionable. For he speaks of the transformation of the bread and wine not into the body and blood of Christ, but into the body of the Logos. And just as Gregory of Nyssa could be thought of as a follower of Origen, Chrysostomus, for all the directness of his language, is also as a member of the Antiochene School, and much too spiritualizing in his thought to be able to think of a transformation of the elements. He speaks only in his liturgical capacity, and as a preacher, when he expresses the expectation that what we really consume in the Eucharist will bring us immortality and bodily unity with Christ. In spite of all the mysterious and magical popular conceptions, a theory of the conversion of the elements did not appear until later.

Theodore of Mopsuestia and Nestorius, as members of the Antiochene School, use symbolic terms throughout: the broken body and the poured out blood of the man Jesus, who was united with the Logos, are symbolically represented by bread and wine, so that we who take these representations into ourselves are made partakers of what the sacrifice of Christ has gained for us. By contrast, the Alexandrines and Monophysites (*cf.* Vol. II *Christology*, II) are pronounced realists: the bread and wine of the Eucharist are the body, which gives life, and the blood, which conveys immortality, of God the Logos. *c.* The victory of the Alexandrine theology paved the way for the elaboration of this *realistic* conception of the Eucharist into a body of scholastic and academic doctrine. Eutychius of Constantinople (*On the Passover and the Eucharist*) still teaches that the exalted body of Christ remains whole and undivided in itself, and is nevertheless received entire by every communicant in the fragment he consumes. Without a real change having taken place in the bread and the wine, they appear as the antitypes of the sacrificed body of Christ. For every realist from the time of Irenaeus on the elements in the Eucharist represent something distinct from the actual body; it is simply that no one was fully conscious of this fact, and a veil was quietly drawn over it. But popular piety went further, and theology followed it. *John Damascene* (*de fide orthod.* 4.13) objected to the view that the consecrated elements were merely antitypes of the body and blood of Christ; this could only be true of the unconsecrated bread and wine; the consecrated elements are rather the deified body of the Lord himself. At the second Synod of Nicaea in 787, this view was officially recognized by the Church: after consecration the body and blood of Christ are really present in the Eucharist. John Damascene is also the source of the doctrine of the conversion of the elements held in the Greek Church. He seeks to explain the process by saying that just as bodily nourishment is converted into the body, and yet does not become another body apart from what it was, so the elements of the Eucharist, through the invocation of the Holy Spirit, are changed supernaturally to the body and blood of Christ, and not to something else. The body of Christ in the Eucharist and the exalted body in heaven must be *one* body, for the incarnate Logos has only *one* hypostasis. Down to the present day the Greek Church holds firmly to the view that it is the invocation (*epiclesis*) of the Holy Spirit which brings about the change. In all other respects, however, the teaching of the Greek Church was gradually assimilated to the Roman idea of transubstantiation between the thirteenth and sixteenth centuries (*cf.* 3*b* below).

3. The Western Church

A dogma of the Eucharist was formulated much later in the *West* than in the East. The idea of *sacrifice* appeared as early as Cyprian (see 1*b* above). He speaks of the sacrificed body and the sacrificed blood in the Eucharist but does not conceive of either as being really present; he regards the Eucharist as a symbolic sacrifice, which recalls the suffering of Christ, by imitating what Christ did on Golgotha. The Eucharist offers to those who partake of it simply what everyone receives who is in union with Christ, that is, the fruit of his redeeming word. But since a purely symbolical conception is altogether impossible for the modes of thought of the ancient world, it is not surprising that the idea of a *change in the elements* in respect of their power occurs again and again. This is true as early as Tertullian, who can scarcely be considered as holding a purely symbolical conception. From the fourth century, therefore, these ideas of a symbolic sacrifice, related to the true body and true blood of Christ, are constantly influenced by the realistic ideas of Greek theology. The conception of being nourished by the life-giving flesh of the God-man became more familiar. This is especially evident in Ambrose. Under the influence of the idea of sacrifice, the way was prepared for a doctrine of the conversion of the elements.

That its progress was not more rapid is explained by the influence of *Augustine*. For him the sacraments are signs and rites, which in association with the word point to something holy which is offered to the believer. They are, so to speak, the word become visible. The Eucharist in particular creates a spiritual unity both with Christ and with the Church of the Saints. For even when Augustine is speaking of a eucharistic sacrifice which takes place both in the offering and the sacrificial meal, he always has the subjective intention principally in mind. Sometimes he uses liturgical turns of phrase, which, however, give no reason to question his undoubtedly symbolic view of the Eucharist. What the sacraments offer is only available through faith. 'Believe and you have eaten' (*in Joh.* 25.12). This use of images similar to those of John 6 is characteristic of Augustine throughout; in fact he regarded the symbolic imagery as part of the sacrament (*Ep.* 98.9). Even what appears to be flesh is intended in the sacrament to be taken as something spiritual (*de catech. rudib.* 26.50). Jesus himself had signified by the words 'This is my body' something that in reality was only a sign of his body (*contra Adimant.* 12.3). There is no doubt that Augustine taught a spiritualizing doctrine of the sacrament. He is followed by the Africans *Fulgentius of Ruspe* and *Facundus of Hermiane*. At the same time, the language of the liturgy gradually made its influence felt. This can be seen in Caesarius of Arles

and *Gregory the Great*. In the latter, the principal thought
is that of propitiatory sacrifice, and other questions fall
into the background. He teaches that Christ suffers for
us again and again, and constantly reapplies the fruit
of his suffering to us; that Christians can influence God
in a magical way with the sacrifice of the Mass, in order
to obtain spiritual and bodily blessing, seems to be more
important for Gregory than the nature of the Eucharist
itself. Thus when the end of the Roman Empire brought
to a halt the development of civilization, it was survived
by the incomplete development of these two parallel
traditions of eucharistic doctrine.

b. At the time of the Carolingian renaissance Augustine
was as it were brought back to life, and as a result the
symbolic conception of the Eucharist once more came
to the fore in the theology of that time. But that the idea
of a real change in the elements was no less alive, is
shown by the conflict into which *Ratramnus* of Corbey
came with his abbot *Paschasius Radbertus*. The thought of
that period was already able to distinguish between
image and reality, between the allegory and the object
it represented. Consequently the elements of the Eucharist ceased to be a mere image to them. A further
influence was the contemporary development of Christology (*cf.* Vol. II *Christology*, II). In the minds of many
the historical Jesus was hidden behind the God who had
merely taken on a human nature. This divine being was
only found in the mysteries of the Church. In this matter
too, Augustine no longer reigned unchallenged. That the
consecration of the elements offered by the priest made
them something which they had not been before, was
universally accepted. For the majority of the faithful,
the true body of Christ himself, and not merely its effects,
was present in the Mass as at the Last Supper. The monk
Radbert answered their needs. His book *De corpore et
sanguine Domini* (831/3) is the first work to deal with the

Eucharist on its own. Every day, almighty God, in answer to the prayer of the priest and by his eternal word in the sacraments, changes the substance of bread and wine into the flesh and blood of Christ—by the same miracle of creation through which he formed Jesus through the Holy Spirit in the womb of the Virgin. After the consecration, therefore, Christ's true flesh and blood are henceforth truly present; though the forms of bread and wine, perceptible to the sense, still remain, this only happens in order to avert our horror, to avoid profaning what is holy, and to exercise our faith. Nevertheless, the saving effects of the Eucharist are only available—here there is a reminiscence of Augustine—to the faithful. Radbert's view was not accepted everywhere without question. Archbishop Hrabanus of Mainz saw in the consecrated elements merely symbols, and talked only of a mystical body of Christ, and not of the historical body of Christ. This idea of Hrabanus was defined and developed by the monk Ratramnus in his treatise *On the Body and Blood of the Lord*, composed at the demand of Charles the Bold. The elements are merely an image. When someone receives what he believes, the body of Christ is present in the Eucharist, not in a way perceptible to the senses, but in reality, as the food of the soul for him who believes. It is a question of something spiritual, but nevertheless real, of which the elements are an image. Here Ratramnus opposes the desire of his time for miracles. He makes a clear distinction between appearances perceptible by the senses and the mysteries of faith that lie behind them. He sought to preserve the older teaching of Augustine, but was unable to present any enduring teaching of his own in opposition to the rapidly spreading doctrine of the Mass. Thus his book made little impression, while Radbert was successful.

The fate of Ratramnus was shared two hundred years later in an ominous way by *Berengarius* of Tours. The clumsy way in which the conversion of the elements was presented at that time, irritated his scholarly mind. He rejected it as absurd. It was impossible for Christ, who was enthroned in heaven, to be taken in all his fullness into a tiny piece of bread, and yet Christ promised himself entirely to the faithful. Thus the elements remained in reality, even after consecration, what they had been before, except that to what was visible something invisible was added, through which the faithful could receive in the spirit the power of the true body of Christ. After this question had been violently disputed for more than twenty years Berengarius once again gave an exhaustive presentation of these views in his work *De coena sancta* (*On the Holy Supper, against Lanfranc*). Amongst his opponents, Guitmund of Aversa, and especially the Scholastic Alger of Lüttich, drew from the view which had become popular conclusions which would have made any spiritual conception of the Eucharist impossible. Berengarius was condemned although he had merely sought to save the mind of the Church from superstition and religious materialism by calling on Augustine. With the formula of Cardinal Humbert (1059) the new doctrine was laid down once for all; any contradiction was regarded as heresy. It passed into canon law, and soon a whole swarm of theologians had gathered to expound and defend its every detail. From the middle of the twelfth century on, the term *transubstantiation* came into use. The substance of bread and wine was changed by the consecration into the substance of the body and blood of Christ. Nevertheless, the accidents of the previous substance remained as before, and continued their own independent existence. Since the historical body of Christ in heaven has become spiritual and inviolable through its union with his divinity, from henceforth he has been able by his omnipotence to be wherever he wished. Thus the whole Christ, God and man, is present in each of the two elements of the Eucharist. This doctrine was given dogmatic status by Innocent III at the fourth Lateran Council in 1215, when it was closely related to the doctrine of the Trinity and the Incarnation of Christ, as the earthly manifestation, as it were, of these heavenly mysteries: from the dogmatic point of view it was the most fateful act of medieval Catholicism. Its liturgical consequences were the withdrawal of the chalice and the adoration of the Host, and it permitted the miracle of the bodily presence of Christ in his Church to be venerated in the feast of Corpus Christi with its procession.

c. In their doctrine of the sacraments the *Scholastic* theologians celebrated the triumph of their method by bringing together into a single system ideas that had previously been held in parallel with each other and unreconciled. At the same time the characteristic differences in the two great teaching orders also made their effects felt in this field. While Thomas Aquinas and his school see in the sacraments a sacred sign which sanctified man, the Franciscans denied the existence of a divine power in the sacrament itself, and saw in it merely a parable of what God is doing simultaneously within the soul. Consequently, Duns Scotus only defended the phenomenon of the conversion of the elements in the Eucharist because it was Church doctrine. In reality he was of the opinion that an act of God took place not through the words of the priest, but in parallel with them, by means of which the body of Christ, spatially present in heaven, at the same time entered into a spatial relationship with the host, as it were entering into the bread and penetrating it to the point where it completely disappeared. That in this process Christ can be present at one and the same time both in heaven and in different places in the Eucharist, he explains simply by the omnipotence of God. In any case the nominalist school of Scholastics lost themselves in innumerable details and unreasonable hypotheses which *Tridentine Catholicism* regarded as of no particular value. *How* Christ can be present was regarded as virtually impossible to express in words. The Council of Trent thought it sufficient to regard the consecration by the priest not merely as the occasion but as the cause of transubstantiation (*per consecrationem conversionem fieri*) a view that in its turn played a predominant part in the glorification of the priesthood.

4. Eucharistic Disputes in Protestantism

a. The Reformers were not able to add much that was new in the doctrine of the Eucharist to the conclusions of the early Church and the Middle Ages. At first they followed Luther's *Prelude to the Babylonian Captivity of the Church* (1520) in merely rejecting certain doctrines. The emphasis was laid on communion, representing a fellowship in love with Christ. But if this fellowship was to be possible, then both the body and blood of Christ must be present at the same time in the bread and the wine. But this fact was sufficient in itself, while the way in which it took place was not regarded as important. Thus Luther opposed both the withdrawal of the chalice, and also the doctrine of the conversion of the elements, which he replaced by a view taken from Ailli of the persistence of the substance of the bread and its union with the body of Christ (Concomitance); he likewise rejected the Mass as a sacrifice and as an *opus operatum*.

But this original point of view underwent a marked change after 1522 as a result of disagreements between the Reformers themselves. Luther began by laying great stress on the words of institution, and tried to achieve a real understanding of the presence of the body of Christ and its relationship to the bread and the wine. For him, the body of Christ is not merely the means by which the gifts of the Eucharist are conveyed, but an end in itself in the Eucharist. This brought about the dispute with Zwingli, who came to grips with the ancient contradictions which the medieval Church had overcome only outwardly and by forced interpretations. From now on he obliged Luther to go over his original view and enlarge upon it in many respects. *Zwingli* made a sharp distinction in Christ between his divine and his human nature (*cf.* Vol. II *Christology*, II); because of its created limitations Christ's human nature could not be present at the same time both in heaven and in the Eucharist. Consequently the Eucharist cannot be intended to be anything more than the remembrance of the fact that we have been redeemed by the death of Christ. The exegesis of Karlstadt, Zwingli, and Oecolampadius, and the abrupt contrast, dear to the Anabaptists, between the action of God and the earthly means used, provided the main reason why *Luther* laid so much emphasis on the true eating of the body of Christ in the Eucharist and on developing a christological justification of this view which made use of the idea of 'ubiquity' (*cf.* Vol. II *Christology*, II). Here Luther adopted Occam's doctrine of the presence of the body of Christ everywhere, thus making as intimate a union as possible between the bread and the body of Christ. Of course anyone who wished to obtain the grace concealed in the Eucharist had also to have faith. But the main concern for Luther was that the Redeemer, truly present, should ratify and seal his redemption for us. The real presence of the body of Christ is necessary, because it is this alone which conveys the salvation brought by the Eucharist, the forgiveness of sins, to each individual. Zwingli's doctrine of the Eucharist also developed rapidly, under the influence of the Dutch theologian Hoen, who took the word 'is' in the words of institution in the sense 'means'. From then on he would not regard either the words of institution or the words concerning the bread of life (John 6) as referring to a sacramental eating of Christ. During the first three years the dispute between Luther and Zwingli was confined to this issue, but after 1527 it became aggravated and personal, and finally led to their total estrangement. Since, as in the early Church, two different views of religion were opposed to each other, not even a personal discussion such as that which took place in Marburg (1-3 October 1529) was able to close the breach entirely. Article 15 of the *Marburg Articles*, which deals with the Eucharist, does assume as common ground the reception of the Eucharist in both kinds, the rejection of the Mass as a 'work', the conception of the Eucharist as 'the sacrament of the true body and blood of Jesus Christ' and an emphasis on the 'spiritual partaking of the same', but has to concede that the two opponents 'had not come to an agreement at this time as to whether the true body and blood of Christ are *bodily* in the bread and wine'. For Luther, however, this last point was of decisive importance, and he insisted on his demand, so ominous for the future, that it was necessary to salvation to accept a definitely realistic doctrine of the Eucharist.

b. Just as Lutheran worship was nothing more than a purification of the Mass (*cf.* V, 1 below), so the Lutherans also took a thoroughly conservative attitude to the Roman conception and practice with regard to the Eucharist, while the difference between them and the Zwinglians and Calvinists both in teaching and practice became more and more noticeable. In Article 10 of the *Augsburg Confession* the accommodation made by the Lutherans and the denials of the others are both clearly visible. For the anathema which went with the article condemned all who did not teach *quod corpus et sanguis Christi vere adsint et distribuantur vescentibus in coena domini*, and this conception of the doctrine of the Eucharist did not exclude transubstantiation and the most thorough-going realism with all its consequences. Consequently, the Lutherans of South Germany (*Confessio Tetrapolitana*) went their own way like Zwingli. A union between those who followed Wittenberg and those of South Germany was achieved in the negotiations arranged by Philip of Hesse between Luther, Melanchton and Butzer in May 1536 at Wittenberg, which led to the important *Wittenberg Concord*. This stated concerning the Eucharist that 'with the bread and wine, the body and blood of Christ are truly and substantially present, and administered and received', and that while there could be no question of a conversion of the elements or a localization, yet by means of a sacramental union the bread was the body, and that the body and blood of the Lord were truly administered even to those who were unworthy, and were received by them. It was a successful attempt both to put forward a cautious exposition of the Lutheran view, and to tone down the Zwinglian view. Nevertheless, the contradictions appeared in an even sharper form.

Melanchthon departed more and more during the next decade from the Lutheran view. Numerous passages from the Fathers had brought him closer to Zwingli's figurative conception. Besides, he disliked Luther's clumsy mode of expression and especially the doctrine that Christ was everywhere (ubiquity). The Wittenberg Concord still had his approval. Finally, however, his desire to meet the South Germans half way led him to alter Article 10 of the edition of the *Augsburg Confession* published in 1540, to teach that the body and blood of Christ were given to those present at the Eucharist 'with the bread and wine', although he refused explicitly to repudiate those who believed otherwise. The unfortunate consequence of this was that the Lutherans became used to regarding those who followed Melanchthon as merely 'crypto-Calvinists'. And theological discussion returned with even greater passion to the question of the Eucharist, and in relationship with it, to the doctrine of the ubiquity of Christ. The *Formula of Concord* was the result of these struggles and taught, following Luther and repudiating the Zwinglians and Calvinists, but also clearly rejecting transubstantiation and its consequences, that according to the words of institution, and through those words, Christ's true body and true blood, united with bread and wine in the sacraments, are received in the mouths of all communicants, even those who are unbelievers, bringing blessing to some, that is the forgiveness of sins, and bringing condemnation to others.

c. By contrast, all other Protestants, whether they were influenced by Zwingli or by Calvin, were agreed in holding that it was only possible to speak of the body and blood of Christ in the Eucharist insofar as one is referring to the salvation in which the believers partake spiritually. For Christ is present in the Eucharist not in a bodily way, but only according to his divine power. Consequently the words of institution must be taken in a figurative sense. This conception demanded a visible expression in the rite. There could be no question of Christ's being bodily present in the Eucharist and partaken of in a bodily way, so that even those who did not believe received him. Both Zwinglians and Calvinists were agreed in this. In some details they disagreed, in that Zwingli regarded the Eucharist as being in the first place an obligatory meal of the community which was a memorial and confession of faith, and in which to eat spiritually meant no more than to believe in the sacrifice of Christ. *Bullinger* had already objected strongly that the Eucharist really gives us something. We appropriate to ourselves in faith what Christ's death has won for us, and by so doing attain to a spiritual union with

Christ. This had been Augustine's view. *Calvin*, however, is easier to understand from the Lutheran point of view than from that of Zwingli, which in fact seemed to him 'profane'. For he rejects Luther's 'monstrous' doctrine of the ubiquity of the body of Christ, and emphasized that we can only receive Christ's body in faith because he is firmly located in heaven and is therefore only present in the Eucharist, as elsewhere on earth, through his power and effect. Thus he shares with Zwingli a figurative interpretation of the words of institution and the view that the Eucharist is an expression of brotherly union, but agrees with Luther in maintaining the presence of the living Christ and a spiritual effectiveness which is not bodily, but nevertheless real. The extent to which Zwingli's ideas gave way under the influence of Calvin is shown by the Zürich Consensus of 1549, which conceded that every communicant, so long as he belonged to the elect, received not merely the signs but Christ himself with all his gifts. The other Reformed confessions of Switzerland, Germany, France and England, especially the Heidelberg Catechism of 1563, also accepted the doctrine of the Eucharist in its Calvinist form.

d. The smaller sects which have developed from Anglo-Saxon Calvinism have adopted a very liberal attitude to the question of the Eucharist, in that, like many of the groups that have broken away from the Orthodox church in Asia Minor, they maintain open communion, that is, they allow anyone to come to the Eucharist who wishes to do so. On the other hand, for the great Christian communions, the Eucharist serves, right up to the present day, as a confession of adherence to a particular denomination (*cf.* VI below). In fact even after the disputes about the Eucharist had died down for almost two hundred years, this view of the sacrament led in the nineteenth century, in consequence of the forced union of the churches in Prussia on the one hand, and in consequence of the newly awakened Lutheran confessional theology on the other, to conflicts and schisms within German Protestantism (*cf.* III, 1 below).

Friedrich Wiegand

III. THE SIGNIFICANCE OF THE EUCHARIST AT THE PRESENT DAY

1. The rationalist course taken by the *Enlightenment* resisted any mystical interpretation of the Eucharist. The Eucharist was regarded as 'a beneficial institution set up by the Saviour of the world in remembrance of his death'. It was not meant to deny by this that the bread and wine mediate the presence of the whole Christ, but *morali quadam ratione* (Wegscheider), that is, by their moral effect. For Kant, the Eucharist was the fraternal meal of the moral community of the citizens of the world. On the other hand, following the tendencies of *German idealism*, Hegel laid stress on the religious significance of the sacrament in terms of his own system of thought; he referred to it as 'the enjoyment of the present actuality of God'. *Schleiermacher* also continued to accept the Church as it had developed historically, and Christian doctrinal belief. As a theologian of the Union of the Churches in Prussia, however, he stressed what Lutherans and the Reformed churches held in common, that is, the establishment of a communion with Christ, and the passage of the life of Christ into ours. Apart from this he held that *historical criticism* should be given its due place. Thus the best way out was not to go back to the interpretation of Luther or Calvin (*cf.* II, 4 above); rather it was to be hoped that exegetical study would arrive at a new interpretation which would not break down on the old difficulties. L. J. Rückert tried along these lines to discover the true meaning of the Eucharist

simply by going back to the original meaning given to it by Jesus. It was firmly believed that this was possible. H. Schultz affirmed that according to Jesus's original intention, the body and blood of Christ were his earthly, physical body and his material blood—but 'they are not meant as some mysterious substance, but as historical realities of enduring power and effect'.

In the meantime, *romantic theosophy* had begun to make use of quite different methods of understanding from those of critical study. Oetinger and Baader had discovered the idea of the equivalence of body and soul, which they felt had its true place in the Eucharist. They regarded it not so much as a visible manifestation of God's grace, but rather as a physical process, the nourishment of the resurrected body. At first people recoiled in horror from the mixing of the Lutheran doctrine of the Eucharist with a nature philosophy of this sort; but then it was seized on in all its details by the leaders of the *Lutheran revival*, who rejoiced at having found a way out of the 'theology of rhetoric' to the 'theology of facts' (Vilmar), to the objectivity of God: it is possible for the word to be spiritualized away, but the sacrament works from below, through our corporal nature, upon our whole personality. A less extreme form of this theory was advanced by such thinkers as Martensen, who believed that in the Eucharist the seed of the future resurrection body was being sown, or Bail, who quite recently described the sacraments as 'the giving of meaning to the created world'.

More recently, especially in the works of A. Schweitzer, Fr. Spitta, A. Eichhorn, and Heitmüller, there has again been a heated dispute as to the meaning of the words of institution (*cf.* I above). An attempt was not made to understand them in the context of their time and of the mystery cults. But Schleiermacher had already shown how uncertain critical study is, by contrast to the *spiritual effect of the celebration of the Eucharist.* Thus an attempt is being made to make the saving gift of unity with Christ and with the Church an object of living experience and assurance. The objectivity of the rite is seen on the one hand as lying in the historical reality and enduring experience of the *Church* (R. A. Lipsius) and on the other hand in *Christ* himself, whose historical person is experienced as being present (Schlatter) or who, as the exalted Lord, acts directly in the Eucharist (Bachmann). From both points of view the Reformation concept of the 'visible word' is emphasized, as also is the community of Christians with one another: the Eucharist is 'the presentation of the gospel in the image of the self-sacrificing Saviour, the representation of the Church as a brotherhood in the image of a common meal' (Troeltsch). A lively emphasis is laid on the idea that the whole person of Christ is involved as the subject of his whole saving work (H. Stephan). Karl Barth accepts with Luther the miracle of God in the Eucharist, but also sets against it the qualifications of the Reformed churches.

While a concern for the Eucharist has clearly reappeared in theology, a new current of theosophical ideas has flowed in on it from outside. Richard Wagner embraced such ideas in his cult of the Holy Grail; the *Christengemeinschaft* (Christian Brotherhood) carries out its 'consecration of man' with great enthusiasm. This shows the deep and real sacramental need of our time, but also manifests an arbitrary lack of historical sense and a psychological excitement produced by autosuggestion.

2. As the *enduring substance of these developments* the following principles can be accepted.

a. The Eucharist is the table of the Lord. The *common meal* has always been a particularly honourable and reliable token of fellowship, and we too should be filled with a proud and reverent joy when we eat the bread that Jesus has broken for us and drink the wine that he has blessed. This brings us directly into contact with him who in his own unique way has made our relationship to God what it is, and has given a decisive form to our faith and hope, our love and our lives. The difference of time and outlook disappears. We are with him and he is with us. This is much more than if we were to have as our guest an exalted and saintly human being. In Jesus God has come to look for us and invited us into a fellowship with him, and so at the table of the Lord we are also aware of fellowship with our God. Surely it is a great festival of Christian faith!

b. An indelible mark has been left upon the holy Eucharist by its relationship to Jesus's *last* meal, to the night in which he was betrayed and to the mysterious words which he spoke at that time over the bread and the wine. However much the meaning of his words may be disputed, one saying, which he added himself as a commentary on his other words, is clear and unequivocal: 'I shall not drink again of this fruit of the vine until that day when I drink it new with you in my Father's kingdom'. Jesus gave himself, in his body and blood, as a *pledge* that his gospel remained the truth, even though outward defeat threatened to cast doubt on all his promises of God's power, grace and kingdom. Even if the desperate course of the world, and the evil in and around us threatens to take away our faith in the reality, the grace and the faithfulness of God, Jesus comes before us in his whole person to show us that he does not deceive us, and that faith in him is the victory which overcomes the world.

c. Even if Jesus himself did not have his death in mind when he spoke the words of the Eucharist, nevertheless this meal was his last; he had in fact to follow the bitter way to the cross, and there he offered his life to his God, to his task, and to his friends as a sacrifice. Thus at every Eucharist we proclaim the *death of the Lord*. We celebrate his total abandonment of himself to the will of God and his sacrificing of himself for his brethren and his enemies, which is capable of overcoming all our estrangement from God, our self-seeking and all our lazy indecision and confusion. We appropriate to ourselves in faith this conquering and atoning power, by partaking of the sacred signs, and we are thereby drawn into the same sacrificial readiness to live for God and our brethren; this is the most valuable sense of the idea of sacrifice in the Catholic Mass.

d. Thus a right participation in the sacred meal, which is a matter both of receiving and of giving, brings about a real *union with the being and work of Christ*. We receive Christ himself, what he desired to be to us and what he is always able to be to us. His love, the love of God for us, is poured out into our hearts; this is the connection between the outward nourishment and the food of the soul. It is true that they remain what they are, bread and wine. But if they are rightly received, they do not merely signify the coming of Christ and God to us, but give this to us in reality. We ourselves become the body and blood of Christ, the manifestation on earth of his being, which should be revealed in all that we are and do, and will continue to be revealed. In spite of all the protest of Reformed theology against a magical view, this is a recognition of the doctrine of the transformation of the elements, the constant renewal of the incarnation of God upon earth.

e. A most important aspect of this is that all who go to the same table of the same Lord, and indeed all without exception who have belonged to him, belong to him now, or who are to belong to him, become *one body of Christ*, united through the same mysterious relationship to God which Christ founded and which is clearly made visible in the common meal; it is not intended for individuals alone, but for the whole Church. Thus the soundest test of whether our reception of the Eucharist is genuine, is not any kind of mystical enthusiasm, but whether true love and fraternal loyalty spring from it. It must also be regarded as of great importance that the Eucharist, which is celebrated by all Christian churches, should no longer divide them, but unite them.

f. But if we partake of the Eucharist in a quarrelsome, arrogant, purely conventional, indifferent and bored fashion, without a serious self-examination and criticism, and if we come closer neither to God and Christ, nor to ourselves, nor to our fellow men, it is not only useless, but leaves a deep mark upon our lives; for we are losing the habit of encountering what is holy with reverence and joyful self-sacrifice; we are eating *judgement* to ourselves.

g. However much intrinsic value is accorded to such a symbol as this, sanctified by tradition and history, and in which—it is surely possible to say this—the sacramental symbolism of all ages and nations has reached its highest point, the greatest treasure of the Church remains the gospel of the power and the grace of God. No sacrament can give us more than the *word* of reconciliation. The sacred meal gives us this word in a distinctive form: the sacrament is a *visible word*. The table of the Lord gives both to each individual and to everyone simultaneously a visible and palpable union with Jesus of Nazareth, with the night in which he was betrayed, with his life and his love even unto death; it proclaims outwardly and inwardly: 'Taste and see that the Lord is good!'

Arnold Meyer

IV. THE LITURGICAL HISTORY
OF THE EUCHARIST

1A. The Breaking of Bread in the Primitive Church

The oldest form of the Eucharist is the breaking of bread
of the primitive Church attested in the Acts of the
Apostles (Acts 2.42,46; 20.11; *cf.* 27.35), which is reflected in the story of the disciples at Emmaus (Luke
24.30,35). Even the apocryphal Acts of the Apostles
belong in part to the same tradition (*Clem. Hom.* 14.1;
Acta Johannis 106-110.85; *Acta Thomae* 27, 29, 49-50, 133).
The celebration took place in a private house (κλῶντες
κατ'οἶκον ἄρτον, Acts 2.46), where the tiny congregation
gathered together. The leader took a loaf of bread,
uttered the blessing for bread which was customary
amongst pious Jews, and then broke the bread, which
was divided amongst those at the table. Each one ate
his portion, and then the common meal began. There is
nothing special about the way the whole ceremony was
performed; every meal took place in the same way as in
any group of Jews; and the absence of wine (*cf.* I, 2
above) gives the whole scene an aspect of frugal simplicity, which carried those who took part back into the
days when they wandered homeless with their Master
through Galilee. But the nature of this celebration is now
obvious. As soon as the appearance of the risen Christ
had given them the certainty that he was not still dead,
the same group gathered together again, and returned
to the *daily table fellowship* which they had enjoyed
before; and they knew that the Lord was seated at the
table with them as he had been before, invisible, but
nevertheless really present. Where two or three were
gathered together in his name, he was there amongst
them (Matt. 18.20), and when the Acts of the Apostles

recalls that this breaking of bread was celebrated 'with glad hearts' (2.46; *cf. Acta Verc. Petri* 5), it is not hard to understand why: the disciples were rejoicing at the presence of the Lord, and were waiting with scarcely restrained exultation for his *parousia* in the immediate future.

1B. *The Eucharist of the Didache*

This original simple form was sometimes slightly expanded. Occasionally *wine* was also drunk, when according to the customs of Jewish households the blessing for wine and the thanksgiving for the meal were pronounced by the head of the house over a last cup of wine at the end of the meal. We find this custom in Corinth (1 Cor. 11.20 ff.). But the prayers soon developed away from their original Jewish form, and were filled with Christian ideas and phrases. It was also possible—according to a rather later Jewish custom—for a solemn blessing to be pronounced over the first cup of wine that was brought to the table. In this way the blessing of the bread and of the wine followed one another, and this distinguished the act, now dignified with a Christian content, from the main course of the meal as a special solemnity. This is the form in which the primitive Christian breaking of bread is presented in the *Didache* (The Teaching of the Apostles) as a *Eucharist* (*cf.* I, 2 above). The blessing of wine with a prayer of thanksgiving for the 'sacred vine of thy servant David' (*cf.* Ps. 80) who has been revealed to us, is followed in turn by the blessing of bread with a thanksgiving for life and immortality, and a prayer for the gathering together of the scattered members of the Church from all the ends of the world into the messianic kingdom. The general thanksgiving for the meal then comes at the end of the meal which followed every 'Eucharist'. In this prayer thanks are offered to God for giving us 'spiritual food and drink and eternal life': thus the Eucharist is already regarded as a heavenly food, which brings about eternal life. This can be seen more clearly in the first half of this prayer of thanksgiving: 'We thank thee, holy Father, for thy holy name (=spirit, power), which thou hast made to dwell in our hearts, and for the knowledge and the faith and the immortality which thou hast made known to us through thy servant Jesus'.

It was required of all who took part that they should be free from sin and from hate towards their brethren. Anyone who was not had first to do penance, before he could come to the sacred meal, which was regarded as a pure sacrifice offered to God. It is clear that ideas from the hellenistic mystery religions have been added to the simple original concept.

There is a supplement at the end of these provisions, in the form of several sentences whose liturgical purpose has been much disputed. According to their content they belong to the point where (at the beginning of the celebration) the blessing of the bread is pronounced and the communicants come up to the leader of the congregation to receive the consecrated portions. Then follow the disputed words, which in all probability form a dialogue:

Grace (=the Lord) shall come, and this world shall pass away!

The congregation: Hosanna to the God (or: son?) of David!

If anyone is holy he may come; if he is not, he must do penance! Maranatha! (i.e. Our Lord, come! or: Our Lord has come!)

The congregation: Amen!

These words undoubtedly belong to the oldest form of the liturgy. They are filled with the enthusiastic expectation of the *parousia* of the Lord and with longing for the passing away of this world. This was the fervent prayer to the Lord that was made in those earliest days. But to this apocalyptic idea there is also linked a mystical theme. The hosanna rings out not merely as an expression of a future hope; it is also a greeting to the Lord manifested amongst his followers at the sacred meal. And that is why we have to give a double sense to the ancient prayer 'Maranatha', which had been uttered by Paul himself (1 Cor. 16.22).

2. *The Pauline 'Lord's Supper'*

While the rite of the 'Lord's Supper' (1 Cor. 11.20 ff.) was celebrated in Corinth in exactly the same way as that of the 'breaking of bread' of the earliest period, and expanded by the addition of the blessing of the wine at the end, we can see from Paul's words that a completely different set of ideas is associated with it. The Lord's Supper does not appear as the continuation, with the exalted Lord, of the previous daily table fellowship, but is related to one single occasion, the last supper which the Lord took with his disciples in the night in which he was betrayed. Paul is acquainted with the same tradition which underlies Mark (14.2,25). But whereas in Mark the fact is merely recorded, and there is no mention of any repetition, Paul adds to his account the decisive words 'Do this in remembrance of me' (*cf.* I, 1 above). There is good reason for regarding this addition as the work of Paul himself: it was this that was revealed to him by the Lord (11.23: παρέλαβον ἀπὸ τοῦ κυρίου). It was he who turned the Lord's Supper from the restoration of the disciples' table fellowship with Jesus to a remembrance of his death and consequently also of his resurrection (*cf.* I, 3 above).

We have seen how even in the *Didache* hellenistic ideas were added to the ancient form of the meal. This naturally took place even more rapidly in the *gentile Churches* which had been set up as a result of Paul's missionary work. The meal was assimilated to the ancient sacrificial meals, and regarded as a means of mystical communion (κοινωνία) with the deity through the partaking of spiritual food (1 Cor. 10.14-21). Paul makes use of this view in order to demonstrate to the Corinthians the necessity of abstaining from all heathen sacrificial meals. The believer eats the body and drinks the blood of the Lord: he cannot at the same time enter into table fellowship with the demons worshipped by the heathens. And if at the Christian celebration he does not 'discern' the body of the Lord, but eats it thoughtlessly like any other form of nourishment, and in general treats the whole ceremony as a good opportunity for a feast, his own body will pay the penalty. Many of the Corinthians have grown sick through unworthily eating the sacred food, and some have even died as a result. There is a heavenly power in the bread and the wine: it brings immortality and eternal life to devout Christians; but it turns to deadly poison for the unworthy person who treats it with contempt. We find here a clear and simple conception: the closest parallels to it are easily found in the ideas held by the ancient world, concerning sacrificial meals (*cf.* I, 3 above).

3. The Formation of the Sunday Morning Celebration

Here as elsewhere in the struggle with Jewish Christianity, the future lay with the Pauline view. Further liturgical development followed Paul. The oldest complete liturgy which we possess, that of the Church Order of Hippolytus, is nothing more than an elaboration of Paul's ideas, and with very few alterations could have been used in the primitive churches of the Pauline mission. The rite is not, as in the time of Paul, linked to a meal taken together by the congregation, nor is it any longer carried out in small groups, but has become *part of the Sunday worship of the whole congregation*. In consequence, the time at which it takes place has been changed from the evening, the normal time for a meal, to the morning. In Justin (*Apology* I 67) we find that this development was already complete in Rome by 150 A.D. The Pauline Eucharist has become separated from the solemn meal and as a remembrance (ἀνάμνησις) of the sacrificial death of Christ (*cf.* also Justin, *Dialogue* 41, 70, 117) in which his redeeming sufferings are re-experienced, has become a climax of the Sunday worship. But the ancient 'breaking of bread' of the primitive Church had not disappeared. As the 'love-feast', that is, as a meal for the poorer brethren at the expense of individual members of the Church, it persisted for a long time. The description of such an *agape* in the Church Order of Hippolytus reflects a custom going back to the life of the very earliest Christian church at Jerusalem; the 'breaking of bread' of the Twelve (*cf.* 1*A* above), took place in essentially the same way. The history of the Eucharistic liturgy now becomes part of the history of the celebration of the Catholic *Mass*, and cannot in consequence be treated here. The Eucharist has no relationship to the Jewish passover and its ritual, as has often been believed. It is true that the last meal of Jesus is presented in the context of the synoptic account as a Passover meal, but there are powerful reasons against the acceptance of this view (*cf.* I, 1 above). And it is an indubitable fact that neither in Jerusalem, nor in its Pauline conception, did the Lord's Supper have any relationship either in form or content with the Passover.

Hans Lietzmann

V. PRESENT-DAY LITURGIES

1. The Historical Origin of the Present Protestant Eucharistic Liturgies

a. Both in the orders of service drawn up by the Reformers, and in the partly official and partly private Protestant service books at present in use, which follow the older usages in this respect, there is a difference between the two great groups of service, the Reformed and the Lutheran, not merely from the dogmatic point of view, but also liturgically. In *Lutheran* practice, the Eucharist is linked to the principal service, so that when there are no communicants the latter remains incomplete, while the *Reformed* churches have separated their preaching service and the Eucharist, in that the Eucharist is not intended for every Sunday, but only for a few (great feast days, days of prayer, once a month, etc.). In reality this great difference no longer exists to the extent which would appear from the orders of service. In by far the greater number of Lutheran churches, the Eucharist does not take place every Sunday for lack of those wishing to communicate. Further, the orders of service belonging to the same group as the Württemberg Church Order laid down from the beginning only a few Sundays of the year for the celebration of the Eucharist. It has also come about in recent times in the Lutheran Church, especially in cities and industrial areas, that in many places, following unwritten usages, a clear preference is given to a number of days (Days of Penance, Good Friday, etc.); one result is that, although these days are not inappropriate in themselves, the large increase in the number of communicants means that the service takes an excessively long time and loses a great deal in consequence. On the other hand the Reformed Churches in their turn have frequently found it necessary to set aside for the Eucharist not merely a regular four Sundays in the year, but also the Sundays before or after, with the result that the number of Sundays on which the Eucharist is celebrated is considerably increased. In Switzerland, in the cities, the Eucharist is celebrated practically every Sunday in at least one church. The situation is naturally different where the total number of communicants forms the congregation as such (Free Churches in Scotland); the whole congregation gathers together several times in the year for the celebration of the Eucharist. Here, as everywhere else where the custom is to sit to receive communion, and not to go up to the altar rails, as in Lutheran districts, and less frequently amongst the Reformed Churches, the difficulties are not so obvious. Nevertheless they do exist. Just as amongst Lutherans, they are a result of an historical development, without a precise knowledge of which it is not possible to evaluate what has been handed down to us by our fathers, nor to understand the numerous questions which arise within the Lutheran and Reformed Churches.

b. The formation of the Protestant eucharistic rites developed through time in such a way that they are now frequently celebrated within the framework of two other services, the *confession* which precedes them, and the *service of thanksgiving* which follows them in the afternoon. This arrangement now seems only to persist in country districts, and is fast falling into disuse. The *confession* was usually held on the previous day and was linked to Vespers, at which appropriate alterations were made in the order of service, and a penitential hymn sung instead of the office hymn; the *confession* was itself a private confession, and the best known of the prayers used come from Naumberg in 1537, and from the Kalenberg Church Order of 1569. Gradually this private confession was replaced by public confession, and transferred to the

Sunday itself, a custom that had long been allowed in country districts on account of distance. In Reformed Church districts there was no confession in the Lutheran sense, but merely what was called the preparation service, which in some places (Scotland, etc.) was held not only on the day itself, but also on the previous Sunday. But with the penitential tone of the Lutheran confession and the warnings against unworthy partaking of the sacrament in the Reformed Church preparation services, both have a very similar atmosphere, and at the present time they are not very different from one another. In fact, the three well-known questions which precede the absolution, and which have passed into Lutheran service books, were taken from the Hesse Reformed order of service of 1657, which in its turn was based on the Palatinate Reformed Church Order of 1563.

c. The *celebration of the Eucharist* itself in *Lutheran* regions is linked, as has been said, to the preaching service, and in fact follows Luther's *Formula missae* of 1523, and his German Mass (*Deutsche Messe*) of 1526, and takes the following form. A transitional hymn (offertory) is followed by the preface with the ancient 'Lift up your hearts' (*sursum corda*). The preface concludes with the Sanctus, to which the Hosanna and Benedictus are often added. Sometimes (e.g. Sweden) the Sanctus is not sung, as in Luther's German Mass, until after the words of institution. What follows the Benedictus, which like the whole preface, is ordered in the Protestant Church Orders to be sung only 'if time permits', has always varied from place to place. In some orders of service, there are prayers or exhortations before the words of institution. Indeed, in spite of the preparation service on the previous day, there is sometimes a general confession and absolution with the Lord's Prayer (Württemberg group); and the Lord's Prayer on its own is also very frequent, occurring particularly in the North German orders of service, which go back to Bugenhagen, before the words of institution, as in Norway, but not in Sweden. Both arrangements are permitted in the Baltic countries, depending on the earlier usage. The words of institution are frequently sung, and linked with them is the so-called consecration (even with the sign of the cross, and elevation, and post-consecration prayers!). The *Agnus Dei* and other hymns of the Passion, eucharistic hymns, and more rarely hymns referring to the Church year, are sung during the distribution of communion. In the country the men come up first, and sometimes, on certain fixed Sundays, follow the traditional order in which the oldest come first; then the women follow, but often in the reverse order, with the youngest first; each group approaches, and with reverence, sometimes also kneeling on kneelers brought up to the altar rails—it is also a widespread custom to kneel during the prayers of confession and the consecration—receives the elements (usually undiluted white wine and special hosts—the Lutheran practice—or bread—leavened in Reformed Church practice, and unleavened amongst the Zwinglians) according to the fixed formula laid down in the orders of service. The conclusion (post-communion) is very simply constructed from a versicle, a collect of thanksgiving and a blessing; it can be expanded by the addition of 'The Lord be with you', a dismissal, etc., as for example in Bavaria and Scandinavia. The basic pattern of the Mass is visible in this form of Eucharistic rite.

d. Amongst the *Reformed* orders of service, that of Zwingli should be mentioned first. It departs entirely from the pattern of the Mass, and gives the rite an entirely new liturgical form, whereas his preaching service is very simple (prayer, Lord's Prayer, sermon, general confession, prayer and blessing; no singing). The eucharistic rite begins with prayer. This is followed by: I Cor.

11, the *Gloria in excelsis* spoken alternatively by the pastor and the congregation, 'The Lord be with you' and its response, John 6, the Creed (again alternated between pastor and congregation), and exhortation with the Lord's Prayer and other prayers, the words of institution, the communion (received seated; the deacons carry the elements round, even up to the balconies, and each breaks his own piece from the loaf, as in Scotland at the present day), Ps. 113, thanksgiving, and 'Depart in peace'. Here again, no singing is provided for. Zwingli's order of service did not continue in Switzerland in this form. An amalgamation with that of Calvin came into use. In particular, it is the practice in many places, not only in the west of Switzerland, to come forward to receive communion. The orders of service of many Reformed Church districts in Germany, which go back to the Palatinate Reformed Church Order of 1563, are also dependent upon Calvin. This pattern is as follows: introductory verse, general confession, prayer including the Lord's Prayer (in place of this, Calvin himself had: words of consolation, Ten Commandments, a psalm, and prayers), sermon, then (in the Palatinate) 'public confession', the Lord's Prayer or a paraphrase of it, the words of institution—together with an admonition of 14 pages!—a prayer of thanksgiving with the Lord's Prayer, a profession of faith, an exhortation to lift up one's heart to God—(A Reformed *sursum corda!*), communion (the congregation goes up to receive communion; the bread which is given to them—not a special host as in Lutheran regions—is taken by each into his own mouth), a reading of the scriptures or a hymn during the distribution, and a thanksgiving. Thus the outward pattern is in some respects assimilated to the Lutheran order. On the other hand the rites going back to Lasco's orders of service of 1550, in use in Holland, on the lower Rhine, in East Frisia, etc., differ markedly; to a large degree the basic principle of table fellowship has been retained, although the Synod of Emden, which made the decisive provisions for this region, permitted communion to be administered with the congregation either going up to receive it, or standing, or seated. Originally there was no hymn during the distribution, but a reading of the scriptures, and this is quite often still the custom. In Scotland, the distribution of communion only takes a short time, because a large number of elders carry the elements to the congregation in their seats, and a solemn silence is maintained.

2. The Reform of the Eucharist

a. There has long been widespread agreement that a *reform is necessary.* All these rites still contain a number of elements from the pre-Reformation medieval rite. In consequence, genuine Protestant ideas were never fully expressed. Further, there are certain external features present which without question have caused a fall in the respect with which the sacrament is regarded. It has been shown from statistics, that from the beginning of the eighteenth century, when accurate registers of communicants began to be kept, that the *numbers taking part in the Eucharist* have constantly fallen, and this is so more in the case of men than of women. Besides the three reasons usually given, of indifference to the Church, class consciousness, and a dislike of the common chalice, must be added a fourth equally important factor, that for many there is a clear contradiction between the Protestant view of the Eucharist and the rite itself. Congregations whose ecclesiastical outlook has unconsciously been affected by catholicizing ideas which have not yet been overcome, are of course less aware of this contradiction. Consequently, the presence of large numbers at the Eucharist is not in itself an exact measure of a truly Protestant Christianity, any more than a markedly low figure in Reformed districts, or districts which have come under the influence of the Reformed churches, is a sign of a lack of spiritual fervour; for here the stress laid on the sacraments as a *mysterium tremendum* in the sense of I Cor. II often frightens away those who are most serious in their intentions. This effect can be so great that often, especially in Scotland, the serious and terrifying tone of the preparation service makes the best people in the congregation, conscious of their own total unworthiness, so afraid that in the end they absent themselves. Thus, with very few exceptions, we have had little success in Protestant Churches in bringing about a truly Protestant celebration of the Eucharist. Thousands have come year after year, and for thousands it has been a living experience. They came and went, restored, strengthened, comforted and armed for the battle of faith. Perhaps they communicated with a small group of their closest relations (*private communion*), or on their sick bed, being prevented by a long illness from receiving with the congregation. They received communion surrounded by those who were dearest to them, and perhaps in company with them, and if it was for the last time, they joyfully prayed: 'Lord, now lettest thou thy servant depart in peace, according to thy word; for mine eyes have seen thy salvation . . .' All these wonderful and blessed experiences enjoyed by individual devout Protestant Christians have shown them the truth of what is constantly emphasized in Protestantism, that by contrast with the *verbum audibile*, which is addressed to everyone at once, the sacrament is a *verbum visibile* directed with its gifts towards the individual, so that its main purpose consists of the 'individual application' of the forgiveness of sins. But the underlying idea of all this is that the Eucharist should be celebrated in the *whole congregation*, something which dogmatic theologians have naturally never completely overlooked (*cf.* for example Baier: *dilectio mutua communicantium,* referring to 1 Cor. 12.13), but have let fall too far into the background. And to some extent this is equally true of the Reformed Church, although it is often said that here, as also in the smaller sects which for the most part have arisen in Reformed Church regions, the idea of the community and the congregation has been better maintained. For the awe which keeps people away from the Eucharist has often made it difficult to realize. But the laity also have an unconscious feeling that in truth the Eucharist can only obtain its full effectiveness when it is celebrated by the whole congregation. This is shown by the regrettable fact, which has often been noticed, that those who communicate as comparative strangers in a city congregation, in an area unknown to them, and especially where there are vast numbers of communicants, can not achieve any true devotion.

Thus one of the first considerations in a reform of the Eucharist must be to bring an end to very lengthy *mass communions*. And in general it can be strongly argued that the days which have become customary, the Day of Penance, New Year's Eve, Good Friday, and the end of the Church year have been responsible for making even narrower an already one-sided conception of the Eucharist, in which the central theme is becoming more and more the idea of penance and forgiveness. Above all, as is implied by the ancient prefaces, the whole Church year, and especially Maundy Thursday, should be restored to its proper place.

b. Another external feature is the question of the *common chalice*. Every one remembers the uproar at the suggestions made at the turn of the century for the institution of the *individual cup*. This usage has finally had to be permitted at occasional celebrations (a formula is given in Smend's Service Book). The present suggestion that 'intinction' should be introduced (the Eastern Orthodox Church already practises this, as is well known, although by a different method) or of the use of a *paten and chalice combined* in which the host, lying on a paten combined with the chalice into a single unit, is dipped into the wine and administered to the communicant, has been received much more calmly. This method was put forward not only to provide for a rather more certain protection against the infectious diseases which have spread so much more rapidly since the war, but also in order to make it possible considerably to shorten the celebration, which would be an advantage in itself. It is significant that in spite of its rejection by the two provincial synods which have discussed motions on the subject, Hanover and Hamburg, which would not even concede the use of the individual cup in certain conditions for sick communicants, this new method has gained adherence in all theological camps, on account of the saving of time. It is to be hoped that it will be permitted to celebrate using intinction, as well as in the way laid down in the Church Orders.

c. More important than these external points are the *inner reasons* which call urgently for a fundamental reform. Even if one is convinced that because of the conservative outlook of congregations in this question, especially when it touches the most intimate personal faith of the individual, there are many things which it will not be possible to achieve for a long time, it must nevertheless be regarded as a sacred duty constantly to draw serious attention to what the celebration of the Eucharist should really be like. May we never lose sight of the ideal! 'Our task today is to exclude many traditions which still remain with us from Catholicism, and to create a truly *Protestant* celebration of the Eucharist. This must represent the congregation taking part in a celebration as a tightly knit fraternity, appropriating to itself in faith and in remembrance of the death of Christ, the grace that is offered to it' (Schian).

In bringing this about the following measures are desirable. The preaching service should be separated from what henceforth would be an independent Eucharist service with a rich liturgical framework, such as Luther already had in mind. It would be celebrated on particularly appropriate Sundays and feast days, and as far as possible, where no excessive distances have to be taken into account, in the evening. The *confession* (the preparation service) should be done away with, a matter on which there is wide theoretical agreement on the basis of the ideas of the early Church and the Reformers (in Norway this can already be left out if desired at week-day celebrations). For the confession anticipates something which is essential to the Eucharist, and thereby deprives the celebration which follows of its value; and it provides no means of excluding those who are unworthy, especially since it is rare that personal application has to be made to come to communion. Besides, the ideas contained in the formal confession can be given sufficient mention in the sermon which should form part of these celebrations. Further, the whole pattern of the liturgy, especially the form in which communion is administered, must give expression to the fact that the celebration is a celebration of the *whole congregation* which is present. This provides an easy answer to the disputed question of the self-administration of communion (a formula for this purpose was provided for example for Hesse and Cassel in 1896). But the service must also be a *true celebration*. The idea of penance and atonement is too prominent at present. A restored form should be like that of the early Church, when it was called 'Eucharist', *a service of praise and thanksgiving (cf. I, 2; IV, 1 above)*. It ought also to be a joyful *profession of faith*; and most important of all, the primitive Christian idea of the *parousia*, which at that early period was so inseparably linked with it, should not be forgotten. We must return to the prayers of the *Didache* (*cf.* IV, 1B. above), and to the pattern of primitive Christianity! This would be the surest guarantee that however gradually the goal was achieved, we would eventually obtain what we seek in the reform of the Eucharist which is so urgently necessary.

Paul Graff

VI. THE EUCHARIST AND CANON LAW

1. In the Catholic Church only the consecrated priest can *administer* communion; in the Protestant Churches normally only those who have been ordained have the right to do this. But amongst the various sects, celebrations of the Eucharist by laymen are widespread. The provincial churches cannot put an end to this state of affairs, although it is in contradiction to their Church Orders. Nor have they entirely succeeded in doing this where new Church constitutions have made it possible for someone other than a regular clergyman to celebrate the Eucharist under certain conditions. In the Catholic Church those who are baptized and have reached the age of reason (the beginning of the age of reason is set at approximately the seventh year by the decree *Quam singulari* of 1910), and in the Protestant Church those who have been confirmed, may *receive* the Eucharist. According to Catholic teaching everyone who has the right to do so must receive communion at least once a year, at Easter time. In the Protestant Churches there are no longer any binding rules concerning the reception of the Eucharist. The obligation of the clergy to receive the Eucharist is virtually without force in the Protestant Churches, but the practice of celebrating the Eucharist

in one's own parish is almost universal. The way the Eucharist should be celebrated is laid down in its main points, and especially with regard to the formula of administration, in the *orders of service* (*cf.* V, 1 above).

2. Because the doctrine of the Eucharist has been hotly disputed, it has become a sign *dividing one Church from another*. Conversion from the Catholic to the Protestant Church takes place (although not as a legal obligation) by taking part in a Protestant celebration of the Eucharist. The union of Churches involves their sharing in each other's eucharistic worship. The removal of the fellowship of the Eucharist signifies a deep schism between Protestant Churches. The German Protestant Churches practically all give hospitality to each other's members at the Eucharist.

3. *Exclusion* from the Eucharist is an ancient means of discipline, but persists in our Protestant Churches. The self-governing bodies of the Church have to decide this for the most part; but for example in East Prussia the pastor has the right to pronounce exclusion on some occasions, and to enforce it until the executive of the local synod has given a decision. But use is rarely made of these provisions.

Martin Schian

BIBLIOGRAPHY

Barth, Karl. *The Teaching of the Church Regarding Baptism.* Translated by Ernest A. Payne. London: SCM Press, 1948.

Bultmann, Rudolf. *The History of the Synoptic Tradition.* Translated by John Marsh. Oxford: Basil Blackwell & Mott, and New York: Harper & Row, 1963.

Primitive Christianity In Its Contemporary Setting. Translated by R. H. Fuller. London: Thames & Hudson and New York: Meridian Books, 1956. Also issued in Fontana Library, 1960.

The Theology of the New Testament. 2 vols. Translated by Kendrick Grobel. London: SCM Press and New York: Scribner's, 1951-55.

Cullmann, Oscar. *Baptism in the New Testament.* Translated by J. K. S. Reid. Chicago: H. Regnery Co., 1950.

Deissmann, G. Adolf. *Paul: A Study in Social and Religious History.* Second edition, revised and enlarged. Translated by William E. Wilson. New York: Harper & Brothers, 1957.

Dibelius, Martin. *From Tradition to Gospel.* Translated, in collaboration with the author, by Bertram Lee Woolf. London: Nicholson & Watson and New York: Scribner's, 1935.

Jesus. Translated by Charles B. Hedrick and Frederick C. Grant. London: SCM Press, 1963 and Philadelphia: The Westminster Press, 1949.

Heschel, Abraham J. *The Prophets.* First edition. New York: Harper & Row, 1963.

Jeremias, Joachim. *The Eucharistic Words of Jesus.* Translated from the German 3rd edition by Norman Perrin. New York: Scribner's 1966.

Kittel, Gerhard. *Bible Key Words* from *Theologisches Wör-*

terbuch zum Neuen Testament. Translated and edited by
J. R. Coates. New York: Harper & Brothers, 1952-64.
A Theological Dictionary of the New Testament. Translated
and edited by Geoffrey W. Bromiley. Grand Rapids:
Eerdmans, 1964-7.

Knox, John. *Jesus: Lord and Christ.* New York: Harper
& Brothers, 1958.

Lietzmann, Hans. *A History of the Early Church.* 4 vols.
Translated by Bertram Lee Woolf. London: Lutter-
worth Press, 1958.

Mass and Lord's Supper. Translated by Dorothea H. G.
Reeve. Leiden: Brill, 1953-64.

Mowinckel, Sigmund. *Prophecy and Tradition.* Oslo:
I kommisjon hos J. Dybwad, 1946.

Nock, Arthur Darby. *St. Paul.* Revised edition. London:
Oxford, 1946. Torchbook edition. New York: Harper
& Row, 1963.

Otto, Rudolf. *The Kingdom of God and the Son of Man.*
Translated from the revised German edition by Floyd
V. Filson and Bertram Lee Woolf. London: Lutter-
worth Press, 1943.

Rowley, Harold H., editor. *Studies in Old Testament Prophecy.* Edinburgh: T. & T. Clark, 1950.

Schweitzer Albert. *The Quest of the Historical Jesus.*
Translated by W. Montgomery. Third edition. Lon-
don: A. & C. Black. Paperback edition. New York:
Macmillan, 1961.

Stauffer, Ethelbert. *New Testament Theology.* Translated
by John Marsh. London: SCM Press, 1963 and New
York: The Macmillan Company, 1956.

Stendahl, Krister. 'Biblical Theology, Contemporary',
The Interpreter's Dictionary of the Bible, I (New York and
Nashville: Abingdon Press, 1962), 418-32.

Wilder, Amos N. *Eschatology and Ethics in the Teaching of
Jesus.* Revised edition. New York: Harper & Brothers,
1950.

Index of Names

Adventists, 275, 374
Aeschylus, 135
Aesop, 87
Ahijah, 47, 60, 77
Akiba, Rabbi, 156
Alger of Lüttich, 371
Alsted, 269
Althaus, Paul, 14, 21, 320
Ambrose, St, 368
Amos, 38, 48, 56, 59, 62, 63, 70, 74, 78, 85, 234-5
Anabaptists, 266, 267, 269, 317
Apollonius of Tyana, 87, 155
Aquinas, Thomas, 15, 266, 372
Archelaus, 113
Arminians, 318
Athanasius, 15, 364
Auberlen, 274
Augustine, St, 15, 264-5, 313, 314, 326, 368, 369, 370, 371, 378

Baader, 380
Bachmann, 381
Bail, 380
Banus, 296, 297
Barnabas, St, 175, 176, 178
Barth, Karl, 12, 16, 31, 381
Baur, F. C., 28, 176

Beck, J. T., 274
ben Zakkai, Rabbi, 156
Bengel, 270, 271
Berengarius of Tours, 370, 371
Berosus, 222, 223, 228
Bertholet, Alfred, 21
Blumenhardt, 274
Bousset, 30
Brandes, Georg, 94
Brenz, 317
Bucer, 331
Buddha, 37
Bugenhagen, 317, 394
Bullinger, 377
Bultmann, Rudolf, 13, 14, 21
Butzer, 376

Caesarius of Arles, 368
Calvin, 15, 317, 332, 377, 378, 379, 395
Carlyle, Thomas, 93
Charles the Bold, 370
Chrysostomus, 365
Cludius, 27
Cocceius, 269, 270
Comenius, 269
Cremer, H., 320
Cyprian, 326, 360, 361, 367
Cyril of Jerusalem, 313, 324, 325, 365

Daniel, 245, 246, 248
Darwin, Charles, 272
David, King, 231, 235, 237, 242
Deissner, Kurt, 21
Deutero-Isaiah, 65, 68, 73, 82-3, 85, 240-1
Deutero-Zechariah, 244
Dibelius, Martin, 22

Dillmann, A., 26
Donatism, 313
Drews, Arthur, 94
Duns Scotus, 372

Eichhorn, A., 380
Elchasai, 304
Elijah, 38, 40, 44, 45, 47, 56, 60, 62, 77, 233, 243
Elisha, 39, 45, 46, 56, 62, 77
Epictetus, 134, 135
Essenes, 295
Euripides, 135
Eusebius, 296
Eusebius of Caesarea, 264, 364
Eutychius of Constantinople, 366
Ezekiel, 51, 52, 53, 56, 61, 62, 64, 65, 67, 75, 81-2, 235, 242, 244
Ezra, 77, 85, 247

Facundus of Hermiane, 368
Faust, Dr, 88
Feine, 30, 31
Feuerbach, 273
Fichte, 272
Francis of Assisi, 88
Frank, R., 320
Fulgentius of Ruspe, 368

Gabler, J. P., 27
Gamaliel, 156, 171
Gerhard, J., 268
Goethe, J. W. von, 105, 272
Graff, Paul, 22
Gregory Naziansen, 313, 364
Gregory of Nyssa, 313, 365
Gregory the Great, 265, 369

Guitmund of Aversa, 371
Gunkel, Hermann, 22
Gutschmid, Alfred von, 247

Habakkuk, 56, 80, 85, 244
Haggai, 75, 83, 242-3
Harnack, Adolf, 14, 25-6
Hauer, 33, 34, 35
Haymann, 27
Hegel, Friedrich, 94, 95, 96, 272, 273, 379
Hegesippus, 296
Heiler, Friedrich, 14
Heitmüller, 380
Hemerobaptists, 296
Heraclitus, 222, 224
Hermas, 310, 312
Herod Antipas, 119
Herod the Great, 113, 117
Herrmann, Wilhelm, 319
Hillel, Rabbi, 156
Hippolytus, 262, 389, 390
Hoen, 374
Hofmann, J. C. K., 28, 31
Hofmann, von, 274
Hohlwein, Hans, 22
Holtzmann, H. J., 29
Hosea, 43, 56, 70, 72, 78, 85, 232, 234-5
Hrabanus, Archbishop, 370
Huck, A., 344
Humbert, Cardinal, 371
Hussites, 266

Ignatius, 30, 312, 357, 359, 360
Ildefonsus, 326
Innocent III, 372
Irenaeus, 15, 262, 312, 313, 362, 363, 364, 366

Isaiah, 43, 52, 53, 56, 60, 62, 63, 64, 70, 72, 79, 83, 85, 236-8, 239, 244
Isidore of Seville, 326

James, St, 116, 250
Jeremiah, 43, 45, 48, 49, 52, 53, 54, 55, 56, 58, 61, 62, 67, 72, 74, 75, 80-1, 83, 85, 239, 240, 241
Joachim of Floris, 266
Joel, 84, 244
Johanan, Rabbi, 156
John Damascene, 366, 367
John, St, 89, 92, 102, 105, 110, 120, 156, 256, 298-9, 342, 357
John the Baptist, 98, 117, 118, 122, 125-6, 127, 132, 133, 134, 156, 166, 256, 297-8, 299, 300, 301, 302
Jonah ben Amittai, 46
Joseph, St, 110, 111
Josephus, 113, 115, 116, 296
Josiah, 239
Judas Iscariot, 165
Justin Martyr, 262, 296, 312, 322, 355, 357, 359, 361, 365, 390

Kähler, M., 319
Kalweit, 320
Kant, Immanuel, 272, 379
Karlstadt, 374
Kautsch, E., 26
Kierkegaard, Søren, 15
Klopstock, 87
König, E., 26

Labadie, von, 270
Lampe, F. A., 270
Lasco, 395
Leo I, 327, 335

Lessing, 272
Lietzmann, Hans, 22
Lipsius, R. A., 319, 320, 381
Ludwig, Emile, 94
Luke, St, 30, 89, 98, 99, 100, 101, 104, 105, 110, 111, 112,
   113, 117, 303, 343-4, 345, 346, 347, 348
Luthardt, 25
Luther, Martin, 15, 266, 267, 268, 270, 273, 316, 317,
   320, 330, 331, 332, 333, 373, 374, 375, 376, 377, 378,
   379, 381, 393, 400

Malachi, 75, 84, 147, 243
Mandaeans, 305
Mara, 115
Mark, St, 89, 99, 100, 102, 104, 105, 106, 110, 157, 189,
   302, 343, 344, 345, 346, 347, 352, 388
Martensen, 380
Marti, K., 26
Martin of Braga, 326
Marx, Karl, 272
Matthew, St, 89, 99, 105, 110, 111, 112, 113, 117, 139,
   302, 343, 344, 345, 346, 347, 352
Melanchthon, 316, 317, 376
Melito of Sardes, 310, 312
Menken, 274
Meyer, Arnold, 22
Micah, 79, 85, 238
Micaiah ben Imlah, 44
Mitsuko, Shimamura, 37
Mohammed, 33, 37
Moravian Brethren, 335
Moses, 48, 77, 85, 140, 232, 243
Münzer, Thomas, 330

Nahum, 56, 80
Nao, Deguchi, 37

Nathan, 77, 231
Nehemiah, 77
Nero, 177
Nestorius, 366
Nietsche, Friedrich, 96, 135

Obadiah, 69
Occam, 374
Oecolampodius, 374
Oetinger, 270, 380
Olrik, Axel, 220
Optatus of Milevis, 326
Origen, 262, 263, 313, 360, 362, 363, 364, 365

Papias, 261
Paschasius Radbertus, 369, 370
Paul, St, 30, 103, 107, 133, 135, 137, 139, 145, 155,
    169-214, 251, 256, 257, 258, 259, 300, 305, 306, 307,
    311, 341, 342, 343, 344, 345, 346, 347, 352-6, 358, 388,
    389
Paul V, 329
Paulinus of Nola, 264
Pelagius, 314
Peter, St, 30, 99, 103, 104, 164, 165, 176, 177, 300
Philip of Hesse, 376
Philo, 146, 170, 190, 207, 261
Pilate, Pontius, 118, 165
Pindar, 36
Plato, 135, 224
Proksch, Otto, 22
Protosurus, Bishop, 327

Quenstedt, 317
Quirinius, 113

Ratramnus of Corbey, 369, 370
Renan, Ernest, 94

Richter, F., 273
Rietschl, 338
Ritschl, Albrecht, 275, 319
Rothex, R., 274
Rückert, L. J., 379

Samuel, 38, 40, 47, 62, 77
Sarcerius, 317
Scheel, 319, 320
Schian, Martin, 22
Schlatter, 30, 31, 381
Schleiermacher, 23-4, 273, 274, 318, 319, 379, 380
Schmidt, Hans, 22
Schmidt, Karl Ludwig, 22
Schmidt, S., 27
Schultz, H., 380
Schweitzer, Albert, 18, 19, 380
Sellin, Ernst, 22
Selnecker, 317
Seneca, 135
Serapion, 115, 325
Silesius, Angelus, 271-2, 277
Smend, R., 26, 338, 398
Socinians, 318
Søderblom, Nathan, 14
Son of David, 166
Son of God, 166
Son of Man, 166, 167
Sophocles, 135
Spencer, Herbert, 272
Spener, 270
Spitta, Fr, 380
Stade, B., 26
Stauffer, Ethelbert, 22
Stephan, H., 381
Stephen, St, 106, 172

Strabo, 223
Strauss, D. F., 273
Suetonius, 115

Tacitus, 115, 155
Tertullian, 311, 312, 323, 326, 360, 362, 367
Theodore of Mopsuestia, 366
Thomasius, G., 320
Thümmel, 338
Tiberius, Emperor, 117
Ticonius, 264
Tillich, Paul, 13, 14
Trito-Isaiah, 84
Troeltsch, 381

Urbanus Rhegius, 317

Vespasian, Emperor, 155
Victor I, 334
Vigilius, Pope, 327
Vilmar, 380
Virgin Mary, 110, 111
Vitringa, 270
Von Oettingen, 320

Wagner, Richard, 381
Wegscheider, 379
Weinel, 30
Weiss, B., 29, 30
Weiss, Johannes, 19
Wellhausen, 26, 232
Wernle, 29
Wesley, John, 15
Wiegand, Friedrich, 22
Wrede, W., 29

Xenophanes, 36

Zarathustra, 36
Zechariah, 65, 83, 85, 243, 248
Zephaniah, 80, 85, 239
Zerubbabel, 83, 244
Zwingli, 317, 332, 374, 375, 376, 377, 378, 394, 395

71 72 73 74   12 11 10 9 8 7 6 5 4 3 2 1